The Princeton Review

More Illustrated Word Smart

A Visual Vocabulary Builder

Morgan Chase
Illustrations by Chris Kane

Random House, Inc.
New York

www.PrincetonReview.com

The Independent Education Consultants Association recognizes The Princeton Review as a valuable resource for high school and college students applying to college and graduate school.

Princeton Review Publishing, L.L.C.
2315 Broadway
New York, NY   10024
Email: booksupport@review.com
Copyright ©2001 by Princeton Review Publishing, L.L.C.

ISBN 0-375-76205-1

Editor: Maria Dente

Illustrator: Chris Kane

Production Editor: Maria Dente

Production Coordinator: Stephen White

Manufactured in the United States of America.

9 8 7 6 5 4 3 2 1

Contents

INTRODUCTION

Learning shouldn't be a chore. No matter how boring a topic seems, there's always some way to make it interesting. For most people, improving their vocabulary is a chore, so they never work at it. Our Word Smart series changed all that.

In 1988, we published *Word Smart*, which included over 800 of the most important words needed for an educated vocabulary. At the time, we thought it would be our only vocabulary book. The overwhelming popularity of *Word Smart*, however, led to *Word Smart II*. People kept asking us to give them more words, so we did. Many people who enjoyed these books wished that there were an easier way to learn and remember words. In response to these requests, we published *Illustrated Word Smart*, which provided cartoons helping to relate words to their definitions. Again, people loved the idea and wanted more.

More Illustrated Word Smart contains 250 words which commonly appear in educated writing. Many of them can be found on such standardized tests as the SAT, GRE, SSAT, and ISEE. For each word, we have provided the pronunciation, definition, and part of speech. We have also provided a mnemonic device—a memory aid—and a cartoon for each word. The mnemonic device will usually be a word or phrase that is similar to the vocabulary word. Let's look at this example:

> ## apex
>
> **definition:** the very highest point (noun)
>
> **mnemonic:** APE

As you can see on page 57, the cartoon shows an ape at the apex of a building. The cartoon connects the mnemonic to the vocabulary word, forcing you to remember the visual image. (If the mnemonic reminded you of the word directly, there would be no point in including the cartoon.) Of course, we tried to make the cartoons as memorable as possible, without making things too complicated. Here's another:

> ## aloof
>
> **definition:** keeping apart from others (adjective)
>
> **mnemonic:** ALONE ON THE ROOF

This mnemonic contains the letters a-l-o-o-f within a phrase which is related to being aloof. For this sort of mnemonic, the cartoon is not as important, but is still helpful.

The following icon is used to introduce the mnemonic device, which is usually both visual and auditory.

LOOKS/SOUNDS LIKE

The cartoon and the mnemonic device provide two extra means of learning each vocabulary word beyond memorizing its definition. The end result, we hope, is a book that is both useful and entertaining. Students preparing for the SAT should find it particularly helpful, but it should also be useful to adults who hope to expand their vocabulary.

HOW TO USE THIS BOOK

This book is divided into 16 chapters of loosely related words (plus one chapter of drills at the end). For example, one chapter will contain words relating to confusion, and another will contain words relating to intelligence. Each chapter provides a manageable set of words that can be learned in one chunk. After 16 sessions with *More Illustrated Word Smart*, you will have learned all of the words in the book.

Unfortunately, if you try to memorize all of these words at once, it won't work. It takes time to transfer knowledge from your short-term memory to your long-term memory, so slow down and read a new chapter every three or four days. Also, each chapter is independent of the others, so you don't necessarily have to go through them in order. However you go about learning these words, we hope that the process will be entertaining as well as educational.

Each chapter is followed by a quick quiz and word puzzle, so that you can test your newfound knowledge. The answers to the word puzzles at the end of each chapter can be found in chapter 17. There are also quizzes at the back of the book, which test your knowledge of all the chapters. The puzzles are similar to crossword puzzles, with a few fundamental differences. The example on the following page will show you how these puzzles work.

For each puzzle, you will fill in each word from that chapter, going from left to right (including the gray boxes). Each row of the puzzle will contain one or more words from the chapter. Clues are provided for each row, in the same order as the words that belong in that row. The vertical gray bars tell you that the same letter belongs in every box within that gray bar.

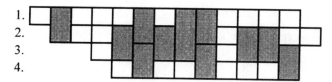

1.   clue for Dread Zeppelin

2.   clue for Rush; clue for Zappa; clue for Ice-T

3.   clue for Cheap Trick

4.   clue for Men At Work

Here's what it looks like with the answers filled in:

Notice that each gray bar has just one distinct letter in it. These gray bars are the keys to solving the puzzles, especially when a number of the words in a given chapter have similar meanings.

PRONUNCIATION

We don't use standard dictionary phonetics in our *Word Smart* books for the simple reason that many people don't understand them. Instead, we use a modified phonetic approach that we believe is largely intuitive. The pronunciation key below should clear up any questions you might have about how to use our pronunciation guide:

The letter(s)	*is (are) pronounced like the letter(s)*	*in the word(s)*
a	a	bat, can
ah	o	con, on
aw	aw	paw, straw
ay	a	skate, rake
e	e	stem, hem, err
ee	ea	steam, clean
i	i	rim, chin, hint
ing	ing	sing, ring
oh	o	row, tow
oo	oo	room, boom
ow	ow	cow, brow
oy	oy	boy, toy
u, uh	u	run, bun
y (ye, eye)	i	climb, time
ch	ch	chair, chin
f	f, ph	film, phony
g	g	go, goon
j	j	join, jungle
k	c	cool, cat
s	s	solid, wisp
sh	sh	shoe, wish
z	z	zoo, razor
zh	s	measure

All other consonants are pronounced as you would expect. Capitalized letters are accented.

CHAPTER 1

DR. FEELGOOD:
Words about doing well and being healthy

accord (uh KORD)

agreement (noun)

 OF COURSE

This word can refer to agreement in general, but it also can refer specifically to an agreement between two nations or groups, such as a peace *accord*.

aspire (uh SPYRE)

to work hard toward or dream of a goal (verb)

ASP + HIGHER

This snake is studying late into the night to further its education, so it can manage other snakes someday. The *spire* part of this word relates to breathing (or respiration). *Aspiring*, or having *aspirations*, often causes you to breathe heavily from exertion.

benefactor (ben uh FAK tur)

one who supports a cause, often financially (noun)

 BENEFits the ACTORs

The Latin root *bene* means good and the Latin root *fac* means make or do. Therefore, a *benefactor* is someone who does good things.

blithe (BLYTH)

carefree (adjective)

 BLIss + smooTH

This word comes straight from Old English. The skater seems to be enjoying herself, with nothing to worry about, because the ice is so smooth.

cathartic (ka THAR tik)

cleansing one's emotions (adjective)

 ARCTIC

Catharsis is a term you may hear when discussing drama in your English class. It's the feeling of peace that can come after going through an intense emotional experience. Swimming in Arctic (or Antarctic) waters would certainly be an intense experience, and after the initial shock, you might feel some inner peace. You probably wouldn't be able to feel your fingers and toes, though.

complaisant (kum PLAY sunt)

willing to please others (adjective)

 CAMP + PLEASANT

As the spelling might indicate, this word comes from French. With a spelling variation, you can see the word *please* hidden within it.

cultivate (KUL tiv ayt)

to help grow (verb)

 CULT IS GREAT AT GARDENING

The most common meaning of this word is to help plants grow, but it can mean to help anything grow. For example, a teacher may *cultivate* an interest in reading in her students.

liaison (LEE ay zahn)

a secret romantic affair (noun)

 RAISIN

These raisins seem to be having quite a date. A *liaison* can also be a person who communicates between two groups. As you might expect, this word comes from French.

nostalgia (nah STAL juh)

a feeling of longing for the past (noun)

 NOt STALe

Someone who is homesick or wishes to return to the past is *nostalgic*, or sentimental. Someone who is overly *nostalgic*—weeping and moaning and putting on a big show—is being maudlin or mawkish.

prolific (proh LIF ik)

very productive (adjective)

 PRODUCTION'S TERR**IFIC**

To *proliferate* means to grow or reproduce quickly. Synonyms for *prolific* include *fecund*, *fruitful*, and *fertile*, which comes from the same root.

revive (rih VYVE)

to regain strength (verb)

 KEEP ALIVE

This word comes from the Latin root *viv*, meaning live. As you can see, a plant can be *revived* with some water. A commercial of a few years ago encouraged people to *revive* with caffeine pills. And when an old play is performed years after it was first produced, it's called a *revival*.

savor (SAY vur)

to enjoy a taste or smell; to keep enjoying a feeling (verb)

 KEEPS ITS FLAVOR

If you *savor* a victory, you enjoy the feeling of it for a long time. The adjective *savory* can mean strong-tasting or pleasant-tasting, but it can also mean morally acceptable. An "unsavory character" is a morally offensive person, not someone who tastes bad.

unscathed (un SKAYTHD)

unharmed (adjective)

 SKUNK + BATHED

Does taking a bath in tomato juice really get rid of the smell of skunk? Personally, we've never had to find out. To come through an experience *unscathed* means to suffer no damage. A related word is *scathing*, which means harmful or bitter—harsh criticism might be described as "*scathing* remarks".

vaunted (VAWN tid)

receiving excessive praise (adjective)

 WANTED

This word implies that something or someone has a greater reputation than it deserves. To *vaunt* means to brag about something, but the adjective *vaunted* is used more often.

verdant (VUR dunt)

covered with green vegetation (adjective)

 coVERrReD WITH plANTs

The Latin word *verdis* means green. Do you know which state's nickname is "The Green Mountain State"? Here's a hint: The word Vermont comes from the French for "green mountain".

DRILLS

Quiz #1

For each question below, choose the word that is LEAST similar to the other two.

1.	a.	verdant	b.	aspire	c.	cultivate
2.	a.	vaunted	b.	nostalgia	c.	savor
3.	a.	cathartic	b.	revive	c.	liaison
4.	a.	blithe	b.	benefactor	c.	unscathed
5.	a.	accord	b.	complaisant	c.	prolific

Puzzle #1

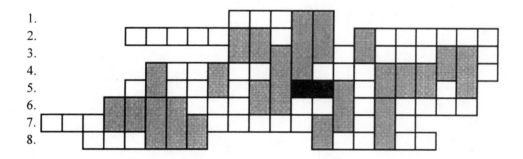

```
1.
2.
3.
4.
5.
6.
7.
8.
```

1. enjoy for a while

2. financial supporter; having a reputation

3. agreement; lush and green

4. bring back to life; eager to please

5. very productive; secret date

6. cleansing the soul; foster the growth of

7. not hurt; longing for the past

8. carefree; pursue a goal

CHAPTER 2

CELEBRATION:

Words about giving praise and having fun

accolade (AK uh layd)

praise (noun)

 A COLA AD

The words *accolade* and *collar* are both derived from the same Latin root, because an *accolade* used to include a hug around the neck. With the cola, clipboard, and pencil, though, it's probably good that there's no hugging here—someone would probably get hurt, or spilled on.

caricature (KAYR ih kuh choor)

a humorous portrait that exaggerates particular features of the subject (noun)

 CHARACTER

This word is derived from the Latin *carrus*, a type of cart used in France. As the word evolves into Italian, it came to mean to overload, and then to exaggerate. You can have your *caricature* done at almost any shopping mall or street fair, but you may not be pleased with the results.

eccentric (ek SEN trik)

strange; unusual (adjective)

 ACCENT TRICK

You can see the word center hiding in *eccentric*. An *eccentric* person is a bit off-center, or unstable. If you've studied ellipses in geometry, you may recall that the *eccentricity* of an ellipse tells how misshapen it is—if the *eccentricity* is zero, the ellipse is actually a circle.

ecstatic (ek STAT ik)

extremely happy (adjective)

 EXCiTing GYMNAsTICs

Ecstasy comes from a Greek word which originally meant insanity or bewilderment. Later, it came to mean a trance, or out-of-body experience. Now, it means supreme pleasure or happiness.

esteem (ih STEEM)

to think highly of (verb)

 BEST TEAM

This word can also be used as a noun. The curator of the locker museum holds the 1976 team "in high *esteem*." A related word is *estimation*—meaning not approximation of a value, but a favorable opinion.

extol (ik STOL)

to praise or speak highly of (verb)

REX TOLD

The Latin root of this word means to lift up. To *extol* something means to put it on a pedestal, then. Maybe the school will erect a statue of Frank, but probably not.

flippant (FLIP int)

overly casual, to the point of disrespect (adjective)

FLIPPER

This dolphin seems to have gone a bit too far while joking around. This word can also be shortened to *flip*. If someone tells you not to be *flip*, replying "Do you want me to be a cartwheel instead"? would be flippant.

homage (OH mij)

respect; reverence (noun)

HOMepAGE

This word is derived from the Latin root *homo*, meaning man. *Homage* is respect paid to a great person.

intriguing (in TREEG ing)

very interesting; fascinating (adjective)

 IN THE TREE aGAIN

This word is related to *intricate*, which means elaborate or complex. Something *intriguing* attracts your curiosity, then entangles you and draws you in.

jocular (JAHK yuh lur)

describing someone who enjoys joking (adjective)

 DISK JOCKEY

You can see that *jocular* and *joke* are derived from the same root. Other related, but less common, words include *jocose* and *jocund*.

panegyric (pan uh JEER ik)

detailed or elaborate praise (noun)

 GYRO

This word is descended from a Greek word meaning a public gathering; a panegyric was originally a public eulogy or speech praising someone.

rhapsody (RAP suh dee)

a state of extreme happiness (noun)

 RAP SODA

This word originally referred to poetry, describing a work full of passion. In music, a *rhapsody* is an irregular work that may seem to have been pieced together—if you've heard Queen's "Bohemian *Rhapsody*," you get the idea. *Rhapsody* is most commonly used to describe a feeling of bliss, though, with no reference to poetry or music.

stimulate (STIM yuh layt)

to arouse interest or excitement (verb)

 MULE

A drug that causes a person to be more energetic is called a *stimulant*. In biology, something that causes some reaction or response is called a *stimulus*.

superlative (soo PUR luh tiv)

of the highest quality (adjective)

 PEARL

This word contains the prefix *super*, meaning over or above. An adjective that ends in "-est", such as highest, cutest, or best, is the *superlative* form of the related adjective (high, cute, or good). For many adjectives with more than one syllable, the word "most" is used to form the *superlative*: most beautiful, for example, not beautifullest.

vivid (VIV id)

brightly colored; very noticeable (adjective)

 VERY INTENSE VIDEO

The Latin root *viv* means life. Something *vivid* is full of life or energy. Since this is a black-and-white book, we couldn't color this picture for you. If this is your book, go ahead and color it in yourself. If this isn't your book, don't you wish you had your own?

whimsical (HWIM zik ul)

unpredictable; fanciful (adjective)

 WHEE + CYCLE

This word describes a person who may like to do weird or funny things, or may just change his or her mind for no apparent reason. If you do something on a *whim*, it means that you do it without thinking about it. Riding a bike with no hands and no helmet probably seems fun and exciting until you hit a stone and kiss the pavement.

DRILLS

Quiz #2

For each question below, choose the word that is LEAST similar to the other two.

1.   a. accolade   b. extol   c. stimulate

2.   a. intriguing   b. flippant   c. jocular

3.   a. homage   b. caricature   c. panegyric

4.   a. rhapsody   b. vivid   c. ecstatic

5.   a. superlative   b. whimsical   c. eccentric

Puzzle #2

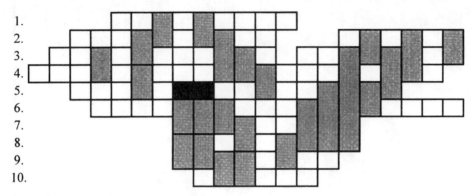

1. awaken

2. very interesting; praise

3. of the highest quality; praise

4. extreme pleasure; very memorable; humorous

5. praise; unpredictable

6. disrespectful; exaggeration

7. elaborate praise

8. strange

9. very happy

10. praise

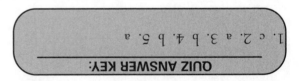

CHAPTER **3**

OVERKILL:
Words about excess

cumbersome (KUM bur sum)

difficult to carry, because of size or weight (adjective)

 cuCUMBER

This word is descended from Celtic; in Middle English, the word *cumbren* meant to annoy. In Modern English, though, *cumber* usually means to annoy by weighing down or getting in the way. To *encumber* means to place a burden on someone.

extravagant (ik STRAV uh gunt)

spending a lot (adjective)

 **EXTRA GIVING**

This word is related to *vagrant* and *vague*. The *vag* part of each word is derived from the Latin word for wandering. *Extravagant* can be thought of as describing someone whose spending habits wander beyond acceptable limits.

frenzy (FREN zee)

a state of wild excitement (noun)

 FREaky aND craZY

The word *frenetic* is related to this word, and they both come from the Greek root *phren*, meaning mind. *Schizophrenia*, the mental disorder, also comes from this root. The obsolete science of *phrenology* is the study of the bumps on a person's head in order to determine the person's mental qualities.

garish (GAR ish)

overly bright or colorful (adjective)

 GLARING-ISH

Synonyms for this word include *flashy* and *gaudy*. All three of these words indicate that something is in poor taste.

horde (HORD)

a large crowd (noun)

 HOw cRowDEd!

Maybe that *horde* is in a Ford. This word can also mean a large group that travels, often with the idea that the members are all moving around and causing trouble; you may have heard of the "Mongol *hordes*." The traveling festival of hippie bands, the HORDE tour, is aptly named.

immense (im ENS)

very large (adjective)

 BIG FENCE

This word is formed from the Latin roots *im*, meaning not, and *mens*, meaning measurable. Another word with the same root is *commensurate*, meaning of equal measure.

inundate (IN un dayt)

to flood (verb)

 IN UNDerwATEr

This word is derived from the Latin word *unda*, meaning wave. To *inundate* originally meant to flood with water, but it can also mean to overwhelm with a great amount of something. For example, a celebrity could be *inundated* with requests for interviews.

litany (LIT uh nee)

a repetitive list (noun)

 LIsT mANY

This word originally referred to a type of prayer in which one person's recitation would be answered periodically by the congregation repeating the same response. It has come to mean any repetitive list or description.

prattle (PRAT ul)

to talk a lot without saying much (verb)

 RATTLESNAKE

This word comes from a less common word, *prate*, which means essentially the same thing.

rampant (RAM pint)

widespread; unrestrained (adjective)

 RAMP ANTs

This word is related to *rampage*, which means a wild spree of violence. *Rampant* can also describe an animal rearing on its hind legs.

surfeit (SUR fit)

an excess of something, usually causing discomfort (noun)

 SURF IT

The prefix *sur* means over, and the *feit* part of this word is derived from the Latin *fac*, meaning to do. *Surfeit*, then, is the result of overdoing something—usually eating too much.

swarm (SWORM)

a large crowd, often of insects (noun)

 SWINGING **ARM**S

This word comes from the Old English *swearm*, meaning a group of bees that leaves its hive in search of a location to begin a new colony. Around 1400, it began to be applied to groups of people. It can also be used as a verb, meaning to move in large numbers.

throng (THRAWNG)

a large crowd (noun)

 A THOUSAND STRONG

Like swarm, this word also comes from Old English, and can also be used as a verb.

verbose (vur BOS)

using many words (adjective)

 oVERBoard prOSE

The Latin root *verb* has a number of English descendants, including *verbal*, *verb*, *verbatim*, and *verbiage*. So what does the root *verb* mean? "Word", of course.

writhe (RYTH)

to move in a twisting motion, usually in pain (verb)

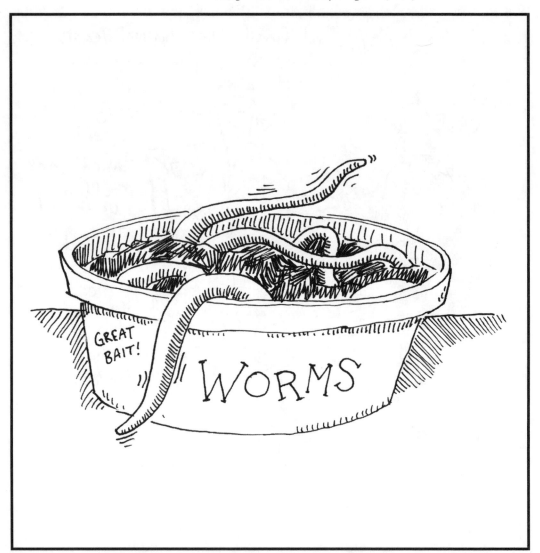

 WRIggle and sliTHEr

This word comes from Old English. (Most of the short words do, if you hadn't noticed.) There are a few related words in English which contain this idea of being twisted. A *wreath* is bent into a circle and can be made of twisted branches. If you feel *wrath*, very strong anger, you feel tormented and emotionally twisted out of shape.

DRILLS

Quiz #3

For each question below, choose the word that is LEAST similar to the other two.

1.	a.	litany	b.	horde	c.	throng
2.	a.	verbose	b.	prattle	c.	rampant
3.	a.	frenzy	b.	inundate	c.	surfeit
4.	a.	writhe	b.	swarm	c.	extravagant
5.	a.	immense	b.	garish	c.	cumbersome

Puzzle #3

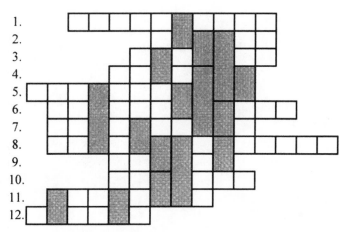

1. difficult to carry

2. wild excitement

3. enormous

4. widespread

5. overly generous

6. a crowd; flashy

7. a crowd; a crowd

8. overindulgence; wordy

9. twist and turn

10. talk at length

11. flood

12. repetition

CHAPTER 4

TAKE ME TO THE TOP:

Words about being large and growing larger

abundance (uh BUN duns)

a great amount (noun)

 A BUNch IN attenDANCE

This word is derived from a Latin word meaning to overflow. The root *unda* means wave, and gives us the words *inundate* (which is listed elsewhere in this book) and *undulate*.

apex (AY peks)

the very highest point (noun)

 APE

This word comes straight from Latin. It can mean a physical high point, such as the top of a building or mountain, or it can have a more abstract meaning, such as the high point of someone's career.

crest (KREST)

to reach the top of (verb)

 CLIMB eveREST

This word can also be used as a noun, often to describe the highest point of a wave. It can also mean the ridge or tuft of feathers on the top of some birds' heads. If someone is *crestfallen*, he or she is sad, with head hung low.

crucial (KROO shul)

very important (adjective)

 YOU SHALL

A related word is *crux*. It usually occurs in phrases such as "the *crux* of the problem", meaning the most important aspect of the problem.

encompass (en KUM pus)

to surround or contain (verb)

 IN COMPASS

This compass *encompasses* a large area. The word *compass* can also be used as a verb, meaning the same thing as *encompass*, but this is rare and sounds old-fashioned.

fortify (FOR tuh fye)

to enrich or make stronger (verb)

FOR YOUR HEALTH...

SUPER 45 VITAMINS

 FORTY-FIVE

You've probably heard various foods advertised as being "*fortified* with vitamins and minerals." This means that the nutrients have been added to the food. If a city is *fortified*, though, it means that defensive walls—*fortifications*—have been constructed to defend against an attack.

garner (GAR nur)

to amass or accumulate (verb)

 GAther in your coRNER

This word is derived from the Latin *granum*, meaning grain. The original sense of the word was related to storing grain, but now can refer to collecting or storing anything. For example, a leader could *garner* support for a cause.

glutton (GLUT un)

one who eats too much (noun)

 BUTTON

You may have heard someone described as a "*glutton* for punishment." This means that the person seems to invite abuse, so it appears that he or she has an enormous appetite for being treated badly. A related word is *glut*, which means an excess of something.

incentive (in SEN tiv)

a motivation or reward (noun)

 ONE CENT GIVE

Although this word would appear to be related to incense or incite, it is actually derived from the Latin word *canere*, which means to sing. An *incentive* sets the tone for your activity.

pigment (PIG munt)

something that adds color (noun)

PIG

This word can describe a substance in a plant or animal that gives it its distinctive coloring. It can also describe a dye or powder used to add color to something such as paint. Interestingly, pigs and humans are the only two species that can suffer sunburn.

prominent (PRAHM uh nunt)

noticeable (adjective)

 PROM kINg AND queEN

Aren't they a cute couple? They sure stand out from the rest of the kids. In case you were curious, *prom* is short for *promenade*, which can mean to take a walk. At the beginning of some formal dances, the guests parade around so that everyone can get a peek at everyone else.

promiscuous (pruh MIS kyoo us)

tending to engage in casual romantic relationships (adjective)

 PROMISE A KISS

This word is descended from a Latin word meaning to mix. A *promiscuous* person tends to mix with—and date—a lot of people.

swell (SWEL)

to increase in size or volume (verb)

 GROWS WELL

This word comes from the Old English *swellan*. It can describe something growing larger, such as a pumpkin, or growing louder, such as music. It can also be used as a noun or an adjective, and has other meanings too numerous to mention here.

troupe (TROOP)

a company of actors or dancers (noun)

 THEATRE gROUP

This is a French word meaning, strangely enough, *troop*. In English, it describes a group of entertainers, often one which travels.

unanimous (yoo NAN uh mus)

in complete agreement (adjective)

 YOU STAND WITH US

This word is formed by the Latin roots *unus*, meaning one, and *animus*, meaning mind. People who arrive at a *unanimous* decision are of one mind—they all think alike.

voluminous (vuh LOO muh nus)

very large (adjective)

 VOLUME Is eNormOUS

The word *volume*, meaning a book, comes from the form of a scroll, which has to be rolled to be read. The Latin root *volv* means to roll, and gives us such words as *revolve* and *convoluted*. Eventually, *volume* came to mean the size of a book, and by extension, the size of anything. *Voluminous*, then, means having great size.

DRILLS

Quiz #4

For each question below, choose the word that is LEAST similar to the other two.

1.   a.   apex   b.   fortify   c.   crest

2.   a.   voluminous   b.   promiscuous   c.   swell

3.   a.   abundance   b.   garner   c.   crucial

Puzzle #4

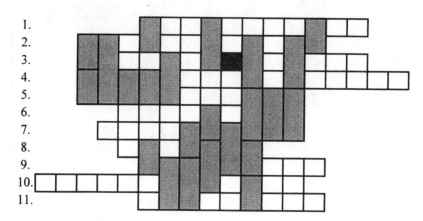

1. grow; collect

2. top; person who takes too much

3. most important; acting company

4. noticeable; strengthen

5. romantically overactive

6. fully agreed

7. gigantic

8. color

9. motivation

10. plenty; top

11. surround

CHAPTER 5

WAR PIGS:

Words about being strong and trying hard

annex (an EKS)

to add on (verb)

 ADD NEXt

This word often refers to adding territory to a country, but is not limited to that situation. It can also be used as a noun, usually to mean an addition to a building. The Latin root *nec* (or *nex*) means to bind together, so *annex* is related to *connect*.

ardor (AHR dur)

strong enthusiasm (noun)

 TRIES HARDER

This word describes a burning desire, which makes sense once you know that it comes from the same Latin root as *arson*.

awe (AW)

respectful amazement; wonder (noun)

 DROP YOUR JAW

This word is descended from Old Norse. If you feel *awe*, you are *awestruck* by something *awesome*. The word *awful* is also related to *awe*, because a feeling of *awe* usually involves some amount of dread.

compel (kum PEL)

to force (verb)

 COME TELL

A number of English words are formed by a prefix and the Latin root *pel*, meaning to force or push. *Repel* means to push away, *expel* means to force out, and *propel* and *impel* both mean to push forward.

conquer (KAHN kur)

to defeat (verb)

 CONCORD

Other related words include *conquest*, *conquistador*, *acquire*, *quest*, and *question*. They all come from a Latin root meaning to seek. When William the Conqueror defeated England in 1066, his invasion continued long after he was crowned king. The French Normans brought their language with them, including the word *conquerre*, marking the end of the Old English period and the beginning of Middle English.

endorse (en DORS)

to give support or approval (verb)

 DEF**END** A H**ORSE**

Around election time, organizations may *endorse* candidates whose views they support. The kind of *endorsement* that you can't escape, however, is that of a celebrity appearing in an advertisement. You can also *endorse* a check by signing it on the back. In fact, the Latin root *dors* refers to the back—the big fin on a shark's back is called the *dorsal* fin.

fervor (FUR vur)

intense enthusiasm (noun)

 FLY FURTHER

This word is descended from the Latin word *fervere*, meaning to boil. If you are *fervent*, you feel hotly about something, and your emotions are boiling over.

forge (FORJ)

to advance, usually with some difficulty (verb)

 FORWARD GOES

To *forge* ahead means to move forward in the face of opposition—perhaps in waist-deep snow, or under the blazing sun, or when no one else agrees with your ideas. This word also has a number of other meanings, such as to hammer metal into shape, or to write a false document.

persevere (pur suh VEER)

to keep trying something difficult (verb)

 PURSE IS HERE

This word is derived from a Latin word meaning very serious. You can see the word *severe*, meaning serious, hiding inside. If you *persevere*, you're taking something seriously and not giving up.

procure (pro KYOOR)

to get, usually through special effort (verb)

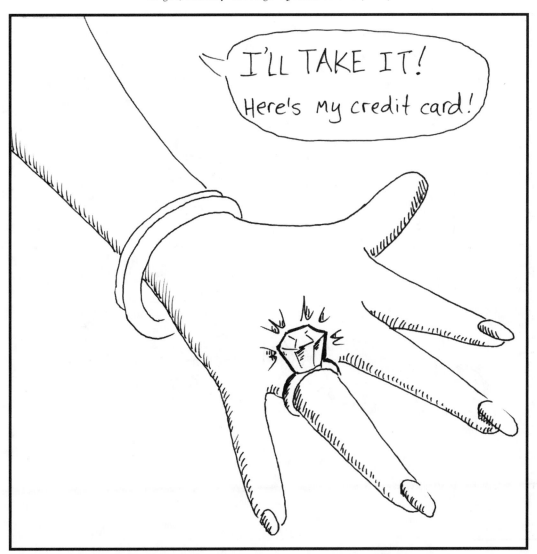

 PROCEED TO ACQUIRE

This word is derived from the Latin root *cura*, meaning care. To *cure* someone is to care for his or her health, and a *curator* takes care of a museum. Let's hope that this woman cares about paying off her credit card bill.

resilient (rih ZIL yunt)

able to recover from trouble (adjective)

 BRAZILIANS

This word is derived from the Latin root *salire*, meaning to leap. This *resilient* team can "bounce back" from a bad situation. Look at that diving stop!

robust (ro BUST)

strong; healthy (adjective)

 NO RUST

Yes, a stainless steel house might not be practical, but it won't rust. This word is descended from the Latin word for the red oak tree—oak is very strong. You may have heard an advertisement for coffee describe it as a *"robust* blend". There is actually a kind of tree, the *robusta*, from which coffee beans can be obtained, but there's no guarantee that a *"robust* blend" of coffee comes from this kind of tree. The advertisers are most likely using the word to mean strong.

skirmish (SKUR mish)

a small battle (noun)

 SKIRt MISsion

This word has a complicated history, coming from a Germanic word, through Italian, and finally through French into Middle English. In the 1400s, it mutated into the word *scrimmage*, which we use now in football to describe the action while the ball is live. The rugby term *scrum* (or *scrummage*) also comes from *skirmish*. These warriors had better hope that their battle doesn't get any bigger than a *skirmish*, seeing as there are only three of them. And yes, technically, a kilt is not a skirt.

stature (STACH ur)

height; level of prestige (noun)

 STATUE

This word can refer to the actual physical height of something, but it is often used figuratively to describe someone's *status*, or level of importance. As a symbol of New York and the United States, the Statue of Liberty has achieved great *stature*.

steadfast (STED fast)

stubborn; unwilling to move (adjective)

 DEAD LAST

This word comes from an Old English compound. If you combine the words *steady* and *fasten,* you'll get the meaning of *steadfast.*

strive (STRYVE)

to make a strong effort (verb)

 STRong drIVE

This word comes from Old French, and is closely related to *strife*, which means bitter conflict. This makes sense when you consider another definition of *strive:* to compete strongly.

DRILLS

Quiz #5

For each question below, choose the word that is LEAST similar to the other two.

1. a. steadfast   b. annex   c. conquer

2. a. fervor   b. ardor   c. skirmish

3. a. forge   b. strive   c. compel

4. a. persevere   b. endorse   c. resilient

5. a. compel   b. stature   c. awe

Puzzle #5

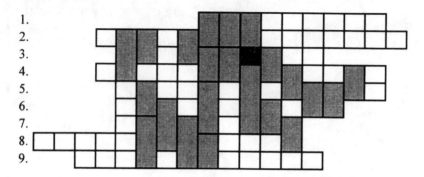

1. strong and flexible

2. obtain; quarrel

3. strong; respect

4. enthusiasm; unmoving

5. force; support

6. move ahead; enthusiasm

7. keep going

8. defeat; keep trying

9. absorb; rank

QUIZ ANSWER KEY:

1. a 2. c 3. c 4. b 5. a

CHAPTER 6

THE SOUNDS OF SCIENCE:
Words about being smart and speaking well

acumen (ak YOO mun)

mental sharpness; keen insight (noun)

 ACcURate MEN

This word describes someone with a sharp or keen mind, because it's derived from the Latin word *acus*, meaning needle. What's the name for a sharp, pointy angle that's smaller than 90 degrees? *Acute*.

adept (uh DEPT)

highly skilled (adjective)

 ABLE DEPuTy

Although this word is not linked to such words as *apt*, *inept*, and *aptitude*, it may as well be. *Adept* and *inept* are direct opposites, but do not share a common history. In the Middle Ages, alchemists were busy trying to perform impossible feats such as turning lead into gold; the word *adept* was used to refer to someone who had (supposedly) unlocked the secrets of alchemy.

adroit (uh DROYT)

cleverly skilled (adjective)

 ADD RIGHT

This is one of those words that helps to keep right-handed people in power. The French word *droit* means right, and is related to a number of words that mean skilled or correct. See the word *gauche* elsewhere in this book for the rest of the story.

articulate (ar TIK yuh lit)

well-spoken (adjective)

 ARe TICks Up LATE TELLING STORIES?

This word can also be used as a verb, meaning to pronounce or express clearly. To *articulate* something, you must pronounce each part separately. This sense of the word explains why a part of a plant or creature having two sections joined by a flexible connection is called an *articulation*.

astute (uh STOOT)

clever; intelligent (adjective)

 A Smart TUTor

Synonyms for this word include *wily* and *cunning*, which indicate craftiness, and *sagacious*, which indicates perceptiveness.

conceive (kun SEEV)

to understand or imagine (verb)

 CAN SEE

The psychic monkey perceives the future by receiving messages in his crystal ball. Or he may be a fraud, intending to deceive his customers.

concoct (kun KAHKT)

to create by mixing together (verb)

 CONFUSING COCKTAIL

This word is related to *cook*. It can mean to create something physical, such as a weird drink, or it can mean to form a strange idea or plan. The bartender may have to *concoct* an excuse to her boss explaining why she can't mix the drinks correctly.

deft (DEFT)

skilled; agile (adjective)

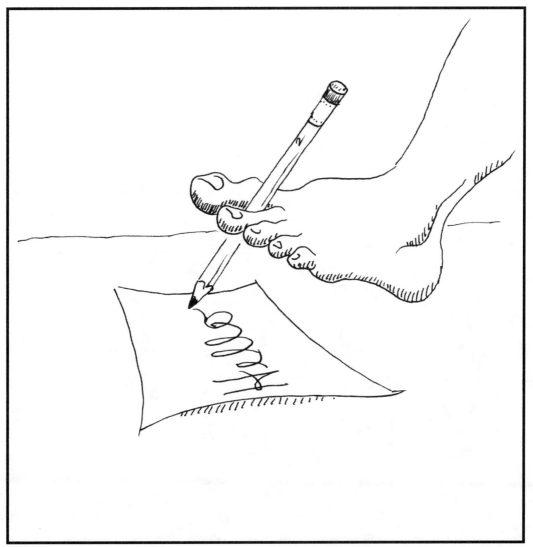

 SKILLE**D** L**EFT** FOOT

This word is descended from the word *daft*, which today means foolish. *Daft* originally meant appropriate or fitting; then, because meekness is fitting behavior, it came to mean gentle or meek. Eventually, people decided that being meek was stupid. *Deft*, however, has come to mean efficient and skillful.

eloquent (EL uh kwunt)

well-spoken (adjective)

 SELL A MINT

The Latin root *loq* (or *loc*) means to talk. Some other words derived from it include *loquacious, elocution, soliloquy,* and *ventriloquism.*

explicate (EK splik ayt)

to explain (verb)

 X INDICATES

Based on its Latin roots, this word literally means to unfold. Now that the map has been unfolded, the location of the treasure can be explained. You may have seen this warning on albums: "PARENTAL ADVISORY: *EXPLICIT* LYRICS." While there it is meant to indicate that the album contains dirty words, *explicit* more generally means expressed clearly. If someone asks you to be more *explicit*, you should explain yourself more fully.

germane (jur MAYN)

connected to the topic being discussed (adjective)

 YOUR MAIN POINT

This word can be traced back to the Latin word *germen*, meaning *bud*. You may know the word *germinate*, which means to sprout or grow. A *germane* comment, then, is related to the main conversation, just as a bud or sprout is related to the main plant.

persuasive (pur SWAY siv)

able to change others' minds (adjective)

 WHISPER SWAYS

The *suas* part of this word (through the *suad* part of the word *persuade*) is distantly related to sweet; if you are *persuasive*, people will swallow your ideas because they're sweet, not bitter.

principle (PRIN suh pul)

a rule that guides one's behavior (noun)

 PRINCE

This word and *prince* are closely related; a *principle* was a law or rule that a leader dictated to his people. Be careful that you don't confuse this word with *principal*, which can mean either most important, or a leader (such as the *principal* of a school).

shrewd (SHROOD)

clever; aware; unlikely to be tricked (adjective)

 SMART DUDE

This word has had a long and varied history, which shows how the meaning of a word can change drastically over the centuries. It has gone through all of the following definitions of these words: *evil*, *stern*, *piercing*, *scolding*, and *cunning*.

subtle (SUT ul)

not obvious; faint (adjective)

 SHUTTLE BUS

Subtle details are easily missed by someone who is not paying attention. A subtlety, like the pronunciation of this word, is something that is not obvious at first glance. The word subtle can also indicate sneakiness, probably because people who don't notice subtleties tend to assume that they are purposefully hidden.

DRILLS

Quiz #6

For each question below, choose the word that is LEAST similar to the other two.

1. a. germane   b. shrewd   c. acumen
2. a. astute   b. concoct   c. adept
3. a. articulate   b. eloquent   c. subtle
4. a. persuasive   b. deft   c. adroit
5. a. conceive   b. principle   c. explicate

Puzzle #6

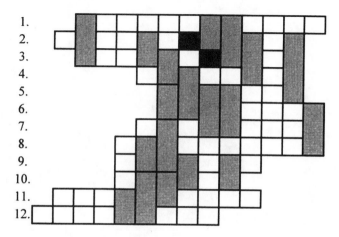

1. clever; skilled
2. clever; skilled
3. not obvious; skilled
4. well-spoken
5. create
6. understand
7. rule
8. convincing
9. relevant
10. skill
11. well-spoken
12. explain

CHAPTER **7**

GIMME THREE STEPS:

Words about not having too much
or too little

acquiesce (ak wee ES)

to agree without protest (verb)

 SURE, I GUESS

This word is related to *quiet*; when you *acquiesce*, you agree *quietly*, without putting up a fight. If you are *acquiescent*, you are willing to go along with something; if you are *quiescent*, you are inactive.

appease (uh PEEZ)

to satisfy or calm (verb)

 APe + PlEASE

This word is descended from the Latin word *pax*, which also gives us the words *peace* and *pacify*. Freeing the pet ape should *appease* the protesters. When Germany was busy absorbing half of Europe in the 1930s, Britain maintained a policy of *appeasement*, trying peacefully to get Germany to promise to stop invading any more countries. Unfortunately, as Britain finally realized, sometimes *appeasement* doesn't work nearly as well as war.

compliant (kum PLY unt)

willing to do what others want (adjective)

 NO **COMPLAINT**

Through the magic of Latin, this word is related to *complete*; to be *compliant* is to fulfill someone's wishes. A similar-sounding word is *pliant*, meaning flexible or easily shaped. Although these two words have different histories, they both can describe a person who does as others say.

concise (kun SYSE)

using few words (adjective)

 ONCE IS NICE

The *cis* part of this word means to cut. It also appears in such words as *incisor*, *decisive*, and *scissors*. A *concise* message is short—all of the extra words have been cut out.

equate (ih KWAYT)

to consider two things equal (verb)

 EQUAL WEIGHT

This word is often used in reference to abstract ideas. For example, you might say that a businessperson *equates* money with happiness, or that a coach *equates* winning with success. What you're hinting at is that money can't always buy happiness, or that winning isn't always the true measure of success.

generic (juh NAYR ik)

not specific; not of a particular brand (adjective)

 GENERal AND basIC

This word is related to *general*, as they both come from the Latin *genus*, meaning kind or type. Something *generic* is not of a particular type, but is representative of a larger group. Many people save money by using the *generic* equivalent when having a prescription filled at the pharmacy—it has the same active ingredients as the name-brand product, but costs less because no money has been spent to advertise it.

imply (im PLY)

to hint at something without clearly stating it (verb)

 **PLY**wood

This word is often confused with *infer*. To *imply* is to hint at something; to *infer* is to figure out what is being *implied*. A related word is *implicit*, which means that something is understood without being stated outright.

latent (LAY tunt)

hidden; beneath the surface (adjective)

 not BLATANT

This word is used in a number of fields. Detectives look for *latent* fingerprints, which are not visible to the naked eye, but which become visible when dusted with powder. Biologists describe a characteristic as *latent* if it is undeveloped but could grow normally. Psychologists use *latent* to describe a subconscious thought.

oblique (o BLEEK)

not clearly stated; indirect (adjective)

 WON'T SPEAK

The original definition of this word referred to lines and angles: An *oblique* line is slanted, not parallel or perpendicular to another line. If you think about some ways to say that someone is being honest or responsible, such as being direct or forthright or confronting something head on, you'll see how *oblique* came to describe remarks that are not straightforward.

opaque (o PAYK)

not letting light through; difficult to understand (adjective)

 STEAK

This word has two related, yet distinct, meanings. The first refers to light: Something *opaque*, such as a thick piece of beef, does not allow light to pass through. The second refers to understanding: Something *opaque*, such as an explanation, is difficult or impossible to figure out. Something *opaque* has *opacity*.

perfunctory (per FUNK tor ee)

done mechanically, or with little attention to the task (adjective)

 NO FUNK

This word comes from the Latin root *funct*, meaning to perform. If something is done *perfunctorily*, it is done in a routine manner, with little thought or feeling. Other related words include *function* and *defunct*.

slake (SLAYK)

to satisfy or lessen (verb)

 DRINKS A LAKE

This word comes from Old English, and is related to *slack*, which means slower or looser. If you *slake* your thirst, it becomes less intense.

soothing (SOO thing)

calming; comforting (adjective)

 SmOOTHING

This word comes from the Old English word *soth*, meaning true. Knowing the truth can put your mind at ease. The word *soothsayer* comes from this same root. A *soothsayer* is a fortune teller, and is so named because he (supposedly) can speak the truth by predicting the future.

sufficient (suh FISH unt)

adequate; just enough (adjective)

 SOME FISH

This word comes from the Latin root *fic* (or *fac*), meaning to make or do. There are many English words descended from this root; the words most similar to *sufficient* include *proficient*, *deficient*, and *efficient*.

tantamount (TAN tuh mownt)

having the same effect; equivalent (adjective)

 EQUIVA**LENT AMOUNT**

This word was formed by the addition of the Latin word *tantum*, meaning so much, to a word which eventually became *amount*. If one thing is *tantamount* to another, they amount to the same thing.

vestigial (ves TIJ ee ul)

left over from an earlier time (adjective)

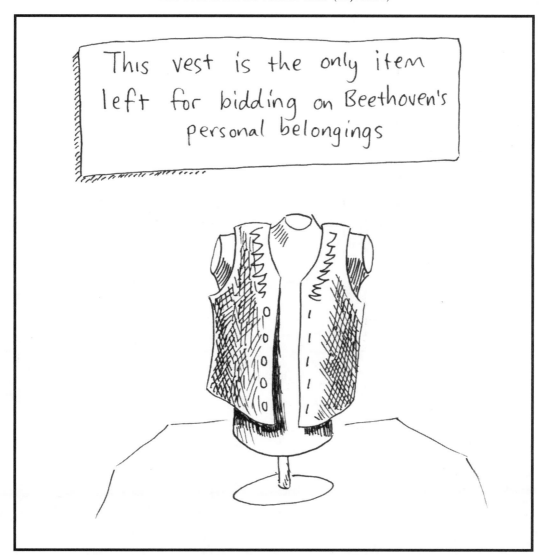

 VEST IS ALL THAT'S LEFT

The Latin word for a footprint is *vestigium*. Like a footprint, something *vestigial* is a clue to the past. Your appendix, for example, is a *vestigial* organ. It was useful many thousands of years ago, but as humans have evolved, it now serves no purpose (except to put you in the hospital if it decides to burst). A *vestige* is a trace or hint of something that no longer exists.

DRILLS

Quiz #7

For each question below, choose the word that is LEAST similar to the other two

1.   a.   compliant   b.   acquiesce   c.   sufficient

2.   a.   sufficient   b.   imply   c.   oblique

3.   a.   soothing   b.   slake   c.   latent

4.   a.   tantamount   b.   vestigial   c.   equate

Puzzle #7

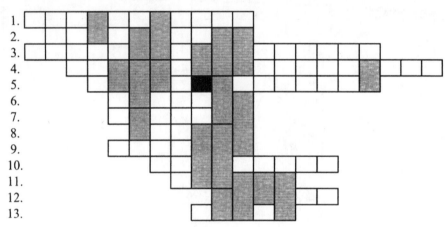

1. done without thought

2. enough

3. not specific; equivalent

4. agreeable; obsolete

5. hint; relaxing

6. satisfy

7. short

8. unclear

9. indirect

10. agree

11. consider the same

12. hidden

13. satisfy

CHAPTER 8

AND JUSTICE FOR ALL:

Words about knowledge and evidence

beacon (BEE kun)

something that guides (noun)

 BACON

A lighthouse is a kind of *beacon*, guiding ships away from dangerous rocks. Airports use radio *beacons*, emitting steady beeps, to guide planes. The word can also be used figuratively—in his "I Have a Dream" speech, Martin Luther King, Jr., described the Emancipation Proclamation as a "great *beacon* light of hope".

cite (SYTE)

to mention as a source of information (verb)

 SHE'S RIGHT

If you are asked to *cite* your sources, you are being asked to tell where you got your information. A *citation* can be a quotation from an authoritative source, but it can also be an order to appear in court.

conclusive (kun KLOO siv)

deciding something without a doubt (adjective)

 CLUE

Conclusive evidence allows something to be *concluded*. The detective has reached the *conclusion* that this is the criminal's footstep. The *clus* part of each of these words comes from a Latin root meaning to close. Case closed!

corroborate (kuh RAH buh rayt)

to confirm an explanation (verb)

 ROBBER

In court, *uncorroborated* testimony is that which cannot be backed up by anyone else. Here, though, the robber holding the pocketbook is *corroborating* the victim's story. This word is related to *robust*, another word in this book. To *corroborate* a story is to strengthen it.

deliberate (dih LIB uh rayt)

to discuss for a long time (verb)

 DELIVER LATE

A jury *deliberates* when it goes off to decide a case. This word is derived from the Latin word *libra*, meaning scales. To *deliberate* means to weigh the different alternatives. As an adjective, *deliberate* means slow and careful or intentional.

elaborate (ih LAB uh rayt)

to explain in detail (verb)

> I wish your boyfriend wouldn't blabber on the machine for hours saying how much he misses you.
>
> BLAH BLAH BLAH BLAH BLAH....

 BLABBER

As an adjective, this word means complicated or detailed. It is related to the word labor—to *elaborate* on something requires more effort.

excavate (eks kuh VAYT)

to dig out; to dig up (verb)

 CAVE

This word comes from the Latin word *cavus*, meaning hollow. Related words include *cave*, *concave*, and *cavity*. To *excavate* can mean to empty something out, such as a buried tomb; it can also mean to remove by digging up, such as the contents of a tomb.

exonerate (ig ZAH nuh rayt)

to free from blame or obligation (verb)

 EGGS + HONOR

An *onus* is a burden or obligation, and something *onerous* is troublesome. The prefix *ex* means not or away, so if you are *exonerated*, you are freed from some responsibility.

hierarchy (HYE uh rar kee)

a group ranked in order of importance or power (noun)

 HIGHER ARE WE

This word is formed by two Greek roots: *hieros*, meaning holy, and *archos*, meaning leader. It originally described a rank of angels, then was extended to describe the rank of a religious group. Eventually, the word lost its connection with religion; it can now be used to describe any group ranked by order.

inquisitive (in KWIH zih tiv)

overly curious (adjective)

 QUIZ

Related words include *inquire*, *inquiry*, *inquest*, *query*, and *question*. An *inquisition* is a ruthless or unfair investigation; this meaning pays tribute to the Spanish *Inquisition*, which was exceedingly harsh in its efforts to punish heresy in the 1500s.

palpable (PAL puh bul)

able to be felt or touched (adjective)

 PULP-ABLE

This word is often used in a figurative sense. You might say that someone's fear was *palpable*, for example, if the fear was so obvious or strong that it almost seemed that you could reach out and touch it.

queue (KYOO)

a line, usually of people (noun)

This word originally meant an animal's tail; then it came to mean a long braid of hair running down the back, like a tail. Eventually, it acquired the meaning of a line of people or objects, the shape of the line suggesting a tail. This picture can help you remember how to spell the word: "Q-you-he-you-he" means "q-u-e-u-e".

refute (rih FYOOT)

to show to be false; to deny the truth of (verb)

 REFUse To AgrEe

This word comes from Latin, and means the same thing as *rebut*, which has a Germanic source. The evidence for these claims is *irrefutable*.

specimen (SPES uh mun)

a scientific sample; an example of a group (noun)

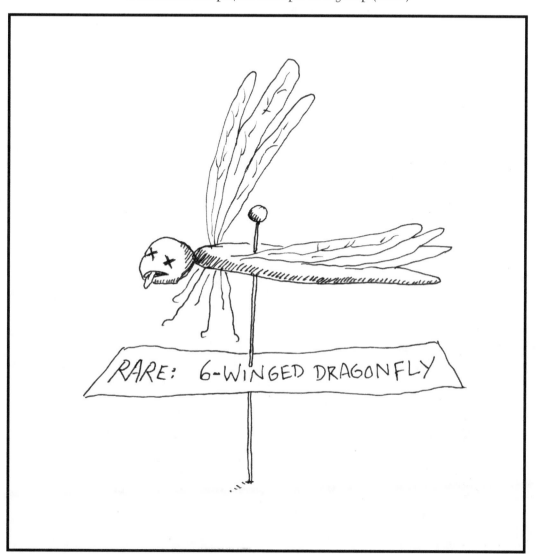

RARE: 6-WINGED DRAGONFLY

 SPECIAL

A *specimen* is something to be observed or inspected. It can be something unusual, such as this dragonfly, or it can be something more common that represents a larger group. If a doctor takes a *specimen* from a patient, for example, the doctor assumes that it will be representative of the patient's health. An unusual *specimen* in this case would be misleading to the doctor.

tactile (TAK tul)

related to the sense of touch (adjective)

 TACK

The *tact* part of this word means to touch; it can also be found in *contact*. *Tactile* describes something related to touch, just as visual does for sight, aural does for hearing, olfactory does for smell, and gustatory does for taste.

tangible (TAN juh bul)

able to be felt or touched (adjective)

TANGERINE

This word means the same thing as *palpable*, which you saw a few pages back, so we decided to continue the citrus fruit theme. The *tang* part comes from the same Latin root as the *tact* part of *tactile*, which you saw on the last page. Something *intangible* has no form or substance.

DRILLS

Quiz #8

For each question below, choose the word that is LEAST similar to the other two.

1.	a.	tangible	b.	elaborate	c.	palpable
2.	a.	deliberate	b.	cite	c.	corroborate
3.	a.	hierarchy	b.	queue	c.	beacon
4.	a.	specimen	b.	exonerate	c.	refute
5.	a.	inquisitive	b.	tactile	c.	excavate

Puzzle #8

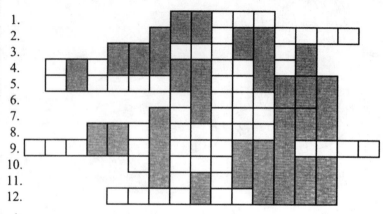

1. line

2. asking questions

3. deciding

4. signal; of feeling

5. disprove; solid

6. solid

7. explain

8. quote; unearth

9. example; layered structure

10. consider

11. free

12. verify

CHAPTER 9

CHANGES:
Words about changing and being different

adapt (uh DAPT)

to change in order to better handle a situation (verb)

 WINGS FLAPPED

This word is related to *apt*, meaning suitable or appropriate. When creatures *adapt* to their surroundings, they develop characteristics that make it easier for them to survive. If all of a species' natural enemies had to walk on the ground, for example, *adapting* to life in the air might be a way to ensure that the species would survive.

ambivalent (am BIV ul unt)

having difficulty making a decision (adjective)

 AM SWIVELING

The prefix *ambi* means both, and the *val* part of this word means strong (as in valor or valiant). To feel *ambivalent* is to have strong feelings in two different directions. Other words with this prefix include *ambidextrous*, *ambiguous*, and *ambience*.

contradiction (kahn truh DIK shun)

two statements that cannot both be true (noun)

![icon] FACT OR FICTION

Based on its Latin roots, the word *contradict* literally means "speak against." Here is a classic *contradiction*, consisting of two sentences that cannot simultaneously be true: "The following sentence is true. The preceding sentence is false." If you assume the first sentence is true, it makes the second sentence true, which means that the first sentence is really false. If you assume the second sentence is true, though, the first statement is false, which means that the second sentence cannot be true.

erratic (ih RAT ik)

unpredictable (adjective)

 AIR + ATTIC

The Latin word *errare* means to wander. Something *erratic*, such as an out-of-control airplane, wanders in different directions. To *err*, or to make an *error*, involves the same idea of wandering away from what is correct. The word *erroneous* is listed elsewhere in this book.

evanescent (ev un ES unt)

likely to disappear (adjective)

 VANISHING SCENT

The verbs *evanesce* and *vanish* both come from the same Latin root, but *vanish* entered the English language much earlier. As Old English mutated into Middle English, the combination *sc* was eventually replaced by *sh*. When *evanesce* entered the language much later, it retained the *sc*.

expunge (ik SPUNJ)

to erase or eliminate completely (verb)

 SPONGE

Although he's doing his best, this daring lad hasn't truly *expunged* the homework assignment—to *expunge* means to remove completely. If the teacher didn't write down the assignment and doesn't remember what it was, and if none of the students speaks up, then the homework will truly have been *expunged*. Otherwise, it's simply been erased.

fickle (FIK ul)

changing one's feelings for no apparent reason (adjective)

 PICKLE

Someone who is *fickle* might love you one day, ignore you the next day, then love you again the day after that. This word originally meant deceitful, but it now means changeable.

fluctuate (FLUK choo ayt)

to change back and forth (verb)

 WHAT YOU ATE

The Latin root *fluct* means to flow, so to *fluctuate* means to flow back and forth. For example, the stock market *fluctuates* as stock prices go up and down. A related word with a number of different meanings is *flux*.

inconsistent (in kun SIS tunt)

unpredictable; not agreeing logically (adjective)

 NEAR AND DISTANT

This word has two important meanings. One meaning is similar to those of some other words in this chapter, such as *erratic*, *fickle*, and *fluctuating*: irregular or unpredictable. The other meaning is similar to that of *contradiction*: not making logical sense.

molten (MOL tun)

so hot as to be in liquid form (adjective)

 MICHAEL BOLTON

This adjective comes from an archaic form of the verb *melt*. Another word in this book, *swell*, has a similar adjective form: swollen. You will most often hear *molten* used in reference to volcanoes; lava is *molten* rock.

motley (MAHT lee)

having many different unrelated parts (adjective)

 MOSTLY DIFFERENT

A *mote* is a speck of dust; something that is *motley* can be thought to look speckled, because it is made up of many unrelated parts. These fellows look like a *motley* crew; let's hope they sound like one, too!

permutation (pur myoo TAY shun)

a rearrangement or reshaping (noun)

 PERM MUTATION

As you probably could have guessed, this word is closely related to *mutation*, an abnormal change. In math, a *permutation* is an arrangement of certain items in which the order of the items is important. For example, there are six *permutations* of the letters A, B, and C written in a row: ABC, ACB, BAC, BCA, CAB, and CBA.

revamp (ree VAMP)

to improve or renovate (verb)

 REVIse A StAMP

A *vamp* is the upper part of a shoe, so to *revamp* really means to fix a shoe. This word had been broadened, of course, to refer to fixing just about anything. It usually indicates that the thing being fixed is being improved in some way, not just restored to its original condition.

supplant (suh PLANT)

to take the place of, usually through dishonest means (verb)

 DIGS UP PLANTs

This word and *plant* actually sprout from the same root. The Latin word *planta* means the sole of the foot, which is what you use to push a shovel into the ground. It's also visible when you trip someone, hoping to take his or her place.

tentative (TEN tuh tiv)

unsure; not settled (adjective)

TENT TO LIVE?

If a situation is *tentative*, you're trying it out temporarily. This couple's plans to buy a house are only *tentative*, because they depend on the bank's decision.

vacillate (VAS uh layt)

to have difficulty making a decision (verb)

 CASTLE GATE

To *vacillate* means to go back and forth between two alternatives. A related word is *oscillate*, which means to swing back and forth steadily, like a pendulum. An *oscillating* fan is one which moves back and forth in order to improve the air circulation.

DRILLS

Quiz #9

For each question below, choose the word that is LEAST similar to the other two.

1. a. fluctuate   b. erratic   c. motley
2. a. revamp   b. adapt   c. evanescent
3. a. tentative   b. contradiction   c. inconsistent
4. a. ambivalent   b. permutation   c. vacillate
5. a. supplant   b. fickle   c. expunge

Puzzle #9

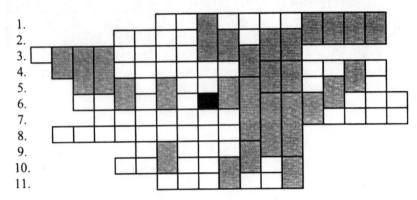

1. arrangement

2. logical impossibility

3. improve; unpredictable

4. short-lived; dissimilar

5. waver; liquid

6. changeable; uncertain

7. undecided; change

8. not uniform

9. replace

10. change

11. eliminate

CHAPTER 10

ALONE AGAIN:

Words about being alone and getting rejected

aloof (uh LOOF)

keeping apart from others (adjective)

 ALone on the rOOF

For reasons too arcane to mention, this word was formed from the idea of a ship sailing into the wind and keeping clear of shore so it didn't run aground. Eventually, it came to describe people who "steered clear" of others or gave them a "wide berth".

arcane (ar KAYN)

known by only a select few; mysterious, because of secrecy (adjective)

 ARCADE

Arcana is secret or specialized knowledge. Both of these words come from the Latin word *arca*, meaning chest. Something *arcane* is kept secret, as though hidden in a treasure chest.

detached (dih TACHT)

not involved; impartial (adjective)

 DEb jusT wATCHED

Detach means to disconnect. Someone who is detached is apart from a group, and is not interested in participating in the group's activities. Deb is emotionally and physically detached from dune buggy racing.

dormant (DOR mint)

asleep; inactive (adjective)

 DOORMAT

The Latin root *dorm*, meaning sleep, also gives us the word *dormitory*. Something that is *dormant* is not necessarily asleep, but may be inactive for some other reason. This word is similar in meaning to *latent*, another word in this book.

embargo (em BAR go)

a ban on trade with a nation (noun)

 END CARGO

This word comes from the Spanish word *embargar*, meaning impede, but (of course) it ultimately comes from Latin. It is related to the words *barrel* and *barrier*, which could be used to *barricade* roads in order to prevent shipments from entering a country.

hermit (HUR mit)

one who lives alone, away from society (noun)

 PERMIT

A *hermitage* is a place of seclusion, where a person can go to be alone. It can also be a place where a group of *hermits* live, such as a monastery or abbey. A *hermit* crab is a soft crab that uses empty snail shells to protect itself. As the crab grows too large to fit inside a certain shell, it abandons it in favor of a larger shell.

inhibited (in HIB it ud)

reluctant to express or enjoy oneself (adjective)

 RIVETED

This word comes from the Latin root *habere*, meaning to hold. An *inhibited* person holds back from having fun. Joe is having trouble getting over his *inhibition*, because it feels as though his feet are *riveted* (bolted or pinned) to the floor.

insular (IN suh lur)

isolated (adjective)

 INSULATED

The Latin word for island, *insula*, give us the words *insular* and *insulated*. Something *insular* is set apart or protected from its surroundings.

quarantine (KWOR un teen)

to isolate something, usually because it has a contagious disease (verb)

 GUARANTEED TIME ALONE

The Latin *quarant*, meaning forty, is hidden in *quarantine*. When a ship coming into port was suspected of carrying some disease, it was kept in the harbor for forty days, presumably until the disease was no longer contagious. Now the word can refer to any period of isolation, for any length of time, but it principally refers to one involving an illness or a dangerous substance.

rebuff (rih BUF)

to refuse, often bluntly (verb)

 BUFFY'S HAD **ENOUGH SHUFF**LING

This word comes from an Italian word, *ribuffo*, which means a reprimand. Essentially, *ribuffo* means "re-puff" or "blow back".

sequester (sih KWES tur)

to isolate (verb)

The jury was kept in trial all semester long, and I missed classes.

 SEMESTER

As shown above, a jury on an important case is sometimes *sequestered*, or kept apart from society, for weeks or months. This is done so that the jurors won't hear (or spread) any rumors about the case. The jury lives in a hotel and can't watch TV, read newspapers, or talk to anyone. In the classic Pauly Shore film *Jury Duty*, his character attempts to drag out a case for as long as possible so that he can keep living in a fancy hotel.

spurn (SPURN)

to refuse; to scorn (verb)

 SPit and tURN

This word comes from the Old English word *spurnan*, meaning to kick. (The word *spur* is also related to this word.) To *spurn* someone would be like kicking or stomping on his or her toes.

stolid (STAH lid)

showing little emotion; expressionless (adjective)

 STERN AND SOLID

This word is distantly related to such words as *stall* (a small area for a horse or cow) and *stale* (not fresh). A *stolid* person is unmoved by emotion, just as an animal cannot move around in its stall.

supine (SOO pyne)

lying on one's back; inactive (adjective)

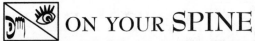 ON YOUR SPINE

This word can describe something such as a person lying down face-up, or a hand with the palm facing upward. It has been generalized from this meaning to describe something that is not active.

transparent (tranz PAR unt)

see-through; poorly disguised (adjective)

 DAN'S PARENTS

This word originally described something that let light shine through, such as glass. It has taken on a figurative meaning; a *transparent* excuse, for example, does a poor job of hiding the truth. The aliens' disguises are *transparent* because you can see right through them—figuratively, of course.

DRILLS

Quiz #10

For each question below, choose the word that is LEAST similar to the other two.

1.	a.	hermit	b.	insular	c.	stolid
2.	a.	quarantine	b.	inhibited	c.	sequester
3.	a.	transparent	b.	spurn	c.	rebuff
4.	a.	detached	b.	aloof	c.	arcane
5.	a.	dormant	b.	embargo	c.	supine

Puzzle #10

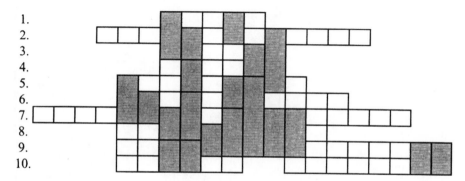

1. uninvolved

2. ban; refuse

3. not widely known

4. reclining

5. isolate

6. refuse; unemotional

7. clear; alone

8. isolate

9. inactive; not moving freely

10. loner; uninvolved

CHAPTER

OOPS, I DID IT AGAIN:

Words about unnecessary or useless things

banal (buh NAL)

not interesting; commonplace (adjective)

 BANANA

This word has three more or less commonly accepted pronunciations; the other two are "BAY nul" and "buh NAHL". Before refrigerated trucks, getting tropical fruit in the north was sometimes difficult. Your grandparents may have stories about being very excited when they got a banana or an orange in their Christmas stocking. However, now we can get just about any fruit or vegetable at any time of year, so no one gets excited about bananas.

cower (KOW er)

to hide in fear (verb)

 COW + fEaR

To cow someone is to frighten with threats. Although the word coward has a different origin from cower and cow, it has essentially the same meaning.

cursory (KUR suh ree)

done quickly and not carefully (adjective)

 CURSOR WILL HURRY

This word comes from a Latin word meaning to run. If your cursor, the marker that shows where you are on a computer document, is moving fast, you must not be reading very carefully; you're taking only a cursory glance at the text. Let's hope that this guy doesn't start cursing at his slow computer.

dilute (dye LOOT)

to make weaker by adding something of lesser quality (verb)

 DULL FRUIT JUICE

Based on its Latin roots, this word means to wash away. It can refer to liquids, of course, but can be applied to other situations as well. For example, a forceful argument might be diluted by the addition of a number of unimportant points that reduce the overall effect.

extraneous (ek STRAY nee us)

unnecessary; not essential (adjective)

 EXTRA TRAIN NEEDLESS

The Latin prefix extra means outside or beyond. Something extraneous goes beyond what is needed.

founder (FOWN dur)

to fail; to sink (verb)

 FLOUNDER

The Latin root fund means bottom. To founder means to sink to the bottom or collapse. Other words with this root include foundation, fundamental, and profound. The verb flounder means to move clumsily or splash about, but does not mean to sink.

inadvertent (in ud VUR tunt)

accidental; unintentional (adjective)

 FALLING ADVERTIsemENT

> An adversary is an enemy, and if someone is being adverse, he or she is acting against you. These words indicate willful opposition or harm. Something inadvertent may be harmful, but it is accidental.

irrelevant (ih REL uh vunt)

not related to the topic being discussed (adjective)

 ELEPHANT

If something is relevant, it is worthy of being "raised" in conversation. This explains its connection to the word relief, which means artwork with some elements raised above a flat surface. Irrelevant means not relevant—so not worthy of discussion.

meander (mee AN dur)

to walk around with little direction (verb)

MEn wANDER

This word comes from the Greek name of the Maeander River (now called the Menderes) in Turkey, which follows a winding course as it approaches the sea.

mimic (MIM ik)

to imitate (verb)

 COPY A **GIMMICK**

Some creatures use mimicry to survive; for example, some species of frogs have evolved to look like other species of poisonous frogs, which keeps them from being eaten by predators. Lots of new TV shows use mimicry, but they generally don't live as long as the original.

redundant (rih DUN dunt)

repeating something already said; unnecessary (adjective)

 RED ANT

This word, along with some others in this book, comes from the Latin word *unda*, meaning wave. If something is redundant, it's like an overflow of information. You may have heard the redundant slogan for a certain brand of insecticide: "kills bugs dead". Well, what else would they be after you had killed them?

sinecure (SYE nih kyoor)

a paying job that requires little effort (noun)

 **SECURE**

This word is formed from a Latin phrase, sine cura, meaning without care. A sinecure is a job that has few responsibilities.

stagnant (STAG nunt)

not moving; not developing (adjective)

 STAG

The Latin word stagnum means a swamp; stagnant water is foul because it isn't flowing. A person (or deer) can become stagnant—or stagnate—by not trying to improve his or her life. Buck is content to do the same old thing, day after day, while his wife is trying to move on to new opportunities.

superficial (soo pur FISH ul)

concerned with only what is on the surface (adjective)

 SUPER-VISUAL

The Latin roots *super*, meaning above, and *facies*, meaning face, combine to form this word. The word *surface* is formed in the same way, because *sur* also means above. This person took a *superficial* glance at the newspaper, and therefore didn't realize that the newspaper itself was *superficial*—that it didn't go into the stories with any depth.

tangential (tan JEN shul)

barely related to the topic being discussed (adjective)

 TAN GENT

The tang part of this word comes from the Latin word tangere, to touch. You may have heard of a tangent line in your math class; a tangent line touches another curve at exactly one point. If someone goes off on a tangent, he or she departs from the topic at hand by discussing something else—following the tangent line, instead of following the curve of the conversation.

tedious (TEE dee us)

boring; slow and dull (adjective)

 TirED and sIck Of US

This word describes something that is long, slow, and boring. Tedium is boredom due to something that is long and drawn-out.

DRILLS

Quiz #11

For each question below, choose the word that is LEAST similar to the other two.

1.   a. mimic   b. extraneous   c. redundant

2.   a. superficial   b. cursory   c. meander

3.   a. tangential   b. dilute   c. irrelevant

4.   a. inadvertent   b. banal   c. tedious

5.   a. stagnant   b. cower   c. founder

Puzzle #11

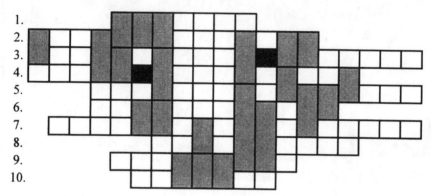

1. hasty

2. easy job; weaken

3. not deep; boring

4. fear; unimportant

5. imitate; accidental

6. not interesting; go indirectly

7. not growing; unimportant

8. unnecessary

9. repetitive

10. sink

CHAPTER 12

ERUPTION:

Words about bad attitudes and getting angry

apoplexy (AP uh plek see)

a fit of rage (noun)

 POP

This word's original meaning described a blood vessel rupturing in the brain. It has been extended to mean an episode of intense anger. Someone who is *apoplectic* is enraged.

brash (BRASH)

insensitive; rudely bold (adjective)

 Big cRASH

This word sounds similar to *brassy* and *brazen*, which also have the same general meaning. This fellow's cymbals are made of brass, which helps to explain where these two words come from. Synonyms for *brash* include *rash*, *presumptuous*, and *impudent*.

calumny (KAL um nee)

false, harmful statements about someone (noun)

 CALL ALUMNI NAMES

To *defame* is to spread falsehoods about someone in order to damage his or her reputation. To *slander* someone is to defame orally. To commit *libel* is to defame someone in print, or some other method that is recorded. *Calumny* can be either spoken or written.

crass (KRAS)

unrefined; insensitive (adjective)

 NO CLASS

This word describes someone with bad—or a complete lack of—manners. Synonyms include *coarse*, *unrefined*, and *vulgar*.

crude (KROOD)

blunt; impolite (adjective)

 CRuel and **R**ude

Like *crass*, this word can also mean unrefined. *Crude* oil is raw oil that needs to be processed in a refinery before it can be used. If a person is described as *crude*, he or she is rude and tactless.

defiant (dih FYE unt)

refusing to do what someone wants (adjective)

 DEaF gIANT

This word comes from the Latin word *fidus*, meaning faithful, but means the opposite because of the prefix *de*. To *defy* someone is to be unfaithful to his or her wishes.

draconian (dray KO nee un)

overly strict; exceedingly harsh (adjective)

 DRACULA

This word is derived from the name *Draco*. *Draco* was responsible for drawing up a set of laws and punishments in the city of Athens in about 621 B.C. His laws were consistent to a fault—nearly every offense called for the death penalty. Most of Draco's laws were repealed about 25 years later, but his name lives on in our word *draconian*.

goad (GOHD)

to push into action (verb)

 TOAD

This word originally meant a pointed stick used to move animals along. It can be used in other situations as well; as a verb, to *goad* means to urge someone to do something, often by harassing or pestering the person (or toad).

infuriate (in FYUR ee ayt)

to make very angry (verb)

 IN FUR I hATE

This word is related to *fury* and *furious*; to *infuriate* means to make someone *furious*.

jeer (JEER)

to taunt or ridicule (verb)

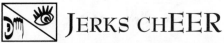 JERKS chEER

Synonyms for this word include *mock*, *gibe*, and *disparage*. It can also be used as a noun.

provoke (pruh VOHK)

to cause a feeling or reaction; to push into action (verb)

 POKE

This word is formed from the Latin roots *pro*, meaning forward, and *voc*, meaning to call. To *provoke* something is to call it forth, to cause it to begin. If you *provoke* someone, you make them angry and cause them to react. If something—such as a story— is *provocative*, it stimulates thoughts or feelings.

querulous (KWER uh lus)

complaining (adjective)

 QUERying tUrtLe grOUSes

This word has a slightly different meaning from its cousin *quarrelsome*. Someone who is *querulous* complains or grumbles, but doesn't necessarily argue or quarrel.

raucous (RAW kus)

loud and unpleasant-sounding (adjective)

 ROCK US

This word comes straight from the Latin word *raucus*, with a minor spelling variation. What a *ruckus*!

sarcasm (SAR kaz um)

humorous comments intended to ridicule (noun)

 SHARK

This word is descended from the Greek word *sarx*, meaning flesh. A *sarcastic* remark can be described as cutting or biting, as though it caused a physical wound. *Sarcasm* contains irony, which is the use of words to mean the opposite of what they usually mean. When the judge says "Nice shark" about this piece of junk, it's clear that the judge is being *sarcastic*, and really thinks that the shark stinks.

truculent (TRUK yuh lunt)

willing to fight (adjective)

 TRUCKers

This word is related to *truncate*, to cut short. To *truncate* something is to defeat it, in a way. Synonyms for *truculent* include *combative*, *pugnacious*, and *belligerent*.

vociferous (vo SIF uh rus)

loud and fierce (adjective)

 VOiCe Is FERociOUS

This word combines two Latin roots: *voc*, meaning voice, and *ferre*, meaning to carry. If you are *vociferous*, your voice carries a long way.

DRILLS

Quiz #12

For each question below, choose the word that is LEAST similar to the other two.

1.   a. provoke   b. goad   c. vociferous

2.   a. sarcasm   b. jeer   c. draconian

3.   a. truculent   b. defiant   c. crass

4.   a. apoplexy   b. querulous   c. infuriate

5.   a. calumny   b. brash   c. raucous

Puzzle #12

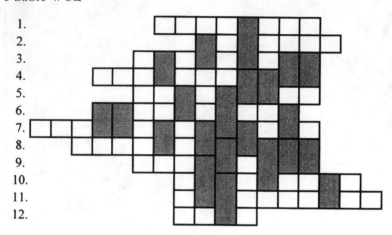

1. rage

2. damaging words

3. warlike

4. make fun of; challenging authority

5. anger

6. loud

7. cause a reaction; biting remarks

8. ill-mannered; loud and unpleasant

9. complaining

10. strict

11. ill-mannered; loud

12. cause a reaction

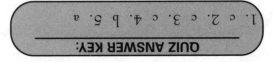

CHAPTER 13

TOTAL ECLIPSE OF THE HEART:

Words about sad or unpleasant situations

chaos (KAY ahs)

complete confusion (noun)

 **STAY LOST**

In math and physics, *chaos* theory is the study of seemingly random behavior, although researchers continue to find interesting patterns within the randomness. In general, though, *chaos* refers to any situation that is totally disordered or confusing.

doleful (DOHL ful)

sad; morose (adjective)

 BOWLFUL

Related words include *dolor* and *dolorous*; all of these words come from the same Latin root, which means to grieve.

dreary (DREER ee)

bleak; dull (adjective)

 DRab and wEARY

This word has softened in meaning over time; it comes from an Old English word, *dreorig*, which meant bloody or gory. In Middle English, *dreri* still meant bloody, but could also mean frightened or sad. Now, in Modern English, only traces of the "sad" meaning remain. *Dreary* is often used to describe a gray, overcast day. If an assignment is *dreary*, it is mind-numbingly boring.

elegy (EL uh jee)

a song or poem for someone who has died (noun)

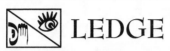 LEDGE

This word comes—through French and Latin—from the Greek word *elegos*, meaning a mournful song. The meaning hasn't changed much since then, although *elegiac* can describe certain forms of poetry, which may or may not be *elegiac* in content.

gaffe (GAF)

an embarrassing mistake (noun)

 GirAFFE

This word describes an error in judgment, usually in a social setting. Synonyms include *blunder* and *faux pas*.

gauche (GOSH)

describing a social blunder (adjective)

 GOAT

Interestingly, the French word *gauche* means left, but also means awkward or tactless. "Normal" people—right-handed people—find it awkward to use their left hands, so the word *gauche* took on this new meaning. Since it's always easier for those in high society to sneer at someone by using a foreign language, the English meaning of *gauche* refers only to social awkwardness.

gloomy (GLOO mee)

partially dark; melancholy (adjective)

 GRAY ROOM

The word *gloom* originally meant partial darkness, but it can also refer to depression. *Gloomy* can mean visually or emotionally dark. It is often used, like *dreary*, to describe a dark, cloudy day. A *gloomy* person could also be described as *glum*.

grimace (GRIM is)

a twisted facial expression of displeasure (noun)

 GRIM FACE

This word can describe a pained look, but it can also be used to describe an expression of mock pain; you might *grimace* when you hear a bad pun, for example. Synonyms include *wince* and *scowl*.

mire (MYRE)

to become stuck (verb)

 MUDDY tIRE

This word comes from an Old Norse word, *myrr*, meaning a bog or swamp. As a noun, it means a deep, soggy area. The verb means to become stuck, as though trapped in *mire*.

noisome (NOY sum)

disgusting; offensive; dangerous (adjective)

 NOSE + TOY

This word is related to *annoy*, which originally meant to make *odious*, which means causing intense dislike. *Noisome* is most often used to described a smell, or fumes in the air.

precipice (PRES uh pis)

a steep cliff (noun)

 SLIP + ICE

This word can also mean the beginning or edge of a dangerous situation; if you act *precipitously*, you are acting hastily, and might fall into such a situation. To *precipitate* something means to cause it to happen suddenly or hastily.

quell (KWEL)

to suppress; to quiet (verb)

 sQUAsh wELL

This word comes from the Old English *cwellan*, meaning to kill. *Quell* has a less intense meaning; it means to put and end to something, often forcefully, but not necessarily to kill.

rout (ROWT)

to defeat decisively (verb)

 dRive OUT

This word comes from Old French, so it has undergone a spelling change that disguises its relation to words such as *rupture*, *erupt*, and *disrupt*. It can also be used as a noun, to describe a crushing defeat.

sordid (SOR did)

filthy; immoral (adjective)

 SORe FROM WHAT I DID

Like many of the words in his book, this word has both a literal and a figurative meaning. If your living conditions are *sordid*, they are extremely dirty or miserable. If your past is *sordid*, you have done a number of morally questionable things. A synonym for this word is *squalid*.

taint (TAYNT)

to make dirty; to corrupt (verb)

 STAINED

This word is related to *tinge* and *tint*, which mean to add a trace of color. To *taint*, though, means to add a trace of something bad. A water supply could become *tainted* by chemicals, or a police department could become *tainted* by corruption.

turbulent (TUR byuh lunt)

not smooth; restless (adjective)

 DISTURB + UNPLEASANT

The Greek root *turb* means confusion or turmoil. If you've ever flown in a plane, you've heard of *turbulence*. The word *turbulent* can describe a physically bumpy ride, such as a flight in a plane, or an emotionally bumpy ride, such as the 1960s. Rufus' rough play is making his owner quite perturbed. Ruff!

DRILLS

Quiz #13

For each question below, choose the word that is LEAST similar to the other two.

1. a. gaffe   b. noisome   c. gauche

2. a. rout   b. gloomy   c. dreary

3. a. mire   b. elegy   c. doleful

4. a. sordid   b. taint   c. grimace

5. a. chaos   b. quell   c. turbulent

Puzzle #13

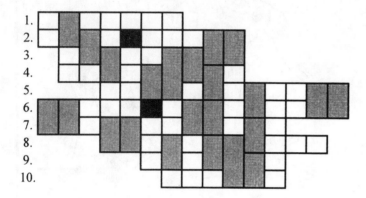

1. depressed

2. defeat; soil

3. unsteady

4. trap; tribute

5. stop; pained look

6. mistake; steep drop

7. awkward; depressing

8. confusion; dirty

9. disgusting

10. depressing

CHAPTER 14

DUST IN THE WIND:

Words about destruction and saying nasty things

abduct (ab DUKT)

to kidnap (verb)

 DUCK

This word is formed from the Latin roots *ab*, meaning away, and *ducere*, meaning to lead. A ventilation *duct* leads air away, and a tear *duct* leads tears out of the body.

bilk (BILK)

to cheat or defraud (verb)

 GOT BOGUS mILK

This word can be a verb, meaning to swindle, or a noun, meaning a swindler. Incidentally, titanium dioxide is often used as an opaque pigment in paint and coffee whitener, so perhaps confusing paint with milk isn't all that unusual. (Don't worry; titanium dioxide is nontoxic.)

diatribe (DYE uh trybe)

an abusive speech (noun)

 TRIBE

The Latin word from which this word comes means an educated discussion, but it now means a hateful or bitter speech. Synonyms include *tirade*, *harangue*, and *denunciation*.

encroach (en KROHCH)

to slowly take or get too close to someone's property (verb)

 ENCouraged ROACH

This word is related to the word for a kind of needlework, *crochet*. They are both derived from a Germanic root *croc*, which means hook. When you *crochet*, you use a needle with a hook on the end. When you *encroach*, you grab onto someone's possessions, as if with a hook. I wonder what this roach's mother would think if she knew he was eating off the floor?

eradicate (ih RAD ih kayt)

to completely get rid of (verb)

 HE RADISHES ATE

This word comes from the Latin word *radix*, meaning root. To *eradicate* means to tear something out by the roots. In math, the symbol for a root ($\sqrt{}$) is often called a *radical* sign.

evict (ih VIKT)

to force someone out of a house (verb)

 BE KICKED OUT

This word has a common root with words such as *victory, vanquish, invincible,* and *convince.*

exterminate (ik STUR min ayt)

to completely get rid of (verb)

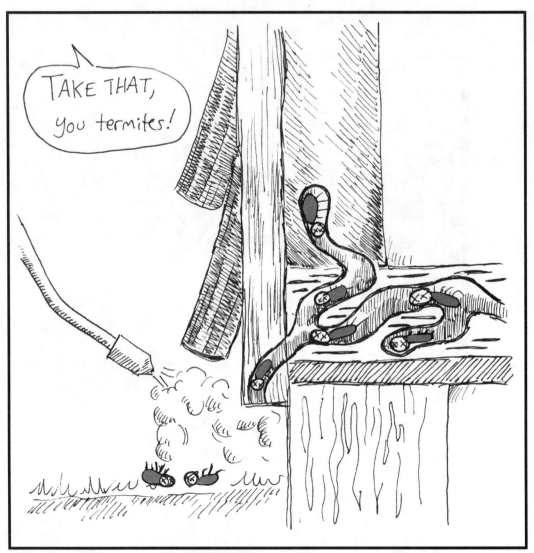

 TERMITES

The Latin word *terminus*, meaning end, gives us a number of words. The *Terminator* movies were about machines designed to *terminate* people—to end their lives. A *terminal* illness is one that will eventually end in death. Some of these words relate to location, not time or death. A railroad *terminal* is a station at the end (or at a major intersection) of the line. The station or town at the end of the line can also be called a *terminus*.

flagrant (FLAY grunt)

obviously bad (adjective)

 FLAG RANT

This word is derived from the Latin root *flagra*, meaning fire. The word *conflagration* also comes from this root. In basketball, a very hard foul is called a *flagrant* foul—the team getting *fouled* gets rewarded with two free throws and possession of the ball.

infringe (in FRINJ)

to violate; to cross a boundary (verb)

 IN + FRINGE

This word is distantly related to the words *break* and *breach*. (The b and f sounds correspond to each other, as do the g and k/ch sounds.) It is more closely related to the words *fracture*, *fraction*, *fragile*, and *fragment*, as they all share the common Latin root *frangere*, which means to break.

malign (muh LYNE)

to speak badly of (verb)

 MAD LYING

The Latin root *mal* means bad, and gives us such words as *malady*, *malaise*, *malcontent*, *malefactor*, and *malevolent*.

malinger (muh LING gur)

to pretend to be ill in order to avoid work (verb)

 MAN WON'T LIFT A FINGER

This word comes from the French *malingre*, meaning sickly. Yes, there's that prefix *mal* again.

ostracize (AH struh syze)

to banish from a group (verb)

 OSTRICH

In ancient Greece, the citizens of Athens would gather once a year to see whether anyone should be banished from the city. Each person would vote by writing a name on an *ostrakon*, a piece of pottery. If one name received a majority of the votes, that person was banished for a time. In modern times, *ostracism* usually refers to exclusion from a social group, not actual banishment from a city.

pilfer (PIL fur)

to steal in small amounts (verb)

 PILL

A related word, which no one uses, is *pelf*, meaning wealth obtained through dishonesty. If you write poetry, you now have another word to rhyme with "self".

propaganda (prah puh GAN duh)

political information reflecting only one viewpoint (noun)

 imPROPER GANDER

This male goose, or gander, wants the other geese to take a look, or gander, at some *propaganda* aimed against the loons. *Propaganda* has been used throughout history, whenever someone has published half-truths in order to further a cause. Throughout the Cold War, the U.S. and USSR used *propaganda* to portray each other as evil monsters bent on world domination.

reproach (rih PROCH)

to criticize (verb)

 REPrimanded ROACH

Well, his mother wasn't happy. If someone's motives or actions are "beyond *reproach*", they cannot be criticized. And really, who are we to criticize a species that's been around for over 300 million years?

DRILLS

Quiz #14

For each question below, choose the word that is LEAST similar to the other two.

1.   a. malign   b. encroach   c. infringe

2.   a. flagrant   b. propaganda   c. diatribe

3.   a. malinger   b. eradicate   c. exterminate

4.   a. abduct   b. reproach   c. ostracize

5.   a. pilfer   b. evict   c. bilk

Puzzle #14

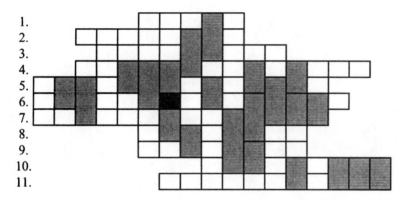

1. remove

2. get too close

3. banish

4. criticize; kidnap

5. defraud; one-sided information

6. steal a little; pretend to be sick

7. speak ill; get too close

8. vicious speech

9. clearly bad

10. destroy completely

11. destroy completely

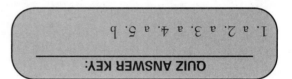

CHAPTER 15

SHUT DOWN:

Words about being empty or shrunken

dearth (DURTH)

a lack or scarcity (noun)

 SCORCHED EARTH

This word comes from the Old English word *deore*, meaning costly or dear. When there is a lack of something, such as food, it becomes more valuable.

detract (dih TRAKT)

to reduce the value or effectiveness of (verb)

Nobody is going to buy our house until they remove that broken-down tractor.

 HIDEOUS TRACTOR

This word comes from the Latin root *tract*, meaning to take. The old tractor *detracts*, or takes away, from the value of the house. Some other words derived from the same root include *extract* (to take out), *retract* (to take back), and *protract* (to take longer).

emaciated (ih MAY shee ay tid)

very thin from lack of eating (adjective)

 SPACE HE ATE

This word is descended from the Latin word *macer*, meaning thin. A related word is *meager*, in short supply.

gaunt (GAWNT)

tall and thin; haggard (adjective)

 AUNT

This word means thin and bony. Its meaning is similar to that of *emaciated*. It can also mean *bleak* or *barren*, often when describing a landscape.

hoary (HOR ee)

ancient; covered in white (adjective)

 OLD **STORY**

This word comes from Old English, and can describe something covered with gray or white hair. *Hoarfrost* is an archaic term for frost; the frost forms a white coating which resembles white hair. *Hoary* also describes something very old, regardless of whether or not it has hair.

lax (LAKS)

not strict or firm; loose (adjective)

 YAKS

It seems that the little yak's mother is too *relaxed*, or *slack*, in her parenting—she lacks control of her child.

lenient (LEE nee unt)

not harsh or strict (adjective)

 LEaNIng + parENTs

This word means much the same thing as *lax*. These parents shouldn't allow their son to lean over and feed the animals. At least that's a dolphin, not a shark.

minuscule (MIH nuh skyool)

very small (adjective)

 MINI-SCHOOL

This word is descended from the Latin word *minor*, meaning lesser or smaller. Other words coming from the same root include *minimum* and *minus*; strangely, *miniature* does not come from this same root.

null (NUL)

empty; invalid (adjective)

NOT FULL

To *nullify* or *annul* means to invalidate or cancel; all three of these words come from the Latin word *nullus*, which means none. Contracts are often declared "*null* and void." In math, the *null* set is the empty set; it has no members.

penurious (puh NOOR ee us)

unwilling to spend money; having no money (adjective)

 PENNILESS

As mentioned above, this word has two different meanings: unwilling, or unable, to spend money. *Penury* is a synonym for poverty.

porous (POR us)

full of holes (adjective)

 POUR

The holes in your skin through which you sweat are called *pores*. If something is *porous*, it has a number of holes, or is easy to pass through. If a team's defense is described as *porous*, it means that it doesn't put up much resistance.

ravenous (RAV un us)

very hungry; greedy (adjective)

 **RAVEN**

This word is descended from the Latin root *rap*, meaning to seize forcefully. A less common synonym is *rapacious*. Other words coming from this root include *raptor*, *rapture*, and *ravage*.

scant (SKANT)

in short supply; barely enough (adjective)

 CAN'T FIND MUCH

This word came into English from the Old Norse word *skamt*, meaning short. "*Scantily*-clad" is an overused phrase that describes someone who isn't wearing much.

shrivel (SHRIV ul)

to dry out and become smaller (verb)

 SHRINK + LITTLE

Synonyms for this word include *mummify*, *wither*, *desiccate*, and *wizen*.

wizened (WIH zund)

dried up and shrunken (adjective)

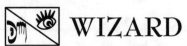 WIZARD

This word comes from the Old English word *wisnian*, meaning to wither or shrink.

DRILLS

Quiz #15

For each question below, choose the word that is LEAST similar to the other two.

1. a. scant   b. detract   c. minuscule
2. a. lax   b. lenient   c. ravenous
3. a. emaciated   b. gaunt   c. penurious
4. a. porous   b. wizened   c. shrivel
5. a. null   b. dearth   c. hoary

Puzzle #15

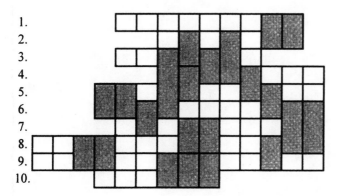

1. very thin

2. shrunken

3. shrink

4. very hungry

5. take away from; empty

6. lack; very thin

7. not strict; not strict

8. very small; scarce

9. poor; ancient

10. easily penetrated

CHAPTER 16

DAZED AND CONFUSED:

Words about complicated or confusing situations

anomaly (uh NAH muh lee)

something unusual or irregular (noun)

 ABNORMALLY

This word comes from the Greek roots *an*, meaning not, and *homalos*, meaning regular. *Homogenized* milk doesn't have a layer of cream on it—it's been mixed in so that all of the milk is of the same consistency.

archipelago (ar kuh PEL uh go)

a sea containing many islands; a group of many islands (noun)

 CHIP + LAGOON

This word comes from *Arcipelago*, an old Italian name for the Aegean Sea. Greece, which lies on the Aegean, has numerous tiny islands. The Italian name, with a minor spelling change, has been extended in English to describe any sea with numerous islands, or the islands themselves.

byzantine (BIZ un teen)

very complicated (adjective)

 BUSY AND TEENY

In *Byzantine* architecture, the walls are covered with complex mosaics. When not capitalized, this word describes anything elaborate, complicated, or confusingly detailed. For example, a secret plan or a set of rules could be *byzantine*.

clamor (KLAM ur)

to complain loudly (verb)

 CLAM

This word is related to *claim*, and other words formed from it, such as *exclaim*, *proclaim*, and *declaim*. The other clams probably wish that the *clamoring* clam would be quiet, or "clam up".

controversial (kawn truh VUR shul)

causing arguments or disagreement (adjective)

 COMMERCIAL

A *controversy* is a dispute or significant disagreement. You can hear this word all the time in the news. To *controvert* is to argue against something.

erroneous (ih RO nee us)

incorrect; mistaken (adjective)

 MACARONI FUSS

As you could probably guess, this word is related to *error*. Other related words include *aberrant* and *erratic* (which can be found elsewhere in this book).

feign (FAYN)

to pretend in order to deceive (verb)

 FAKING

If something is *feigned*, such as an illness, it isn't real. This person is probably going to pretend to faint if his headache excuse doesn't work. A closely related word is *feint*, which is to pretend to attack in one direction before attacking in another. A football player may *feint* to the left, then run to the right. A boxer may *feint* with one hand to set up a punch with the other hand.

figment (FIG munt)

something imaginary (noun)

FIG

This word is related to *fiction* and *fictitious*. A *figment* of your imagination is not real.

garble (GAR bul)

to make something impossible to understand (verb)

MARBLES

Although this word isn't related to garbage, *garbled* speech sounds like it. *Garbled* means mixed up, scrambled, or distorted.

implausible (im PLAW zuh bul)

unlikely; not believable (adjective)

 PLAZA

According to the Latin origin of the word, *plausible* means worthy of *applause*, and therefore means believable. As you'll notice over the course of the next few pages, the prefix *im* or *in* turns a word into its opposite.

impractical (im PRAK tih kul)

difficult to use or apply (adjective)

 TIM'S CACTUS BALL

If something is *practical*, it is easy to put into *practice*. Something *impractical* would be possible, but difficult or expensive.

incoherent (in ko HEER unt)

unable to be understood; not connected (adjective)

 DRINK A BEER RANT

To *cohere* means to stick together. We remember doing experiments in seventh grade testing the *cohesion* of different liquids—whether the liquid tended to stay together in one blob, or run all over the place. *Coherent* speech is logically connected; it makes sense.

incongruous (in KONG groo us)

not fitting; inappropriate (adjective)

 IN CONGRESS

The Latin word *congruere* means to agree. If two things are *congruous*, they go well together. You may have heard the term *congruent* in your math class. *Congruent* segments have equal lengths, and *congruent* angles have equal measures.

inscrutable (in SKROO tuh bul)

difficult or impossible to understand (adjective)

 SCREW + TABLE

To *scrutinize* means to examine or search carefully. Something *inscrutable*, though, cannot be examined or understood.

pandemonium (pan duh MO nee um)

noisy confusion (noun)

 PANDA

In *Paradise Lost*, John Milton invented a name for the capital of Hell—he combined the prefix *pan*, all, with *daemonium*, demon, and formed *Pandaemonium*. Soon, this word was being used to represent any place of uproar and wickedness; it eventually came to represent the uproar itself.

tortuous (TOR choo us)

very complicated; twisting and turning (adjective)

 TORTOISE

The Latin root *tort* means to twist or turn. Although *torturous*, meaning causing great pain, comes from this same root, these two words are distinct. Other words descended from this root include *extort*, *contort*, *retort*, *distort*, *torture*, *torque*, and *tort*. Each one has some connection to twisting, turning back, or causing pain.

DRILLS

Quiz #16

For each question below, choose the word that is LEAST similar to the other two.

1.   a. garble   b. incoherent   c. impractical

2.   a. controversial b. byzantine   c. tortuous

3.   a. incongruous   b. implausible   c. anomaly

4.   a. clamor   b. inscrutable   c. pandemonium

5.   a. figment   b. erroneous   c. archipelago

Puzzle #16

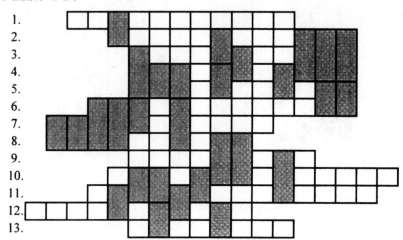

1. island group

2. shout; distort

3. not understandable

4. unlikely

5. not useful

6. causing argument

7. not fitting

8. disconnected

9. complicated

10. dream; unusual occurrence

11. pretend; incorrect

12. confusion

13. complicated

CHAPTER 17

PUZZLE ANSWERS

ANSWERS

PUZZLE #1

```
1.                          S A V O R R
2.        B E N E F A C T O R R   V A U N T E D
3.                    A C C O R D V E R D A N T
4.            R E V I V E C O M P L A I S A N T
5.          P R O L I F I C     L I A I S O N
6.        C A T H A R T I C C U L T I V A T E
7.    U N S C A T H E D N O S T A L G I A
8.        B L I T H E       A S P I R E
```

PUZZLE #2

```
1.              S T I M U L A T E
2.          I N T R I G U I N G     H O M A G E
3.        S U P E R L A T I V E   A C C O L A D E
4.    R H A P S O D Y V I V I D J O C U L A R
5.          E X T O L     W H I M S I C A L
6.          F L I P P A N T C A R I C A T U R E
7.                P A N E G Y R R I C
8.                E C C E N T R I C
9.                E C S T A T I C
10.               E S T E E M
```

PUZZLE #3

```
1.        C U M B E R S O M E
2.                F R E N Z Y
3.              I M M E N S E
4.            R A M P A N T
5.    E X T R A V A G A N T
6.      T H R O N G G A R I S H
7.      H O R D E S W A R M
8.      S U R F E I T V E R B O S E
9.          W R I T H E
10.         P R A T T L E
11.    I N U N D A T E
12. L I T A N Y
```

PUZZLE #4

1. S W E L L G A R N E R
2. C R E S T G L U T T O N
3. C R U C I A L T R O U P E
4. P R O M I N E N T F O R T I F Y
5. P R O M I S C U O U S
6. U N A N I M O U S
7. V O L U M I N O U S
8. P I G M E N T
9. I N C E N T I V E
10. A B U N D A N C E A P E X
11. E N C O M P A S S

PUZZLE #5

1. R E S I L I E N T
2. P R O C U R E S K I R M I S H
3. R O B U S T A W E
4. A R D O R S T E A D F A S T
5. C O M P E L E N D O R S E
6. F O R G E F E R V O R
7. P E R S E V E R E
8. C O N Q U E R S T R I V E
9. A N N E X S T A T U R E

PUZZLE #6

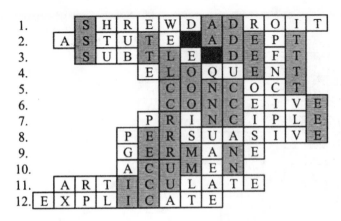

1. S H R E W D A D R O I T
2. A S T U T E A D E P T
3. S U B T L E D E F T
4. E L O Q U E N T
5. C O N C O C T
6. C O N C E I V E
7. P R I N C I P L E
8. P E R S U A S I V E
9. G E R M A N E
10. A C U M E N
11. A R T I C U L A T E
12. E X P L I C A T E

PUZZLE #7

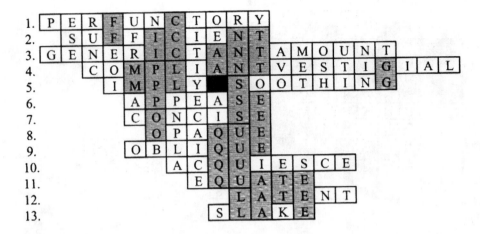

1. P E R F U N C T O R Y
2. S U F F I C I E N T
3. G E N E R I C T A N T A M O U N T
4. C O M P L I A N T V E S T I G I A L
5. I M P L Y ■ S O O T H I N G
6. A P P E A S E
7. C O N C I S E
8. O P A Q U E E
9. O B L I Q U E
10. A C Q U I E S C E
11. E Q U A T E E
12. L A T E N T
13. S L A K E

PUZZLE #8

1. Q U E U E
2. I N Q U I S I T I V E
3. C O N C L U S I V E
4. B E A C O N T A C T I L E
5. R E F U T E T A N G I B L E E
6. P A L P A B L E
7. E L A B O R A T E
8. C I T E E X C A V A T E E
9. S P E C I M E N H I E R A R C H Y
10. D E L I B E R A T E E
11. E X O N E R A T E E
12. C O R R O B O R A T E E

PUZZLE #9

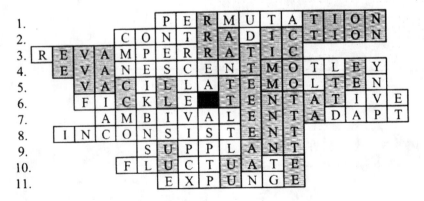

1. P E R M U T A T I O N
2. C O N T R A D I C T I O N
3. R E V A M P E R R A T I C
4. E V A N E S C E N T M O T L E Y
5. V A C I L L A T E M O L T E N
6. F I C K L E ■ T E N T A T I V E
7. A M B I V A L E N T A D A P T
8. I N C O N S I S T E N T
9. S U P P L A N T
10. F L U C T U A T E
11. E X P U N G E

PUZZLE #10

1. ALOOF
2. EMBARGO REBUFF
3. ARCANE
4. SUPINE
5. SEQUESTER
6. SPURN STOLID
7. TRANSPARENT INSULAR
8. QUARANTINE
9. DORMANT INHIBITED
10. HERMIT DETACHED

PUZZLE #11

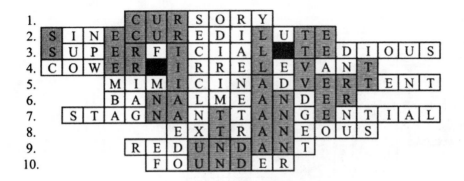

1. CURSORY
2. SINECURE DILUTE
3. SUPERFICIAL TEDIOUS
4. COWER IRRELEVANT
5. MIMIC INADVERTENT
6. BANAL MEANDER
7. STAGNANT TANGENTIAL
8. EXTRANEOUS
9. REDUNDANT
10. FOUNDER

PUZZLE #12

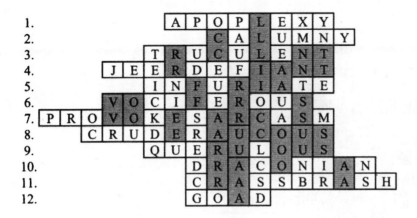

1. APOPLEXY
2. CALUMNY
3. TRUCULENT
4. JEER DEFIANT
5. INFURIATE
6. VOCIFEROUS
7. PROVOKE SARCASM
8. CRUDE RAUCOUS
9. QUERULOUS
10. DRACONIAN
11. CRASS BRASH
12. GOAD

PUZZLE #13

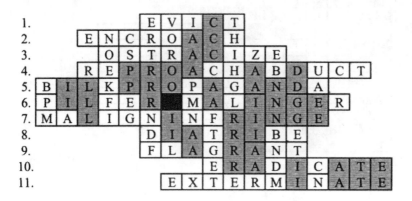

1. D O L E F U L
2. R O U T [ ] T A I N T
3. T U R B U L E N T T
4. M I R E E L E G Y
5. Q U E L L G R I M A C E
6. G A F F E [ ] P R E C I P I C E
7. G A U C H E D R E A R Y
8. C H A O S S O R D I D
9. N O I S O M E
10. G L O O M Y

PUZZLE #14

1. E V I C T
2. E N C R O A C H
3. O S T R A C I Z E
4. R E P R O A C H A B D U C T
5. B I L K P R O P A G A N D A
6. P I L F E R [ ] M A L I N G E R
7. M A L I G N I N F R I N G E
8. D I A T R I B E
9. F L A G R A N T
10. E R A D I C A T E
11. E X T E R M I N A T E

PUZZLE #15

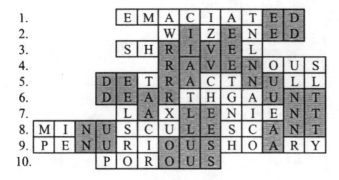

1. E M A C I A T E D
2. W I Z E N E D
3. S H R I V E L
4. R A V E N O U S
5. D E T R A C T N U L L
6. D E A R T H G A U N T
7. L A X L E N I E N T
8. M I N U S C U L E S C A N T
9. P E N U R I O U S H O A R Y
10. P O R O U S

PUZZLE #16

1. ARCHIPELAGO
2. CLAMORGARBLE
3. INSCRUTABLE
4. IMPLAUSIBLE
5. IMPRACTICAL
6. CONTROVERSIAL
7. INCONGRUOUS
8. INCOHERENT
9. BYZANTINE
10. FIGMENTANOMALY
11. FEIGNERRONEOUS
12. PANDEMONIUM
13. TORTUOUS

CHAPTER 18

FINAL DRILLS

MATCHING QUIZ #1: ANTONYMS

For this quiz, match each word on the left with the word most nearly opposite in meaning on the right. (The words may have different parts of speech.)

1. homage	a. porous
2. spurn	b defiant
3. appease	c. inhibited
4. resilient	d. articulate
5. incoherent	e. calumny
6. concise	f. savor
7. promiscuous	g. accord
8. evanescent	h. verbose

MATCHING QUIZ #2: SYNONYMS

For this quiz, match each word on the left with the word most similar in meaning on the right. (The words may have different parts of speech.)

1. chaos	a. expunge
2. irrelevant	b. prolific
3. compel	c. vociferous
4. eradicate	d. draconian
5. abundance	e. vaunted
6. compliant	f. tangential
7. clamor	g. complaisant
8. esteem	h. pandemonium

MATCHING QUIZ #3: ANTONYMS

For this quiz, match each word on the left with the word most nearly opposite in meaning on the right. (The words may have different parts of speech.)

1. endorse		a.	transparent
2. compliant		b.	irrelevant
3. germane		c.	wizened
4. fervor		d.	refute
5. ravenous		e.	stagnant
6. swell		f.	surfeit
7. aspire		g.	detached
8. opaque		h.	querulous

MATCHING QUIZ #4: SYNONYMS

For this quiz, match each word on the left with the word most similar in meaning on the right. (The words may have different parts of speech.)

1. immense		a.	inscrutable
2. malign		b.	voluminous
3. garner		c.	impractical
4. arcane		d.	annex
5. caricature		e.	latent
6. dormant		f.	mimic
7. founder		g.	calumny
8. cumbersome		h.	mire

MATCHING QUIZ #5: ANTONYMS

For this quiz, match each word on the left with the word most nearly opposite in meaning on the right. (The words may have different parts of speech.)

1. extol	a. crucial
2. acquiesce	b. blithe
3. extraneous	c. malign
4. unanimous	d. intriguing
5. abundance	e. dearth
6. apoplexy	f. controversial
7. tedious	g. immense
8. minuscule	h. rebuff

MATCHING QUIZ #6: SYNONYMS

For this quiz, match each word on the left with the word most similar in meaning on the right. (The words may have different parts of speech.)

1. motley	a. nostalgia
2. glutton	b. explicate
3. feign	c. surfeit
4. truculent	d. evict
5. elaborate	e. fortify
6. elegy	f. bilk
7. robust	g. incongruous
8. supplant	h. skirmish

MATCHING QUIZ #7: ANTONYMS

For this quiz, match each word on the left with the word most nearly opposite in meaning on the right. (The words may have different parts of speech.)

1. gloomy
2. extravagant
3. scant
4. cultivate
5. detract
6. robust
7. lenient
8. ardor

a. fortify
b. dilute
c. aloof
d. draconian
e. rampant
f. penurious
g. exterminate
h. ecstatic

WORD SEARCH #1

This grid contains fifteen of the words featured in this book, going left, right, up, down, or in any of the four diagonal directions. To help you find the words, the following clues are arranged to give the words in alphabetical order.

1. One who benefits the actors
2. Fact or fiction?
3. To discuss at length, then deliver late
4. To make dull fruit juice
5. Strict, like Dracula
6. Extra giving
7. One who eats too much and pops a button
8. To engage in mad lying
9. Detailed praise for a gyro
10. To steal a small number of pills
11. Describing the red ant's unnecessary speech
12. A special example of a species
13. Just enough fish for dinner
14. You stand with us in agreement
15. Describing a vest that is left over

T	B	E	T	A	L	P	A	S	C	N	E	A	G	M
E	H	C	N	Q	U	I	E	S	C	G	X	N	R	O
R	I	R	O	K	U	L	A	I	G	I	T	S	E	V
J	P	B	E	N	E	F	A	C	T	O	R	I	A	L
N	R	C	G	P	T	E	I	V	N	Y	A	E	T	S
D	E	L	I	B	E	R	A	T	E	E	V	D	S	I
O	S	O	F	J	Y	P	A	S	I	C	A	R	P	S
H	I	P	B	G	N	E	L	D	C	H	G	A	I	U
A	T	R	E	X	I	O	S	T	I	R	A	C	W	O
E	R	N	L	C	A	D	T	P	F	C	N	O	S	M
N	A	C	K	U	I	P	E	T	F	D	T	N	N	I
P	N	G	I	L	A	M	I	N	U	W	K	I	R	N
L	A	Q	U	T	L	R	E	H	S	L	F	A	O	A
S	V	T	W	I	B	Z	O	N	A	Y	G	N	H	N
R	E	D	U	N	D	A	N	T	E	O	S	H	R	U

WORD SEARCH #2

This grid contains fifteen of the words featured in this book, going left, right, up, down, or in any of the four diagonal directions. To help you find the words, the following clues are arranged to give the words in alphabetical order.

1. Don't pop a blood vessel in a fit of anger
2. Ordinary, like bananas
3. To confirm an accusation against a robber
4. The cucumber is very heavy
5. Lying still, like a doormat
6. He was very thin, because he only ate space
7. A roach gets too close to a candy bar
8. Vanishing scent
9. Flipper the dolphin was casually disrespectful
10. Uproar involving a panda
11. Don't give up looking—your purse is here
12. To squash well
13. The Brazilians always bounce back
14. Describing a bumpy and disturbing situation
15. Free of the skunk smell after he bathed

C	F	T	N	E	C	S	E	N	A	V	E	T	I	R
P	O	U	L	X	A	E	L	D	S	T	A	P	F	C
A	I	R	S	E	N	C	R	O	A	C	H	T	F	D
N	R	B	I	J	T	K	C	R	P	A	I	N	U	W
D	E	U	R	N	I	I	O	M	O	P	D	U	R	C
E	C	L	M	E	L	B	U	A	P	E	N	S	I	T
M	N	E	E	C	O	A	Q	N	L	D	F	I	N	O
O	D	N	H	R	K	U	H	T	E	A	L	E	A	H
N	B	T	R	Y	E	P	N	T	X	N	I	D	R	L
I	R	O	C	L	I	V	A	O	Y	L	P	N	I	E
U	C	B	L	A	W	I	E	S	I	W	P	E	N	G
M	L	A	Y	N	C	F	Z	S	C	H	A	I	A	U
U	N	S	C	A	T	H	E	D	R	A	N	T	V	L
S	C	U	M	B	E	R	S	O	M	E	T	H	E	F
T	R	E	C	S	T	O	W	E	R	I	P	I	R	D

WORD SEARCH #3

This grid contains fifteen of the words featured in this book, going left, right, up, down, or in any of the four diagonal directions. To help you find the words, the following clues are arranged to give the words in alphabetical order.

1. To kidnap a duck
2. Exaggerated drawing of a character
3. The clam is making a lot of noise
4. The psychic monkey can see and understand
5. Explain that the X indicates the location on the map
6. To destroy termites
7. A very thin aunt
8. Unpredictably near and distant
9. The raven is very hungry
10. Smoothing the road makes drivers more calm
11. Lying on your spine
12. Digs up plants, trying to gain power
13. The tortoise followed a winding path
14. Truckers willing to fight
15. Voice is ferocious

S	R	N	I	T	A	L	D	E	T	N	L	S	U	H
P	M	E	L	I	C	Q	A	R	N	S	O	N	A	I
E	E	C	O	S	U	P	I	N	E	T	C	D	F	N
L	X	A	B	D	U	C	T	I	L	E	B	E	R	C
T	F	T	J	Q	M	O	N	Q	U	A	L	K	M	O
U	L	A	E	C	H	N	U	D	C	Y	I	T	L	N
R	S	C	A	R	I	C	A	T	U	R	E	N	A	S
D	O	A	G	P	M	E	G	R	R	E	R	A	E	I
I	R	I	N	D	S	I	A	L	T	O	I	L	W	S
M	A	T	I	L	A	V	N	P	M	Z	T	P	C	T
B	C	O	H	R	E	E	T	A	C	I	L	P	X	E
S	R	X	T	N	T	N	L	O	T	N	I	U	Q	N
S	E	I	O	L	A	C	D	N	R	E	L	S	H	T
V	S	U	O	R	E	F	I	C	O	V	E	T	E	D
E	S	Q	S	I	V	U	M	F	A	L	T	E	R	C

WORD SEARCH #4

This grid contains fifteen of the words featured in this book, going left, right, up, down, or in any of the four diagonal directions. To help you find the words, the following clues are arranged to give the words in alphabetical order.

1. Describing old arcade games
2. The island group is like chips of land
3. The large compass surrounds us
4. A dream about a fig
5. The giraffe made an embarrassing mistake
6. Something accidental in an advertisement
7. Intensely quizzing someone
8. Hidden, not blatant
9. Some parents lean over too far and spoil their children
10. The school of fish was extremely small
11. The perm caused a mutation in the shape of her hair
12. A whisper sways your opinion
13. The steep cliff was covered with ice
14. The sense that allows you to feel a tack
15. Very intense video

E	R	S	R	C	M	S	P	A	C	M	A	N	C	G
V	I	S	E	A	J	I	H	S	O	E	B	O	A	R
I	N	A	D	V	E	R	T	E	N	T	R	F	L	I
T	A	P	Y	O	E	U	Q	A	X	A	F	I	O	S
I	H	M	I	N	U	S	C	U	L	E	N	G	P	A
S	U	O	V	E	R	T	B	A	T	A	M	W	D	
I	M	C	R	I	A	C	K	E	Y	L	O	E	T	N
U	R	N	E	T	N	E	I	N	E	L	I	N	G	U
Q	T	E	N	A	W	O	S	P	R	O	P	T	T	N
N	C	A	E	T	I	D	I	V	I	V	L	A	D	I
I	O	M	L	U	N	H	T	N	E	C	C	E	S	M
F	R	A	P	M	C	Q	U	A	R	T	E	F	O	R
E	L	P	E	R	S	U	A	S	I	V	E	R	N	I
O	C	E	A	E	G	E	R	L	Y	I	H	W	P	K
M	I	L	W	P	T	N	E	T	A	L	D	O	U	S

ANSWERS

MATCHING QUIZ #1

1. e 2. g 3. b 4. a 5. d 6. h 7. c 8. f

MATCHING QUIZ #2

1. h 2. f 3. d 4. a 5. b 6. g 7. c 8. e

MATCHING QUIZ #3

1. d 2. h 3. b 4. g 5. f 6. c 7. e 8. a

MATCHING QUIZ #4

1. b 2. g 3. d 4. a 5. f 6. e 7. h 8. c

MATCHING QUIZ #5

1. c 2. h 3. a 4. f 5. e 6. b 7. d 8. g

MATCHING QUIZ #6

1. g 2. c 3. f 4. h 5. b 6. a 7. e 8. d

MATCHING QUIZ #7

1. h 2. f 3. e 4. g 5. a 6. b 7. d 8. c

WORD SEARCH #1

WORD SEARCH #2

```
C F I N E C S E N A V E T I R
P O U L X A E L D S T A P F C
A I R S E N C R O A C H T F D
N R B I J T K C R P A I N U W
D E U R N I I O M O P D U R C
E C L M E L B U A P E N S I T
M N E E C O A Q N L D F I N O
O D N H R K U H T E A L E A H
N B T R Y E P N T X N I D R L
I R O C L I V A O Y L P N I E
U C B L A W I E S I W P E N G
M L A Y N C F Z S C H A I A U
I N S C A T H E D R A N T V L
S C U M B E R S O M E T H E F
T R E C S T O W E R I P I R D
```

WORD SEARCH #3

```
S R N I T A L D E T N L S U H
P M E L I C Q A R N S O N A I
E E C O S U P I N D T C D F N
L X A B D U C T I L E B E R C
T F T J Q M O N Q U A L K M O
U L A E C H N U D C Y I T L N
R S C A R I C A T U R E N A S
D O A O P M E G R R E R A E I
I R I N D S I A L T O I L W S
M A T I L A V N P M Z T P C T
B C O H R E E T A C I L P X E
S R X T N T N L O T N I U Q N
S E I O L A C D N R E L S H T
V S U O R E F I C O V E T E D
E S Q S I V U M F A L T E R C
```

WORD SEARCH #4

E	R	S	R	C	M	S	P	A	C	M	A	N	C	G
V	I	S	E	A	J	I	H	S	O	E	B	O	A	R
I	N	A	D	V	E	R	T	E	N	T	R	F	L	I
T	A	P	Y	O	E	U	Q	A	X	A	F	I	O	S
I	H	M	I	N	U	S	C	U	L	E	N	G	P	A
S	U	O	V	O	E	R	T	B	A	T	A	M	W	D
I	M	C	R	I	A	C	K	E	Y	L	O	E	T	N
U	R	N	E	T	N	E	I	N	E	L	I	N	G	U
Q	T	E	N	A	W	O	S	P	R	O	P	T	T	N
N	C	A	E	T	I	O	I	V	I	V	L	A	D	I
I	O	M	L	U	N	H	T	N	E	C	C	E	S	M
F	R	A	P	M	C	Q	U	A	R	T	E	F	O	R
E	L	P	E	R	S	U	A	S	I	V	E	R	N	I
O	C	E	A	E	G	E	R	L	Y	I	H	W	P	K
M	I	L	W	P	T	N	E	T	A	L	D	O	U	S

INDEX

About the Authors

Morgan Chase has a pair of degrees in mathematics education, and has obviously spent too much time studying defunct languages. He has taught, tutored, and developed course materials for The Princeton Review, and was its Director of K-12 Program Development the last time he checked. He lives in Vermont with his wife and three cats.

Chris Kane is a graduate of the School of the Museum of Fine Arts, Boston, with a combined degree from Tufts University. He has worked on various projects, from computer graphics and animation to traditional illustration. He currently lives in New York City.

Morgan and Chris met in their ninth grade English class, and have spent the intervening years collaborating on inscrutable comics, playing old video games, and rocking out.

Acknowledgments

Thanks to The Princeton Review, especially Evan Schnittman and John Katzman, for giving us the opportunity to work on this exciting and fun project. Thanks also to our editor, Maria Dente, for letting us get away with a lot of goofy stuff.

Thanks to our parents, families, friends, and teachers for their support and encouragement.

The Bible Challenge

Read the Bible in a Year

Edited by Marek P. Zabriskie

The Bible Challenge

Read the Bible in a Year

Edited by Marek P. Zabriskie

Second Edition

Forward Movement
Cincinnati, Ohio

Library of Congress Cataloging-in-Publication Data

The Bible challenge : read the Bible in a year / edited by Marek P. Zabriskie.—2nd ed.
   p. cm.
 ISBN 978-0-88028-350-2
 1. Bible—Devotional use 2. Bible—Reading. I. Zabriskie, Marek P.
 BS617.8.B555 2012b
 220.071—dc23

2012031124

ISBN: 978-0-88028-350-2

Second Edition

Printed in USA

Forward Movement
412 Sycamore Street
Cincinnati, OH 45202-4195
www.forwardmovement.org

Table of Contents

Foreword

In most churches, portions of the Bible are selected for use in the course of public worship. As a result, the vast expanse of Scripture is reduced to a series of selected texts. *The Bible Challenge* is an invitation to journey with fellow believers from across the world through the entire length and breadth of the Bible, and to experience the full sweep of the biblical record. But, in order to undertake such a journey, it may be helpful to reflect upon how we, as faithful readers of God's word, might orient our hearts and minds as we approach the text before us.

The Word and the Spirit

"Indeed, the word of God is living and active, sharper than any two-edged sword, piercing until it divides soul from spirit, joints from marrow; it is able to judge the thoughts and intentions of the heart" (Hebrews 4:12). These words from the Letter to the Hebrews, which predate the establishment of what we know as the New Testament, apply to the various ways in which the early Christian community experienced the word of God in its various forms beginning with the Hebrew Scriptures and extending to the preaching and teaching of the apostles and their followers. The word of God took the form not only of speech, it also "happened." It took the form of events and encounters, visions, and words heard with the ear of the heart.

All this was enabled by the Holy Spirit, "the Spirit of truth." Who, Jesus said, would "take what is mine and declare it to you" (John 16:15). In the Acts of the Apostles, which is the account of "the Spirit of Jesus"—the Spirit of the risen and ascended Christ, inhabiting the hearts and minds of the disciples and the infant church—we read of the ceaseless activity and urgency of the Holy Spirit. The Spirit "falls upon…fills…sends…speaks… snatches up…forbids…" All the while, empowered by the Spirit, the word of God "continued to spread…to grow mightily…to prevail."

The vitality of Scripture and its capacity to impart life flows from Jesus' resurrection. In the twenty-fourth chapter of the Gospel according to Luke, we are told that when the risen Lord encountered two grieving disciples on the way to Emmaus, "beginning with Moses and all the prophets, he interpreted to them the things about himself in all the Scriptures." Later on, looking back on the encounter, the disciples exclaim, "Were not our hearts burning within us while he was talking to us on the road, while he was opening the Scriptures to us?" (Luke 24:13-32). It is the continuing ministry of the risen Christ, through the agency of the Spirit, to open the Scriptures to us in order that our hearts might burn within us with the living truth of his presence. Christ is the "Word of God" (Revelation 19:13) whom we encounter at the heart of the scriptural word.

Approaching Scripture in Expectation and Joy

This notion of a living encounter mediated by the words of Scripture is wonderfully captured in a hymn written in the fourth century by the deacon Ephraim of Edessa: "I read the opening verses of the book, and was filled with joy, for its verses and lines spread out their arms to welcome me. The first rushed out and kissed me and led me on to the next."

To approach Scripture in such a spirit of expectation opens us to the possibility of our being surprised and accosted by the Spirit who draws continually from "the boundless riches of Christ," (Ephesians 3:8) and makes them present to us through the words of Scripture.

The fathomless depths of Scripture are suggested by well-known twelfth-century commentator and preacher Bernard of Clairvaux, who describes Holy Scripture as "a vast sea in which a lamb can paddle, and an elephant can swim."

These words from the past provide a helpful way of approaching Scripture that counterbalances the critique offered by R. M. Benson, the Founder of the Society of St. John the Evangelist, reacting to what he considered to be an overdependence upon biblical criticism. He wrote, "I think the joy of Holy Scripture is very much hidden by the joylessness of commentators who write about it with no sense of supernatural delight."

There are, of course, different ways in which to approach Scripture. The early commentators made a distinction between a literal and a spiritual reading of the text. According to Origen, a biblical commentator of the third century, not everything in Scripture is true in a historical sense, but nonetheless all Scripture conveys truth in a spiritual sense. It is, therefore, not a question of either/or—either something is true in an empirical sense, or it is not true at all—but of both/and: an ability to approach a passage on a literal and a spiritual level at the same time, and in the process honor both dimensions.

An example might be helpful. Let us take the Song of Mary recorded in the Gospel of Luke (Luke 1:46-53). Who but Mary's kinswoman, Elizabeth, was present to hear it, let alone record it? Further, in examining the text, it appears that it bears a strong relationship, if not dependency, upon the Song of Hannah recorded in the First Book of Samuel (1 Samuel 2:1-10). At the same time, the song can be allowed to address us on its own terms, and Mary's cry of humility and thanksgiving for the "great things [the Mighty One] has done for me," can become our own cry in the face of God's remembered mercies in our own lives.

Bishop Charles Gore, who unsettled late Victorian England by suggesting that the account of creation in the Book of Genesis was not literally true, went on to observe that myth and poetry in the pages of the Bible can as easily convey truth as those portions of Scripture that can be regarded as historical. This then brings us back to Origen and the need to approach scriptural texts on both a literal and a spiritual level.

Scripture Encounters Us

In addition, we must let Scripture accost us on its own terms. And, to that end, we must give room to the risen Christ, through the agency of the Holy Spirit, to address us through the words of the text before us, as the Word at the heart of the word freely wills. The following prayer may help us in preparing for that encounter:

Take away, O Lord, the veil of my heart while I read the Scriptures.
Blessed are you, O Lord: teach me your statutes: give me a word,
O Word of the Father: enlighten the understanding of my heart:
    open my lips and fill them with your praise.
Let me show forth your truth in my life by the life-giving power of your Holy Spirit.

—AFTER LANCELOT ANDREWES

—The Rt. Rev. Frank T. Griswold
25th Presiding Bishop of The Episcopal Church

Introduction

In the beginning…

The idea for *The Bible Challenge* was born after Christmas 2010, when I read that a friend was inviting members of his church to join him in reading a One Year Bible. I was exhausted after leading six worship services in three days. But my own Bible reading had become sporadic, so I decided to read the entire Bible in a year.

I began reading Genesis by the fireside. The next morning I fixed a cup of tea and continued reading. I soon added a psalm each day and a chapter from the New Testament. After a few days, I felt very spiritually alive. God nudged me to invite a few members of the church I serve to share this experience.

What began as a simple invitation grew rapidly into a ministry that began transforming many lives. Over 180 church members and more than 90 friends committed to read the entire Bible in a year. We read stories that are never read aloud in church. Some stories were very challenging and even disturbing. Some provoked great theological questions and made us realize how much the Bible relates to current events. Because so many church members were participating, *The Bible Challenge* began to transform our church.

Episcopalians and Anglicans are not the best evangelizers, but reading God's Word daily is so powerful that *The Bible Challenge* began to spread naturally. God nudged us to share this ministry beyond our church. So we created the Center for Biblical Studies to promote *The Bible Challenge* nationally and globally. We received wonderful support.

About this book

We developed this book to help Bible Challenge participants. We invited 103 archbishops, bishops, cathedral and seminary deans, Bible scholars, and priests from around the world to each write three meditations along with questions and prayers to stimulate reflection on the readings and help readers apply God's wisdom to their daily life.

The authors of these meditations used a variety of Bible translations. While we recommend reading the New Oxford Annotated Translation of the Bible, you may use any Bible translation that you desire. Our website offers many resources and tips to help you participate in *The Bible Challenge* as an individual or with your church, school, or diocese. We welcome hearing about your experience reading God's Word. Visit us at www.thecenterforbiblicalstudies.org.

How to begin The Bible Challenge

You can start *The Bible Challenge* at the beginning of the year or anytime of your choice. Some find it helpful to begin at Lent or Advent, or at the start of summer. The schedule of this book works best if you begin "Day 1" on a Monday. We encourage readers to read portions of the Bible Monday through Saturday, and assume that on Sunday they will be in church hearing the Scriptures read aloud.

Read the Bible slowly and meditatively, as if it were a love letter written by God especially to you. Our prayer is that *The Bible Challenge* will transform your life and help you to develop a lifelong spiritual discipline of daily Bible reading.

With every blessing,

—The Rev. Marek P. Zabriskie

Founder of *The Bible Challenge* and the Center for Biblical Studies

Rector of St. Thomas' Church, Whitemarsh Fort Washington, Pennsylvania

Visit www.thecenterforbiblicalstudies.org for:

- Tips on how to make best use of the daily meditations
- Reading schedules to start at several different times (e.g., Lent)
- Resources to learn more about the Bible and *The Bible Challenge*
- Ways to connect with other readers

Forward Movement also offers resources for Scripture study and prayer at www.forwardmovement.org.

The Rev. Scott Gunn   **Day 1**
Executive Director of Forward Movement
Cincinnati, Ohio

Genesis 1–3, Psalm 1, Matthew 1

Today is all about beginnings. It's the start of our great adventure reading the Bible. Even the texts set beginnings before us. Genesis famously opens with "In the beginning. …" Chapters 1–2 tell the story of creation. Here we encounter a God who brings into being a world that is wholly good.

But humanity as we know it comes into being in Genesis 3. In the sixth verse, the newly created woman and man both eat forbidden fruit. The rest of the Bible is the story of God's relentless love for a people who never quite manage to live as God intended. As you read the sweeping narrative of the Bible, it's startling how many times and how many ways God reaches out to humanity in love.

Many Christians will regret what we now call "the Fall," that time when humanity first sinned against God. But there is a medieval English carol about the Fall, which ends, "Blessed be the time / That apple taken was. / Therefore we moun singen / *Deo gratias*!" Why would we bless this disobedience? Because it is precisely our disobedience that brought about the need for our redemption through Jesus Christ. No apple, no Jesus.

And this brings us to Matthew. Chapter 1 is the genealogy of Jesus and his birth. It would be tempting to skip past the genealogy, but then we would miss an important point. Even a casual glance at the list of names reveals what is for me an inspiring picture. The Incarnation of Jesus Christ was brought about through a rogue's gallery of imperfect people. While Jesus himself did not sin, his forbearers certainly did.

If God can work through ordinary, flawed people to bring about extraordinary things, then God can work through us.

QUESTIONS

As you read the Bible, where do you see yourself in this vast, sweeping story of God's love for humanity?

Look up a few people in the Matthew 1 genealogy (e.g., "the wife of Uriah"). What does it say about God and about us that God could use ordinary people to bring about the salvation of us all?

PRAYER

God of light and life, open my mind and my heart to your gracious love, and use me for your saving purposes; through Jesus Christ our Lord. Amen.

Day 2

The Rev. Scott Gunn
Executive Director of Forward Movement
Cincinnati, Ohio

Genesis 4–6, Psalm 2, Matthew 2

With today's readings, things start to go awry in a big way. We encounter the Bible's first murder. As people multiply on the face of the earth, their evil deeds increase. But we also get our first real hero, as Noah follows God's commandments.

In the New Testament reading, our curtain opens on the scene with the wise men visiting the child Jesus. The message is clear: this savior is not just for a few people in one particular nation, but for the whole world. But that same fact represents a threat to the established order; Herod's fear runs to epic proportions.

Puzzling out the murder of innocent children is enough to keep a reader up at night. How could God allow this? Why do the pages of the Bible contain these grim stories? Where is God in great tragedy? Of course, these questions are not just for the pages of the Bible. The front page of any newspaper reveals a world of violence, fear, and exploitation. Where is God in *our* world?

As we read the Bible, we have an opportunity to step back to see a God whose saving purposes for humanity are evident over the sweeping range of the biblical story. This same God gives humanity the freedom to worship, to love God. And God leaves us the choice to disobey, at great cost to ourselves and to our world.

We do well to read very difficult passages in the context of the wider narrative. This will not excuse or minimize every terrible act. But we can see a loving God, who at the very least weeps with us and with all those who suffer. Seeing God at work in the Bible can help us see God in our world, too.

QUESTIONS

Do you find the violence of some biblical stories disturbing? Is this more or less troubling than violence in a newspaper? Why?

We don't focus much on the flight into Egypt and the slaughter of innocents at Christmastime. How might our image of Jesus be different if these parts of his life's story were more prominent?

PRAYER

God of love, reveal yourself to me even when it seems that the world has turned far from you, through Jesus Christ, the Prince of Peace. Amen.

The Rev. Scott Gunn
Executive Director of Forward Movement
Cincinnati, Ohio

Day 3

Genesis 7–9, Psalm 3, Matthew 3

A few years ago, I asked a group of church leaders to name their favorite story from the Bible. As we went around the table, over half of the people said "Noah's ark." Certainly it's a story rich with visual imagery. Walking through a large hardware store at Christmastime not long ago, I saw an inflatable lawn decoration. It depicted the ark, with some cute animals. Over the ark was a large banner: "Joy!"

Joy? Really? I wonder if people who love the story of Noah and the ark have read the story. It is fundamentally a story about God drowning almost every living creature on earth. Noah and his family would have heard the screams of women, men, and children.

It's not a very joyous story. And yet this tale of a fresh beginning for God's creation has a hold on us and our culture. Aside from the potential to inspire fanciful murals, the story concludes with God's promise to spare humanity this terrible fate in the future. God, it seems, was also horrified by how things turned out.

Most biblical scholars agree that the story of the flood is not history in the sense of scientific fact. Rather, it is a story about God's care for creation and God's desire to form a covenant with us. It is a story of *meaning* that teaches us something about ourselves, our world, and our God.

It is ironic that in the same day we read about water used as a means of death, we also read about John the Baptizer, who used water as a sign of new life. But in both cases, water brings about new beginnings, new life. It cleanses us and our world, making us ready for a fresh start.

QUESTIONS

Do you think the story of Noah's Ark is a story of joy? Why or why not?

How would a man such as John the Baptist be received by today's church? Are his startling words about Jesus relevant today?

PRAYER

Cleanse my heart and my life today, Lord God. Make me ready for fresh starts with each day's grace. Amen.

Day 4

The Rev. Dr. Walter Brueggemann
Author, Old Testament Scholar, and Theologian
Cincinnati, Ohio

Genesis 10–12, Psalm 4, Matthew 4

These readings strike me as an honest acknowledgement of the force of ambiguity before which we live out our faith. Even Jesus, at the outset of his ministry, faced ambiguity, whatever his specific experience might have been. He was tempted by the devil, but before he left the wilderness, "Angels waited on him" (Matthew 4:11). This strange mix, I suspect, is an epitome of his life, for he was sustained in amazing ways by God, yet was endlessly at risk.

Jesus is no exception to the rule of faith. The same mix is voiced in Psalm 4. The psalmist in confidence will lie down and "sleep in peace" (v. 8). But this same person is vexed by social shame (v. 2) and is disturbed at night (v. 4). That is how our sleep may be—disturbed and at peace. In the Genesis reading, the long genealogies of place and continuity are disrupted by the narrative of Babel (Genesis 11:1–9). So it is with our certitudes and our routines, interrupted by foolish yearning.

In these readings, faith seems to have two fronts. There is honesty about lived reality, a candor about how it is. But faith promises to override our conflictedness through trust in God's good gifts. Either feature without the other makes faith thin. It is not a bad way to begin the new year in faith—honest about the life we live, while at the same time on the receiving end of gifts that bring us to well-being, even in the face of such vexation.

QUESTION

Can you think of a time in your life when your cherished beliefs have been challenged by your experience? Were you able to trust in God in the midst of the ambiguity?

PRAYER

In our can-do society, make us grateful receivers. We do not doubt your gifts, but we manage often to live without them. Give us freedom to match your generosity with our own gratitude. Amen

The Rev. Dr. Walter Brueggemann
Author, Old Testament Scholar, and Theologian
Cincinnati, Ohio

Genesis 13–15, Psalm 5, Matthew 5

Faith is a summons to be different, to have a different buoyancy and to live a different ethic. That difference is visible in Psalm 5. After the psalmist in verses 4-6 details all kinds of ignoble conduct on the part of the wicked and evil-doers (such as being bloodthirsty and deceitful), then comes, "But I" (v. 7). The "I" of faith acts from the assurance of God's loyal love (v. 7) and is led by God to a straight, safe path (v. 8).

Father Abraham is described in these Genesis narratives as being different and making a difference. In Genesis 13:8-9 he commits an act of uncommon generosity by letting his nephew, Lot, choose the land he wants. In response, Abraham receives a sweeping promise from God to receive the land of promise (13:14-17). That divine promise, moreover, is verified in the remarkable covenant-making ritual of chapter 15. Abraham and his family are marked as carriers of a difference that is grounded only in God's promise.

In the Sermon on the Mount, Jesus instructs his disciples on making a difference by loving one's enemies. That difference is the vocation of the church. The church faces two temptations: one is to give up difference and fade into the social landscape along with everyone else. The other is to separate from all the others to be safe, pure, and unvexed by social reality. Neither choice is faithful. Rather, this community is dispatched to be engaged in transformative, reconciling generosity, the only difference that finally matters.

QUESTIONS

How have you experienced your Christian faith as a summons to be different?

How has your faith empowered you to make a difference in the world?

PRAYER

We pray for courage to be different. In our self-indulgence, we do not want to be different. In our fearfulness, we cringe from our vocation. Give us hearts shaped by courage and resolve that persists. Amen.

Day 6

The Rev. Dr. Walter Brueggemann
Author, Old Testament Scholar, and Theologian
Cincinnati, Ohio

Genesis 16–18, Psalm 6, Matthew 6

These texts ponder what the disciplines are for women and men of faith. Principal among such disciplines is prayer, the opening of one's life in honesty in the presence of God. Our classic prayer, the Lord's Prayer, is found in Matthew 6. Many interpreters believe the prayer pivots on debts to be forgiven in a bold practice of Jubilee. In any case, it is a prayer that eagerly awaits the full rule of God in the world.

Psalm 6, also filled with petition, is a zealous complaint to God in a context of deep need. The key imperative is "turn" in verse 4; the psalmist urges God into transformative action. Remarkably, the prayer ends in confidence that "God has heard" (v. 9). This is a God who hears, answers, and acts. The boldness of the prayer in its demand is anticipated in Abraham's exchange with God in Genesis 18. Both Abraham and God are vigorous bargainers in this text. Such prayer is more than just pious recital of familiar innocuous mantras. It is, rather, down and dirty engagement with God.

In our society, where we imagine we may be (or must be!) on our own, prayer is the core acknowledgement that in fact our lives are referred beyond ourselves. It is for that reason that Matthew 6 can end in an invitation to move out of anxiety and into glad obedience (vv. 33–34). Such prayer that moves us beyond anxiety is sometimes submissiveness to God and sometimes defiant insistence upon one's own need. Father Abraham knew what he wanted and insisted upon it.

QUESTIONS

What bold petition to God have you not yet voiced?

What might you make of prayer that is engaged dispute with God?

PRAYER

God, teach me to pray to you honestly and boldly, trusting in your transformative power. Amen.

Day 7: Enjoy hearing the Scriptures read aloud in church.

The Rev. Dr. C. K. Robertson
Canon to the Presiding Bishop
of The Episcopal Church
New York, New York

Genesis 19–21, Psalm 7, Matthew 7

Sodom and Gomorrah! Even for those who have never opened a Bible, the names are famous—or, rather, infamous. They are synonymous with depravity and lawlessness. Yet what is perhaps more remarkable is that even the hero of the tale, Lot, does not appear to be very heroic. Indeed, looking back from our twenty-first-century vantage point, some of his behavior would be described as questionable at best. True, compared to his neighbors, Lot practically wears a halo, but that's not really saying much.

And this is not just in the case of Lot. Many—perhaps most—of the protagonists we encounter in Genesis (and also in the biblical books that follow) say things and do things that might shock, embarrass, or even anger us. Polygamy, concubinage, drunkenness, and incredible violence all form part of the saga of God's "faithful" leaders. We might be pardoned, therefore, for judging Lot and company fairly harshly, but as Jesus reminds us in Matthew 7, looking back in judgment does little good.

Rather, we can note that the stories in Genesis, like this one about Sodom and Gomorrah, are really about the choices people make, both then and now. Lot, his spouse, and his neighbors all made fateful choices that resulted in consequences of one kind or another. The reason that judging others does little good is precisely because, in the end, it is what we ourselves do or do not do that really matters. Then what exactly should we do? Again, it is Jesus who answers that question in words that have been immortalized as the Golden Rule: "Do unto others what you would have them do unto you." Now that is a daily choice worth making.

QUESTIONS

What have you read so far in the Bible that has shocked or disturbed you? What things happening today might be shocking or disturbing to Abraham, Sarah, or Lot if they could visit us?

Radical hospitality is a recurring theme in several parts of Scripture. How can you and your church community display such welcome in fresh, tangible ways?

PRAYER

God of welcome, bless us and others through us, that they might see you in all that we say and do, through Jesus Christ our Savior and Host at the heavenly banquet. Amen.

Day 9

The Rev. Dr. C. K. Robertson
Canon to the Presiding Bishop
of The Episcopal Church
New York, New York

Genesis 22–24, Psalm 8, Matthew 8

The story of Abraham and Isaac is hardly a feel-good tale. In fact, you might well find yourself calling out to the boy, "Run, Isaac, run! Don't let him get you!" You might even feel some consternation with the lad. After all, how dense can he be? He's carrying the wood for his own sacrifice. It doesn't help that this passage holds such an important place in the Episcopal tradition, being read each year during the Easter Vigil service.

But as should be obvious by now in this journey through Genesis, a literalistic reading of the biblical texts will not prove very helpful for us. Rather, we are called to do as the Prayer Book says, "to read, mark, learn, and inwardly digest" Holy Scripture. The Word of God is not cotton candy; it is something to be chewed on.

So as we come to the tale of a father asked to sacrifice his son, we must move beyond our repugnance and instead consider the deeper realities to which the story calls us. "God will provide," the father tells the son. These words are not some trite religious sentiment, but a bold assertion of faith in the face of life's very real struggles.

This does not mean that we are free from struggle, from worry, from pain. No, for as we are reminded in Matthew's story of the frightened disciples on the water, when we are in the very heart of the storm, and it seems as if Jesus is asleep and unaware of all that we face, the reality is that he is right there with us, providing peace and calm and presence. The problems of life are legion. The potential sacrifices we face are great. But God's presence and God's provision are greater still. Thanks be to God!

QUESTIONS

The story of Abraham and Isaac clearly resonates for Christians in New Testament texts such as, "For God so loved the world that he gave his only Son." What do these words mean for you? How do you share the good news of God's love?

When have you felt most alone, as if God were asleep, and unaware of your struggles? How did God's presence and peace become known to you?

PRAYER

O God who provides, be with us in the midst of the storms of life, and help us to share your peace and presence with others, for the sake of your Son, Jesus Christ. Amen.

The Rev. Dr. C. K. Robertson
Canon to the Presiding Bishop
of The Episcopal Church
New York, New York

Day 10

Genesis 25–27, Psalm 9, Matthew 9

Abraham, Isaac, and Jacob—their names are legend. Indeed, in later books of the Old Testament and again in the New Testament, the Lord is often referred to as the "God of Abraham, Isaac, and Jacob." And yet it has already been noted that the first of these great figures, Abraham, the "Father of Faith," was far from perfect. Now, with his passing, the spotlight turns first to Isaac, whose brief time on the biblical stage is hardly impressive, and then moves to Jacob.

Abraham and Isaac resort to deception when faced with threatening situations. Jacob takes lying and cheating to a whole new level. His very name meaning "supplanter," Jacob supplants Esau through an elaborate deception that secures for himself the birthright and blessing that should have gone to his brother. Jacob will do whatever it takes to fulfill his ambitions, even if that means spending much of the rest of his life on the run. It is difficult, perhaps, to see why God might choose to raise up "a chosen people, a holy priesthood" through such a morally questionable character.

Turning to Matthew's Gospel, it seems that not much has changed. Instead of going for the best and brightest to be his disciples, Jesus unexpectedly calls Matthew the tax collector to join his ragtag group of unlearned fishermen. Matthew, or Levi as he is sometimes known, is not that different from Jacob. He cheats—in fact, he cheats for a living!

Eventually, Jacob spends a night wrestling with God and emerges a new person. Matthew leaves his old life behind and becomes a new person. Both then and now, God does not wait for any of us to be perfect before calling us to follow. And somewhere along the way, when we least expect it, we are born anew.

QUESTIONS

What do you think of Jacob, of Esau, of Isaac when you read these stories? Why does God sometimes work through questionable people?

When have you experienced God through an unlikely person?

PRAYER

God of new beginnings, meet us where we are in our journey, imperfect as we are, and use us in ways we cannot imagine to make a difference in the world for you, through Jesus Christ our Lord. Amen.

Day 11

The Rev. Dr. Francis H. Wade
Interim Dean
Washington National Cathedral
Washington, D.C.

Genesis 28–30, Psalm 10, Matthew 10

We would probably not like to have Jacob as an influence on our children. He was a liar and cheat who found his match in his Uncle Laban. These two rogues swindled one another back and forth, riding roughshod over the feelings of Rachel and Leah, to say nothing of poor Zilpah and Bilhah. It is natural to wonder what rogues like this are doing in the Bible. And how did Jacob get to be a patriarch, mentioned in solemn tones along with Abraham and Isaac?

The gospel lesson does not help us out very much, as the twelve disciples are introduced with a tax collector (a profession then based on extortion) and a traitor prominent among them. They are sent into a world of wolves where betrayal, slander, and discord are to be expected.

Thoughtful modern readers stand with the psalmist asking, "Why?" Why does God let the arrogant, the wicked, and the deceitful seem to have free reign? Why isn't the Bible full of saintly folk who set us a good example?

The answer is that our ancestors knew that the Bible is not a book about people but a book about God. They did not go out of their way to make the people of the Bible appear any more saintly than anyone else. The wonder is that the glory of God is able to shine through sinful humanity. The wonder is that God does beautiful things with rogues, misfits, and bumblers, as well as the occasional saint. That is what God was doing in ancient times, and it is what God is doing today.

QUESTIONS

How might the glory and goodness of God shine through sinful people?

How might God be working through you—in spite of yourself?

PRAYER

God of glory and goodness, let your light shine through my life in ways beyond my knowing, and help me to always be ready to see that light shining through others. Amen.

The Rev. Dr. Francis H. Wade
Interim Dean
Washington National Cathedral
Washington, D.C.
Day 12

Genesis 31–33, Psalm 11, Matthew 11

The story of Jacob's return to face the brother he had cheated twenty years before is a powerful one by any standard, but it also provides a significant insight into our Judeo-Christian tradition. Jacob did all that he could to protect himself from the righteous anger he expected from Esau. Lavish gifts were sent ahead, and he divided his household into two groups, thinking that if one was attacked the other might escape. Still, the fact that Esau was coming with four hundred men was worrisome. You and I would probably say that Jacob was left wrestling with his conscience, but in the narrative terms of ancient storytellers we are told that he wrestled with a strange man who turned out to be God. One result of the match was that Jacob was given a new name, something that often accompanied turning points in life. The new name was "Israel" which means "one who strives or wrestles with God."

What is especially revealing about this story is that when our faith had developed to the point where it needed a name, there were many options. The people of God could have been named for obedient Abraham or faithful Isaac or Moses the Law Giver. But the chosen name was Israel because the people of God continually wrestle with God about almost everything in life—faith, morality, sin, forgiveness, etc. We wrestle with God partly because, as the psalmist says, God tests the righteous along with the wicked. We wrestle as John the Baptist did when he lost his confidence in Jesus as the messiah and sent a deputation to ask if he really, really was the Anointed One.

The name Israel was not lightly chosen but rightly chosen because the people of God must always wrestle with God.

QUESTIONS

How do you wrestle with God?

What happens if we stop wrestling with God?

PRAYER

Challenging Lord, you come to us in the still of night when we are alone by our own River Jabbok. Help us to engage with you as our ancestor Jacob did that we might greet the dawn with your blessing in our ears. Amen.

Day 13

The Rev. Dr. Francis H. Wade
Interim Dean
Washington National Cathedral
Washington, D.C.

Genesis 34–36, Psalm 12, Matthew 12

Those who navigate rely on fixed objects to help them find their way. The North Star, mountains, rivers, and longitude and latitude provide points of certainty for people venturing on unfamiliar paths. Those who undertake spiritual journeys tend to seek similarly reliable points as they (we) try to be faithful in a changing landscape that rises into an unknown future.

The genealogies that tend to confuse the modern reader were part of our ancestors' attempts to establish fixed points for their journey. These lists sought to establish the true owners and, therefore, the true inheritors of property both temporal and spiritual. In Jesus' day the Pharisees relied heavily on certain fixed dogmas that told them whether they were on the right path. One of these was the sanctity of the sabbath, another was predictable pre-established signs of God's favor, and a third was one's place in family life.

Unfortunately, Jesus shows that none of these provide the certainty that the faithful expected from them. In today's reading, Jesus says that he has greater authority than sabbath laws; refuses to give a traditional sign; and rates his spiritual community above his nuclear family.

Lest we feel we are being left to wander, Jesus affirms in each instance that he is the fixed point. Our ongoing, living relationship with Jesus is what guides us on our journey.

Today's texts also remind us of a constant in that relationship: God's concern for what the psalmist calls the despoiled poor and the groaning needy; the sick to whom Jesus responded; and, even in their rough way, the justice sought by Israel's sons. When God's concerns are ours, we have a fixed navigational point.

QUESTIONS

What have people relied on in the past to tell them that they were being faithful?

How does Jesus provide guidance for our spiritual journeys?

PRAYER

Blessed Lord, you have set us on a journey into an unknown future. Sharpen our eyes to see the path you have chosen for us, attune our souls to recognizing the Spirit that goes before us, quicken our hands to reach out to those who struggle beside us, and keep us in living relationships as we make our way. Amen.

Day 14: Enjoy hearing the Scriptures read aloud in church.

The Rt. Rev. Stephen Platten
Bishop of Wakefield
Wakefield, England

Day 15

Genesis 37–39, Psalm 13, Matthew 13

Our readings today begin with the saga of Joseph, one of the most beautiful narratives in the Old Testament. Joseph's handsome appearance and attractive personality make others jealous. The interpretation of the dream that shows Joseph as master over his brothers is the final straw. He is thrown into the pit and left to die. Later he will thrive in Egypt and become the salvation of his family who become the model Israel.

Christians down the ages have often seen Joseph as "a type of Christ," one who suffers and then brings salvation. Our psalm echoes a similar theme—how long will we be forgotten and left to suffer? Despite feelings of despair, the psalmist remains faithful, for he knows in his heart of God's enduring love.

In Matthew's Gospel we read Jesus' parables describing the nature of the kingdom of heaven. Of all the versions of the parable of the sower (it is found in Mark and Luke as well), Matthew's is perhaps the most elaborately drawn. Here Jesus is the teacher of the kingdom of heaven in all its richness. The same temptations and dangers seen in the Joseph stories are there, and they are set in the images of the parable: evil can snatch away the seeds, and people will not root themselves deeply in the life of the kingdom. But ultimately it is a gospel story, a tale of the good news, offered graciously by God in Jesus, bringing forth fruit.

Here too is a feast of shorter parables, of the wheat and the weeds, the mustard seed, the yeast, the treasure hidden in a field, the pearl of great price. Each helps fashion a picture of the kingdom that Jesus himself inaugurates. The trials and temptations of our own lives are not far away in these vivid stories and they connect us with the gospel of hope.

QUESTIONS

How can we offer hope to others as we read these vivid stories of Joseph and from Jesus' parables?

Reflect upon the variety of images of the kingdom of heaven in Matthew's chapter 13. How do these images build a three-dimensional picture of God's will for us upon which we can place our own experience?

PRAYER

Father, through your gracious generosity we are created and redeemed; open our hearts to be channels of your love that our lives may be fashioned in the pattern of Jesus Christ our Lord. Amen.

Day 16

The Rt. Rev. Stephen Platten
Bishop of Wakefield
Wakefield, England

Genesis 40–42, Psalm 14, Matthew 14

We pick up the story of Joseph, with him now in Egypt. As in the earlier part of the narrative, there are ups and downs. Joseph's talent and wisdom always provoke jealousy and suspicion. So Pharaoh throws him into jail. Not long after, however, his skill as an interpreter of dreams comes into its own again, and this time he advises Pharaoh himself. The interpretation sets out a strategy enabling the Egyptians to preserve sufficient food for their needs. Then follows the moving episode of Joseph meeting with his brothers, giving them a tough time, and then relenting.

This entire narrative is part of a tapestry of "wisdom" writing that weaves in and out of the texture of the Old Testament. The psalmist picks up similar reflections, but in song form as part of the worship of God. Today's psalm implicitly contrasts wisdom with foolishness. The fool's lack of wisdom is rooted in lack of faith: "Fools say in their hearts, 'There is no God'" (Psalm 14:1).

Faith and our lack of faith appear again as themes in the passage from Matthew's Gospel. Peter sees Jesus walking toward him on the water and attempts to do the same. Peter fails, and Jesus speaks of faith in our relationship with God. Such faith allows Jesus to nourish the hungry in the classical story of the feeding of the five thousand. This also looks forward to the eucharist, to the Last Supper, and to God's feeding of all his people. Finally, the terrifying story of the death of John the Baptist shows how the faithful servant of God endures even unto death.

Faith is at the heart of the Christian life; and the experiences of Joseph, John the Baptist, and Jesus himself tell us so much of how faith, worship, and prayer can shape our lives and the manner in which we mediate that life to others.

QUESTIONS

In which ways does the lens of faith transform our actions and attitudes in the light of these narratives?

In your reading of the Bible, where else have you encountered suffering for faith and a response to that suffering?

PRAYER

Open our hearts, O Lord, and give us strength under suffering and wisdom to inform our faith in Jesus Christ our Lord. Amen.

The Rt. Rev. Stephen Platten
Bishop of Wakefield
Wakefield, England

Day 17

Genesis 43–45, Psalm 15, Matthew 15

Yesterday's reading ended with the extraordinary story of Joseph's brothers finding the money they had taken with them to buy grain in their bags when they arrive home. When they return for more grain, Joseph tricks them again, packing a silver cup in their luggage. Benjamin, the youngest son, is then to be held as hostage. Joseph breaks down with emotion, revealing his true identity, and sends his brothers back to bring Jacob, their father. They are then given land in Egypt. The story's underlying message is of generosity. As with all of the Joseph saga, it is a tale about the goodness of God to his people.

Today's psalm is a well-known piece of poetry. It describes the pattern of a godly life. In Matthew's Gospel we encounter Jesus in dispute with the scribes and Pharisees. The dispute is about purity laws, but Jesus uses it to pick up a similar theme to our psalm. It is not the flouting of laws of purity that are the key issue—instead, we are defiled by failing to live a godly life. In contrast to those pious Jews, known to follow the law, the next story sees Jesus encounter a foreigner, a Canaanite woman. Her faith and her humble answer to Jesus' question mark her out as a true follower. These two contrasting tales take us into a second feeding, this time of four thousand people, not dissimilar to the story we read two days ago about the five thousand.

One of the abiding truths about the Bible is how we learn of God's ways with humankind through story. The Joseph narratives and the gospel stories offer us a similar way of learning of God's love and of the life he would have us live. Today's psalm is a commentary on just this manner of learning.

QUESTIONS

How is Joseph's trickery of his brothers still part of the generous tale of God's love?

How do we square the Pharisees' true piety with the more radical command of Jesus about defilement?

PRAYER

Loving Father, you show your love for us through those who nurture us and care for us along the way. Give us the generosity to allow that same love to pour out to others in the service of our Saviour Jesus Christ. Amen.

Day 18

The Very Rev. Ian Markham
Dean of Virginia Theological Seminary
Alexandria, Virginia

Genesis 46–48, Psalm 16, Matthew 16

The tragic haunts every human life. We all have to cope with mortality, loss, and failed relationships. Learning to cope with the difficulties of life can be a challenge. One important feature of Scripture is the way in which the tragic is recognized. Embedded in the famous and familiar story of Joseph, we see the human family in all its complexity. In today's reading, a father is reconciled to a son he thought dead, and a brother forgives the rest of his siblings and provides land for the family to occupy. The drama is intense. Underneath the text is deep hurt and pain—a feeling that to an extent we all recognize.

Our gospel weaves together the tragic with Christian hope. The tragic is captured in the anxieties around having sufficient food to eat (after all, the disciples did not bring along any bread) and the predication from Jesus that he must go to Jerusalem to suffer and die. Christian hope is captured in the powerful confession of Peter. Jesus in so many ways did not fit the classic Messianic expectations, but Peter gets it right and tells Jesus that he is "the Messiah, the Son of the living God." The tragic is intermingled with the hope—indeed, the hope partly depends on the tragic coming to pass.

Scripture does not evade the reality of suffering. Like the psalmist, we pray for God's protection but know that such protection cannot mean a pain-free life or a promise of uncomplicated relationships. Instead, protection means that we trust that God will be with us in the difficult times. It means that God supports us through the complexities of our relationships. It means that we find grace and hope even in the moments of deepest despair.

QUESTIONS

Reflect on the tragic in your life. Search for the moments of grace embedded in those tragic seasons.

Reflect on the question: "Who do people say that the Son of Man is?" Who is Jesus for you?

PRAYER

Loving God, we pause and remember the tragic moments in our lives. We offer the pain of those moments to you. Please enter into those memories and allow your hope and your grace to be present. Help us, loving God, to cope with all the challenges of being human. In Christ we pray. Amen.

The Very Rev. Ian Markham
Dean of Virginia Theological Seminary
Alexandria, Virginia

Day 19

Genesis 49–50, Psalm 17, Matthew 17

Gathering around the bedside of someone dying is an important moment. This poem, where Jacob blesses his sons, plays a crucial role in the Genesis narrative. Here we have the fortunes of the different tribes anticipated; the older sons have fallen out of favor and one of the younger sons, Judah, is described in very positive terms. The author of Genesis invites us to recognize how the past shapes the future and how decisions now can impact generations to come. The narrative stresses how interconnected we all are. For this author, Reuben's actions during his life (see Genesis 35:22) had an impact for centuries. The ripples from a certain action can extend a long way.

The past meets the present in a very striking way in Matthew's Gospel. Jesus takes Peter, James, and John up a high mountain. These three disciples then witness the Transfiguration of Jesus, who is then joined by Elijah and Moses. Elijah is important as a prophet; Moses is important as the giver of the law. This is Matthew's way of letting us know that Jesus stands on the achievements of the past; Jesus is in continuity with the past. In the same way that sin has consequences that can shape generations to come, so faithfulness and service to God can create opportunities for good in the future.

Jesus in this passage is very conscious of the passing of time. This is the second predication of his betrayal "into human hands," which will lead to his death. He has so much to teach the disciples. The need for them to cultivate a faith sufficient to bring God's presence to a difficult situation is stressed. Jesus wants us to grow in our relationship with God so we can be a vehicle for God's grace.

Every second that passes is a second that has gone forever. The invitation today is to reflect on the passing of time and use every moment to build possibilities that God can use in the future.

QUESTIONS

What would you like to say to loved ones when you are near death? What is stopping you from saying some of those things now?

Think a little on your use of time. Set yourself the goal of using every moment for God.

PRAYER

Holy One of love and light, I give you this moment and this day. Please use every moment of this day for your glory. May your Son be seen in me. In the name of Jesus I pray. Amen.

Day 20

The Very Rev. Ian Markham
Dean of Virginia Theological Seminary
Alexandria, Virginia

Exodus 1–3, Psalm 18:1-20, Matthew 18

Children often have a hard time. When Jesus explains that real greatness in the kingdom requires us to become "like children," he was being deliberately shocking. Children are vulnerable and weak; they are easy to abuse and hurt. Jesus makes it clear that those who have the lowest status in society are much closer to being great in the kingdom.

Back in the opening chapters of Exodus, children are the primary victims. Joseph has been forgotten. The leadership of Egypt has turned the Hebrews into slaves. To maintain their superiority, the Egyptians are attempting to eliminate male babies. In this tragic situation, a young Hebrew mother places a baby "among the reeds on the bank of the river." Through God's grace, one child is saved.

Jesus is very clear about the value that God places on a child. To hurt a child is a wicked sin. Children have a special place in the kingdom. The sense that everything around us is a gateway to the spiritual comes easily to children. Adults lose that sense of wonder and awe, but children have it all the time. The miracle of a flower growing and the mystery of the stars are understood by children; adults can so easily take it all for granted.

It is a great gift and responsibility to care for children. Whether as a friend, parent, or grandparent, we are invited to strive to be a good and constructive influence on children. Today's gospel invites us to meditate on what we can learn from children. Perhaps we need to recover some of that childlike appreciation of this remarkable world that God has made.

QUESTIONS

Recall your own childhood. Reflect on those moments when you learned about the world around you. Are you still amazed by the miracle of life and being?

Think about your friendships with children. Spend a few moments considering how you can have constructive relationships with children.

PRAYER

Holy and Loving God, thank you for the gift of children. Help me to retain a childlike appreciation of this remarkable way. For Christ's sake. Amen.

Day 21: Enjoy hearing the Scriptures read aloud in church.

Dr. Deirdre Good
Professor of New Testament
The General Theological Seminary
New York, New York

Day 22

Exodus 4–6, Psalm 18:21-50, Matthew 19

In today's reading from Exodus, God calls Moses to lead the Israelites out of slavery into freedom. In this role, Moses will not only deliver God's people into the promised land, but will also deliver the law (Torah). The best known part of the Torah, the ten commandments, are not simply rules but a framework to form and maintain a new kind of society.

Every community has to have rules, and communities around Jesus are no exception. Keeping God's commandments, namely, the law is a hallmark of Matthew's community. "Don't think that I have come to destroy the law and the prophets," Jesus says in Matthew 5:17. "I have come not to destroy but to fulfil them."

Obedience to God is central to being part of a community. At the heart of Psalm 18, verses 30–31 explain that God's way is perfect and that God is a shield for all who take refuge in him. Keeping the commandments of God is a way of being obedient to God.

Matthew's nineteenth chapter occurs in a section of the gospel in which a community, having been formed around Jesus, begins to regulate itself. The practice of praying the Lord's Prayer (Matthew 6) has already identified community members as siblings addressing God as Heavenly Father. Chapter 18 identifies both membership and mechanisms for discipline in the community in the case of a brother or sister sinning against a community member, while chapter 19 seeks to regulate divorce in a context of marriage and children.

Jesus prohibits divorce in Mark 10. But in Matthew 19, we hear teaching on divorce that moderates Mark 10 and lets us see that Jesus's teaching on divorce was not univocal. Characters in the narrative include Matthew's Pharisees, who question Jesus on a controversial topic, and Matthew's disciples, who seek to understand Jesus' teaching. Topics in the narrative that fall under the rubric of Jesus' instruction to disciples about entering the kingdom of heaven by keeping the commandments include divorce, eunuchs, and children.

Like Moses who delivered the law, Jesus reminds his first followers—and reminds us— that our relationships with one another are integral to our relationship with God.

(continued on next page)

Day 22, continued

QUESTIONS

How does your Christian community regulate itself?

Are there ever circumstances in which someone might be exiled from a community?

How does your Christian community reflect diversity, including unmarried people?

PRAYER

O God, you have bound us together in a common life. Help us, in the midst of our struggles for justice and truth, to confront one another without hatred or bitterness and to work together with mutual forbearance and respect; through Jesus Christ our Lord. Amen.

Dr. Deirdre Good
Professor of New Testament
The General Theological Seminary
New York, New York **Day 23**

Exodus 7–9, Psalm 19, Matthew 20

The psalmist of Psalm 19 delights in the Torah, the law of God, and expresses joy in God's instruction that sets Israel apart from other nations. Meditation on the Torah here and in other psalms (see, for example, Psalm 1) involves reflection on study and practice of Torah-obedience. Reading and memorizing psalms is something Jesus did. Psalms 18 and 19 are also profound meditations on the ideal orientation of a person in authority toward God. The readings from Exodus show a struggle between Pharaoh and God concerning the exercise of power over others.

Matthew's parable of the laborers in the vineyard of the kingdom (20:1-15) describes the means by which those who came late to the employment office for the vineyard are paid the same as all-day laborers on the basis of God's generous justice. It provides analogies for many situations and circumstances on which we are invited to reflect, all of which involve the inclusion of latecomers to the rewards of labor.

Those who were able to commit early to the labor of the vineyard might well resent that others added to the workforce receive, at the end of the day, the same wages as those who "bore the burden of the day and the scorching heat." But as the vineyard owner explains, they are not unjustly treated: "Am I not allowed to do what I choose with what belongs to me? Or are you envious because I am generous?" What is given is not only generous, but as it is given by God, it is also just.

Those who challenge generous justice, having already been paid, seem greedy and their envy would deny God's generosity to all who need it. Those who receive generous justice as the (unexpected) reward of their labors have only gratitude for God. So it is with those who come later to labor in the vineyard. We as latecomers are the recipients of God's surprising generosity, for which we have nothing but gratitude. And in the end, whether we work early or late, aren't we all laboring side by side in the vineyard of the kingdom?

QUESTIONS

What are the shortcomings of "equal work for equal pay"?

How has God's justice been manifest in human history?

PRAYER

Grant, O God, that your holy and life-giving Spirit may so move every human heart, and especially the hearts of the people of this land, that barriers that divide us may crumble, suspicions disappear, and hatreds cease; that our divisions being healed, we may live in justice and peace. Amen.

Day 24

Dr. Deirdre Good
Professor of New Testament
The General Theological Seminary
New York

Exodus 10–12, Psalm 20, Matthew 21

Today we reflect further on the exercise of power, whether that of God or of human rulers like Pharaoh or any other leader. The readings from Exodus relate the origins of Passover as the story of the deliverance of Jews from Egypt, celebrated today as Pesach.

In Matthew 21, Jesus enters Jerusalem as a king. Images of "the triumphal entry" show Jesus on a donkey entering the holy city to universal acclamation. People wave palm branches and shout approval. Contrast this with the flight of the Holy Family into Egypt in silence and terror (Matthew 2) when Jesus fled for his life with his mother Mary and Joseph. Now Jesus rides into Jerusalem, not as a triumphant ruler in a victory procession but as a meek king fulfilling the prophecy of Zechariah for Jerusalem crowds and gospel readers. (Modern translations prefer the word "humble.") Contemporary treatises on Hellenistic kingship in Jesus' day describe a meek king as a noncoercive leader who practices disciplined calmness over himself and is benevolent and magnanimous to others. Since the Roman Empire was the dominant power in Jesus' day, rulers and kings were not autonomous. As a client king, Jesus looks to God for help in time of threat and success in struggle (Psalm 20) and brokers God's kingdom to others.

Entering the temple, Jesus overturns the money changers' tables, thus symbolically reforming the space. Jesus welcomes into the temple hitherto marginalised and excluded groups: the blind, the lame, and the children, and it is this that causes the temple authorities to become angry. Upon leaving the temple, and finding no fruit on a fig tree, Jesus curses it and it immediately withers. This is a symbolic comment on the ineffectiveness of temple leadership.

Within the temple courts Jesus then instigates five controversies with the Jerusalem temple's religious elite. Such controversies characterise Jesus' speech with opponents in the gospels. These encounters end with the silence of opposition and Jesus' last words.

Discussions about exercising power do not belong to ages past. In the 1993 movie *Schindler's List*, Oscar Schindler, a Jewish businessman, discusses power with the prison camp leader Amon Goeth. He is trying to persuade Goeth to release Polish Jews from the Warsaw Ghetto into employment in his factory and so save them from death.

> Schindler: They fear us because we have the power to kill arbitrarily.
> A man commits a crime, he should know better. We have him killed

Day 24, continued

and we feel pretty good about it. Or we kill him ourselves and we feel even better. That's not power, though, that's justice. That's different than power. Power is when we have every justification to kill— and we don't.

QUESTIONS

Where in your life and in the world have you seen power exercised through submission or weakness?

How can apparent powerlessness be a sign of strength?

PRAYER

O God, you declare your almighty power chiefly in showing mercy and pity: Grant us the fullness of your grace, that we, running to obtain your promises, may become partakers of your heavenly treasure; through Jesus Christ our Lord, who lives and reigns with you and the Holy Spirit, one God, for ever and ever. Amen.

—*THE BOOK OF COMMON PRAYER*, P. 234 (PROPER 21)

Day 25

Dr. Christopher Wells
Executive Director
The Living Church Foundation
Milwaukee, Wisconsin

Exodus 13–15, Psalm 21, Matthew 22

The famous story of the Israelites' exodus, via miraculous escape from pursuing Egyptian armies through a parted Red Sea, culminates in the Song of Moses. Anglicans may know this as a canticle for Morning Prayer: a hymn to the Lord's power and might, his faithfulness to the people he redeemed (Exodus 15:13).

It's worth reflecting on the liturgical fact that as Christians sing this song, just as when we pray the psalms, we add at the end a Trinitarian coda: "Glory to the Father, and to the Son, and to the Holy Spirit: as it was in the beginning, is now, and will be for ever. Amen." This frame of Christian prayer underlines the consistency of God's character in all of Scripture, across time and space. God is the same yesterday, today, and tomorrow. Thus, God is ever interested in saving and perpetuating a people, across many generations, who may learn to say of their own life: I also came up out of Egypt (Exodus 13:8). Or, as in Jesus' wedding banquet parable: I was one whom God found on the street and rescued and am now, by grace, clothed in life and light (Matthew 22:9-14).

In this way, we become scriptural people: a people who, by knowing the Scriptures, know the power of God, as Jesus repeatedly demonstrates to the baffled Pharisees and Sadducees.

QUESTION

When have you, like the Israelites, experienced God's redeeming power in your life?

How have you been rescued by Christ?

PRAYER

Lord, shine the light of your Word on my life. Help me to understand and live by your teaching. Make me your humble child, glad with the joy of your presence. Amen.

Dr. Christopher Wells   **Day 26**
Executive Director
The Living Church Foundation
Milwaukee, Wisconsin

Exodus 16–18, Psalm 22, Matthew 23

Again, Scripture echoes from "old" to "new" and back again. We discover that Jesus' familiar cry of dereliction on the cross comes in the words of Psalm 22 (we may recognize other parts of this psalm that are read in Lenten services of the Stations of the Cross). As ever, the prayer opens out to the universalizing vocation of Jacob/Israel, not least as we Gentiles gratefully join the chorus: *"All* the ends of the earth shall remember and turn to the Lord, and *all* the families of the nations shall bow before him" (v. 27)—an extraordinary prophecy of missionary success, especially fit for meditation in the season of Epiphany. Imagine the people of God stretched out across the earth, incorporating every nation and people. This is the church, the reconciled community of Jew and Gentile (see Ephesians 2; Roman 9-11), the communion of the whole world.

Jesus' in-your-face polemic against the religious authorities of his day gathers prophetic steam in this light. Do what they teach you and follow it, but do not do *as* they do (Matthew 23:3), for Jesus came not to abolish but to fulfill the law. In this way he calls "Jerusalem" back to her roots, in an apocalyptic anticipation of the end, when the figures of old will find their fulfillment in the words of Psalm 118, adopted as the *Benedictus* of the Mass: "Blessed is he who comes in the name of the Lord" (23:39). Speaking of our sojourning Israelites, Saint Paul explains in 1 Corinthians 10:4, "They drank from the spiritual rock that followed them, and the rock was Christ," in a boldly Christological rendering of Exodus 17:6. What does this mean? That Jesus Christ comprehends history, as Word of God. All the rest is commentary.

QUESTIONS

When have you, like Jesus, found that words from the psalms resonate with and express your own prayers?

Is there a psalm that articulates your prayer today?

PRAYER

Lord Jesus, prepare us for your return, and make us capable of caring for the world, as members of your universal family. Amen.

Day 27

Dr. Christopher Wells
Executive Director
The Living Church Foundation
Milwaukee, Wisconsin

Exodus 19–21, Psalm 23, Matthew 24

Perhaps no psalm is better known than the twenty-third, for good reason. Many children and new believers learn it as an introduction to the Lord of heaven and earth: God is our tender father and protector, Jesus is our good shepherd (see John 10), and the Holy Spirit is our ever-present comfort in time of need. Once we know this, it is hard to forget, and so mature believers rightly return to these words for the personal reassurance of God's promises, as we place our trust in him: "I shall not be in want…I shall fear no evil…your goodness and mercy shall follow me all the days of my life" (Psalm 23:1, 4, 6).

This being the case, it may be jarring to read Jesus' rather different assurance to his disciples: "All will be thrown down" (Matthew 24:2). And he spends some time here (as in Luke) elaborating on the nature and extent of the trials to come, as signs of the long-awaited messianic age about which Jesus had queried the Pharisees several days prior (22:41ff.). War, famine, and earthquake will mark the birth pangs, followed by necessary persecution and martyrdom of the faithful and a thinning of their ranks—truly, a time of great suffering, unlike any other. "This gospel" will, however, "be proclaimed throughout the world," says Jesus, "as a testimony to all the nations; and then the end will come" (24:14).

Here is the good news, consonant with the psalm: that our end will be in Christ, albeit not without pain and difficulty. This world will end, before it is re-made as the kingdom. The words of God, however, will not pass away (Matthew 24:35), and in these we hide our hearts. "Do not be afraid; for God has come only to test you and to put the fear of him upon you so that you do not sin" (Exodus 20:20).

QUESTIONS

How have the words from Psalm 23 spoken to you in the past? How do they speak to you today?

How have you experienced God as shepherd and protector?

PRAYER

Lord Jesus, stay with us, for evening is at hand and the day is past; be our companion in the way, kindle our hearts, and awaken hope, that we may know you as you are revealed in Scripture and the breaking of bread. Grant this for the sake of your love. Amen.

—Collect for the Presence of Christ,
The Book of Common Prayer, p. 124.

Day 28: Enjoy hearing the Scriptures read aloud in church.

The Rt. Rev. C. Andrew Doyle
Bishop of Texas
Houston, Texas

Day 29

Exodus 22–24, Psalm 24, Matthew 25

Christians begin with a very important assumption that God created the world. Certainly this notion of God as Creator of all things is found in our creedal statements, which are rooted in the first followers' experience of Jesus and echo our earlier Abrahamic tradition. Today we read in Psalm 24: "The earth is the Lord's and all that is in it, the world, and those who live in it."

As creatures in this world, we are reminded that we are his and we are made as members of a wider creation. The temptation is to believe that God has given all of this to us to manipulate for our own purposes. The truth is, and we confess it regularly, that God creates all things (including us) and that all things belong to God.

When we open the gates of our hearts and souls to this reality, we find that we must respond. We respond not by negotiating percentages and ownership with God or others, but by being stewards of God's whole world. Out of this understanding we care for the poor, we share our goods, and we remember our neighbor and especially God's favorite people, the alien in a strange land. All things belong to God, as do we. Out of this stewardship comes a call to sow and multiply God's grace and the wealth within his creation. We see not a world of scarcity, but rather a world of abundance, and out of that abundance we are able to share with others. We are able to feed, clothe, and shelter Christ in the form of the other. Stewardship is not a self-interested negotiation with the Creator.

QUESTIONS

What am I doing with God's things? How am I using them?

Am I creating a sustainable world where all have enough and the riches of the kingdom of God are multiplied?

PRAYER

Heavenly Father, Creator of all good things, we know you reap where you did not sow and gather where you did not scatter; help us to be stewards of your creation in all aspects of our life. Amen.

Day 30

The Rt. Rev. C. Andrew Doyle
Bishop of Texas
Houston, Texas

Exodus 25–27, Psalm 25, Matthew 26

Psalm 25 implores God to help us know and learn his ways. Abiding in the grace of God means to dwell under an outpouring of love. When we dwell and abide in this grace, it is natural for us to wish to respond in some feeble way.

In Exodus, God asks the Israelites to make a tabernacle, altar, and some very fine vestments. We are invited to respond to God by giving God the very best of ourselves and to tend this sacred space. Exodus also tells us that in the midst of this priesthood and tending of the sanctuary, God is present.

We find God through the struggle of tending to God's ways. "Tending" involves setting apart time and space in our lives to follow him. It is the pressure of God's grace that invites us to respond by molding our actions, words, and time into a place where God is experienced.

The woman with the oil and the alabaster jar is responding to God's grace as experienced in the person of Jesus and his ministry. In setting apart her life, her wealth, and her time, she bears witness to God. She challenges others to see and rethink their commitment to Jesus.

Not everyone is able to do this. Not everyone is interested in this prayer or this work. As Christians we recognize that the lives we lead in community reflect our desire to live in God's ways. Our Episcopal rule of life (the Baptismal Covenant) offers a shape to our lives that invites us to live in the grace of God and to respond in word and action to that grace in our everyday lives. Whether we are receiving food for our spiritual journey through the remembrance of Jesus' own sharing of bread and wine, participating in regular worship, or sharing in outreach, service, and evangelism, we are tending to God's things. We are anointing the body of Christ with fine oil—a life lived for God in Christ Jesus alone.

QUESTIONS

What can I do in my life today that will worship God?

How will this witness to God's invitation to live differently change my life?

PRAYER

Heavenly Father, we give you thanks for inviting us to make room in our life to worship you. We ask that you will help us to see opportunities to live out your overflowing grace in a world desperate to see your hand at work. Amen.

The Rt. Rev. C. Andrew Doyle
Bishop of Texas
Houston, Texas

Day 31

Exodus 28–30, Psalm 26, Matthew 27

One of the apostolic fathers said (paraphrasing Genesis 3:8), "God wishes to walk with his creatures in the eve of the day." Jesus said, "How long have I wanted to gather you under my wings like a hen gathers her chicks?" (Matthew 23:37). In response to this desire of God and his choosing to be with us, people have long responded with words reminiscent of Psalm 26 wherein the author sings of his desire to walk with God in integrity.

From the verses in Exodus, we can see that for a long time, people have walked with God in the safety of a sanctuary, where people worship and wear different things. I force my youngest one to get cleaned up for worship. We have a rule: no holes in your clothes when you go to church. We do and act differently in the sanctuary when we go there and walk with God for a little while.

God comes into the creation that he loves. He enjoys walking with us in the cool of the evening breeze. And he invites us to live out our Christian lives in the world. We are called not only to dress up and go to church but to leave the church and take God with us, so that God may walk with us and talk with us as we make our pilgrim journey through the course of our day. We are to take God with us and introduce God to our family and friends, our neighbors and coworkers. We are to take God into the tabernacle of our souls and meet the poor, hungry, and homeless who live along the path of our life.

When we do this work of worship in the midst of our living, what we find is that God is already there and has been waiting for us all along. God is already there in our lives and the lives of those we would seek to help. He is already there. We find it was us and our need to walk worshipfully through life that was the missing piece.

I think when we do this we cannot help but see God in Christ Jesus, and we cannot help but say after everyone we meet, "Truly this is the son of God" (Matthew 27:54).

QUESTIONS

What would happen if you wrote down the names of everyone you saw today? Write down the names, and then write "Jesus Christ" next to each name. When you are done, spend thirty minutes and pray quietly. What was your experience?

PRAYER

Jesus Christ comes into our midst and opens his arms to us on the hard wood of the cross. Help us to worship God by opening our arms as God's saving embrace to the world around us. Amen.

Day 32

The Rev. Barbara Cawthorne Crafton
Author and Retreat Leader
Newark, New Jersey

Exodus 31–33, Psalm 27, Matthew 28

It was a miracle that Moses even lasted forty years in the wilderness with the Israelites. What with their steady whining and frequent backsliding, leading them was no picnic. And his brother Aaron, whom he trusted, was little better—here, for instance, we read about the golden calf he and the others make while Moses is up on the mountain talking with God.

There is something distinctly familiar in Aaron's response when his brother catches him in the act: "Then they gave me the gold, and I threw it into the fire, and out came this calf!" (Exodus 32:24). Well, that's not exactly how it went down, is it? The writer of Exodus makes sure we know that Aaron worked pretty hard himself on that golden calf ("fashioning it with a tool"). It didn't just pop out of the fire like magic—Aaron *made* it.

Forming a golden idol out of people's melted earrings is not a sin we're likely to commit today. But minimizing our own role in the sins we do commit is alive and well. We see it on the news all the time: "Mistakes were made," someone in public life says carefully, which falls considerably short of saying, "I made a mistake." And all of us know what it is to avoid owning up to our own less-than-holy moments. Even to ourselves.

Just come clean, we silently beg the straying politician as he parses his words ever so carefully into the forest of microphones facing him and his frozen-faced spouse. Get it over with.

Yes. Do it. However much a truth hurts, avoiding it will hurt more, in the end.

QUESTIONS

There has been much discussion about the relationship between private morality and fitness for public office. How do you respond to it?

Have you ever been caught in a web of your own falsehood? Or caught someone else? How did the decision to take responsibility—or not to do so—play out in that instance?

PRAYER

Merciful God, you know the secrets of our hearts. Give us the integrity and the courage to be what we seem to be, and lead us back to the truth when we stumble and fall short of it. For you never turn away when we turn to you, and for this we give you humble thanks. Amen.

The Rev. Barbara Cawthorne Crafton
Author and Retreat Leader
Newark, New Jersey

Day 33

Exodus 34–36, Psalm 28, Mark 1

"Then Moses gave an order and they sent this word throughout the camp: 'No man or woman is to make anything else as an offering for the sanctuary.' And so the people were restrained from bringing more, because what they already had was more than enough to do all the work" (Exodus 36:6-7).

Can you imagine—a capital campaign so wildly successful that people must be ordered to stop contributing? Neither can I.

Human beings form societies in order to accomplish things that are too big for one person to do alone. We reach out for help when we can't do it by ourselves. We make teams, sell shares, set up committees, hire assistants. Many hands make light work, we say.

Unless they don't.

One of the great truths of life together is that it always causes friction. We can't read each other's minds. We each have our own vision. A great leader communicates her vision in a way that others can see and embrace it, but there is usually a slip or two along the way—nothing fatal, usually, but different enough from what we expect to require a little more flexibility than we thought we'd need when we began. If you are undone by the unexpected, life will make you a nervous wreck in no time. If we want to accomplish anything in life, we'd better surrender at least some of our rigidity.

We must also be ready to move through our projects. The people who brought in all those things for enhancing Israel's worship of God were so excited about the first stage of the effort that they wanted to stay there. They would have brought in fancy fabrics forever. But now it was time to stop collecting goods and begin deploying them—a different activity altogether.

We can't prepare forever. Eventually it's time to take the plunge and use what we have.

QUESTIONS

Have you ever gotten stuck in the preparation phase of something you cared about? How were you helped to move on?

PRAYER

God of all our blessings, I want to help. Help me do so cooperatively, with an open mind and a listening heart. Help me not to take it personally when someone tempers my enthusiasm. Help me to entrust the outcome of all human effort to you. Amen.

Day 34

The Rev. Barbara Cawthorne Crafton
Author and Retreat Leader
Newark, New Jersey

Exodus 37–39, Psalm 29, Mark 2

It's not always easy to see—the biblical writers were human beings, as we are, and sometimes confused their own customs and preferences with the divine will, as we sometimes do. But a thread of blessing winds through the laws laid on Israel: it is for our good and for our joy that God makes demands on us. At bottom, the law is for us, not against us.

Often we see Jesus interacting with people who have lost sight of this. Grimly competitive in their by-the-book fidelity to the letter of the law, they react with violence to the intimacy with God upon which Jesus bases his own relationship: "The sabbath was made for man, not man for the sabbath. So the Son of Man is Lord even of the sabbath" (Mark 2:27-28). For Jesus, the law points consistently to a loving God. For some, it has become an end in itself.

Many Jewish writers speak of the enormous blessing of sabbath, a blessing which continues through even the most secular life. They get up from a meeting and take their leave, take an early train home, breathe deeply of a weekly rest—a rest like the one which even God embraced. From it they emerge to face another challenging week, knowing that the blessing of sabbath will come again, and soon.

QUESTIONS

Have you ever found a freedom wrapped in a restriction? Something you would not have seen were it not for being unable to do what you wanted to do?

Have you ever broken a rule for a good reason?

PRAYER

O God, we thank you for the things we can do and the things we can't. Help us to see the freedom wrapped in our restrictions, and to look beneath the surface of our rules to discern their spirit. Amen.

Day 35: Enjoy hearing the Scriptures read aloud in church.

The Rt. Rev. Kirk Stevan Smith
Bishop of Arizona
Phoenix, Arizona

Day 36

Exodus 40, Psalm 30, Mark 3

This section of Exodus ends with details for setting up the tent of meeting with its vessels, vestments, and sacred objects of worship. For these writers, God's divine presence was thought to physically dwell in the "Holy of Holies," in the temple. In our worship, God is not more present in church but we are more present to God. The Hebrew people trusted that God would be a constant presence in their lives, guiding and directing them (we would say "24/7") as a "pillar of fire by night and pillar of cloud by day" (Exodus 13:21).

Psalm 30 is a joyful outburst of gratitude for rescue from danger. How wonderful we feel when we are on the mend from an illness or when a crisis is past! Then it is easy for us to say, "Weeping may linger for the night, but joy comes in the morning." This is not just a cliché that clouds often have a silver lining, but rather that deliverance belongs to those who actively call upon God.

Each of the sections of this chapter of Mark begins with a geographic location: synagogue, seashore, mountain, home. In the synagogue Jesus heals on the sabbath. Some of us are old enough to remember when most stores and entertainments were closed on Sundays. Jesus' actions remind us that doing the work of God is more important than following rules and regulations, no matter how well-meaning. The narrative then turns to the Sea of Galilee where crowds seeking healing are so great that Jesus is forced to preach to them from a boat offshore. Interestingly, it is the demons who know who he is—the Son of God—and they are the first to confess him! This will not be the first time.

From the seashore, Jesus goes up on a mountain (mountains for Mark being the scene for important teachings and revelations). There Jesus calls his apostles—twelve of them (the same number as the tribes of Israel)—and sends them out. It is an interesting list of names; many we don't hear much more about, but they clearly had a supportive role, just like those unsung members of the church who humbly serve.

By the end of the chapter Jesus is again home, there to encounter the charge that he is crazy, charges made both by the religious leaders and by his own family. Jesus' answer to the scribes contains a mysterious allusion to "the (unforgivable) sin against the Holy Spirit" (Mark 3:29). This probably means the sin of attributing evil motives to good actions, just as the scribes felt compelled to attribute the healing Jesus performs to satanic motives.

continued on next page

Day 36, continued

In any event, Jesus' real family are not those who are related to him by blood but "those who do the will of God" (Mark 3:35).

QUESTIONS

Do we spend too much time in our churches focusing on the externals of architecture, liturgy, and vestments? How can the materials we use in worship be a means to an end and not a distraction?

Who are the people in our congregations who "do the will of God" and not just profess their beliefs? Are you one of them? Do you practice what you preach? If you were arrested for being a Christian, would there be enough evidence to convict you?

PRAYER

Oh God, you have promised to deliver us from all our infirmities and to guide us into the paths you would have us walk. Give us strength and courage to do your will and not ours in every aspect of our lives, trusting in your ever-present care and goodness. Amen.

The Rt. Rev. Kirk Stevan Smith
Bishop of Arizona
Phoenix, Arizona

Day 37

Leviticus 1–3, Psalm 31, Mark 4

Today we begin a book that may strike readers as both strange and barbaric. Written late in the Old Testament period by a priestly caste, Leviticus contains the rules and regulations for temple worship. The first section focuses on procedures for animal and grain sacrifice. In today's section, three of these five temple offerings are described—burnt (or whole) offering, cereal offering, and peace offering. The minutiae of butchering and burning animals is likely irrelevant to our contemporary needs. What *is* relevant to us is that our sacrifices to God must come from our first fruits and reflect the true sacrificial giving of our time, talent, and treasure.

Psalm 31 is generally labeled as a lament, but it sounds more like a desperate cry for help. It is very personal in nature, with the psalmist begging for help from God against personal enemies. Who at some time in their life has not felt like a broken pot, shunned and rejected by those who used to be friends? And yet there is hope for those who trust and who wait upon the Lord.

The fourth chapter of Mark begins with three parables, all of which have to do with seeds and planting, and it ends with a miracle. Exactly what Jesus intended by his use of parables has generated much scholarly debate. In verse 11, Jesus implies that he uses them not to be understood, which can hardly be the case! Most likely these words reflect Mark's explanation of why Jesus' earthly ministry was not more successful—people just didn't "get" his teaching. The parable of the sower (also found in Matthew and Luke) seems to stress that, like Jesus, our task is to preach the gospel, realizing that our efforts may often fall on deaf ears (or, in the language of the parable, on "bad soil"). Yet the promise is that enough of our efforts will bear fruit that there will be a miraculous harvest.

QUESTIONS

What can ancient temple sacrifice teach us about our own "sacrificial giving" to God, to the church, and to others?

What are the obstacles that stand in the way of God's purposes? What is the "bad soil" that you encounter in your own life and in the life of your community? How might these obstacles be overcome?

PRAYER

Oh God, you so generously sow your blessings in our lives. We thank you for the gifts of life, love, and laughter which we enjoy every day. Help us in turn to live generous, outwardly focused lives, giving to others of our whole being in thanksgiving and gratitude to you. Amen.

Day 38

The Rt. Rev. Kirk Stevan Smith
Bishop of Arizona
Phoenix, Arizona

Leviticus 4–6, Psalm 32, Mark 5

Today's Old Testament reading has more instructions on sacrifices offered at the temple, specifically the sin offering and the guilt offering. The first is to be performed when anyone—priest, ruler, or common person—"sins *unwittingly* in any of the things the Lord has commanded." This could include having contact with unclean objects (Leviticus 5:1-4). There is no provision for sins done deliberately. In addition to the ritual of sacrifice, confession is expected (5:5). Guilt offerings are similar to sin offerings, but require that restitution be made to the injured party.

Note how atonement—the reestablishment of a right relationship with God and the community—is always done through the agency of a priest. This idea carries over in our church's hierarchical structure and specifically in the sacrament of penance, which must be performed by a priest. In Anglican theology, only God forgives sins, but priestly absolution is the means through which that occurs.

Psalm 32 is a song of thanksgiving for healing. There is a clear connection for the psalmist between sin and disease, a "mind-body connection" that is increasingly recognized by modern medicine. The psalmist has been healed from infirmity because of a willingness to confess his or her sinfulness.

The fifth chapter of Mark contains three vivid healing stories, those of the Gerasene demoniac, the daughter of Jairus, and the woman with the flow of blood. The first of these strikes us as quite odd: a man possessed by thousands ("my name is Legion") of demons raving among the tombs, whose tormenting spirits Jesus exorcises into a herd of pigs who then jump into the sea. Especially interesting is the fact that the same evil spirits who possess the man are the first to recognize Jesus as the Son of God (Matthew 5:7), a reminder that simply recognizing Jesus as divine is not enough; one must follow him as well.

In contrast to this rather bizarre account are the tender and compassionate healing of a poor woman who dares only to touch Jesus's garment and of the little daughter of the ruler of the local synagogue. In an especially vivid touch, Mark even quotes Jesus' healing words to her in Aramaic, the language Jesus would have spoken, "Talitha cum."

Day 38, continued

QUESTIONS

N. H. Smith in *Peake's Commentary on the Bible* writes of the ritual temple sacrifice described in Leviticus: "Behind all these regulations there lies the conviction that repentance is not enough. Something must be done and must be seen to be done. The ritual is not to please God, who requires only repentance and faith, but for man's sake so that repentance shall be real and not submerged in a wave of undefined sentiment." Do you agree?

What, for you, is the difference between *believing* in Jesus and *following* him?

PRAYER

Oh Lord, we know that your wish for us is health and wholeness. Take away those infirmities of mind and spirit that keep us from loving you with all our heart. Amen.

Day 39

The Rt. Rev. James Tengatenga
Bishop of Southern Malawi
Blantyre, Malawi

Leviticus 7–9, Psalm 33, Mark 6

I have just finished reading Kierkegaard's *Purity of Heart Is to Will One Thing*. This book talks about the importance of preparation for confession: preparation for an encounter with God. Putting oneself in the right kind of frame of mind, desiring nothing but God. Putting oneself in a position to receive the one thing that is needful.

However, the readings for today go to town in discussing the preparation for delivering God's mercy; in fact, delivering God to his people. We talk a lot about the recipients of God's presence, but seldom talk about the preparation needed to be the vessel through which the means of grace flow. Think of all the things that Aaron had to go through in his ordination—clothing, cleansing, anointing with both oil and blood, and then seven days in the presence of God—all this to make him fit to be the priest that he was called to be. On the eighth day, as Aaron was to offer the sacrifices for his people, he also needed to make offerings for himself. Only then was he worthy to be the vessel through which the grace of God flowed.

Those of us whose calling and "job" it is to bless others have a tendency to get so used to it all that we neglect to follow the orders and directions and all the "pain and trouble" it takes for us to be truly worthy of that calling. Not that we can make ourselves worthy by "works" of obedience, but a little care and a little preparation and lots of obedience make all the difference—accoutrements and all. In Mark 6, Jesus's disciples put themselves in a position to be used by God through obedience. Very different from Aaron and his sons: the disciples were ordered to take nothing save the clothes on their backs. No accoutrements; just obedience! As Marks tells us, "they drove out demons and anointed many sick people with oil and healed them" (Mark 6:13).

QUESTIONS

In what other ways do biblical characters prepare to be the vehicles for God's grace?

How do we prepare for blessing others?

PRAYER

Oh God of grace, prepare me to receive your grace so that I can be fit to share it with others; through Jesus Christ our Lord. Amen

The Rt. Rev. James Tengatenga
Bishop of Southern Malawi
Blantyre, Malawi

Day 40

Leviticus 10–12, Psalm 34, Mark 7

Yesterday it was "no haggis" and "no uwende" (a special dish of blood, belly fat, and organs that those who slaughter animals, in some of our cultures, boil and eat while they skin and quarter the carcass), but today the list has grown long. What's with food anyway? All over the world there are all sorts of prohibitions of one food or another. Delicacies in one part of the world make some on the other side of the globe feel queasy. Whole foods, organic foods, vegetarian, vegan—the list goes on. We seem to be obsessed with food and the kinds of food we eat.

Well-being and wholeness and (dare I think it) holiness are closely connected. God cares about what we stuff ourselves with, but then Jesus comes along and seems to say that that is not the case. As he does so often, Jesus, in Mark 7, raises the stakes. It's not just the food or what we stuff ourselves with that matters. It's what comes out of us that matters: it's what we harbor in our minds and hearts, what we say. Words people use say a lot about them. Language is a big deal in our age, to the degree that sometimes we go overboard and prize political correctness above all else. We can either build people up or destroy them by our words. God created through the spoken word; Jesus is the Word Incarnate. I suppose it is time to mind my p's and q's!

QUESTIONS

Search through the Bible for the use of the words "word," "words," and "speech" and find out what they mean and how they are used. It may also be helpful to look for "curse," "blessing," and even the concept of naming.

Apart from hate speech, in what way do words dehumanize people?

PRAYER

Only say a word, O Lord, and I shall be healed! Amen.

O Incarnate Word, grant by your gracious Spirit that I may speak a blessing to all I meet today and always, so that I may please you and in the life to come enter into your kingdom where you, with the Father and the Holy Spirit, live and reign forever. Amen.

Day 41

The Rt. Rev. James Tengatenga
Bishop of Southern Malawi
Blantyre, Malawi

Leviticus 13–15, Psalm 35, Mark 8

After reading these chapters in Leviticus, I am left wondering what they are saying to me. Are they a kind of checkup guide for states of holiness or, rather, ritual cleanliness? Or more like a check of one's state to find out whether one is clean or unclean ritually? By the end of Chapter 15, I am curious as to whether some healing will be administered. To my surprise, nothing of the sort is done. One is only pronounced either clean or unclean and given some instructions about what to do about one's status. One lot is even required to go about calling out "Unclean, unclean." What a humiliation! To what end I wonder? Ritual purity was important, and the possibility of "contaminating" others all too real, a situation which would affect the wholeness/health/purity of the community and in turn affect their relationship with their God. Those who have to shout "unclean, unclean" are of particular interest to me in my Malawi context of HIV and AIDS and the consequent imperative to know one's status for one's own good and that of one's neighbour.

It may sound immoral to require people to test themselves for HIV and broadcast their status; however, I am convinced that each of us has a moral duty not to infect another (willfully or inadvertently). We have an obligation toward ourselves, our neighbour, and God to know our serostatus, and our conscience should move us to declare the same. These biblical passages are talking about people who suspect that they may have a skin disease. Testing for HIV does not necessarily mean that one suspects that one is positive, but I believe that knowing is better than not knowing, because not knowing does not mean that one is clean. I would take it as a religious duty to be tested and be declared one way or the other. Once I know, I also know what I ought to do.

QUESTIONS

What can give us a status of uncleanness before God and our neighbour?

What benefits would it be to us if we were to "come clean" with our neighbour on whatever matter there is between us?

PRAYER

O most holy God of life and wholeness, grant me the desire to know how I stand with you and my neighbour so that I may hear your word to me and so seek salvation in this life and the next; through Jesus Christ our Lord, by whose stripes we are healed. Amen.

Day 42: Enjoy hearing the Scriptures read aloud in church.

Dr. Jenny Plane-Te Paa
Dean of Tikanga Maori
The College of St. John the Evangelist
Auckland, New Zealand

Day 43

Leviticus 16–18, Psalm 36, Mark 9

Often seen as the definitive "law book" of the Bible, Leviticus narrates how God separated and sanctified Israel to himself as a holy people, expecting them in turn to reflect the nature of God's holiness by separating from all that was unholy. The holiness called for in Leviticus was not merely for individual or private piety but was a holistic and inescapable expectation covering all spheres of human activity.

The people of Israel were, however, prone to human failings just as we are today. It was for this reason that the Day of Atonement (Leviticus 16) was implemented as a priestly responsibility intended to address the "impurities" that potentially endanger community.

While the impurities listed in the book of Leviticus provide us fascinating examples of what was once considered utterly profane, the march of scientific and moral progress since that time now leads us *in some instances* to very different understandings. As God's twenty-first-century Christian people, we are nevertheless still challenged to discern and to act against the "impurities" of our times—those things which create and sustain grave social disorder—and thus put distance between ourselves and God.

Mark's Gospel provides some dynamic examples of how it is that we are to be as Christ's witnesses in the world. Mark highlights the age-old universal impurities of superficial spirituality, of hungering for power, of insider arrogance, of the misuse of power.

As with the disciples we, too, need constant reminding of the behavioural and attitudinal standards expected in return for our unconditional acceptance as members of the beloved community. Our task then is to act constantly and faithfully against those things that are life-denying, life-diminishing, or dishonouring of the God-created humanity of any in the global village.

QUESTIONS

What are some of the impurities listed in Leviticus 16–18 that you feel can no longer be realistically upheld?

How do you, in your day-to-day faith journey, live out your belief that the first must be last and servant of all?

PRAYER

How precious is your steadfast loving, O God? All people may take refuge in the shadow of your wings....For with you is the fountain of life: in your light we see light. Amen.

Day 44

Dr. Jenny Plane-Te Paa
Dean of Tikanga Maori
The College of St. John the Evangelist
Auckland, New Zealand

Leviticus 19–21, Psalm 37:1-18, Mark 10

In today's Leviticus readings are echoes of the Ten Commandments, those good and enduring rules for living an exemplary and obedient Christian life. I take Walter Brueggemann's point (in *Theology of the Old Testament*) that God's people Israel were here being enjoined to order their lives in such a way that they would be qualified for communion with God, even as simultaneously they were also to practice justice for the sake of the entire community.

The call was not simply to passive obedience but to impassioned advocacy for the poor, the vulnerable, for those oppressed. It is surely the same for us in our time, to ensure that it is by our good works and not simply our pious proclamations that our faith can be seen as authentic.

The demands of doing God's justice can often be very costly because they place us directly up against both people and systems, which are inherently wicked. The psalmist, however, assures us that ultimately good will triumph over evil. We are encouraged to be patient, to refrain from anger, to simply "Trust in the Lord, and do good!" (Psalm 37:3).

As a teacher I am often frustrated by my seeming inability to always make theology ever more accessible and profoundly understandable to students. In particular I often encounter either indifference or opposition to my theological claim that all Christians are called to be instinctive activists for God's justice.

Today's gospel reassures me that my struggle to be a more effective teacher of theology has its roots in the days of Jesus' earthly ministry. Mark illustrates how even the disciples, those closest to Jesus himself, were frustratingly slow to understand the teaching of the One who came in order that we might have life and have it in abundance.

Daily Bible studies such as these provide us the chance of more readily understanding Jesus' teachings. For in these precious daily moments of biblical reflection we are provided timely scriptural reminders, the opportunity to pray, and time to develop the very necessary faith-based discipline to be truly as servant disciples, especially with and for those who are the least among us.

Day 44, continued

QUESTIONS

How many of the Ten Commandments can you recite by heart? How relevant/ influential are these commandments to be in your life and in your context in the twenty-first century?

What are some examples from your context where the church has been especially influential in advocating for social justice for those most vulnerable in your community?

PRAYER

Loving God, you call us your servants to model your holiness in all we say and do. Help us in our daily worship of you to become ever more humble, ever more willing to give freely of ourselves to meeting the needs of those who suffer so disproportionately in our communities. Amen.

Day 45

Dr. Jenny Plane-Te Paa
Dean of Tikanga Maori
The College of St. John the Evangelist
Auckland, New Zealand

Leviticus 22–24, Psalm 37:19-42, Mark 11

Throughout the world, more especially in the United States, there are many examples of so-called mega-church leaders who have amassed obscene levels of personal wealth. This wealth has usually been made solely at the expense of their followers. I have never been able to understand how such leaders can reconcile their unadulterated greed with Jesus' insistence that such "trade" in the name of the church, whether in human or in strictly economic terms, nonetheless makes the church itself into "a den of robbers."

Today's gospel confronts the reality that too many in authority in the church completely misunderstand the moral and ethical stewardship responsibilities inherent in their leadership. It also points toward what many still do when confronted with the challenge to be demonstrably and authentically Christ-like—they will move first to remove the threat to their own hypocrisy.

In chapter 22 of Leviticus, we are treated to a very stern reality check for those in church leadership about what might be considered a more proper use of holy offerings. While the text invokes a standard of no less than perfection for the offerings made to God, we are left in no doubt whatever about what is expected. The overarching principles of excellence in our worship, proper observance of the holy days, and our continued selfless offering of ourselves as servants for God's mission remain completely relevant in our time.

As frustrating as poor church leadership can be, the psalmist provides a cautionary reminder. Patient waiting for the Lord to act is our proper attitude, not querulous anxiety!

QUESTIONS

How does your church actively demonstrate its gospel commitment to alleviating local and global poverty and suffering?

What reasonable faith-based standards of professional accountability does your church have in place for those in church leadership?

PRAYER

Loving God, you alone anoint men and women to positions of leadership responsibility. Help those whom you choose to always be people of deep faith and unquestioned moral and ethical integrity. Protect your church from the unscrupulous and the greedy so that the needs of those who suffer are never to be compromised. Help us always to remember your house is only ever to be a house of prayer for all the nations. Amen.

The Rev. Hillary T. West
Associate Rector
St. Thomas Church, Whitemarsh
Fort Washington, Pennsylvania

Day 46

Leviticus 25–27, Psalm 38, Mark 12

As the Holiness Code of Leviticus 25–26 comes to a close, we're reminded that all that we are and all that we have is God's. We honor God's covenant promise with sabbath rest for God and the observance of a Jubilee year that frees and liberates, establishing God's justice, creating something much greater than a second chance. God remembers, and so must we. Chapter 27 closes out Leviticus with vows, voluntary promises made to God. These chapters list option after option of God's desire for us to repent (change), to obey, to respond to God's holiness.

Psalm 38 laments that sickness, suffering, and even death are signs of our true humanness, and awaiting God is our only comfort and relief. Again, God remembers, and God saves. When will we remember God?

In Mark's Gospel, after the heroic entrance into Jerusalem, Jesus teaches to church authorities in the age-old rabbinic parabolic pattern, but they fail to understand. Again, we're reminded from Jesus' words, "Pay to Caesar what belongs to Caesar and what belongs to God belongs to God" (Mark 12:17), that all that we are and all that we have comes from God. We fail to recognize the power of God through Jesus Christ. An ever-present, patient Jesus/God reminds us to trust by following the great commandment. Finally, we're reminded again of the reward given in our humble obedience to God through the vivid story of the widow's mite.

QUESTIONS

What prevents us from receiving the freedom of God's love?

God remembers us. Why are we not able to remember God?

What price are we willing to pay in response to God's grace and mercy?

PRAYER

God of promise and passion, remember us as we disregard and distance ourselves; rescue us from our own selfishness and self-assuredness; remind us over and over again of the miracle blessing of your saving grace. Amen.

Day 47

The Rev. Hillary T. West
Associate Rector
St. Thomas Church, Whitemarsh
Fort Washington, Pennsylvania

Psalm 39, Mark 13*

Mark 13 is the continuation of Jesus' journey to the cross in the final week of his life and includes his eschatological discourse. Eschatological means end times. The chapter is marked by language about the end of things: the destruction of the temple (where God is housed in Judaic tradition), wars, famines, and earthquakes. Falsities will prevail and trust will be violated. Hatred will ensue and families will disband. Disgusting and destructive things will stand where they should not. Suffering will endure and darkness will spread throughout. All this will happen and then the Son of Man will appear with great power and splendor and gather his people from the four corners of the earth. This passage is also referred to as the "little apocalypse," as compared to the "big apocalypse" in the book of Revelation.

In Googling "end times," I found 177,000,000 links to the causes of our evil and destruction and, most important, the date of our demise, even though Jesus clearly states, "But nobody knows when that day or hour will come." For most of us, I imagine that Tim LeHaye's fast-paced, action-packed *Left Behind* series is the most popular fictionalization of the end times. Most likely, this is not what Jesus is preaching about in Mark 13.

Historically, we remember the Gospel of Mark is written just after 70 C.E. and the siege of Jerusalem and capture of the temple by Roman armies under the leadership of Titus and Tiberius Julius Alexander. Terror and horror are fresh in the author's mind. Jesus, in typical Markan form, is painting a picture of God's splendorous saving grace in the midst of our struggles and troubles. He cautions us to stay alert, to watch out. God saves, no matter what, over and over again.

* There is no Old Testament reading assigned for this day. Please reread a favorite passage from the first three books of the Old Testament.

QUESTIONS

In times of despair, how have you reached for hope?

What must you release in suffering to know Jesus' saving grace?

Jesus says, watch out, stay alert, get ready. How do you want to equip yourself for Jesus' love and mercy?

PRAYER

Let us pray: My God, here I am, my heart devoted to you. Fashion me according to your heart. Amen.

—Brother Lawrence (1611–1691)

The Rev. Hillary T. West
Associate Rector
St. Thomas Church, Whitemarsh
Fort Washington, Pennsylvania

Day 48

Numbers 1–3, Psalm 40, Mark 14

If we're going to say anything about the beginning chapters of Numbers, we would say they are about divine holiness: the holiness of God and our response to God's holiness as God's holy people. In Numbers, God first identifies God's holy people, setting them apart with a census, numbering more than 600,350. Next, God equips each and every person in her or his mission as one of God's holy people.

Psalm 40 reminds each of us of our devotion to and trust in God. We're always grateful for the blessing of God's saving grace. But then another thing comes along, a new obstacle, a calculated threat, and there we are once again, on our knees, begging God. What an amazing God we have, who patiently, lovingly listens to our words and our pleas and in our need gives us full life with all its ups and downs, loving us in the midst of it.

Mark 14 is an emotionally heartwrenching chapter that leads us to the climax of God's purpose for us: holy life in the life, death, and resurrection of Jesus Christ. The ambiguity of our ability to honor our holiness is truthfully told in the vivid tale of the devotion of the wasteful, anointing woman, the deception of greedy Judas, the denial of pitiful Peter, the naked desertion of faithful followers, and the frightened falseness of the religious authorities, as Jesus is led away in the midst of verbal and physical abuse. Always, we are challenged in Mark's Gospel with the glory of God's salvation shining through the pain of struggle and suffering. We finish the chapter recognizing all too clearly the thinness of our faith. And yet, it is Christ who believes so fully in us. The words "Take, eat,…drink this" are Jesus' words for us, not just to remember but to know fully: the very holiness of God, given to us at creation and promised to us in the Exodus, is holiness in us, with us, and through us in the institution of the Lord's holy meal.

QUESTIONS

Consider how God has set you apart and named you as God's holy one. What does God expect of you?

Who are you in Jesus's story in Mark 14? What do you want to say to Jesus? What do you hear Jesus saying to you?

PRAYER

Glorious Lord of all, we pray and give thanks that you call us to be your holy people. Fill us with all truth and peace. Where we are right, strengthen us; where we are in want, provide for us; where we are divided, reunite us; inspire us and guide us that in all things and in all places, we will glorify your holy name. Amen.

Day 49: Enjoy hearing the Scriptures read aloud in church.

Day 50

The Rev. Dr. Lydia Mwaniki
New Testament Scholar
St. Paul's University
Limuru, Kenya

Numbers 4–5, Psalm 41, Mark 15

Mark 15 presents the most difficult experience of Jesus in his earthly life. This experience was a consequence of betrayal, which Jesus had predicted in Mark 14:18; "I tell you the truth, one of you will betray me." The prediction came to pass in Mark 14:43 when Judas, one of the Twelve and his betrayer, came for Jesus with an armed gang as though to arrest a criminal. They then handed him to the authorities to be tried. In Mark 15, the Good Friday experiences of Jesus include trial, beating, mocking, crucifixion, and finally death.

We may never know quite the same agony of betrayal. But many have known similar Good Friday experiences: the author of Psalm 41, for example, bemoans the agony of betrayal by friends who rejoice in his sickness and wish him dead.

What are your own Good Friday experiences? Have you suffered betrayal and rejection by a close friend? Jesus understands what you are going through. He is journeying with you in your pain and sorrow so that you are never alone. Like the psalmist who shows his total dependence on God, our help is in the Lord. Just put your total trust in him. He will deliver you because he has trodden the same path.

QUESTIONS

Recount your own past Good Friday experiences of agony and distress. How were you able to get through them?

From your experiences, what good do you think can come out of a Good Friday experience?

PRAYER

Lord Jesus, I rejoice in my Good Friday experiences because I know you are with me. May those who rejoice in my troubles confess your goodness and faithfulness to me and turn to you for forgiveness. Amen.

The Rev. Dr. Lydia Mwaniki
New Testament Scholar
St. Paul's University
Limuru, Kenya

Day 51

Numbers 6–8, Psalm 42, Mark 16

A story is told about tiny frogs who organized a competition. The goal was to climb up a very high tower. At the foot of the tower there was a huge multitude who had come to watch the race and to cheer on the competitors. Very many tiny frogs started the race. But meanwhile, they could hear some voices from the multitude saying, "No one can make it! The tower is very tall. No one has ever climbed up there. You will not make it!"

The tiny frogs began to give up one by one as the voices from the multitude became louder and louder. After a while, all had given up except *one* tiny frog who made it to the top. This was a big surprise to the multitude, who decided to investigate in order to find out how the tiny frog managed to get to the top. Guess what? The tiny frog was *deaf!*

Today's gospel reading (Mark 16) brings us Good News of Resurrection. There is life beyond the Good Friday experience of death. Jesus persevered to the end in order to accomplish his mission and goal of reconciling humanity with God and with one another. The road to success is difficult. But like Jesus, we must be determined to accomplish our goals. It doesn't matter how dark our Good Friday experiences are. We need to focus beyond them to the day of victory—the day of resurrection. We must live beyond the grave. Like the deaf frog, we need to be deaf to the voices of discouragement from within us and around us that come between us and our success. Move on with Jesus!

QUESTIONS

In your own experience, who represents the multitude that pulls you back down the tower?

What lessons do you learn from Jesus' Resurrection and the tiny deaf frog about how to deal with the multitude?

PRAYER

Why are you downcast, O my soul? Why so disturbed within me? Put your hope in God. For I will yet praise him, my savior and my God. Amen.

—Psalm 42:5, 11

Day 52

The Rev. Dr. Lydia Mwaniki
New Testament Scholar
St. Paul's University
Limuru, Kenya

Numbers 9–11, Psalm 43, Luke 1

A Chinese pastor once gave his testimony of having spent eighteen years in prison for the sake of his faith. His task was to empty the human waste cesspool:

> Because the pit was so deep, I could not reach the bottom to empty; I had to walk into the disease-ridden mass and scoop out successive layers of human waste, all the time breathing the strong stench....So, why did I enjoy working in the cesspool? I enjoyed the solitude....I could be alone and could pray to our Lord as loudly as I needed. I could recite the Scriptures, including the Psalms I still remembered, and no one was close enough to protest. Also, I could sing loudly the hymns I still remembered... again and again...I experienced the Lord's presence. He never left me nor forsook me. And so I survived and the cesspool became my private garden. (Sam Storms, "Praise God in the Midst of Your Darkness")

Both the psalm reading and Luke 1 bring examples of two different people who find it possible to praise God and serve him in their cesspool experiences. Psalm 43 is the prayer of someone in exile. Like the Chinese pastor, the psalmist is in the hands of the ungodly, who treat him in a cruel way. He longs to go back to Zion, his homeland. However, in this cesspool, he says, "I will put my hope in God, and once again I will praise him" (v. 5).

In Luke 1, we learn Zechariah and Elizabeth did not have children. This would be enough reason to doubt God's love and faithfulness and be lax in his service. But, on the contrary, when the angel Gabriel comes to break the good news that they will bear a son, he finds Zechariah deeply involved in God's service in the temple (1:8). Then the angel says to him, "God has heard your prayer, and your wife Elizabeth will bear you a son." (1:13).

Our praise and service to God is not conditioned by our circumstances, whether good or bad. We praise and serve God for who God is. Try praising God in your cesspool!

QUESTIONS

What is your cesspool experience like?

What will you do *now* to ensure that you continue praising and serving God despite your strong feeling that God has abandoned you?

PRAYER

God, we give you thanks for your loving presence, even in the cesspools of our lives. Help us to keep praising you even when life is hard. Amen.

The Rt. Rev. Henry N. Parsley Jr.
Retired Bishop of Alabama
Birmingham, Alabama
Day 53

Numbers 12–14, Psalm 44, Luke 2

As we "read, mark, learn, and inwardly digest" the Holy Scriptures, it is helpful to ask, what does this text tell us about God and about ourselves? At its deepest levels, the Bible reveals both the nature of God and the reality of us.

Numbers 12–14 continues Israel's wilderness journey. It is a story of profound doubt and fear. The peoples' resources are challenged. There is distrust of Moses. Unrest is rampant. The people complain that God is not with them. It would be better to "go back to Egypt," where life—even in slavery—seemed safe.

So it is with us. In the deserts of the heart, we wonder if God is really there. Fear is endemic to our nature, tempting us back to wherever "Egypt" is for any one of us.

Moses reminds his people again and again that God is with them on the journey. God "abounds in steadfast love" (14.18). Such *hesed* is tough love sometimes, holding us accountable. But it is always faithful. If we but trust, God's steadfast love will always see us through.

Luke 2 tells us of the birth of the One who is Emmanuel, *God with us*. Here is the account of angels appearing to shepherds in a blaze of glory. "Do not be afraid…I am bringing you good news of great joy," an angel says (Luke 2:10). The joy is that Jesus, God in the flesh, is the incarnation of the divine steadfast love.

Shockingly, the Messiah is laid in a manger. Jesus' birth in a poor stable is a sign that no place is too lowly for him to be, no person too unworthy of his embrace, no fear unable to be cast out by his love.

In the deserts of the heart, God's steadfast love and grace are ever present. It is our nature to doubt, but God's nature to be faithful. Because of this, hope is real, and where there is hope there is life.

QUESTIONS

Reflect on your fears. Is there a persistent thing that makes you afraid, and tempts you to go back to "Egypt"? Reflect on it.

Be still and imagine that Jesus is beside you. He asks, "What can I do for you today?" How would you answer?

PRAYER

God, in Jesus you have come among us and showered us with your steadfast love. In the desert journeys of our lives, keep us moving forward in faith. Come to us at the point of our greatest need and help us; through Jesus Christ our Lord. Amen.

Day 54

The Rt. Rev. Henry N. Parsley Jr.
Retired Bishop of Alabama
Birmingham, Alabama

Numbers 15–17, Psalm 45, Luke 3

Luke, like all good physicians, paid attention to detail. In his gospel, our Lord's life is richly grounded in historical fact. Chapter 3 begins by Luke's telling us exactly when the ministry of John the Baptist began—in the fifteenth year of the reign of Emperor Tiberias, when Herod was ruler of Galilee. The gospel opens on the great stage of the ancient world.

Luke stresses Jesus' absolute immersion in the whole human story. He is being clear that Jesus' mission of bringing the good news of grace is not just for Israel but for all. He is "a light to enlighten the Gentiles," as old Simeon put it in his beautiful song. His humanity is our humanity.

Similarly, in verses 25-38 Luke gives us the genealogy of Jesus traced through David, Jacob, Noah, and ultimately "Adam, the son of God." For Luke Jesus is the "new Adam," the Son of God who gives us back our true nature and shows us how to be fully human.

At Jesus' baptism the Spirit descends on him and he hears the words, "You are my Son, the Beloved; with you I am well-pleased" (Luke 3:22). There are few more eloquent, life-transforming words in the Bible. Our baptisms participate in Jesus' baptism. As we participate in Christ, we can hear God say to us, too, "You are my son, my daughter, the Beloved."

This is not easy to hear. Like the people of Israel in the wilderness, we doubt. We experience moments where we know that we have missed the mark. We lose our way. But when God looks upon us, he sees Christ in us. He sees not our imperfection, but our Lord's perfection, imputed to us. "You are the Beloved," he says. That is the deepest truth about you.

The gospel invites us to see ourselves as God sees us in Christ—as the Beloved. This frees us to live as Christ lived from his baptism: to live beyond fear, in abundance and overflowing joy.

QUESTION

Is there a particular person, or persons, in whose presence you feel beloved? Recollect what that feels like, and imagine how God holds you even more in love.

PRAYER

Gracious God, we thank you for this magical and fragile world in all its detail and richness. Open our eyes to see your grace in all things. Open our ears to hear you call us in Christ the Beloved. Open our hands that we may offer the same love to others, to the glory of your Name. Amen.

The Rt. Rev. Henry N. Parsley Jr.
Retired Bishop of Alabama
Birmingham, Alabama

Day 55

Numbers 18–20, Psalm 46, Luke 4

In today's readings, two wildernesses meet: the Sinai, where the Israelites continue their difficult journey, and the Judean desert, where Jesus endures temptation. Both stories remind us that the vocation of God's servants is always tested and purified. The ordeal is part of the journey.

Oscar Wilde wrote, "I can resist anything but temptation." This reality of our nature has been evident since the primordial fall in Eden. It is tough to resist the seductive delights that would lead us astray. It is the Spirit, no less, who leads Jesus into temptation. He must experience all that we experience if he is to be our Savior. His temptations are ours as well: to be heroic, to be all-powerful, to be sensational.

Jesus counters each temptation with words of Scripture, affirming that only God is God, not us. His profound humility and obedience overcome the will to power. So Augustine could write that in Christ, "The pride of man is healed by the humility of God."

From this soul-searching ordeal, Jesus emerges ready for his ministry. In Nazareth he radically identifies himself as the servant in Isaiah, whose work is to bring good news to the poor and healing to the hurt and outcast. He proclaims God's Jubilee of forgiveness and restoration for all. His messianic vocation is about love, not power. This inclusive love is scandalous to his countrymen, and, not for the last time, they try to get rid of him.

The readings in Numbers include the pivotal moment when Moses strikes the rock at Meribah, and water flows forth for the parched pilgrims. In the midst of the desert, new life is born. So it is with Jesus' wilderness experience. Through suffering he is formed for a servant life through which the living water of grace flows for all people.

QUESTIONS

Do you remember a time of ordeal that tested your faith? Recall both its difficulty and any gifts you received through it.

It has been said that the opposite of love is not hate, but power. Do you agree?

PRAYER

Gracious God, as your Son endured the temptations and ordeal of the desert, grant that amid the temptations of the world we may hold fast to you and find your love sufficient to complete and purify us for your service; through Jesus Christ our Lord. Amen.

Day 56: Enjoy hearing the Scriptures read aloud in church.

Day 57

The Rev. Frank Allen
Rector, St. David's Church
Radnor, Pennsylvania

Numbers 21–23, Psalm 47, Luke 5

Today's readings speak to the paradox of our life with God: the mixed experiences we all face. God is moving in our lives and in the lives of those around us, and in the sweet moments, God even intervenes from time to time to change our minds or our circumstances. Yet in the midst of our experience of God alive and at work in us and around us, our lives are not always easy. We struggle; we fall. We face great difficulties and challenges that lead us to a greater dependence on God, or to a faith that wanes.

In the reading from Numbers, the Hebrews are on the verge of entering the Promised Land; but as it had during other times on their travels, grumbling erupts over God's inability to give them what they think they want when they want it. God is with them, but there are still struggles to face and hurdles to overcome. Those are the snakes that attack them as they follow after God—real snakes, no doubt, but spiritual snakes as well.

And what a funny way God uses to offer salvation from the attacks! Moses is commanded to make an image of a snake and hold it before those who have been bitten, and they are healed—healed in the midst of hardship. God brings us delivery from enemies but doesn't remove them completely, leaving room for a life of faith and dependence.

And to this life, we, like Jesus' first followers, are called in Luke. The call of God in Jesus Christ is compelling and brings miraculous catches of fish, people healed of leprosy, and paralytics restored. It also brings conflict with the powers and authorities of Jesus' day, and ours. Miraculous events are coupled with the challenges of living in the everyday world.

Like Jacob wrestling with the angel, we, too, are called to wrestle with the challenges and blessings that are ours in God.

QUESTIONS

Where in your life do you see God at work in the midst of life's struggles?

What would you tell someone about this life with God and the blessings and trials that come for all of us?

PRAYER

Blessed Lord, you promise life to all who answer your call; give us confidence and faith to trust in you, though the road ahead of us appears dark and difficult, and bring us home in safety at the last; through Jesus Christ our Lord. Amen.

The Rev. Frank Allen
Rector, St. David's Church
Radnor, Pennsylvania

Day 58

Numbers 24–26, Psalm 48, Luke 6

Each day brings the opportunity for us to grow more adept, more confident, in our following after Jesus into a life that's really *life*. We may struggle and even fail today. Our growth and confidence may grow in increments so small that we think we are standing in place or even receding, but by God's grace, this is not so. Take heart, for by God's choosing and God's mercy, we are becoming the persons God has called us to be.

Today's task is to pay attention to God's purposes—not just our own—for our lives. God has called us to live a certain way and to build a certain kind of community, a community that exists in such a way that we remain close to God and draw others by the way we live.

The Hebrews discover this dual purpose as they come into closer contact with their neighbors, the Moabites. Living in the midst of people who don't know the one true God, they forget the kind of life God has called them to; they begin to intermarry and even worship other gods. The result is a swift and harsh judgment that leaves many Christians uncomfortable and wondering if this is the same God whom Jesus calls "Father." Rest assured that it is, and that God's discipline, harsh though it is, is meant for the Hebrews' good, so that they may return to the lives that God has meant for them.

Jesus' followers face a different challenge regarding the worship of other gods, gods more subtle than the gods of the Moabites. Too easily we mistake religion and religious practices for God's purposes at work in our lives. The sabbath is nothing to be worshiped, nor are other religious laws or practices. They are the means to the ultimate end—God.

So today, let's remember to live as God has called us to live in spite of the temptations of other ways of being.

QUESTIONS

Do you share your faith by the way you live your life? What does that look like?

Where are the practices of Christianity getting in your way of living as a Christian?

PRAYER

Merciful Lord, give us strength for today to acknowledge you in all our ways. And though we may forget you, please do not forget us; for the love of your Son, our Savior Jesus Christ. Amen.

Day 59

The Rev. Frank Allen
Rector, St. David's Church
Radnor, Pennsylvania

Numbers 27–29, Psalm 49, Luke 7

God's ways are not our ways, the prophet Isaiah will tell us later this year. God's ways are different from our ways of power and prestige and physical vitality. And it's not that God has a particular prejudice against power or prestige or physical strength—it's just that God approaches them from the back side, as though they are of secondary importance.

The pleas of Zelophehad's daughters concerning what property in the Promised Land would be allotted to their family (since their father has no male heirs) appears to be a fairly cut-and-dried issue. It is unusual for women to own property in the time of Moses, so the laws of the day dictate an easy decision: none. On the other hand, the God of justice might grant the land in the name of fairness. Moses brings the matter before God and awaits God's decision. He is a man of God because he relies on God first and foremost. The Lord speaks to Moses, and the matter is decided with a wisdom that is far beyond most of us.

Psalm 49 is the most proverbial of all the psalms, reminding us of the importance of wisdom and the fleeting reality of life. Neither power, nor prestige, nor long life compares to the true riches found in the wisdom and the life lived with God.

In Luke, it is the faith, not the worthiness of the centurion, that brings healing to the centurion's servant. It is faith, not the importance or unimportance of the widow of Nain, that empowers Jesus to bring her son back to life. It is faith that brings forgiveness to the sinful woman who anoints Jesus' feet with oil and tears. It is faith that saves us.

God's ways may not be our ways, but when we seek the Lord and offer what little faith we have, God will give us the answer and change the circumstances of the world around us. It is the opening of the door of our lives that gives God permission to enter in.

QUESTIONS

When was the last time you asked God to help you with a question or difficulty you were facing?

Where could you open the way for God to heal you?

PRAYER

Lord God, we trust that you are a God who provides us all we need; help us to set aside our reliance on earthly power and prestige and prosperity and put our trust in you first; in the name of Jesus Christ our Lord. Amen.

The Very Rev. June Osborne
Dean of Salisbury Cathedral
Salisbury, England

Day 60

Numbers 30–32, Psalm 50, Luke 8

This chapter of Luke ends with three vivid stories of Jesus bringing liberty and assurance to anguished people. We are drawn into the troubles they face and are amazed by the way Jesus meets them in the midst of their very specific needs.

First, the disciples face the danger of a storm at sea. We all know what it's like to panic in the face of fear and for anxiety to overwhelm us. Jesus' question—"Where is your faith?" (v. 25)—may seem like a harsh response, but isn't it exactly what we need to ask ourselves when we are trapped by fear?

The Gerasene demoniac was also imprisoned, but by a form of mental torment. Jesus' rescue of him, involving as it does a herd of pigs rushing into the lake, couldn't be more dramatic, but the story focuses not on the lost herd but on the wonder of how much God has done for the tormented man.

And then we have the parallel needs of Jairus's twelve-year-old daughter and the woman who had bled for that same length of time. They were victims of chronic and acute illness, and Jesus takes time with them and heals them.

In our psalm, God says to those who follow him, "Call on me in the day of trouble, I will deliver you and you shall glorify me." Some of the troubles of our world seem beyond our control, and the account in Numbers of the aggression against the Midianites reminds us of the misery and cruelty of war. Anyone can become a victim of fear, torment, or illness. Yet Jesus' encounters with suffering individuals remind us of how he wishes liberty for each of us. In our troubles, we should not forget God or what God wants to do for us.

QUESTIONS

Which of the people that Jesus meets in Luke 8 do you best relate to, and why?

What binds and limits your life, and how might you find greater liberty?

PRAYER

O God our Father, you are the comfort of the sad and the strength of those who suffer. Hear the prayers of all your children who cry out to you in their troubles, and to every soul that is distressed today grant mercy, refreshment, and liberty; through Jesus Christ our Lord. Amen.

Day 61

The Very Rev. June Osborne
Dean of Salisbury Cathedral
Salisbury, England

Numbers 33–35, Psalm 51, Luke 9

It is believed that Psalm 51 was composed by David after the prophet Nathan had rebuked him for his desire of Bathsheba and all that followed from it. We know that after the destruction of Jerusalem in 586 B.C.E., the king entered into penitential rites on behalf of his nation, and this text may have been part of that corporate confession.

We often use this psalm, with its language of contrition, in our Lenten journey of worship. "Wash me thoroughly from my iniquity, and cleanse me from my sin." Few men or women lead their lives without some sense of failure or remorse, and all of us have a great need of being forgiven, not just by others but by our own selves.

It was the good news of forgiveness and a changed life that Jesus' disciples took with them on their missionary endeavours. You can imagine that when they return, they would want to share their exploits and their growth in faith. They are thwarted, first by the crowds who demand Jesus' attention and need feeding. But then Jesus himself begins to explain that his messianic calling is one of suffering, not triumph, and they, too, must "take up their cross." That cross will be different for each of us. Denying ourselves is a long and challenging path, and it isn't easy to absorb how it brings us life.

As we come toward the end of Numbers, we find a recollection of the forty-two stages of Israel's journey from Egypt through the wilderness, anticipating settlement in a new land of promise. Our own journey of learning how to be true followers of a suffering Lord sometimes feels just as arduous, but through it God creates in us a clean heart and puts a new and right spirit within us.

QUESTIONS

What do you think might be the cross that you have been asked to take up in order to follow Christ?

Is there something that you wish to confess or express penitence for today?

PRAYER

Loving God, you hate nothing that you have made and forgive the sins of all who are penitent. Create and make in me a clean heart that I may obtain from you a knowledge of your mercy and a deep sense of your forgiveness; in your holy name I pray. Amen.

The Very Rev. June Osborne
Dean of Salisbury Cathedral
Salisbury, England

Day 62

Numbers 36, Psalm 52, Luke 10

At the end of the tenth chapter of Luke, Jesus engages with two people who seek to justify themselves. The lawyer wants an individual religion that would guarantee his eternal destiny and make him feel that he'd ticked all the boxes for what was required. The disciple Martha similarly wants everything to be tidy and perfectly ordered and is prepared to tire herself to the point of resentment in order to achieve that.

Jesus confronts both of them, but only when they indicate that they're discontented with the framework they've built for themselves and need his help. What he offers each of them is a different starting point.

To the lawyer, he tells a wonderful story which has reinforced for every generation that religion is about right relationships, not based on prejudice or systems that exclude but on common humanity and compassion. The law requires love of God *and* neighbour. Both of the Old Testament readings for today show us how easily those human relationships can become corrupted; for society to be good, it needs the love that we call justice, without which there can never be peace.

To Martha, he gives a tender rebuke and steers her toward a different set of priorities. We know that in other places in the gospels, Jesus enters into theological dialogue with Martha, and in John's Gospel it is Martha, not Peter, who recognises Jesus as the Messiah and gives voice to that conviction.

Perhaps fostering the love of God and our neighbour also requires us to stop justifying ourselves and to consider our own starting points?

QUESTIONS

Consider the issues that you find difficult to deal with and ask yourself, "What are the starting points that are preventing me from making progress?"

Where do you try to justify yourself, and what might Jesus have to say about it?

PRAYER

Lord God, you know that it is often my starting points that lead me astray. Help me to always sense your priorities and to foster your love, so that worldly cares and a desire to justify myself may not distract me from doing your will. Amen.

Day 63: Enjoy hearing the Scriptures read aloud in church.

Day 64

The Rev. Dr. Peter Enns
Old Testament Scholar and Author
Pennsylvania

Deuteronomy 1–3, Psalm 53, Luke 11

Today's reading in Deuteronomy is a new beginning for Israel. We are picking up the story of Israel's trek from slavery in Egypt to its entrance into the land of Canaan, the land God promised to Abraham back in Genesis 12.

But the Israelites took a bit of a detour. What was to have been a fairly quick move wound up being delayed forty years. The Israelites rebelled at the moment they were about to enter Canaan. Spies had reported to them that the land was indeed lush but was also populated by a strong warring people, including the dreaded and ancient Nephilim, a race of giants. They were afraid, and so that generation was made to wander in the desert to allow time for the distrusting element to die off.

That episode lies in the background of Deuteronomy 1–3. Now we see Israel poised to enter the land, forty years later, in a second try to trust God and go forward. But before they do, Moses has a few things to say.

He reminds them of the past—not as a dig, but to make sure the mistakes of forty years earlier aren't repeated. He reminds them of all that happened, and how their lack of trust landed them in a long trek through the desert. Even Moses was denied entrance to the Promised Land.

Remembering past spiritual failings is part of spiritual growth, although brooding about them is spiritually harmful. Sometimes you have to be reminded of the past and repent before you can move forward.

QUESTIONS

As you read the Bible, do you see this sort of focus on failings to be spiritually depressing or something to learn from in your own life?

Have you looked honestly at spiritual areas you need to work on as a means of true spiritual growth?

PRAYER

Patient Heavenly Father, show me where I have not been faithful to you, and in your great love and forgiveness, show me the path forward; through Jesus Christ our Lord. Amen.

The Rev. Dr. Peter Enns
Old Testament Scholar and Author
Pennsylvania

Day 65

Deuteronomy 4–6, Psalm 54, Luke 12

No one likes to be wronged or falsely accused. No one likes to be treated unjustly or be taken advantage of. Many psalms, like Psalm 54, deal with this theme.

Psalm 54 is a psalm of David. According to its "superscription" (that bit just before the psalm begins, that was added at a later point in time), David is reflecting on a specific moment in his life when he was in a tense relationship with Saul, whom he would soon replace as king. David's life is being threatened (v. 3). Rather than take matters into his own hands, he looks to God to vindicate him (v. 1). Then he will give thanks to God for his deliverance (vv. 6-7).

But this psalm was not included in the Psalter to give us a glimpse into David's life. Whatever personal issues might have driven David or other psalm writers, their works were assembled in a collection that was meant to apply to other readers. That is why you never see specific names and incidents in the psalms. They are supposed to be "mirrors of the soul," as John Calvin put it, not accounts of one person's experiences.

Feeling wronged is part of everyday life—no one really relishes such experiences, and no one would go out of their way to make threats and slander part of their lives. Yet this is precisely what Jesus did. He willingly chose a life where he was slandered, misunderstood, and threatened. Jesus did this for us. And, as David prays in this psalm, Jesus was also vindicated by God, for even though he died, he was raised to life.

QUESTIONS

Have you ever been wronged by others? Have you brought this matter to the Lord in prayer or tried to manage the situation on your own? How do you feel when you handle things this way?

Have you ever considered that you may be more like Jesus during times of intense struggle than when times are going well? Have you ever seen your suffering as something that connects you to Jesus?

PRAYER

Lord, my protector and comforter, I lay before you my fear, my anger, and my desire to get even with others. Vindicate me, in your time and place; through Jesus Christ our Lord. Amen.

Day 66

The Rev. Dr. Peter Enns
Old Testament Scholar and Author
Pennsylvania

Deuteronomy 7–9, Psalm 55, Luke 13

Jesus speaks a lot about the kingdom of heaven (or of God). This has nothing to do with "going to heaven," as we today sometimes think of it, or with what many in Jesus' day expected: a new kingdom ushered in by a military king, a Messiah (anointed one), who would defeat the Romans and assume the throne in Jerusalem. It has everything to do with a here-and-now kingdom that has come down *from* heaven. Jesus' kingdom is about inner transformation by God.

A kingdom like that might be hard to see, and the parable we find in Luke 13:18-21 talks about its inconspicuous beginnings. The mustard seed was considered the smallest seed in Jesus day (2 mm, or about .08 inches), but it grew into a large tree several feet high. Similarly, the kingdom of heaven begins with one person, Jesus, who, like a seed, is placed in the ground (in death), but then grows into an immense people of God. People from all nations will come and "perch" in the "branches" of the kingdom. So, the kingdom starts small but grows beyond measure.

A small amount of yeast makes dough rise, as we all know. Just as the mustard seed is small, the yeast is inconspicuous. A pinch is mixed in thoroughly with the flour, and the dough rises. Without yeast, the dough remains flat. So, the gospel begins to grow inconspicuously but has a permeating influence wherever it is found.

What God is doing in our lives and through us often seems tiny and unimportant, but over time the results are much bigger and more astounding than we could ever imagine.

QUESTIONS

Is there an incident you can look back on that didn't seem like much at first, but had a big impact on your spiritual life years later?

Why do you think God works this way, making something grand out of the small and inconspicuous?

PRAYER

Lord, I am part of the kingdom you have built that started small and grew large. Thank you for letting me rest in your branches. Give me eyes to see and ears to hear the inconspicuous ways you are moving in my life now; through Jesus Christ our Lord. Amen.

The Rt. Rev. Shannon Johnston
Bishop of Virginia
Richmond, Virginia

Day 67

Deuteronomy 10–12, Psalm 56, Luke 14

Chapters 10 and 11 of Deuteronomy stand at the very heart of the story of Israel's journey of faith. Here is the telling of the restoration of the covenant between God and the people God has chosen for a special relationship. This is established by the replacement of the original tablets upon which the Ten Commandments were written and the construction of the wooden Ark of the Covenant. God has heard Moses' intercession on behalf of the offending people and will bring Israel into the Promised Land after all. What is required of the people is their complete faithfulness.

Chapter 12 is a key section in Deuteronomy's prescription of law, beginning with the definitive new principle of a single established place for Israel's worship. Finally, there is stern warning against idolatry. Israel must not be enticed into following foreign gods or imitating the practices associated with them. There is but one God who seeks our hearts.

Psalm 56 is a lament. The psalmist describes a desperate situation against many foes who perpetrate all manner of injury and evil. Yet this text is notable for repeated expressions of confidence and trust in God. One is struck by the realism of the psalmist—the dangers are real and many—but courage and faith win the day. Only God can offer true protection and deliverance. Come what may, we may offer thanksgiving.

Luke 14 has two sections. Verses 1-24 contain four stories, quite distinct from each other in their message. What unifies them is a meal. This cannot be overlooked. In Jesus' world, meals were occasions of great meaning, giving the subject of conversation real weight. Healing on the sabbath, humility, and responsiveness to God's invitation (along with God's provision for the outcast) are all addressed to show what fellowship in God's kingdom looks like. Verses 25-35 ask us to consider that discipleship has costs and consequences. The final, urgent plea to "listen!" should make us take note and wonder if we really do.

QUESTIONS

What are the specific ways in which you act upon your devotion to God?

How do you take the time and effort to examine your life of faith?

PRAYER

O Lord my God, give me a heart that longs for you at any cost, in Jesus Christ my Lord. Amen.

Day 68

The Rt. Rev. Shannon Johnston
Bishop of Virginia
Richmond, Virginia

Deuteronomy 13–15, Psalm 57, Luke 15

The overarching message of Deuteronomy 13 is the sovereignty of God: any source that seeks to lead the Israelites into following other gods must be utterly destroyed so that the people are completely purged of the evil that threatens Israel's pure faith and devotion. The severity of these penalties is counterbalanced by the compassion that God will show to the faithful.

Chapter 14 begins with details of the dietary laws that mark a people who are separated to be a holy people, that is, a people who live in the nearest possible relationship to God. Some of this may seem esoteric to us, but we must remember that the world of ancient Israel was absolutely defined by "sacred" vs. "profane," clean and unclean, and to take part in the sacred and clean was a question of nothing less than knowing God or not. The same was true with regard to stewardship of all possessions, and so the first fruits and the tithes were strictly holy and dedicated to God.

Chapter 15 poses the premise that there would be no chronic poverty if God's will is always fulfilled and then provides a scheme for the remission of debts (note the psychological realism of vv. 9-10). It is acknowledged that there will always be poverty among the people, but the point here is our own ungrudging imitation of God's grace toward those indebted. If only we were indeed so divinely disposed!

Psalm 57 is a combination of supplication in time of trouble and statements of steadfast trust. In the face of difficulty and even terror, affirmation of the life of the human spirit that knows God's presence is beautifully expressed: God's loving kindness is greater than all else.

In three of the best known and most loved of all parables, Luke 15 examines the question, "Does God care about those who have lost their way?" Jesus leaves no doubt: not only does God care about the lost but also seeks, finds, and embraces them (us). The redemptive lesson could not be more clear: joy in heaven trumps judgment when the lost are found and restored.

QUESTIONS

In what ways do Deuteronomy's rules about purity and stewardship still matter?

Why are these parables about "the lost" in Luke so enduring and popular?

PRAYER

Be my strength, O God, and find me when I cannot find my way. Amen.

The Rt. Rev. Shannon Johnston
Bishop of Virginia
Richmond, Virginia

Day 69

Deuteronomy 16–18, Psalm 58, Luke 16

Deuteronomy 16 sets forth the observance of three festival times: Passover, Weeks, and Booths (Tents, Tabernacles). Passover, held during March or April, must be celebrated at the central sanctuary; therefore, it is a pilgrimage time. The Feast of (seven) Weeks was a wheat harvest festival culminating in our month of June. Booths, an ingathering festival held in the autumn, was what we may term the New Year; it was the most popular of the feast times. We see that it was most important for the common life of Israel to be regulated by the regular and rhythmic—indeed, sanctified—cycles of the annual calendar.

There follows (16:18–17:20) a section of laws dealing with the administration of justice, with warnings against corruption so that justice and only justice is pursued. Chapter 18 begins with the rights of the Levitical priests; these priests may not hold or inherit wealth and so are entitled to support. The chapter closes with warnings against the practices of pagan religions and their rites as well as discussion of proper and authoritative prophecy.

How does one address the problem of unjust, unrighteous rulers? The author of Psalm 58 composed what is technically a "lament" and yet it reads as a condemnation and contains ancient elements of a curse (vv. 6-9). The unjust rulers receive their just deserts in the triumph of the sovereignty of God.

Luke 16 has two parables dealing with questions of personal wealth translated into spiritual terms and realities. The dishonest manager proves to be shrewd in securing his future; believers must be prudent in living so as to obtain eternal life. Material things have eternal consequences! The haunting parable of the rich man and the beggar strikes us much more personally, if only because it seems more straightforwardly understandable. Though our personal details may be less dramatic, we might easily worry if we're in this parable and on the wrong side.

QUESTIONS

What kind of authority does the Christian liturgical calendar have in your life?

Are you generous with your wealth? How do you provide for the poor?

PRAYER

O Lord, may your grace shape me into the person you created me to be. Amen.

Day 70: Enjoy hearing the Scriptures read aloud in church.

Day 71

The Rev. Canon Dr. Titus Presler
Principal of Edwardes College
Peshawar, Pakistan

Deuteronomy 19–21, Psalm 59, Luke 17

What does it mean to be a disciple of Jesus in the new era that Jesus called the kingdom of God? Jesus offers a number of perspectives in today's reading from Luke's Gospel. A disciple builds up the faithfulness of weaker and more vulnerable disciples. A disciple meets repentance with forgiveness. A disciple serves without expecting reward. A disciple is prepared to let go of this life in the transition to God's full glory.

The disciples' plea to "Increase our faith!" is one any of us might echo. In Jesus' exaggerated response, we learn that faith is not a quantifiable commodity but a quality of relationship. As we trust, God can do great things through us.

Think about the grateful leper's identity as a "foreigner" healed by Jesus. Mission means crossing boundaries into communities that feel "foreign" to us. Just as the foreigner alone returned to give thanks, so we are often blessed by the people to whom we go in mission. They help us grow in understanding God and ourselves.

The chapters from Deuteronomy offer a fascinating glimpse of the Hebrews' nation-building in the promised land of Canaan. Underlying the command to destroy cities within Canaan was a concern to preserve the new nation's faithfulness to God. Provisions about boundary markers and rights of first-born children in a polygamous society seem reasonable, and cities of refuge seem creatively merciful. The punishment for rebellious children, by contrast, seems harsh today.

Biblical psalms befriend us by coming alongside and articulating our moods with God. Today the psalmist helps us express the lonely anguish we may feel when beset by people who wish us harm. As we cry out in our suffering, we realize that God holds our lives, and we respond with praise.

QUESTIONS

Try thinking about faith as trusting relationship rather than as theological belief. How does this affect your spiritual life?

Have you experienced "cities of refuge"? Have you been a city of refuge for people at odds with each other? Have you ever needed a city of refuge?

PRAYER

Thank you, God, for inviting me to share myself with you. I offer you my trust—and do help me to trust you more. You desire for me more than I can ask or imagine. Help me to trust that this is true, through Christ Jesus the trustworthy savior. Amen.

The Rev. Canon Dr. Titus Presler
Principal of Edwardes College
Peshawar, Pakistan

Day 72

Deuteronomy 22–24, Psalm 60, Luke 18

Deuteronomy is the statute book of ancient Israel, comparable to the books of laws in the office of your lawyer or solicitor. A difference between the ancient statutes and civil law today is that Israel was a theocracy, a nation ruled by God, so the Israelites believed their laws were generated by God. Those laws were enshrined in Scripture.

In Deuteronomy we experience the mixture of divine inspiration and human agency characteristic of all our Scriptures, a mixture we see also in God's incarnation in Jesus. In our very different cultural situations today, some of Israel's laws seem harsh, others patriarchal, some commonsensical, others touchingly compassionate, and some just plain puzzling. Underlying a number of laws in today's reading are such principles as respect for nature's differences, support for family structure, protection of the weak, and mercy for the poor.

In Psalm 60 the community not only mourns a military defeat but also concludes that disaster signifies God's rejection, a belief common among Muslims and Christians alike in Peshawar today. Eternal human questions arise: Does my relationship with God guarantee success? If not, what is the use of God?

Equating worldly success with God's favor was the stance of those who mocked Jesus at the crucifixion that he predicts in today's reading from Luke. The truth is that God, enfleshed in Jesus, lived through the human experience of weakness, rejection, and pain, both physical and psychic. In the stories he tells and the work he does in today's gospel, Jesus acts out that solidarity by lifting up a poor widow, commending a repentant tax collector, blessing little children, directing a rich man to help the poor, and healing a blind beggar. God's centrality in existence is shown not in control, but in loving companionship with us in suffering.

QUESTIONS

A skeptic recently asked me, "In such an infinitely large universe inhabited by such chaos, how can you believe that God is there, and in charge?" How would you respond?

PRAYER

I want to partner with you, God, in your patient and sacrificial mission of love in this hurting world. I ask you to broaden my vision, intensify my vulnerability, and deepen my compassion, so that I can work with you, and you can work with me, in the way of Jesus. Amen.

Day 73

The Rev. Canon Dr. Titus Presler
Principal of Edwardes College
Peshawar, Pakistan

Deuteronomy 25–27, Psalm 61, Luke 19

Jesus' triumphal entry into Jerusalem, followed by his weeping over the city and clearing of the temple, sets the stage for the culmination of his ministry. Christians often wonder, "Did it have to happen this way?"—too often the response is, "Yes, it was all preordained!"

No, it was a drama of choices. As one catechism puts it, being created in God's image "means that we are free to make choices." God chose to come to us in Jesus. Jesus chose to be faithful, and others chose to oppose him. Jesus chose to confront the temple marketplace, and the authorities chose to plot his demise. Jesus' words as he wept over Jerusalem mean basically, "It did *not* have to come to this!"

"Where is God?" people often ask accusingly, in response to the poverty, wars, terrorism, and ecological crises of today's world. "Right here, weeping over the world," might be our answer. It does *not* have to be this way. Following Zacchaeus, we can choose repentance and amendment of life. Following Jesus, we can work sacrificially for the justice and peace of the realm of God.

Psalm 61 stresses the choice of depending on God, certainly "when my heart is faint," but also at all other times. Self-reliance is a virtue only as long as it is grounded in reliance on God, who all of us need to "lead me to the rock that is higher than I."

The long recitation of laws in Deuteronomy concludes today with exhortations to offer first fruits and tithes in gratitude to God, both to support worship and to help the marginalized. The covenant between Israel and God signified that Israel was God's "treasured people" as they prepared to take possession of the land God was giving them.

QUESTIONS

What choices do you have in your life? How are your choices limited? Within your constraints, how might choosing God change the environment for your other choices?

If Israel was a "treasured people," you must be a treasured person, treasured by God. Take that fact into your prayer and see if it makes a difference.

PRAYER

Loving God, you chose me long before I chose you, so I know you treasure me and cherish me. That's often hard to believe. So I want to rest in you and let your cherishing wash over me, that I may know deeply how I am a treasure to you and be transformed. All this I pray through Jesus, your revelation of how you cherish us all. Amen.

The Rt. Rev. Pierre Whalon
Bishop of the Convocation of
Episcopal Churches in Europe
Paris, France
Day 74

Deuteronomy 28–30, Psalm 62, Luke 20

Today is all about tests. Not school exams, of course, but the kinds of experiences that put our values to the test: Do we live according to our proclaimed values? And how can we know how to apply those values to any morally ambiguous situations we face?

The Second Law (which is what "Deuteronomy" means) refines and reiterates the Law of Moses, which is summed up in the Ten Commandments. In these chapters, we are repeatedly told to choose between blessing and curse, life and death. The author, who is supposed to be the Lawgiver himself, tells us in graphic detail what life will be like after we make that choice. In short, it will be delightful or gruesome.

The psalmist has a different slant. He places his trust in God, even as enemies try to knock him down. They speak blessings upon him but really mean curses. Lest we be tempted, he warns us that status in human society, wealth, and power are of no consequence. Like the Deuteronomist, the psalmist tells us that our choices do matter.

Luke 20 is about Jesus being tested. He confounds those who would trip him up by reframing their questions in terms of God's intent. As he was during the temptation in the desert, Jesus is successful because he sees everything through the lens of God's mission—his mission—in creation.

The Scriptures remind us to see our own lives, and the often-difficult choices we must make, from the perspective first of God's intent for us, both individually and as a race.

Take a moment to read the closing verses of each of today's chapters. They weave together with subtle power.

QUESTIONS

What in your life can you name as an authentic blessing?

And what would be a "curse"?

PRAYER

Lead me not into temptation, O Lord, and do not put me to the test. In difficult choices, let your Spirit ever guide me in the path you would have me take. You have promised to be always with us—do not forsake me, Lord our God. Amen.

Day 75

The Rt. Rev. Pierre Whalon
Bishop of the Convocation of
Episcopal Churches in Europe
Paris, France

Deuteronomy 31–33, Psalm 63, Luke 21

There are odd resonances between the Deuteronomy chapters and Luke. Moses is predicting the Exile; Jesus is describing not only the Last Day but also the fall of Jerusalem. Both passages were written after those historical events, and they seek to help people understand the shocking calamities that seem so at odds with what we expect from God, whom the psalmist says he loves more than life itself.

Both texts tell us that we must hold firm to what we believe, for in various ways we will be tempted to forsake the faith we share. If we give in to that temptation, there will be consequences. While God is ever ready to forgive our sins, the consequences of our actions or failures to act will inevitably come home to roost. In God's providence, the Holy Spirit will make something out of them for good. Better to try and avoid such situations altogether, however.

The longing for God that David describes—like a wanderer in the desert who seeks a drink; like a dry land that needs water—is what we should strive to cultivate, in good times as well as in bad: longing for justice and peace in our time, for right doing, and for Jesus Christ to fulfill completely the kingdom of God, through the creation of new heavens and a new earth.

QUESTIONS

Moses is not allowed to enter the Promised Land, for he doubted God at Meribah. He seems to think that God is dealing fairly with him. What do you think?

Compare Luke 21 with Mark 13. What is the same, and what is different? Why do you think that is so?

PRAYER

O God, you have always forgiven my sins when I have asked. I pray that your Holy Spirit will make those consequences that I know only too well the instrument of my transformation from strength to strength, through Jesus Christ, who lives and reigns with you and the same Spirit, one God, now and for ever. Amen.

The Rt. Rev. Pierre Whalon
Bishop of the Convocation of
Episcopal Churches in Europe
Paris, France

Day 76

Deuteronomy 34, Psalm 64, Luke 22

God allows Moses a glimpse of the Promised Land, from east to west and north to south. Then, despite his good health at a very advanced age, Moses dies and the Lord buries him. It is a poignant moment in a relationship that began back in Egypt, with Moses' faithful mother serving as his nurse. Moses was alone with God at the burning bush, on the height of Sinai, and in the Tent of Meeting. Now he dies with God seemingly at his side, and God alone buries his body in a place only God knows.

Luke 22 is an amazingly rich passage, with much material for prayer and meditation. Like Moses, Jesus is finally alone with God, in the garden. While Moses seems serene, Jesus is tormented by the knowledge of his impending rejection and death. One textual variant says that he was so overwhelmed that the capillaries on his face burst from the pressure of his blood, and drops of blood fell onto the ground, a rare but medically plausible condition.

Throughout the chapter, Jesus keeps pointing ahead. He will drink wine again only when the kingdom has come; there the Twelve shall sit on thrones; Peter will recover his faith after his betrayal, but "alas for Judas"; the Son of Man will come in glory. The contrast between Jesus' confidence with others and his private agony is striking.

QUESTIONS

How do you envisage your death? Are you serene when you think about being dead one day (as opposed to the process of dying)? Why or why not?

Do you think Jesus is being hypocritical with his public confidence and private agony? What does it remind you of in your own life?

PRAYER

Lord Jesus, I am so grateful that you were willing to stoop down to my level and suffer what I must endure. Always give me the faith that will allow me to trust in you, even when I am being torn apart by suffering and doubt, especially at the hour of my death. This I ask for the sake of the love you have shown for me and for all people. Amen.

Day 77: Enjoy hearing the Scriptures read aloud in church.

Day 78

The Very Rev. Douglas Travis
President and Dean of the
Seminary of the Southwest
Austin, Texas

Joshua 1–3, Psalm 65, Luke 23

An innocent man—a man utterly undeserving of death—dies the cruelest death of all. Why? Indeed, Pilate (a man scarcely known for showing mercy!) himself protests that "he has done nothing to deserve death"! And yet this man must die.

Perhaps the greatest challenge of a follower of Jesus is to hope for what Jesus hopes for. Jesus proclaimed the kingdom—the very reign of God *present now*! Jesus declared that the promises human hearts yearn to see fulfilled were fulfilled in him, but the fulfillment was not what people expected. If you make me a promise but do not fulfill it as I expect you to, you have betrayed me! "Crucify him! Crucify him!"

Make no mistake about it. Jesus died because we—you and I—hung him on the cross. Though this particular man died that particular death at that particular time and in that particular place, you and I continue to hammer the nails into his hands and feet whenever we refuse to see the reign of God present with us now because it isn't what we wish it to be. We continue to execute the Innocent One whenever we are disappointed that he is not the Messiah we yearn for.

The point of these comments is not to instill guilt or sorrow. The point is to encourage us to wake up! To watch! To see! A god that I define is no god and cannot satisfy. The God who satisfies my heart loves me and you so much that this God will die for us, but this God will not let us define God. Indeed, this God loves us so much that he would rather die than let us define him. God knows that if we define God we lose God, and God's paramount desire is to give God's very self to us.

QUESTIONS

How can we relate the invasion of Canaan by Joshua and the Israelites to the crucifixion of Jesus?

How does the death of Jesus serve God's fulfilling of the divine promise of the Messiah?

PRAYER

God of love, in your presence and your love, grant us the power to hope for what you hope for! Amen.

The Very Rev. Douglas Travis
President and Dean of the
Seminary of the Southwest
Austin, Texas

Day 79

Joshua 4–6, Psalm 66, Luke 24

"If for this life only we have hoped in Christ, we are of all people most to be pitied" (1 Corinthians 15:19).

"[T]o your faithful people, O Lord, life is changed, not ended; and when our mortal body lies in death, there is prepared for us a dwelling place eternal in the heavens" (*The Book of Common Prayer*, p. 382).

A great deal rests upon our embracing that the Resurrection of Jesus is true, that the tomb really was empty, and that Jesus truly appeared to his disciples. But we must be wary of thinking that by believing something which otherwise seems absurd (namely, that dead people rise) we've somehow cut a bargain with God to secure our salvation. One does not bargain with God, even in believing the truth about God. All that we have— our souls and our bodies—are pure gifts from God. The challenge is not to believe the absurd but to embrace with all our hearts the *presence* of the Risen One.

For in the power of the Holy Spirit the Risen One is still available, but we may not recognize his presence. The first witnesses to the Resurrection did not always recognize the One in their midst. We do not know how long the conversation on the road to Emmaus lasted, but it was obviously more than just a few minutes. Luke tells us that Emmaus was seven miles from Jerusalem, and the unrecognized Jesus had sufficient time to interpret "to them the things about himself in all the Scriptures." And yet, even though the speaker was engaging enough to hold their attention for several miles and elicit from them an invitation to stay for supper, they did not know with whom they were talking until he "took bread, blessed and broke it, and gave it to them."

In the power of the Holy Spirit the Risen One is still very much with us, especially in the meal he himself established for your sake and mine. The challenge is not so much to *believe* this as it is to *know him*. In coming to know him one cannot but believe!

QUESTIONS

What does it mean to "believe" in the Resurrection? What does it mean to trust in the Resurrection?

How can we know the Risen Lord?

PRAYER

O God of the Risen Lord, assure me of your Presence, that I may know you, trust you, and always walk with you. Amen.

Day 80

The Very Rev. Douglas Travis
President and Dean of the
Seminary of the Southwest
Austin, Texas

Joshua 7–9, Psalm 67, John 1

I conceive a thought. I articulate it by breathing air over my vocal chords and moving my lips just so. You hear my words.

"In the beginning was the Word, and the Word was with God, and the Word was God. He was in the beginning with God."

In Luke 23, on day 78 of the Bible Challenge, we read of the Innocent One crucified. In Luke 24, on day 79, we read of the Dead One Risen and with us still. Today we discover that this One who died and was raised has not only always been with us, but has always been with God and is, in truth, himself God! Indeed, this One is the very Word of God Himself. This One is God, and God expresses God's very self in the world!

What's more, this One has intention for you and for me. "[T]o all who received him, who believed in his name, he gave power to become children of God, who were born, not of blood or of the will of the flesh or of the will of man, but of God" (John 1:12-13).

It is the will of God—the same God who creates the world through his Word—that we should be born of God, if we *trust* in his name. It is fitting that the first chapter of John should describe the calling of the first disciples, the first ones to trust in his name. The challenge that Philip issues Nathanael rings true to the ear twenty centuries later: "Can anything good come out of Nazareth?" "Come and see" (John 1:46).

Come and see, but see deeply! This is not merely a good man, nor even merely a miracle worker. The One through whom all things came into being has become flesh! Become one of us, "full of grace and truth" (John 1:14).

QUESTIONS

What does it mean to say that Jesus is the "Word of God"? Is this different from saying that Jesus is the Messiah? Is this more than saying that Jesus is the Messiah?

PRAYER

Word of God, speak yourself into my heart and the hearts of those around and about me, that together we may know you, the only Son of God, full of grace and truth. Amen.

The Rt. Rev. Michael Curry
Bishop of North Carolina
Raleigh, North Carolina

Day 81

Joshua 10–12, Psalm 68, John 2

What kind of God orders people to conquer and kill? The first twelve chapters of Joshua are narratives of the conquest of the Promised Land under the leadership of Joshua. The stories are brutal. They seem contrary to our Christian understanding of the God who is love (1 John 4:8). And when I think of the conflicts in Israel/Palestine today, I wonder, "Do these sacred stories help? Hurt?"

Psalm 68 seems to continue the same troubling thread. "Let God arise, let his enemies be scattered" (v. 1). But later in the psalm there is a hint that may help us to understand: "Father of the fatherless and protector of widows. God gives the desolate a home to dwell in" (vv. 5-6). Here the brutal war language has a moral purpose: to defend those who have no defenders, to provide for those who have not, and to set the prisoners free, as the rest of the psalm says. The God who emerges here is one who cares passionately for a homeless band of newly freed slaves (as described in Joshua) and all those oppressed or disposed. And while the methods may be troubling, the motives are not.

That is where the story of Jesus' miracle in John 2—changing water into wine—may help. The miracle does not happen out of thin air. Jesus takes water that *is* and transforms it into something new, the wine that *shall be.* That may be a pattern of God's way of being in the world. God takes what is and works to transform what is in the direction of what is meant to be. Another way to say it is that God, working with fallible human agents, takes what is a nightmare and transforms it into something closer to what God dreams and intends for creation and the human family.

QUESTION

In your own life, how has God taken what is difficult or painful and transformed it into something positive?

PRAYER

Eternal God, open our eyes to see your hand at work in the world about us. Amen.

Day 82

The Rt. Rev. Michael Curry
Bishop of North Carolina
Raleigh, North Carolina

Joshua 13–15, Psalm 69, John 3

It is not known for sure, but some scholars theorize that the Book of Joshua was composed during the exile of the Jews in Babylon. Others suggest that it was written during the period of the Persian dislocation, when a small community of Jews was exiled under the rule of the Persian Empire. In either case, it is possible that Joshua was written when the Jewish people of God were in exile, without a home, lost in lands not their own.

I can only imagine how a Jew would hear these stories of Joshua distributing the land to the tribes of those who formerly had no home. Imagine hearing that your ancestors were given land by Joshua, with God guiding Joshua in the distribution. Imagine. Imagine. Imagine.

What appears to be a narrative of land distribution would likely have been heard as a hymn of hope—a hymn quickening the imagination to dream beyond the reality of what is and in the direction of what God dreams and intends for the human family and all creation. Imagine.

George Bernard Shaw had it right when he said, "Some look at things that are and ask why. I dream of things that never were and ask why not." Only those who dream, those who imagine, those who, as the old spiritual sings, "look over Jordan," find the courage to pray and labor for a different, a new, a better world, a new and different self. Imagine.

That's what Jesus was teaching Nicodemus. "You must be born anew, again, from above," he says (John 3:7). And Nicodemus replies, "How can a man be born when he is old? Can he enter a second time into his mother's womb?" (John 3:4). And Jesus points to the Spirit, to the kingdom of heaven, to the ultimate horizon and reality of God. *New birth. New possibility. New heaven. New earth.* Imagine.

QUESTION

What would change in your life if you took seriously God's dream for you? Imagine.

PRAYER

Dear Lord, help me this day to see beyond what is and to behold your dream for what is meant to be. Amen.

The Rt. Rev. Michael Curry
Bishop of North Carolina
Raleigh, North Carolina

Day 83

Joshua 16–18, Psalm 70, John 4

In Joshua, the tribal lands are distributed by the casting of lots. I guess that is where we get language about allotments and "lot" as a designation for land. In biblical times, the casting of lots was not like a roll of the dice to us. Today, the roll of the dice is seen as a matter of random luck, though probability can be approximated. But few in Las Vegas seriously think of the roll of the dice as a providential act. Not so in the biblical consciousness, where lots were cast in prayer. In the New Testament, the apostles cast lots to select Matthias to replace Judas as one of the Twelve (Acts 1:26).

There is some ancient wisdom here. By casting lots a decision is taken out of the hands of humans, away from factions, interests, and political control. Everyone has an equal opportunity. Joshua and the leaders did their part and left the final decision to God.

The late Benjamin Elijah Mays served as president of Morehouse College in Atlanta and was a mentor to Dr. Martin Luther King Jr. and countless others. He was fond of saying, "Faith is taking your best step and leaving the rest to God." Interestingly enough, that was the experience of the Samaritan Woman who met Jesus at the well in John 4. She gave her best, courageously facing the truth about her life and making a decision to trust, and Jesus did the rest.

QUESTION

The idea of casting lots is an ancient way of giving the ultimate decision to God. What are some ways we can do our best and then leave the rest to God? Imagine.

PRAYER

Gracious God, please grant me the wisdom and strength to do that which accords with your will. And then give me the grace to move out of the way for you. Amen

Day 84: Enjoy hearing the Scriptures read aloud in church.

Day 85

The Very Rev. Mark Pendleton
Dean of Christ Church Cathedral
Hartford, Connecticut

Joshua 19–21, Psalm 71, John 5

At the end of the violence that followed the invasion of Canaan, the Israelite tribes received their portion of the spoils of war: land. Promised Land. Holy land. "Thus the Lord gave to Israel all that land that he swore to their ancestors that he would give them; and having taken possession of it, they settled there" (Joshua 21:43).

One of my most vivid childhood memories occurred each year on Halloween night after the annual frenzied havoc that my friends and I would bring upon our neighborhood. Our unabashed goal was to collect bags and bags of candy. We were motivated, organized, and ruthless. We had a well-thought-out plan, and we executed it each and every year: we knew which houses to skip and which would yield vast rewards of large hauls of candy. At the end of the night, we dumped our sweet treasure out on the living room floor and then began to sort, categorize, negotiate, and trade.

Unlike the Halloween candy of childhood memories, there are few things in this world that get divided up so cleanly. Colonial powers create artificial but lasting borders that haunt local populations for generations. In prosperous societies, those with a head start do not always leave enough for those who might follow. Those upstream—on the map and in life—often fail to think of those downstream.

QUESTIONS

What is the inheritance you have received—from family, from friends, from God—that has nothing to do with the material world?

Have you ever felt that you were given something in this life that you did not deserve? A leg up? A head start? A second chance?

PRAYER

To the God of land, water, and air, help us be wise inheritors of what we have received from our ancestors in faith and family. May we receive gratefully all that you give us. And for what we do receive, may we remember that it is never fully ours alone. Give us the courage to share, conserve, and pass on your goodness to your children yet unborn. Amen.

The Very Rev. Mark Pendleton
Dean of Christ Church Cathedral
Hartford, Connecticut

Joshua 22–24, Psalm 72, John 6

"Enough!" What a powerful word, which can be used in all kinds of ways. I use it when I am at the end of my rope and have exhausted all of the patience that God has given me to handle a situation, calm down an unhappy camper, or rein in a headstrong teenager. "No more!" You have exceeded your limit, and it is time to call off the charge.

When an elderly Joshua reminded the people of all that the Lord God had done for them, and how each tribe had been allotted an inheritance of land, one can only imagine that the knowledge of such good fortune should have been enough to ensure their faithfulness and obedience. But we know that even having all the land in sight was not enough to keep the people on track. In his final farewell to his people, Joshua sensed the uncertainty of the future: "Be very careful, therefore, to love the Lord your God" (Joshua 23:11).

In John 6, Philip said that six months' wages would not buy enough bread for the vast crowd of some five thousand people that was amassing to listen to Jesus.

When is enough ever enough? Enough insurance to protect what we own and the lives of those we hold dear? Enough patience and grace to make it through a day without blowing our stack at innocent people who simply find themselves between us and where we want to go? Enough abundance to make sure no one goes hungry in our nation and world?

Perhaps the only way one can know when enough is truly enough is if there is something left over for others. Food for the hungry. A decent job for the unemployed. A home for the homeless.

QUESTION

In John's telling of the feeding of the five thousand, the boy with the five loaves of bread and the two fish is the hero of the moment. His preparedness and free offering of what he had led to a multiplication and sharing beyond his imagining. Can you think of a time in your own life when what seemed like too little turned out to be more than enough?

PRAYER

To the God of abundance, plenty, and overflowing mercy, grant us moments when our desire for enough is tied less to the things that rust and wither and more to having enough faith in you to trust through the good times and bad times. May your son Jesus, who made much out of little, be always enough to draw us more deeply into your heart. Amen.

Day 87

The Very Rev. Mark Pendleton
Dean of Christ Church Cathedral
Hartford, Connecticut

Judges 1–3, Psalm 73, John 7

The Book of Judges tells the story of the season of change that was underway in the lives of the Israelites. It was a frightening and unsettling time after the deaths of Moses and Joshua and before the glory days of David and Solomon. It is never easy to live in a time between strong leaders.

Some political commentators have asked if leaders bring about momentous and historic times, or do events and challenges rise up and propel great leaders into fame? Is it the man (or woman) or the movement? I believe it is the latter that prevails most often. Winds blow, hearts stir, and people find their way to leaders who arrive on the scene inspired and dedicated, who have something to say and who propose a path forward.

There is a great deal of conversation today about our nation, our culture, The Episcopal Church, and other churches being in the midst of a season of change. In John 7, Jesus finds himself in an in-between place and time. Galilee was home and safe, but Judea and Jerusalem were where the action was—in this case, the Festival of Booths. Jerusalem was also filled with people who sought to kill Jesus. Even in the face of this threat, Jesus' brothers thought it might be the right time for Jesus to show his stuff for the whole world to see. But Jesus wasn't so sure at first. He held back. He waited.

QUESTIONS

When do we know if it is our moment to step from behind the curtain or out of the pew, throw caution to the winds, and speak out? When do we hold back, waiting for the time to move?

How do we claim the voice and authority, as one of Christ's own, to speak and do what Jesus himself would do?

PRAYER

Almighty and all compassionate God, help us to find our time, our voice, and our audience to risk becoming a leader in uncertain times. May you grant each one of us vision, hope, and the thick skin that comes with the territory of taking our rightful place in the community of believers. Amen.

The Rev. Dr. A. Katherine Grieb
Professor of New Testament
Virginia Theological Seminary
Alexandria, Virginia

Day 88

Judges 4–6, Psalm 74, John 8

Today's lessons deal with conflict. Judges 4–5 recount the battles between the Israelites and the Canaanites in the time of the prophet Deborah. Psalm 74 appeals to God for help after enemies have ravaged the Jerusalem temple at the time of the exile (587 B.C.E.). John 8 describes a polemical debate between Jesus and "the Jews," reflecting tensions between Christian Jews and non-Christian Jews after the destruction of the temple by the Romans in 70 C.E.

Judges 4 provides an account of the victory of Deborah and Barak over the powerful Canaanite army and the death of its general, Sisera. Judges 5, the ancient "Song of Deborah" is a poetic version of the same story. In verses 28-30, we are invited to imagine Sisera's mother waiting for her son to return victorious from the battle. We readers know that he will never return. Even as the desire for revenge is expressed ("so perish all your enemies, O Lord" says verse 31), the Bible reminds us that for every victor in battle, there is also a vanquished soldier on the other side, who had a mother, a spouse, children.

Psalm 74 expresses faith in God's saving power even as it describes atrocities done to the temple. The same God who created the universe also defends the poor and needy. In tender love language, Israel is described as God's pet dove, in danger of being devoured by wild animals.

John 8 also describes Israel: this time Israel divided over the question of the identity of Jesus Christ. The bitter debate here reflects severe tensions between two groups of Jews after 70 C.E.: Jews who believe that God's Messiah has come in Jesus, and Jews who do not. The consequences of this argument would be played out for centuries to come with tragic results. As with every passage in Scripture, this chapter needs to be read carefully in the context of prayerful study. Only then can we continue in God's word and know the truth that will set us all free.

QUESTIONS

Elsewhere (e.g., Matthew 5:44), Jesus tells us to love our enemies. How are all of these Scripture passages to be read together? Where am I called to be a peacemaker or to engage in conflict? Can there ever be justification for violence performed in the Name of God?

PRAYER

Lord, make us instruments of your peace. Help us, as we struggle for truth, to confront one another without hatred and teach us to work together for the common good of all. Amen.

Day 89

The Rev. Dr. A. Katherine Grieb
Professor of New Testament
Virginia Theological Seminary
Alexandria, Virginia

Judges 7–9, Psalm 75, John 9

Today's lessons are best considered by combining the first two readings and treating the gospel separately. Judges 7–9 describe Gideon's triumph over the Midianites and the attempt of Gideon's son Abimelech to set himself up as king of Israel. Gideon requests food for his exhausted soldiers from the people of Succoth and Penuel, in order to hunt down the two kings of Midian who had killed his brothers, and is refused by them. He manages to kill the two kings anyway and exacts bitter revenge on the people of Succoth and Penuel. When the Israelites ask Gideon to rule over them, because he has delivered them from the Midianites, Gideon feigns humility and piety, saying, "I will not rule over you, and my son will not rule over you; the Lord will rule over you" (8:23). But even as he says this, he collects 1,700 shekels of gold from them and makes an *ephod* (breastplate) that probably contains an idol, since the narrator comments that "all Israel prostituted themselves to it there, and it became a snare to Gideon and to his family" (8:27). Upon Gideon's death, the Israelites formally make Baal-berith their god.

Gideon leaves seventy sons from multiple wives and one son, Abimelech, from a concubine whose family are Shechemites. Abimelech enlists the support of his relatives from Shechem, who give him money to hire a band of thugs, and promptly kills his seventy brothers, except for Jotham, the youngest, who hides himself and survives the great slaughter. Jotham warns the Shechemites about Abimelech's ambition in the famous parable of the trees: the olive, fig, and vine are all content to serve others; only the invasive, good-for-nothing bramble aspires to rule over others. Jotham predicts that Abimelech and the Shechemites will destroy each other, which is exactly what happens. The narrator provides a theological summary at the end of chapter 9: thus God repaid Abimelech for murdering his seventy brothers, and God destroyed the Shechemites for their wickedness.

Psalm 75 could well serve as further theological commentary on all the political intrigue, the struggles for power, and the violence of Judges 7–9. The psalmist warns against those who exalt themselves, for "it is God who executes judgment, putting down one and lifting up another" (v. 7). Both the Judges reading and Psalm 75 remind us that not all the characters in Scripture are heroes; God works out Israel's history through villains and murderers as well as through the righteous.

By contrast, the man born blind in John 9 becomes an example of the ideal disciple, gradually deepening his understanding of the identity of Jesus Christ and growing

Day 89, continued

more and more bold to confess his own discipleship. Neither the religious leaders nor his own fearful parents can keep him from proclaiming that Jesus is a prophet and finally confessing him as Lord.

QUESTIONS

Where in my culture do I see political power based on greed and violence?

What pressures in my life keep me from confessing Jesus as my Lord?

PRAYER

Lord God, help us to remember that all power belongs to you. and teach us to use whatever influence we have in ways that honor you and to serve others in your Name. Amen.

Day 90

The Rev. Dr. A. Katherine Grieb
Professor of New Testament,
Virginia Theological Seminary
Alexandria, Virginia

Judges 10–12, Psalm 76, John 10

By now the literary structure of Judges is clear: minor characters like Tola and Jair the Gileadite (at the beginning of chapter 10) and Izban of Bethlehem, Elon the Zebulunite, and Abdon, son of Hillel (at the end of chapter 12), serve as judges of Israel without major incident. But after the repeated refrain "the Israelites again did what was evil in the sight of the Lord" (see 10:6; 13:1), we hear how God gave the people into the hands of a foreign power—the Ammonites in Judges 10–11—and Israel was cruelly oppressed until God raised up someone to deliver them. Here it is Jephthah, a son of Gilead who was driven out by Gilead's other sons—a good thing for him, since they were all slaughtered by Abimelech (9:5).

Now, in the time of Israel's danger at the hands of the Ammonites, the elders of Gilead are eager to patch things up with Jephthah: they promise that if he rescues them from the Ammonites, he will rule over them. In chapter 11, we have a lengthy account of the diplomatic arguments Jephthah attempts with the Ammonites, but when diplomacy fails, Jephthah prepares for war. The narrator tells us that the Spirit of the Lord falls on Jephthah as he travels toward the battle. We are also told that Jephthah makes a vow so foolish that it has prompted generations of Jewish and Christian sages to wonder whether he should have broken it. He promises that if God gives the Ammonites into his hand, he will sacrifice whatever or whoever first greets him upon his return home. God gives him the victory, and when he returns home, his little daughter, his only child, comes dancing out to greet him. We hear how she prepares for death and is duly sacrificed to fulfill his foolish vow.

Psalm 76 praises the God of Israel who puts an end to war and dwells in Jerusalem, the city of peace. The "human wrath" that serves only to praise God in verse 10 may refer to Israel's enemies; but it is unlikely that the sentence "make vows to the Lord your God and perform them" (v. 11) refers to vows like Jephthah's because God is described as the One who rises up in judgment "to save all the oppressed from the earth" (v. 9), which surely includes young children like Jephthah's daughter.

In John 10, Jesus describes himself as the good shepherd who watches over the sheep and protects them from wolves and thieves. Unlike the hired hand who does not care and runs away, the good shepherd lays his life down for his sheep. He knows them all and calls them by name. We are reminded of this passage later in John 20 when Jesus calls Mary Magdalene by name. It is only then that she recognizes the risen Lord and greets him joyfully.

Day 90, continued

QUESTIONS

When, if ever, is it right to break a vow made to God or to others in the presence of God? (This question arises even for vows that were not made foolishly, such as marriage vows or vows taken by those in religious orders.)

What is your first memory of Jesus the Good Shepherd? How has he called you by your name? In what ways has God shepherded you through difficulties or dangers?

PRAYER

Dear Lord, watch over us now as you have watched over us in the past. Keep us from all harm and bring us safely to places of rest and refreshment. Watch especially over the children of the world, who are so often sacrificed to human greed, ambition, and violence. Amen.

Day 91: Enjoy hearing the Scriptures read aloud in church.

Day 92

The Rev. Samuel T. Lloyd III
Priest-in-charge
Trinity Church
Boston, Massachusetts

Judges 13–15, Psalm 77, John 11

Maybe the biggest and best claim our Scriptures make is that God is there in the darkness and struggle of our lives. John 11 gives us the unforgettable story of Jesus raising his old friend Lazarus out of death. When Lazarus is stricken, his sisters Mary and Martha send for Jesus, who doesn't arrive in time. "If only you had gotten here sooner!" they exclaim (v. 21).

"If only…" Isn't that what we so often think? "Things could have been different if only God had been there for me." In our world there are losses and sadness aplenty. Every flower fades, every human being dies, every newspaper brings reports of tragedy.

But into this death-haunted world God breathes new life. Jesus arrives at his old friend's tomb and commands, "Lazarus, come out!" Then, as the mummy-like figure emerges, Jesus booms, "Unbind him, and let him go!"

Something about Jesus hates death. "I am the resurrection and the life," he says to Martha. "Those who believe in me, even though they die, will live" (John 11:25). He's about to go into death himself, but here he is saying that to be close to him, to know and trust him, is to be in touch with a power greater than any dying.

Even when God seems far away, Psalm 77 says, we can trust the One who has never deserted us. "Stay close to me," Jesus is telling us, "and you can go through anything."

QUESTIONS

What are the tombs you have faced in your life?

Where are you bound now?

What would it mean for Jesus' resurrection to come alive in your life?

PRAYER

Lord Jesus, you are the Lord of life and death. Give me the grace to trust you in my hardest times and to cling to you and the power of your Resurrection; in your Holy Name I pray. Amen.

The Rev. Samuel T. Lloyd III
Priest-in-charge
Trinity Church
Boston, Massachusetts
Day 93

Judges 16–18, Psalm 78:1–39, John 12

You can feel the tension rising in John 12 as Jesus rides into Jerusalem on what we now call Palm Sunday. But don't miss the moving moment as the chapter opens, with Jesus at dinner with his close friends—Mary, Martha, and Lazarus. To everyone's amazement, Mary goes over and pours a jar of expensive perfume oil on Jesus' feet and then bathes his feet with her hair.

Judas Iscariot, the disciples' treasurer, is outraged: "What a waste! Shouldn't this be used for the poor?" (John 12:5). "No," Jesus says, "leave her alone. She is anointing me for the burial ahead" (John 12:7).

Mary can't resist giving Jesus the deepest expression of love she knows. Her response is excessive, over the top, completely unnecessary. Love is wasteful like that.

Extravagance, going for broke, putting our hearts and souls on the line—those are things that don't come naturally to most of us prudent folks. We like to be measured and careful, especially in things spiritual and religious.

But Jesus has lived God's love flat out, in ways that will soon have him hanging on a cross. If he were careful he would turn around now and go back to Galilee. But instead he rides on.

He's going for broke. What a wasteful, extravagant thing to do, for us.

QUESTIONS

When have you felt called to take a risk, to put yourself out there, for God?

When you watch Jesus put everything on the line for God, what desire does that stir in you to give more, to go further?

PRAYER

Lord Jesus, you gave up everything for us; help me to love you with the extravagance of Mary, and to take up my cross and follow you right here in the middle of this day; I ask in your Holy Name. Amen.

Day 94

The Rev. Samuel T. Lloyd III
Priest-in-charge
Trinity Church
Boston, Massachusetts

Judges 19–21, Psalm 78:40-72, John 13

John 13 gives us probably the most intimate moment Jesus has with his disciples. He knows the end is near and that this will be his last time with his friends. How can he sum up everything he has been trying to teach them? To do that he leaves them with three gifts to sustain them when he's gone.

An Example. Without saying a word, Jesus takes a towel and basin and washes the feet of his disciples. Everything he has been teaching finally comes down to this: just serving one another, getting our pride out of the way and giving of ourselves, not just to the worthy but to everyone.

A Command. Jesus leaves his friends a new commandment: "Love one another, as I have loved you." Love was Jesus' meaning. Not the feelings of being "in love," but the hard business of caring for people we don't like or admire or approve of, even people we fear or hate.

But Jesus knows the disciples won't be fully able to live that way. They are all too frightened, too self-absorbed, too busy—like us. And so Jesus gives one more gift.

A Meal. Jesus feeds them with the bread and wine that would ever after become his Body and Blood. From that time forward, when they shared this meal they would be united to him and filled with his love.

An example, a command, a meal. These have been shaping our lives ever since.

QUESTIONS

When and where have you experienced servant love in ways that have made a difference? When and where have you given this love?

How has Christ met you in his holy meal?

PRAYER

O Lord of love, help me to be your servant, an instrument of your love, day by day; hold me close to your church, your meal, and above all to you, I ask in your name. Amen.

The Rev. Whitney Altopp
Vicar
St. Thomas Church, Whitemarsh
Fort Washington, Pennsylvania

Day 95

Ruth 1–4, Psalm 79, John 14

The Book of Ruth tells of the plight of two women who have no one to care for them. In a patriarchal society, women found security only in the men of their family. In an effort to provide for herself and Naomi, Ruth takes to gleaning in the fields, that is, following behind the reapers, gathering any harvest they have left behind.

John 14 is referred to as the beginning chapter of Jesus' Farewell Discourse. Over the next three chapters, Jesus tells his disciples of how he has cared and is caring for them, even as he knows that he must say good-bye.

These chapters from the Old and New Testaments tell of God's provision and care for God's people. There is a resounding emphasis through the laws of the Old Testament (leaving some of the harvest for the gleaners, looking to the next-of-kin to provide for the needy in the family) and the law of the New Testament ("love one another") that God remembers the needs of the people. God trusts people to demonstrate God's care for all by carrying out the commandments they have been given by God. This requires discipline on our part.

QUESTIONS

How have you come to know that your security is in God?

What are some ways that you are carrying out Jesus' commandment to love one another? What is one way that God is inviting you to do that better today?

PRAYER

God of All, you provide for all that you have made; increase my faith in your provisions. Give me opportunities to rely on you so that I can know most deeply the security that you provide through Jesus Christ our Lord. Amen.

Day 96

The Rev. Whitney Altopp
Vicar
St. Thomas Church, Whitemarsh
Fort Washington, Pennsylvania

1 Samuel 1–3, Psalm 80, John 15

Hannah's fervent prayer for a child reminds us that God, as described in the Old Testament, was intimately connected with his people. Having just finished Luke, you might recognize the similarities between Hannah's prayer and Mary's song of praise in Luke 1:46-55. There are also similarities between the description of Samuel in 2:26 and the description of Jesus in Luke 2:52. Both boys were set apart for service to God. As Christians, however, we understand Jesus to be more than human. Jesus is fully God and fully man.

In John 15, we hear the heart of Jesus' message, that we love one another. This is part of Jesus' Farewell Discourse to his disciples. For the first seventeen verses of this chapter, Jesus tells his disciples of what it means to be a part of his work of love in the world. The remaining ten verses highlight our interconnectedness, as Jesus' disciples, with him and the message that has been foundational in his ministry. It is because of our interconnectedness that God responds to our requests. God desires to bring glory to himself through our lives.

QUESTIONS

What phrase in Hannah's prayer grabs your attention? Sit with that phrase for a few minutes, allowing God to pray those words in you.

What would God say happens in your life that gives God glory? Spend a moment in thanksgiving for that opportunity.

PRAYER

Loving God, you invite us to allow our lives to be in service to you; give me an opportunity this day to respond to that invitation, in the name of the One God. Amen.

The Rev. Whitney Altopp
Vicar
St. Thomas Church, Whitemarsh
Fort Washington, Pennsylvania

Day 97

1 Samuel 4–6, Psalm 81, John 16

The ark of God was the most prized possession of the Israelite people, giving them a sense of place and identity wherever they might be. As with all things of value, the fine line between reverence and idolization was sometimes hard to observe. The desperation of the Hebrew people in their battle against the Philistines led them to reach for the power of their most prized possession in order to survive. Instead, they lost it all, the reality of which was too much for Eli and his daughter-in-law to bear. The unfortunate illness of the Philistines and the ability for the milch cows to find the Hebrew people without any direction illustrate God's supreme power, which will not be thwarted. Indeed, a lack of reverence of God leads to certain death.

Psalm 81 echoes this same point, reminding people to listen to God.

In John 16, still giving his Farewell Discourse, Jesus prepares the disciples for what lies ahead. He assures them of his presence through the Spirit's coming when he is gone. Knowing that they will find the future disorienting and difficult, he offers them something to hold onto by telling them of what is to come. Jesus goes ahead of them into their unknown future and provides for them there through the presence of the Spirit.

QUESTIONS

What in your life reminds you of the supreme power of God?

What unknown future event do you need the Spirit to go into ahead of you?

PRAYER

God of power, nothing diminishes you; give me strength to acknowledge your power and presence in my life so that others might see your glory, through Jesus Christ our Lord. Amen.

Day 98: Enjoy hearing the Scriptures read aloud in church.

Day 99

The Rev. John Peterson
Former Secretary General
of the Anglican Communion

1 Samuel 7–9, Psalm 82, John 17

One of my favorite psalms, if not my favorite, is number 82. It is my favorite because this psalm helps us to understand how God does God's business.

The setting is a courtroom which is called the Divine Council. In the midst of other gods (notice that the psalmist does not deny the existence of other gods—they are simply inferior), God "holds judgment." Why is God witnessing in the courtroom in the first place?

Because the other gods have been judging unjustly. It is here that we see what God expects from us: "give justice to the weak and the orphan; maintain the right of the lonely and destitute. Rescue the weak and the needy; deliver them from the hand of the wicked" (Psalm 82:4).

It is interesting that in Jesus' first sermon in the synagogue in Nazareth (Luke 4), the same themes were at the core of Jesus' ministry.

In his High Priestly Prayer in John 17, Jesus picks up on the concerns of the Divine Council. Here Jesus gives us a new understanding of how we should live. Here Jesus is the perfect embodiment of God, "so that the world may know that you have sent me and have loved them even as you have loved me" (John 17:23b). In other words, Jesus witnesses to the truth of the righteous God who loves us and calls us to be a part of God's nature—to live in the perfect image/icon of God.

QUESTIONS

Have you ever thought about the Divine Council in the context of Jesus' High Priestly Prayer, particularly in the light of the gods or "the evil one"?

In the church today, could God bring a lawsuit against us because we act like gods?

PRAYER

Open my heart today so that I can hear the argument that God has with me. Amen.

The Rev. John Peterson
Former Secretary General
of the Anglican Communion

Day 100

1 Samuel 10–12, Psalm 83, John 18

Today's readings from 1 Samuel and John 18 are juxtaposed to each other. On the one hand, Samuel is presented as a "righteous judge," one who has neither defrauded nor oppressed; nor has he taken a bribe. Samuel is preparing to go to the Divine Council, where the Lord will be his witness. In John 18, we find Jesus in the garden of Gethsemane being betrayed by Judas. Jesus, a righteous man, will have to take the stand before the Roman tribunal.

In the gospel, the debate with Pilate is really over kingship. There are two interesting conversations going on here: If Jesus is the king of the Jews, why is he in the Roman Antonia Fortress (Praetorium) being tried by Pilate? If he is a Jew, why is he not being tried in the Jewish legal system? From the perspective of the Roman legal system, Pilate can "find no case against Jesus," but the religious authorities do not want Jesus to be released; instead they shout that they want Barabbas, a bandit, to be freed instead of Jesus.

What is so interesting in John 18 is that the whole text hangs on verse 32: "This was to fulfill what Jesus had said when he indicated what type of death he was to die." The Evangelist here believes that crucifixion was the Roman form of capital punishment. According to John, had the Jewish religious authorities (the Sanhedrin) sentenced Jesus to death, the death would have been by stoning (like Stephen, the first martyr of the church).

In tomorrow's gospel, the Divine Reversal takes place, when God turns upside down what we normally would consider "truth."

QUESTIONS

Why do you think the Jewish religious authorities wanted the Romans to try Jesus and not the Sanhedrin?

The Jewish religious authorities were complicit with Rome's desire to crucify Jesus. Have there been times when the church has been complicit with the "Roman authorities" as well?

PRAYER

Give me strength, O Lord, to stand up to the religious authorities as well as to the political authorities, so I will have the courage to testify to the truth. Amen.

Day 101

The Rev. John Peterson
Former Secretary General
of the Anglican Communion

1 Samuel 13–15, Psalm 84, John 19

In yesterday's gospel, the Jews replied to Pilate, "We are not permitted to put anyone to death," when he urged the religious authorities to use their own law.

In today's gospel, the chief priests and the temple police are both shouting, "Crucify him! Crucify him!" Pilate responds to the crowd by saying, "Take him yourselves and crucify him; I find no case against him." John then quotes the religious authorities as saying, "We have a law, and according to that law, he ought to die because he has claimed to be the Son of God" (John 19:6-7).

In John 18 and 19, the evangelist gives us two different understandings of the law. In chapter 18, the religious authorities say they are not permitted to put anyone to death, but in chapter 19, they say that according to their law (Leviticus 24:16), Jesus should die because of his blasphemous claim that he is the Son of God.

On Good Friday, as we reflect on this most solemn chapter in John's Gospel, I suspect in our most honest moments we, too, have to confess that often we are as conflicted as were the Jewish religious authorities.

This is the Divine Reversal, God turning upside down everything we hold to be so important in our lives: power, authority, wealth, and prestige. Kings and queens wear crowns of gold and silver, adorned with diamonds, emeralds, and rubies, but the King of Kings and the Lord of Lords ultimately wears a crown of thorns that will pierce the skin and cause blood to flow.

There has never been a divine drama like it.

QUESTIONS

As you read the Passion Story, how do you reflect on the tension between the religious authorities and the state authorities?

Have you ever felt conflicted about this Jesus of Nazareth who "claims" to be the Son of God?

PRAYER

When I am conflicted, God, open my heart so that I will always be prepared to reach out to the despised and rejected in society with love and compassion. Amen.

The Very Rev. Samuel G. Candler
Dean of the Cathedral of St. Philip
Atlanta, Georgia

Day 102

1 Samuel 16–18, Psalm 85, John 20

"You never get a second chance to make a first impression" goes the old adage. According to the Gospel of John, Jesus said three "first" words to his gathered disciples in the upper room after his Resurrection. These were the statements that would continue Jesus' ministry, through the disciples, and into the future church.

The first word: "Peace be with you." Jesus appears as a man of peace, especially since the disciples were huddled together, maybe even hidden, out of fear (John 20:19). "Be at peace," Jesus advises. The words indicate a presence of peace as well. The resurrected Jesus enters the world in peace.

The second word: "Receive the Holy Spirit" (John 20:22). Ah, this word is delivered with a corresponding action; Jesus breathes on them. According to John, this is the moment—before the Day of Pentecost—when the disciples receive the power of the Holy Spirit. The physical and historical ministry of Jesus is now completed. In the power of the Spirit, the disciples will continue the ministry of Jesus.

The third word: "If you forgive the sins of any, they are forgiven" (John 20:23). Here, we might have the heart of the Christian church. Sure, the church's power to forgive sins has been exploited, and even abused, over the centuries. Despite our mishandling of the gift, however, the gift is still here. In the Spirit of Jesus, the community of faith has the power to forgive sins.

Oh, yes, there is one more element to Jesus' Resurrection words: "As the Father has sent me, so I send you," he adds. We are now included in the disciples of Jesus. We are to be sent in the same Spirit as Jesus was. And his Resurrection words indicate that way: peace, the Holy Spirit, the forgiveness of sins.

QUESTIONS

Martin Luther once said that every morning was like an Easter morning, an experience of resurrection. What are the first words you say in the morning?

How does your community of faith, whether it is a church or not, forgive people?

PRAYER

Lord Jesus Christ, you are the Resurrected One who appears to us in peace, in the Holy Spirit, and in the forgiveness of sins. Send us forth into the world in the same way you appeared to your disciples. Amen.

Day 103

The Very Rev. Samuel G. Candler
Dean of the Cathedral of St. Philip
Atlanta, Georgia

1 Samuel 19–21, Psalm 86, John 21

At some point in our Christian lives, we will hear that the New Testament uses several different Greek words for the English word "love. "Love" can be *phileo*, which refers to familial or brotherly/sisterly love, or *agape*, which refers to divine, self-giving love.

When Jesus asks Peter, three times, "Do you love me?" (John 21:15-17). Jesus uses the word for agape love the first two times. Do you love me with divine, self-giving love? But Peter responds using the phileo form of the word; "Yes, Lord, you know that I love you with familial, brotherly/sisterly love" (John 21:17).

What is going on? Is good old Peter, the representative par excellence of human discipleship, unable to achieve or admit divine love? Maybe so. When Jesus asks the question a third time, it is Jesus who changes the form of the word to phileo love. Jesus adapts the question to the way Peter has been answering it. Maybe that is why Peter is hurt.

Still, Jesus loves Peter. And Peter loves Jesus. What if, at root, love is the same no matter how it is expressed? For instance, isn't familial love also a self-giving love? God desires our love, no matter how we define it. Indeed, in the grace of God, our various definitions may all lead to the same place.

"Tend my sheep," Jesus advises Peter after each question. Love, no matter how we define it, is not only a feeling. It is an action. Love, whether divine or human, results in activity and behavior. In the grace of God, all our definitions of love do lead to a similar place: they lead to action.

QUESTIONS

Does God love you like a brother or sister? How?

What is the best way to tend, or to feed, sheep?

PRAYER

Most gracious God, you love us with a love that penetrates deeper than any definition of ours. Help us to turn your love for us into an active love for our neighbor; through Jesus Christ, our Lord. Amen.

The Very Rev. Samuel G. Candler
Dean of the Cathedral of St. Philip
Atlanta, Georgia

Day 104

1 Samuel 22–24, Psalm 87, Acts 1

"In the first book, O Theophilus…" The first book was the Gospel of Luke. It is broadly understood that the person who wrote the Gospel of Luke also wrote the Acts of the Apostles. Both books are addressed to "Theophilus," which means, literally, "God-lover." Perhaps Luke and Acts are addressed to any of us who want to love God.

We have four different gospels, but only Luke tries to write about what happened immediately after the life and resurrection of Jesus. Jesus lived and taught and died and was resurrected. So what? In the Book of Acts, Luke provides a model of how disciples might act after the time of Jesus.

It is Acts 1:8 that provides the entire title, the entire purpose, of the book: "You will receive power when the Holy Spirit has come upon you, and you will be my witnesses in Jerusalem, in all Judea and Samaria, and to the ends of the earth." After the Spirit falls upon the disciples in Acts 2, the book takes exactly that route. Acts describes power starting in Jerusalem, then moving to the neighboring regions, and finally ending with Saint Paul in Rome—a long way away.

Saint Paul was not there in chapter 1 of Acts, even though much of the book will describe him. We were not there in chapter 1 either. But we are meant to be no less disciples than Paul or the others. Yes, we are meant to be "Theophilus," the "lover of God" who takes a place among the disciples. We, today, are meant to be numbered with the disciples.

Wait for power. Then, be witnesses to Jesus to the furthest reaches of the world.

QUESTIONS

What does it mean to love God? Are we "Theophilus"?

What power do you need today in order to witness to the loving power of Jesus Christ?

PRAYER

Lord Jesus Christ, we wait for power. Send us your Holy Spirit of power and direct us into the world in your name. Amen.

Day 105: Enjoy hearing the Scriptures read aloud in church.

Day 106

The Rev. Canon Martyn Percy
Principal of Ripon College
Cuddesdon, England

1 Samuel 25–27, Psalm 88, Acts 2

Pentecost commemorates a number of events. Principally, it marks the coming of the Holy Spirit after the resurrection and ascension of Jesus. A frightened group of bereft disciples are suddenly empowered by the Spirit, resulting in the birth of the church. Luke, the writer of the Book of Acts, begins his work by describing the phenomenon, the Spirit settling on disciples like "tongues of fire." The disciples become apostles, sealed by the Spirit.

The use of the word "tongue" is important here, for what follows in Acts provides a narrative link. From tongues of fire, we move to speaking in tongues. According to Luke, the disciples are able to stand before a vast and cosmopolitan crowd and address each person in his or her own language.

But this account in Acts is best read analogically. In the Old Testament (Genesis 11), the story of the tower at Shinar tells of how all the different languages in the world came to be. Once upon a time, all nations spoke with one voice. But then people got ideas above their station and decided to build a tower to heaven in order to get on God's level. God, who liked privacy and primacy, sowed dissension amongst the ranks of builders by inventing new languages that hampered the construction. Shinar became Babel, from which we derive the word the English word "'babble." Not for the last time, an ambitious building project was scuppered through poor communication.

The account in Acts is probably an attempt to redeem and reconfigure this fable. The message is this: In the church, a construction of the Spirit—all languages are recognised and spoken. The spirit is universal, not local: the gospel is for all people. So the first act of the Spirit is to reverse the tragedy of Babel: God now speaks to everyone, and the church becomes a global lingua. The language is that of the Spirit.

QUESTIONS

When you consider the account of Pentecost today, how do you think unity and diversity should be expressed in the church?

Look up the story of the tower of Babel in Genesis 11. What lessons might the church and the world learn from it?

PRAYER

Set our hearts on fire with love for thee, O Christ, that in that flame we may love thee and our neighbors as ourselves. Amen.

The Rev. Canon Martyn Percy
Principal of Ripon College
Cuddesdon, England

Day 107

1 Samuel 28–30, Psalm 89:1-18, Acts 3

Jesus' healing ministry appears to be extremely discriminating. On only four occasions—out of well over forty recorded in the gospels —does a healing occur in a building used for religious purposes (see Mark 1:23-27, Mark 3:1-5, Matthew 21:14, and Luke 13:10-13). In two of these cases, the person healed is a woman whose actual right to be there is in some question. In every other case, healings by Jesus take place outside any community of faith, except where crowds of people or the poor are deemed by the gospel writer to constitute a group of the faithful. Jesus' friends or relatives are not usually the beneficiaries of his healing power either. In fact, of those who are healed, we know little, not even a name, and certainly nothing of their long-term response. This may be partly because those who are healed are uniformly poor, voiceless, marginalised, or despised within society. The healing offered by Jesus is socially deep and extensive, not just physical. The impact of the healing always extends well beyond physical changes.

It is interesting, then, that Peter and John pick up the healing ministry of Jesus exactly where he left off. We note that the cripple—unnamed and unknown—catches the disciples before they get inside the temple. This is yet another healing outside a religious building: on the street, with the people, is where God meets the needs of our most needy.

Peter and John, now that they are touched and charged by the Holy Spirit, heal in the way that Jesus taught. And the first person to be healed after Pentecost is an unknown individual, marginalised from society, and outside the temple. We find the Holy Spirit at work in the way that Jesus showed us. Not in places of comfort, safety, and faith, but in the places where God is not known—yet where the people long to be touched.

QUESTIONS

How can the church be an agent of Christ's healing today?

Where outside the church is Jesus calling me to serve?

PRAYER

Lord, help us to follow you in faith and hope and love; and grant us the courage to live faithfully amongst those who need your healing most, and to love, serve, and heal as you taught us. Amen.

Day 108

The Rev. Canon Martyn Percy
Principal of Ripon College
Cuddesdon, England

1 Samuel 31, Psalm 89:19–52, Acts 4

I like the fact that the Christian life does not give you shortcuts. Our contemporary culture is besotted with a desire for the "quick fix." But the Christian life is slow work. It is a work of patience, grace, and growth—in courage and in fortitude.

Today we find Peter and John before the council. They must have been afraid, even though Acts speaks warmly of their courage and their boldness. But they are human, too. Their lives are on the line. And there is no quick exit.

Like many people, I spend much of my life living on the cusp of anxiety and hope. Woody Allen is perhaps not best known for his contributions to theology, but he has a nice line for all of us facing a challenge, whether it is at work, college, or even before the council: "How do we make God laugh? Tell him our future plans."

One of our best-known psalms (23) captures the essence of assurance. God will be with us, in whatever shadows or valleys we walk through. But we are not offered a detour. There is no way around the difficulties we face in life. Rather, faith offers a way *through* these things. So, as we face the challenges ahead, we step out in trust and in hope. As poet Marie Louise Hoskins put it:

> I said to the man who stood at the gate of the year
>> "Give me a light that I may tread safely into the unknown."
> And he replied,
>> "Go out into the darkness and put your hand into the hand of God.
>> That shall be to you better than light and safer than a known way."
> So I went forth and finding the Hand of God, trod gladly into the night.

Peter and John do just that in our reading today. They follow the lead of the Holy Spirit, not because it will take them to any kind of easy success, but because they are faithful to a calling. A calling, indeed, that will in the end lead to their martyrdom.

QUESTIONS

Why does God sometimes lead us into difficult situations?

How can we stay faithful to God when the going gets tough?

PRAYER

May God grant me the serenity to accept the things I cannot change, courage to change the things I can, and wisdom to know the difference. Amen.

The Rt. Rev. James Mathes
Bishop of San Diego
San Diego, California

Day 109

2 Samuel 1–3, Psalm 90, Acts 5

One king dies in battle; another, on a cross. One king's death is met with bloody retribution and lamentation, and he remains dead. The other king, the true anointed, does not remain dead but defeats death. His disciples follow on the way and proclaim that his kingdom continues. They preach peace to those who are far off and to those who are near. In the end, Saul's kingdom is an earthly realm that passes away. Jesus' kingdom is imperishable, and his disciples cannot forsake their citizenship in it.

These apostles, through their mere presence, bespeak of the risen Jesus. To be with them is to experience "signs and wonders." Even to have Peter's shadow merely fall upon the sick is enough. But for some, change is so fearful that they cannot sense this new life in their midst. Their answer to the healing, transformational power of Jesus manifest in these apostles is to try to lock it up. But the jails are as ineffective a container of the King's power as the tomb.

And just as with Jesus, the apostles are brought before Jerusalem's religious leaders. In this moment, a voice of wisdom is heard. The great teacher of the law, Gamaliel, famously says of the apostles' proclamation, "If this plan or understanding is of human origin, it will fail; but if it is of God, you will not be able to overthrow them—in that case you may even be found fighting against God."

Gamaliel was right. Earthly kings will rise and fall. But Jesus will reign forever.

QUESTIONS

In what ways do we need to alter our daily lives to shift our allegiance from the kingdoms of this world to the kingdom of Christ our King?

How do we share in and show forth the risen Jesus in our lives? Do people want to dwell in our shadows because Christ's transforming power abides there?

PRAYER

Life-giving and transforming God, you call me to be a citizen of your kingdom. Give me the courage to forsake all but you and your anointed, Jesus, my risen Lord. Teach me your ways that I may be a source of your light and your grace of new life. Amen.

Day 110

The Rt. Rev. James Mathes
Bishop of San Diego
San Diego, California

2 Samuel 4–6, Psalm 91, Acts 6

Several years ago, Alan Greenspan, then chair of the U.S. Federal Reserve, made a speech in which he memorably described investors exhibiting "irrational exuberance." That might be the way that Michal, the daughter of Saul, described David's leaping and dancing as the ark of the Lord was brought into Jerusalem. In another time in Jerusalem, others might have said the same thing about Stephen as he lived into his diaconal vocation, "full of grace and power," doing "great wonders and signs among the people" (Acts 6:8).

But this is as it should be. David's rejoicing was rooted in thanksgiving. At least for a time, peace was at hand. And Stephen knew the risen Christ. He could sense the power of the resurrection as he brought the good news to the people.

Investors in the stock market evaluate risk and reward. They buy *and* sell. But David bet everything on God's providence and promise. Perhaps this is why the psalms are attributed to him. They so often seem to belong on the lips of a grateful ruler: "For he will command his angels concerning you to guard you in all your ways" (Psalm 91:11). And the arrested but unrestrained Stephen would likewise echo the psalmist: "You who live in the shelter of the Most High, who abide in the shadow of the Almighty, will say to the Lord, 'My refuge and my fortress; my God, in whom I trust'" (Psalm 91:1-2).

Like David, Stephen bets everything, his whole life, on Jesus. Some called it blasphemy. Others might say it was irrational exuberance. Stephen does what the rich ruler cannot do. He gives it all up for Jesus.

QUESTIONS

How much am I willing to give up for Jesus and the gospel?

What does it look like to be irrepressibly exuberant in my discipleship to Jesus?

PRAYER

Almighty God, the source of all that is good and true, teach me to be complete in my devotion to you, following the way of Jesus, which is irrational to the world but perfect in your sight; through Christ our Lord. Amen

The Rt. Rev. James Mathes
Bishop of San Diego
San Diego, California

Day 111

2 Samuel 7–9, Psalm 92, Acts 7

We are made to worship God. It is in our DNA as creatures to love our creator and to give thanks for all that we receive—food, shelter, families, and companionship, every grace and goodness. And so we sing with the psalmist, "For you, O Lord, have made me glad by your work; at the work of your hands I sing for joy. How great are your works, O Lord!" (Psalm 92:4).

The summer before my wife and I were married, we taught Vacation Bible School. My wife taught the four-year-olds. As part of one lesson, they created a little altar with candles. One of the learners apparently went home and told his mother that God had moved to their classroom. The next day the child's mother suggested that the teachers might want to mention that God was everywhere.

David thought that God could be contained in cedars. Stephen knew and preached otherwise: "The Most High does not dwell in houses made by human hands" (Acts 7:48). For our God is a wandering God. The tent in the wilderness is a much better image than the temple of Solomon, the temple sanctioned by Cyrus, or even Herod's grand but transitory renovated version of the same.

I am always struck that the Feast of Stephen is the day after Christmas. Immediately after celebrating the birth of the Messiah, we remember the first martyr. It feels unsettling, which is probably a good thing. We do well to remember that John's Gospel says of the Incarnation that "the Word became flesh" and "pitched his tent" among us. Stephen would likely have agreed. Jesus is God among us. This is the One we worship. And so we sing with the psalmist, "For you, O Lord, have made me glad by your work; at the work of your hands I sing for joy. How great are your works, O Lord!" (Psalm 92:4).

QUESTIONS

In what ways do we try to contain, restrict, or domesticate God?

Where is God to be worshiped in the world around us?

How might we worship God in the wilderness places?

PRAYER

O God, who is before us and with us, help me to remember that you are always with me. Give me the courage to go where I must go and the confidence to speak your word wherever that place may be; through Jesus Christ our Lord. Amen.

Day 112: Enjoy hearing the Scriptures read aloud in church.

Day 113

Dr. Esther Mombo
Deputy Vice Chancellor
St. Paul's University
Limuru, Kenya

2 Samuel 10–12, Psalm 93, Acts 8

Today's Old Testament text begins with the resumption of the war with the Ammonites at the beginning of the new year. The men going to war included Uriah, a Hittite who left his wife, Bathsheba, at home. David did not join the men for battle. While he was walking on the roof of his house, he saw Bathsheba bathing and admired her. He had an affair with her, and she became pregnant—a fact he tried to conceal by asking that her husband be sent home. Uriah returned but chose to be faithful to the code of conduct of war rather than lie with his wife. When Uriah thwarted David's plans, David arranged for him to be killed on the battlefield, and he took Bathsheba as a wife. These actions angered God, and Nathan was sent to confront David.

Why did Bathsheba give in to David's attentions? What choice did she have, when she was dealing with the most powerful man in the nation? Why did David stay behind when his men were at war? He had so much power, and he could decide what to do with it—until God reminded him that power is not to be abused.

David misused his position of power and authority and could no longer fool himself or those around him or, above all, fool God. He paid for his mistakes by losing the son who was born to Bathsheba. David did not remain in his state of sin but later repented.

Many are the times that we find ourselves in the shoes of David, and we abuse our power because we are mortal. We are called to listen attentively to people of integrity, people who expose the truth, and to repent and join David in asking for forgiveness.

QUESTIONS

How do we challenge misuse of power in our church or society?

How can we raise up leaders of integrity?

PRAYER

God, help us to act with integrity and courage, especially in times when we are tempted. Amen.

Dr. Esther Mombo
Deputy Vice Chancellor
St. Paul's University
Limuru, Kenya

Day 114

2 Samuel 13–15, Psalm 94, Acts 9

During sixteen days of activism calling attention to violence against women, a female student was asked to read the lesson of the day, which was from 2 Samuel 13. After the reading she was supposed to say, "This is the Word of God," but she did not say those words, and there was an unusual silence. Following the service, I spoke with the students about the reading, and most of them said they had never heard this story read and preached about in a service. I asked them why this was the case, and some said it is a very painful story, while others said it reflected what is happening to many girls.

Tamar, the daughter of David, was raped by Amnon, her half-brother, "who was so tormented that he made himself ill" (2 Samuel 13:2) because he desired her so much. He sent for Tamar, tricked her into caring for him, and then overpowered her because he was physically stronger. But after raping her, Amnon hated Tamar, and he had his servant expel her from his house. Tamar protested, saying that he should take responsibility for his actions by marrying her in accordance with the Law (Deuteronomy 22:28-29, Exodus 22:16). But Amnon did not change his mind. Tamar lived in shame for all her life.

In this narrative, Tamar is an example of a woman who tried to resist the act of rape and attempted to bring her perpetrator to account. The biblical record of the rape of Tamar shows God's intention to make sexual abuse and any other form of abuse a subject for public discussion.

QUESTIONS

Are there women like Tamar in your church?

What can we do to support women like Tamar?

PRAYER

God, we pray for all who are oppressed and especially for women who are victims of violence. Give us compassionate hearts and the will to speak and act on their behalf. Amen.

Day 115

Dr. Esther Mombo
Deputy Vice Chancellor
St. Paul's University
Limuru, Kenya

2 Samuel 16–18 Psalm 95, Acts 10

Before the election of the chairman of our parish, Nito was nominated for the post. A group led by Tundo reacted strongly against Nito's nomination, arguing that he came from a community that did not practice circumcision, and they could not be led by a "Gentile" (uncircumcised man). The church was split into two bitter factions that could not be reconciled. This split led to the creation of two parishes that later became two dioceses.

In the early chapters of Acts, we saw that the church was launched as an institution that sought to do away with all oppressive social categories such as age, class, race/ethnicity, and gender. We see how the disciples struggled to discover what this meant for the development of the church, and in chapter 10 we see Peter and Cornelius being taught that the church is a place of inclusion.

Peter is initially presented as very traditionalist, but in Acts 9:32-42, he had already begun to be more inclusive: he was staying in Joppa in the house of Simon the tanner (tanning was viewed as an unclean trade). In today's reading, Peter has a vision of a sheet with all sorts of animals in it, and he is asked to kill and eat them; he then says nothing unclean has entered him. The Spirit was prompting him.

Cornelius was a Roman captain who worshipped God and gave generously to the poor. He had a dream in which an angel of God told him to send for Peter. When Peter arrived at the house of Cornelius, he found many people waiting for him; and after he spoke with them, they believed and were baptized, becoming the first non-Jewish group to be converted to Christianity.

Peter and Cornelius received confirmation from God that the church was not to be an exclusive Jewish sect in which people would be members by birth. The church was different, having been inaugurated by the coming of the Holy Spirit, and all who believed were accepted.

Day 115, continued

QUESTIONS

What are some of the things that make us exclude others from full participation in our churches and society?

How does the story of Peter and Cornelius help us to see that the church is a place to embrace all people?

PRAYER

O God, you made us in your own image and redeemed us through Jesus your Son: Look with compassion on the whole human family; take away the arrogance and hatred which infect our hearts; break down the walls that separate us; unite us in bonds of love; and work through our struggle and confusion to accomplish your purposes on earth; that, in your good time, all nations and races may serve you in harmony around your heavenly throne; through Jesus Christ our Lord. Amen.

—For the Human Family,
The Book of Common Prayer, p. 815

Day 116

The Rt. Rev. Justin Welby
Bishop of Durham
Bishop Auckland, England

2 Samuel 19–21, Psalm 96, Acts 11

Seeing what God is doing, discerning the reality of God in the midst of the busyness of the world, is such a challenge. This bit of David's life retold in Samuel is full of the chaos of low politics and high treachery. It is similar to many countries today: back the wrong person, give in to human impulses, rebuke the ruler, and you are in grave danger. This is the chaos that followed the fall of Baghdad in 2003. It takes us straight to a tale of normal humanity. David wants to mourn his son but must congratulate his troops. Joab deals murderously with anyone who challenges his power. David faces aging and weakness.

In the reading from Acts, the greatest theological revolution since the Exodus, the opening of Christian faith to Gentiles has to be swallowed by an astonished Jerusalem church.

Busyness is not an enemy; it is a reality. Saint Benedict calls for us to find stability in the midst of anything, and stability is found in God alone. David's actions are horrific in modern terms, but he is not a modern man but a man of his time, whose genius is that he kept his eyes on God, even amidst the troubles of war. The psalm has the answer: in starting with the glory of God, we find the source of stability.

QUESTIONS

What is your experience, whether making big decisions, or coping with immense pressure and even danger, of still staying aware of God's purposes?

Chaos and evil do not deny the presence of God but they certainly test our ability to see him. Do you have a group of friends who will strengthen you when, like David, you are weary and fading? If not, begin to seek such a group.

PRAYER

"All the gods of the peoples are idols, but the Lord has made the heavens." Strengthen me, O Lord, to seek you as the one who does not fail, and to cast aside idols of security and safety for the presence that is eternally with you. Amen.

The Rt. Rev. Justin Welby
Bishop of Durham
Bishop Auckland, England

Day 117

2 Samuel 22–24, Psalm 97, Acts 12

What did David do wrong? Every scholar has a different answer, but probably the spiritual reality is that David sought to demonstrate his own strength and not rely on God. God had given him rest from his enemies. He was secure; he had nothing to prove. The psalm he sings shows his true spirituality, his reliance on the God who rescues. The list of mighty men shows his strength. But he could not see that.

We are dealing in terms of a belief that, as they say in Nigeria, the fish rots from the head. In other words, bad rulers bring misfortune on their people. We know that is true, and this passage ascribes responsibility to God. Peter also could not see this was God. He saw and did not believe. In biblical terms that is not seeing. Nor did Rhoda see.

The psalm is one of rule and glory for God. Put alongside randomly cruel Herod and irresponsible David, that seems to make little sense, but it is this truth that has held the prisoner secure under persecution and inspired those struggling with injustice. God's perspective and ours are utterly different. What counts is our final trust in him, not only in this world but in the face of losing it.

The second key point is prayer. David turned to prayer; the church prayed for Peter; the psalmist expresses confidence in God. And things changed. It is easy to believe in prayer as therapy, and less so to hold on to the truth that prayer is both action and obedience, trust and intervention. Prayer aligns us to God and intercedes for an issue or situation to be aligned by God.

QUESTIONS

What do you rely on more than God, if anything?

If you are in the place of Peter, literally or figuratively imprisoned by suffering and circumstances, are you as honest with God as you can be, not only declaring his praise but also telling him of your lament?

PRAYER

O God, you know that we can do nothing for ourselves to help ourselves. Give us strength both to bear the struggles and injustices of this world and also, trusting in your grace, to resist wrong and serve truth; in Jesus' name. Amen.

Day 118

The Rt. Rev. Justin Welby
Bishop of Durham
Bishop Auckland, England

1 Kings 1–3, Psalm 98, Acts 13

Today I am going to alight on the issue of choice. Who chooses what in each story? There is choice by the bucket load. In the Old Testament reading, Adonijah chooses rebellion and disloyalty. Those with him choose to back him in the growing power vacuum that is typical of the declining years of a great ruler. Everyone chooses politics, and one could (wrongly) analyse the narrative only in political and dynastic terms. But above all, God chooses Solomon. Why? Well, who knows? The son of an adulterous and murderous relationship, whose mother does not come across as one of the Bible's heroines, is chosen above his obviously gifted (but ruthlessly ambitious) half-brother. It is clear that the editor of Kings sets his favour on Solomon. But the favour is because he was favoured. David had promised, and the Lord had witnessed to the promise.

In the chapter from Acts there is also choice. Barnabas and Saul are commissioned for perhaps the most important of the missionary journeys, pioneering their way across what is now the Levant and Turkey, as well as Cyprus. They are chosen in prayer and sent out. They choose where to go. They choose to move on, how to minister, and what to say.

Choice is always something that God involves us in. He chooses, and we choose whether to cooperate with his choice—and, of course, as all of Solomon's enemies find, as well as those who oppose or disregard Paul, choices have consequences. God treats us as adults.

QUESTIONS

List five really important choices you have made, for yourself or for others.

Where was God involved in them? How did you get him involved or fail to do so? Reflect on what enables you to make choices that are God-centred.

PRAYERS

Be, Lord Jesus, a bright flame before me, a guiding star above me, a smooth path below me, a kindly shepherd behind me: today, tonight, and forever.

—Prayer of Saint Columba

I will be busy O Lord, you know how busy I must be this day. If I forget you, do not forget me.

—Sir Jacob Astley,
before the Battle of Edgehill, 1642

Day 119: Enjoy hearing the Scriptures read aloud in church.

The Rev. Brenda Husson
Rector
St. James' Church
New York, New York

Day 120

1 Kings 4–6, Psalm 99, Acts 14

King Solomon is celebrated for his wisdom, but clearly he had a talent for organization as well. As today's chapters in 1 Kings begin, we have an accounting of the people who administer the kingdom. It was a system that worked, and we are assured that just as Solomon and his court were well provided for, so all the people of the kingdom also "ate, drank and were happy." Finding himself in the enviable position of having neither adversaries nor misfortune, Solomon sets himself the task of building a house for the name of the Lord. The construction of the temple begins.

Seven years in the making, the temple is described in loving detail in chapter 6. Clearly, no expense is spared: the wood is from Lebanon, and gold is everywhere. But costly as the materials are, there are other costs as well: a single verse in chapter 5 tell us that the work required forced labor.

Magnificent as the temple is, its creation is a source of misery for some. That misery may be an unintended consequence of Solomon's great building project, but it is a consequence nonetheless.

Paul and Barnabas, in their ministry among the Greeks, also learn about unintended consequences. Healing a man in Lystra, they are mistaken for the Greek gods Zeus and Hermes. Yet Paul and Barnabas insist that all glory go to the "living God" and are content to be mortals, just like those to whom they preach, so that those they encounter will look past them and see Jesus, the Christ. Their clarity about who they are and who they are not sustains them through both mistaken adoration and violent rejection.

Psalm 99 proclaims the Lord alone as king. Paul and Barnabas know that; the truth held in Solomon's heart is perhaps less certain. What of us?

QUESTIONS

Have there been times when your longing to do great things, even for God, brought forth unexpected or disturbing consequences?

Paul and Barnabas are steadfast in their focus on Christ both when all goes well and when nothing does. What helps you stay focused on Christ in good times and bad?

PRAYER

God of both majesty and mercy, help me to seek you in all times and seasons and to know that all that I offer is made possible only through your grace; in Jesus' name. Amen.

Day 121

The Rev. Brenda Husson
Rector
St. James' Church
New York, New York

1 Kings 7–9, Psalm 100, Acts 15

As we reach the end of chapter 7 in 1 Kings, the temple and Solomon's own palace have been completed. Solomon, delighting in having fulfilled his father David's intention to build a house for the name of the Lord, brings in the vessels for worship that David had dedicated during his reign. But it is Solomon's special joy to preside as the priests bring in the Ark of the Covenant, containing the two stone tablets that Moses brought down from Mount Horeb. The glory of the Lord fills the temple, and Solomon is in his glory as he declares, "I have built you an exalted house…for you to dwell in forever."

Solomon is wise enough to know that not every day will be as grand this one. So his prayer of dedication also speaks of those times when the people will sin, when drought and famine come, battle rages, or the people are led into exile, and he asks that the Lord, in those days, hear and respond to the prayers of the people. In chapter 9, the Lord responds with both reassurance and warning, promising to dwell with the people but demanding that the people serve the Lord alone.

Paul's mission to the Gentiles has been successful—maybe too successful. Some of Christ's followers back in Jerusalem think that these new Christians must become Jews first, "circumcised according to the custom of Moses." Paul and Barnabas cite signs and wonders occurring among these new converts, and Peter, recalling the gift of the Holy Spirit and the saving grace of the Lord Jesus given to him, sees those same gifts at work among these new Christians. The Gentile believers find themselves welcomed into Christ's saving embrace. And they rejoice.

QUESTIONS

We human beings seem to want to define who's in and who's out in many parts of our lives. How have you found your own views of who is part of God's kingdom challenged?

We know that we are meant to serve the Lord alone. What are some of the other gods that seek to lay claim to your allegiance? How do you dedicate yourself to the Lord?

PRAYER

Dearest Lord, help us to worship you with gladness and come into your presence with thanksgiving, trusting always in your steadfast love made known to us through Christ our Savior. Amen.

The Rev. Brenda Husson
Rector
St. James' Church
New York, New York

Day 122

1 Kings 10–12, Psalm 101, Acts 16

The tension between fulfilling our vows to the Lord and pleasing those we love comes into sharp focus as Solomon's story continues in 1 Kings. Although celebrated for his wisdom and his wealth, Solomon just can't resist the requests of his admirers. The Queen of Sheba visits, swooning over his kingdom, and we're told that he gives the queen "every desire that she expressed" (1 Kings 10:13). For the more than one thousand women in his life, he gladly builds sites for the worship of their foreign gods.

Despite his dedication of the temple, Solomon has forgotten his dedication to the Lord. The response is clear as the Lord tells Solomon that the kingdom shall be taken from him, though not in Solomon's lifetime. Solomon must live (and die) knowing that his actions have changed and diminished the future.

Solomon's son, Rehoboam, makes matters worse. Solomon consorted with idolatry; Rehoboam adds injustice to the mix. Solomon was willing to use forced labor; Rehoboam gleefully chooses to burden the people. As we read this portion of the Bible, we may be tempted to bewail the growing wickedness of the kings as the kingdom is divided and idolatry wins the day. But these stories tell us that our choices matter and remind us how easy it is to give in to sin when it is personally or politically expedient.

Taking the easy way out doesn't seem to be an option for Paul in chapter 16 of Acts. The Lord directs his path, opening the door to some areas for ministry and closing others, and Paul obeys. When his ministry lands him in jail, and an earthquake makes escape easy, he stays put. By staying the course, Paul leads another family to be baptized and forces the authorities to admit to their wrongdoing. Justice and faith are both exalted.

QUESTIONS

Do you find the desire to meet the expectations of others gets in the way of your dedication to God? In what ways does your community of faith help you to walk in the way of the Lord?

Have you experienced Jesus closing a door that you felt called to walk through? Have other opportunities for ministry opened unexpectedly?

PRAYER

Open my heart and steady my feet, dear Lord, that I might walk in the way that you would have me go and share your goodness and grace with all whom I meet; through Jesus Christ. Amen.

Day 123

The Rev. Simon Barnes
Executive Vice President of the
American Bible Society
New York, New York

1 Kings 13–15, Psalm 102, Acts 17

"He reasoned with them from the scriptures explaining and proving that the Christ had to suffer and rise from the dead.…So he reasoned in the synagogues with the Jews and the God-fearing Greeks as well in the marketplace" (Acts 17:17).

"It's not what you say but rather what others overhear that speaks of the gospel," said a wise Christian friend. An authentic Christlike faith is one that can face the challenges head-on with grace, equanimity, and a sense of ever-abiding peace. Paul did not seem unduly perturbed by the opposition he faced: he reasoned, he explained, and some got it and others didn't.

Often, as the psalmist illustrates, it's in our darkest moments that the true nature of our faith is tried and tested. The opposition Paul faced seemed to spur him to act with even greater zeal to make the Good News known. Paul did not appear to question; rather he held on to his "Road to Damascus" experience and allowed this to be the anchor for all that followed.

Sometimes our first formative Christian steps are ones that remain with us for the rest of our lives, and at other times God drops in "mountaintop" experiences along the way. In either case, they form the "Ebenezer stones" that we can hold on to in the face of challenges and opposition.

QUESTIONS

As you look back on your Christian life thus far, what are the "Ebenezer stones" that you recognize? Reflect on how these have spurred you on in your own faith, recall the impression that they have left with you, and be grateful for how they have shaped your journey thus far.

PRAYER

Father, thank you that throughout our lives you seek ways to encourage us; help me to remember those times when I have felt your presence in a real way, and give me the strength and courage to face the challenges, trials, and disappointments with a faith that is sure. Amen.

The Rev. Simon Barnes
Executive Vice President of the
American Bible Society
New York, New York

Day 124

1 Kings 16–18, Psalm 103, Acts 18

"But from everlasting to everlasting the Lord's love is with those who fear him" (Psalm 103:17).

Love and fear are not two words that readily go together; yet throughout the Old Testament, the women who drew close to God understood the careful and sometimes complex balance between the two. Paul similarly was compelled by love, yet he fully understood the consequences that could ensue from not pursuing God wholeheartedly.

How easy it is for me to take my relationship and the many blessings that I have received from God for granted! How often I find myself approaching God as if our relationship were no different than any other relationship I have. Yet I know God's love for me is truly incomprehensible, never failing, never varying, never lost. How often I forget that perfect love, that extraordinary balance between a loving Father and mighty Creator God.

I need to step back from time to time to reevaluate my relationship with God (remembering it is I who got it wrong), reflecting again on his love for me, his love as my Heavenly Father, his love as my Redeemer God, his power as Creator God, and, ultimately, my right fear of a God before whom one day I shall have to give account.

QUESTIONS

How will the realities of the complex relationship you have with God manifest itself today in what you say and do? Are there some things that might need to change?

PRAYER

Lord God, help me this day to have a right fear of you as God and to know your love for me as my Heavenly Father. Amen.

Day 125

The Rev. Simon Barnes
Executive Vice President of the
American Bible Society
New York, New York

1 Kings 19–21, Psalm 104, Acts 19

How often we have sung the words, "God moves in a mysterious way, his wonders to perform," and tried to take to heart the reality that God's economy is not our economy. There are times in my life when I have found myself asking, "Exactly what I am doing here?" Both Elijah and Paul were trying so very hard to do what they genuinely believed God had called them to do, and like so many who desire to follow the Spirit's leading, they found that the going was far from easy. Patience, stamina, and physical well-being were challenged in ways that Elijah and Paul had not anticipated. Theirs was a tough assignment and one that required absolute trust in God.

In my own experience, often it is only when we look back through the years that we can begin to see God's hand so evidently at work and can appreciate that even in those times when we felt God to be far off, the reality was that God was much nearer than we had imagined.

It is while we are laboring in the midst of these struggles that we find it so very hard, as indeed Elijah and Paul did, to understand God's plan for our lives. Like Elijah and Paul, sometimes our only option is to "set our face like flint," to listen as attentively as we can, and to remain faithful to what we genuinely believe God has called us to do.

QUESTIONS

Think back to a time in your life (it may be now) when you felt as though God was calling you to swim against the popular tide. How close to God did you feel, and what were the hallmarks of your relationship with him? What would you want to remind yourself of today as you think back to that time?

PRAYER

Father God, thank you for being a sovereign God who cares for us as individuals and has a plan for each of our lives. Help me to walk before you in righteousness and to follow you in all humility and obedience this day. Amen.

Day 126: Enjoy hearing the Scriptures read aloud in church.

The Rev. Loren Mead
Author and Consultant,
Founder of the Alban Institute
Washington, D.C.

Day 127

1 Kings 22, Psalm 105, Acts 20

In the Old Testament reading, the prophets are torn by different interpretations of God's will as they are tasked to choose military strategy by uncertain kings. The prophet Micaiah, seen as a troublemaker by Ahaz, disputes the consensus of the school of prophets who counsel attack. Micaiah foresees disaster and predicts it—the forces of Judah and Samaria are defeated and Ahaz killed by the Amareans. The question of who can speak for the Lord is raised. What are the consequences of true prophecy and false prophecy?

When do prophets prophesy what the king wants, and when do they truly speak for God? How can the people know? How can even the prophet know?

In our New Testament reading, it is Paul seeking to understand the will of God, pulling against the will of the people of the church who are conflicted, some disagreeing with Paul's teaching and many wanting him to stay, not go. Paul's clarity that he must go to Jerusalem is mixed with his uncertainty about what it will mean to go there. How can he be sure he is doing what God wants him to do?

Both of these story lines emphasize the basic themes of scripture—that what we choose and what we do is related to God's will and God's call to each of us. And it isn't easy to be sure…

Psalm 105 reinforces the importance of all the events and things—no matter how insignificant—that are part of our lives.

QUESTIONS

What happens when different people disagree about what God's call really is?

How do you decide between alternatives you have to choose between?

PRAYER

Lead us, Heavenly Father, lead us,
o'er the world's tempestuous sea;
guard us, guide us, keep us, feed us,
for we have no help but thee,
yet possessing every blessing,
if our God our Father be. Amen.

Day 128

*The Rev. Loren Mead
Author and Consultant,
Founder of the Alban Institute
Washington, D.C.*

2 Kings 1–3, Psalm 106, Acts 21

Our Old Testament reading has more of the story of the early life of the Israelites in the promised land, featuring all sorts of mighty and supernatural acts by the representatives of God—Elijah, the elder prophet, and Elisha, the disciple who moves into the senior role when the chariot "swings low" and takes Elijah to God. Again, the prophets are tasked to support the people against their enemies, who, this time, are mostly the Moabites. (The enemies of the people or the prophets get spectacular recompense for their lack of faith!) But generally the people of Israel prevail.

In Acts, Paul continues his journey "home" to the homeland of the church, facing challenges but also connecting with old and new compatriots. Signs of a growing storm of opposition begin to show up.

QUESTIONS

How do we manage when we have to be part of a change of leadership? Do we fight it? Do we help the change take place and support the new leader?

PRAYER

May we all find our way home from the far places to which we are called; and when we get there, may our Lord himself welcome us home. Amen.

The Rev. Loren Mead
Author and Consultant,
Founder of the Alban Institute
Washington, D.C.

Day 129

2 Kings 4–6, Psalm 107, Acts 22

Great classical stories abound in these Old Testament readings about Elisha and his servant Gehazi. They visit Shunem and minister to the Shunemite widow, who in turn ministers to them; they encounter the great Aramean general Naaman and cure him of pride and leprosy; and they engage in other roles with the people and leaders of Israel.

In Acts, Paul continues with the beginning of his testimony about his conversion, a dramatic, first-person telling of his extraordinary journey to Damascus—the story that is one of the most central to the early church. And the readings take him on toward Rome.

QUESTIONS

How is Paul's story of his background like or unlike Naaman's pride in his authority and lineage?

What is your testimony of how you "found" yourself in Christ? Where did you begin, and where are you now?

PRAYER

O God our help in ages past,
our hope for years to come.
Be thou our guide when life shall last,
and our eternal home. Amen.

Day 130

The Rev. Dr. James Lemler
Rector
Christ Church
Greenwich, Connecticut

2 Kings 7–9, Psalm 108, Acts 23

Psalm 108 acknowledges the sovereignty and power of God. The psalmist offers thanksgiving and song for the victory that originates from and belongs to God. God's love is steadfast. The psalm calls for human beings to fix our hearts on that love. The issue before us is whether or not we will do that. Will we trust in God? Will we believe that God is sovereign, active, and purposeful in our lives?

Certainly that is the continuing issue for God's people as it unfolds throughout the books of Kings. Will God's people trust God, or will they put their faith in human agency, in kings good or bad? In today's reading, we encounter Elisha, the prophet of God, who recounts great deeds of God's love and healing and advises kings while calling them to account. Elisha trusts God. Even his Hebrew name means "God has granted salvation." So, the question of trust unfolds in these chapters. There are machinations galore. There is rebellion and intrigue. There is deliverance and new beginning. Always Elisha represents the question: Will God's people trust their Creator and Redeemer?

It's the same question for Paul, standing accused before the judgment council in Acts 23. He is challenged and even struck. A conspiracy emerges to take his life. Will he trust God? God encourages him, and Paul believes. He stands firm and fast in the steadfast love of his Creator and Redeemer. He walks his walk, living into what God has told him: "Just as you have testified for me in Jerusalem, so you must bear witness also in Rome."

It has been said that the greater problem facing Christians today is not theological atheism but functional or practical atheism. We may have a sense that God exists, but we find it difficult to trust in God's efficacy and power. We believe that we have to make things happen, that everything depends on us. The invitation of Scripture this day is to believe and trust in God's presence, power, and steadfast love. It is to fix our hearts on the God who loves us.

QUESTIONS

Where is your heart "firmly fixed" in your life? Who are the prophets that point you toward truth and trust?

Where is God calling you to move on in your faith? What is one way that you can grow in trusting the love of God?

PRAYER

Gracious, loving God, help me to trust in you more fully. Enrich and strengthen my faith, and let my heart be firmly fixed on your steadfast and efficacious love this day. Amen.

The Rev. Dr. James Lemler
Rector
Christ Church
Greenwich, Connecticut

Day 131

2 Kings 10–12, Psalm 109, Acts 24

"Do not be silent, O God of my praise. For wicked and deceitful mouths are opened against me, speaking against me with lying tongues!" (Psalm 109:1-2).

The psalmist minces no words. They are out to get me! There is falsehood, enmity, accusation, and deceit all around me! Just read…just pray the words. They are heartfelt and poignant. Now, thanks be to God, our lives generally do not have the intensity of opposition expressed in Psalm 109, but we do know the effect that opposition, rejection, and cutting words have on us.

Opposition and intrigue, sometimes open rebellion and war, were the daily lot of the ancient kings of Israel. Today's reading tells the story in vivid detail. Jehu continues his murderous action against the descendants of Ahab and those who oppose him. He uses force to slaughter the worshipers of Baal. The destruction continues as Jehu's sons meet opposition and threat. Sometimes there is victory, and sometimes the kings are faithful. At other times, there is defeat, and the kings fall short. They meet opposition, but they do not rely on God.

Paul takes a different approach, relying consistently on God even in the face of relentless accusation and opposition. His opponents speak all manner of evil against him. Falsely, they accuse him of sedition and perverting the truth. Paul defends himself by telling his story and relying on God. He stands before those who have opened their mouths against him, and, in face of this opposition, he gives voice to hope in God.

It is true. All of us can pray the words of today's psalm. There is a temptation to respond like the kings of ancient Israel, by attempting to control and counter harsh words and actions with harsh words and actions. Paul beckons us to something different. "I have hope in God," he says. When we are hurt, when we are opposed, we can enter the hope of God's love and life.

QUESTIONS

When have you experienced opposition in your life? What are the challenges that face you now? How do you attempt to deal with them: denial, anger, sadness?

Where do you perceive God's gift of hope for you? How might you embrace and enter that hope more fully?

PRAYER

Blessed God, you know about bitterness and opposition and have walked the way of ridicule and accusation. Be with me when I face such things and give me the faith to hope in you with heart and soul, I pray. Amen.

Day 132

The Rev. Dr. James Lemler
Rector
Christ Church
Greenwich, Connecticut

2 Kings 13–15, Psalm 110, Acts 25

Today's readings include a royal psalm, probably used for the crowning of a king or the gathering of the royal house in the great temple of God. The psalmist sings praise of God the Sovereign of the universe and of the earthly king who is God's representative. The psalm alludes to a mystical and marvelous king, Melchizedek, and says that the royal one of God is anointed as both king and priest.

Melchizedek, by tradition both king and priest of Salem, met Abraham and offered bread and wine in thanksgiving for the rescue of Lot. His name means "king of righteousness." He is the prototype of what a king ought to be.

Well…there are kings, and there are kings. Some live into the aspiration of royal and priestly kingship. Others don't. Welcome to the thirteenth through fifteenth chapters of 2 Kings! Jehoahaz is identified as evil. Joash does better. In the midst of it all, the prophet Elisha dies. There is war. There is palace intrigue. There are good and bad decisions. Sometimes there is conflict between the earthly king and the Sovereign of the universe.

Acts 25 describes a whole tapestry of royal power. There is the local king, Agrippa. There is the great emperor of Rome, to whom Paul eventually appeals his case. But behind and underneath it all is the great King and Sovereign of life and hope, God the Creator and Redeemer of the universe. Jesus is the Christ, the "Christos" or one anointed with the royal and saving power of God. Jesus is the Lord of life who lives the role and life "after the order of the anointed Melchizedek" (Hebrews 5:6). Paul knows that and bets his life on it.

There are many things that claim sovereignty, power, and allegiance in modern life. Our call as people of faith is to embrace and be embraced by the sovereignty of God and to recognize the one who is "King of kings, and Lord of lords."

QUESTIONS

What claims sovereignty in your life? How do you live amidst the powers of modern life that claim attention and allegiance?

Where do you see the sovereign love of God in your daily living?

PRAYER

Sovereign God, you are the King of kings and Lord of lords. Grant that I may recognize you and serve you, and anoint me with your love and Spirit for your mercy's sake. Amen.

Day 133: Enjoy hearing the Scriptures read aloud in church.

Dr. Zebedi Muga
Head of Biblical Theology and Philosophy
St. Paul's University
Limuru, Kenya
Day 134

2 Kings 16–18, Psalm 111, Acts 26

The Old Testament reading describes issues affecting Israel in the period just before the fall of the Northern Kingdom. It shows how the kings of the time went about managing their political affairs, such as establishing alliances with superpowers such as Assyria and Egypt. Examples of social, political, and religious integrity set by the political leadership were wanting. Rulers did not keep the law and did not govern justly or listen to God's voice.

The text considers how foreign political and religious influences impacted local society and spiritual life. The example set by the king should have been emulated by the people, but according to the writer, this does not seem to have been the case. Instead, the king, for the sake of his political survival, opened the door to negative foreign influences.

The text raises questions of greed, personal survival both social and political, intrigue at the expense of personal integrity, and good relations with humanity and the divine. God does not appear as central for the rulers, who focus on personal and political survival.

Psalm 111 emphasizes the sovereignty and the omnipotence of God, which we need to remember: it is God who is above all gods and does that which humans cannot do; in all our issues, God must be at the center.

Paul in Acts 26 challenges the status quo of his time. The reading shows how he is put on the defensive, and how he responds cogently to the issues raised. Can we, too, stand up to scrutiny?

QUESTIONS

What are the sociopolitical issues raised by the Old Testament text? Who are the main characters? Is God at the center of their activities?

How does Psalm 111 demonstrate the centrality of the divinity?

What can we learn from Paul's defense of the faith?

PRAYER

God, we pray for all leaders in the world today, that they might set aside selfish interests and work for the good of all people. Amen.

Day 135

Dr. Zebedi Muga
Head of Biblical Theology and Philosophy
St. Paul's University
Limuru, Kenya

2 Kings 19–21, Psalm 112, Acts 27

The Old Testament text shows how a new king reacts to the taunts of the invaders and their intended colonization of the land: he demonstrates reliance and dependence on God. The king receives a message from the Assyrians and seeks the help of the Lord. Perhaps our political leaders can learn from this text how to respond to the issues of our time. The empire and its killing machines have come to our doorstep: how do we respond? King Hezekiah gives a good example as he goes about meeting the challenges, encouraged by the prophet of God. He does not ignore the prophet, as his predecessors had done before, but addresses the situation with the guidance of the prophet.

The psalm demonstrates that keeping the law of God brings joy and exultation in the land. The text illustrates the benefits of adhering to the demands of the law of the Lord. In verse 5, the psalmist mentions particularly the benefits that accrue to those who practice social justice. The rest of the text serves as an encouragement in the face of difficulty.

The reading from Acts focuses on Paul's journey to Rome under guard. He is put in chains to travel to the emperor and defend himself against the charges that have been brought against him. It is interesting to note that his advice is ignored by the centurion, who prefers to listen to the ship's captain (the professional). Paul's reaction is not "I told you so" when things go bad; he is tactful and continues to encourage in the face of an adverse situation.

Today's prophets have the task of learning from Paul's example. When the empire comes to the doorstep, how do men and women of God practice their ministry and faith? Can the people of God intelligently address the issues that arrive with the coming of the empire to our doorstep?

QUESTIONS

How do we react as men and women of God in the face of adversity? What can we learn from King Hezekiah?

What lessons does Psalm 112 teach about our commitment to live by the word of God?

PRAYER

God, we pray that we might learn from the example of King Hezekiah as we face the challenges of our own day. Amen.

Dr. Zebedi Muga
Head of Biblical Theology and Philosophy
St. Paul's University
Limuru, Kenya

Day 136

2 Kings 22–24, Psalm 113, Acts 28

The reading from 2 Kings contrasts Josiah and Jehoiakim, showing the achievements and demise of both. The former is faithful and committed to the ideals of God, while the latter leans more toward political survival and personal greed. During Josiah's reign, a scroll (thought to be the Book of Deuteronomy) is found in the temple. Based on this document, Josiah is credited with returning the nation to the ways of God. Jehoiakim does not show any commitment to sustaining these achievements and ideals. His punishment comes when the nation is overrun and his people are taken into exile.

Psalm 113 celebrates the sovereignty and the omnipotence of God and attributes all political power to God. God is active on behalf of those at the periphery and the king is expected to act on behalf of the poor and the lowly. Today, there is a need for political leaders to act on behalf of those at the periphery, but instead we find them focused on their own needs and wants. This text challenges this failing and demonstrates that all things emanate from God.

The reading in Acts 28 illustrates Paul in situations where he is thought to have extraordinary powers, and then engaging in a dialogue of faith with the Jews. Though their reaction is negative, he does not give up but is emboldened to continue preaching. How do we manage potentially adverse situations in our own lives? Paul could have been tempted to focus on the personal benefits he could accrue from his powers of healing, but he does not. Instead, he points his subjects to God and continues with his ministry of encouragement. It is my prayer that when God uses us in a situation, we will give all the glory to God and not to ourselves.

QUESTIONS

What examples can we learn from the lives of Josiah, Hezekiah, and Zedekiah?

What can we learn from Paul's experiences in Malta?

PRAYER

God, we give you thanks for the examples of our ancestors in faith. Guide us in the church today as you guided Josiah in his temple reforms and Paul in his steadfast faith. Amen.

Day 137

The Rev. Jay Sidebotham
Rector
Church of the Holy Spirit
Lake Forest, Illinois

2 Kings 25, Psalm 114, Romans 1

Not with a bang but a whimper. That's how the second book of Kings seems to end. Could it get any worse? Chapter 25 describes the fall of Jerusalem—heartwrenching destruction, followed by the deportation of the people into Babylonian exile. It's the stuff of Shakespearean tragedy, as King Zedekiah tries to flee, a foolish and futile effort. He is captured and forced to watch the execution of his sons before his own eyes are put out. The people are carried off, and that's almost the end of the story. But not quite.

In the final verses of the book, a small ember suggests a fire could be rekindled. The promise to David that his royal lineage would continue is kept alive—barely. King Jehoiachin of Judah is released from the Babylonian prison. The Babylonian ruler speaks kindly to him and gives him a seat above the other kings. Jehoiachin puts off prison clothes, and he dines with the king. He gets a regular allowance for the rest of his life.

If this were a movie, that last detail would signify a sequel. There is more to come. Today, as we come to the conclusion of this sad history in which power dissipates, we are called to hold it in tension with the first chapter of Paul's letter to the Romans. This letter, the longest of those attributed to Saint Paul, has been instrumental again and again in the renewal and reformation of the church, especially when hope seems lost. It lays bare the power of the gospel, as seen in verses 16-17, which declare the theme of the letter: "For I am not ashamed of the gospel of Jesus Christ. It is the power of God for salvation to everyone who has faith."

As you come to the end of the story described in 2 Kings, as you simultaneously begin Paul's letter to the Romans, claim the power of God to work even in—especially in—the brokenness of the human condition.

QUESTIONS

Have you ever experienced a glimmer of light in situations that seem beyond hope?

What resources do you have in your own life to help you move forward? Where do you find your power?

PRAYER

Eternal light, even in the moments when hope seems to have been extinguished, help me to remember the power of your love revealed in Jesus Christ. Amen.

The Rev. Jay Sidebotham
Rector
Church of the Holy Spirit
Lake Forest, Illinois

Day 138

1 Chronicles 1–3, Psalm 115, Romans 2

I sometimes compare the spiritual journey to a road trip on the highway of life. In order to move forward, it helps to keep one eye on the rearview mirror. In other words, if we're trying to anticipate the way God will act in the future, embracing courage to move forward with hope, it's helpful to look back at the ways God has acted in the past. Perhaps that is why, again and again in Scripture, a retrospective view is indicated through genealogies, a way of remembering God at work in history.

The first and second books of Chronicles run on a parallel track with the first and second books of Kings. But while first book of Kings starts with King David, the first book of Chronicles takes us all the way back to Adam, in perhaps the most extensive genealogy in all of Scripture. Truth be told, this kind of biblical material, name after unpronounceable name, can derail the most well-intentioned Bible reader. Some might wave the white flag. Others might just fast-forward. Some names are familiar. Many, if not most, are not.

But as you make your way through the Bible, take the time today to read the names in these three chapters, perhaps out loud. If you come to a name that is hard to pronounce, say it with conviction. (As Luther said, sin boldly.) If you have a Bible you don't mind marking up, highlight names you know. If you run across names that spark curiosity, investigate. As you read aloud, imagine those names read in an ancient gathering. Imagine the meaning and purpose people could find in that retrospective glance, reminded through the reading of names that God has been active in their community for generations.

Celebrate the good news that God has acted throughout the generations. Let that celebration help you move forward in your own journey today.

QUESTIONS

It's been said that in the journey of faith, we don't need so much to be instructed as reminded. In what ways has God acted in your own history and in the history of those you love?

Who are the people you have known, who have paved the way for your own forward movement?

PRAYER

Gracious God, we give thanks that we are surrounded by a great cloud of witnesses, encouraging us in the journey of faith. May we live this day as a witness for those who surround us. Amen.

Day 139

The Rev. Jay Sidebotham
Rector
Church of the Holy Spirit
Lake Forest, Illinois

1 Chronicles 4–6, Psalm 116, Romans 3

Perhaps one of the reasons for the extensive genealogy in Chronicles is to make the point that we are all in this together, one big family. That's a source of comfort and possibility, for sure. It also bears challenge. It's been said that the Bible is a story of sibling rivalry, notably beginning with Cain and Abel, continuing with Jacob and Esau, and unfolding in the drama between Joseph and his eleven brothers, representing the human family getting along, or not.

Today the readings from 1 Chronicles begin to name the descendants of Jacob's twelve sons. Chapter 4 gives us the descendants of Judah and Simeon, two of the twelve tribes that were closely related. Chapter 5 presents the descendants of Reuben, Gad, and Manasseh. Finally, in chapter 6, we come to the lineage of the Levites. You've got a few more chapters with a lot of names in days ahead, twelve tribes in all. It's a mosaic of generation upon generation, people in relationship with God and with each other, lives marked by joy and challenge, community and conflict.

As you read these many names, hold them in tension with the third chapter of Romans, which paints a powerful picture of the human family and the human condition. We are all in this together. Paul writes: There is no distinction. All have sinned and fallen short of the glory of God. Paul gives an honest assessment of our experience, contrasting human frailty and shortcomings with the faithfulness of God. Watch for the ways that the letter to the Romans tells the story of all of us, all in this together, and ultimately on the receiving end of mercy, a love from which we can never be separated.

QUESTIONS

Why are these genealogies important for a community of faith? Do we have a comparable resource in our own time?

Sin has been described using the metaphor of archery, that is to say, it is a matter of missing the mark. How do you understand the meaning of sin? What can we do about its power in our lives?

PRAYER

Create in us clean hearts, O God, and renew right spirits within us. Amen.

Day 140: Enjoy hearing the Scriptures read aloud in church.

Canon Vicki Garvey **Day 141**
Associate for Lifelong Christian Formation
Diocese of Chicago
Chicago, Illinois

1 Chronicles 7–9, Psalm 117, Romans 4

In Herb Gardner's play *A Thousand Clowns,* Murray Burns worries about the future of his ward, Nick, if Child Services determines that Murray is an unfit guardian. Precocious Nick, already too prone to particulars, might end up with a family of list-makers, and that would break Murray's heart. Murray knows that Nick counts and wants to be sure that he appreciates the "special thing he is."

Murray's right. People count. And sometimes we count people. I'm thinking here of family reunions when we tell the old stories of our kin to remind us of whom we are. Or of those rituals during which we name aloud and so remember those who have died and now form part of the great cloud of witnesses.

By this time in 1 Chronicles, we might be a little wearied by all those listings of endless names. Murray would throw up his hands at the lists—or perhaps not. Because that stream of names represents rivulets of stories of people who count. To the scattered community of Israel in the grim days after the Exile, those names and those stories forge a bridge to the past. The people in the Chronicler's audience need such memories and connections to the people who have, in a sense, made them who they are.

So do the new Christians in Rome. But Paul, instead of trotting out a genealogy, chooses to remind his hearers and overhearers of one figure from their past: Abraham. Behind his lauding Abraham as model, undergirding the Chronicler's endless lists, and embedded in our exceedingly brief psalm, is the most prominent character of all: the God who is and was and will be faithful to everybody, righteous ancestors, and bumblers, and list-makers.

QUESTIONS

Who among your ancestors do you "reckon as righteous" (Romans 4:22), and how does that person assist you in your own journey of faith?

Paul, quoting Genesis 15:6, says that Abraham's "faith 'was reckoned to him as righteousness.'" If you look at the whole of Abraham's life as told in Genesis 12–25, what else might you learn about the life of faith, its valleys as well as its peaks?

PRAYER

God of the ancestors, remind me to be grateful for those in my family tree who model for me a life of faithfulness and wonder in your presence. Amen.

Day 142

Canon Vicki Garvey
Associate for Lifelong Christian Formation
Diocese of Chicago
Chicago, Illinois

1 Chronicles 10–12; Psalm 118; Romans 5

Henry David Thoreau is credited with having remarked, "Many people go to their graves with the song still in them." That would not be true of some of the characters we meet in our texts of the day.

To begin with, our psalmist is downright ebullient with thanks and praise. A song of thanksgiving for deliverance from some unnamed foes, today's psalm is a giddy sigh of release, a drawn-out "aaahhh" beginning and ending with the assurance that God hangs in there with us no matter what. The psalmists, even the grittiest of the lamenters, were besotted with God. They were convinced that God cared and that there was a "Thou" out there not only ready but eager to converse with people, no matter their mood or their virtue.

And that's also at the heart of a portion of the good news that Paul has for his Roman congregants: "Christ died for the ungodly" (Romans 5:6), he insists, and then seems to turn this awesome piece of news over in his mind as an unnamed secretary tries to follow his thoughts. God proves that "steadfast love" which the psalmist praised, Paul says, because Christ died not only for the heroically righteous, or even for the casually pious, but for sinners as well. Good news, even great news for those of us who seem more comfortable "bewailing our manifold faults" than believing that God loves us, is besotted with us.

That includes a David whose checkered career, though cleaned up for the Chronicler's audience, must still have been remembered—David, sinner and saint, whom God chose and with whom God continued to abide even in David's less ideal moments.

QUESTIONS

What's the song in you that wants to be sung aloud? How do you give voice, as the psalmists do, to your excitement or remorse or pain or exaltation?

What does it mean to you that God loves you, even on the days when you are your most curmudgeonly, unhelpful self?

PRAYER

God of love, teach us to see in those around us, as well as in ourselves, the image of yourself that you have planted there. Help us to live into it, through the One who taught us the way, Jesus, your son and our brother. Amen.

Canon Vicki Garvey
Associate for Lifelong Christian Formation
Diocese of Chicago
Chicago, Illinois

Day 143

1 Chronicles 13–15, Psalm 119:1-32, Romans 6

Back in chapter 5 of Romans, citing Adam and Christ, Paul argued that grace trumps sin. Maybe somebody overhearing that argument thought, "Whoa, good idea. Sin more and help grace along!" I'm struck by the way Jesus's parables often end with no ending, really. For instance, we don't know how the story we call "the prodigal son" concluded. I wonder if the older kid accepted Dad's advice and joined the party or lurked outside to punch his wayward brother in the nose. And did that younger sibling "come to himself" again and think, "That worked really well: party, new clothes, and prime beef; I think I'll do it again. Sin big! Grace—and presents—abound."

Which is perhaps why—getting back to Paul—chapter 6 opens the way it does. "You got that all wrong," he says. Baptism makes a difference. Now we're new. Now we've come through death to life. Now we're members of God's family and related to Christ in a new way. We're part of God's tribe, of whom Jesus is the firstborn. As family members, as "Christ's own," we're his hands and feet in the world. As poet Gerard Manley Hopkins says, "Christ plays in ten thousand places / lovely in limbs and lovely in eyes not his." Sin is part of the old us; sin is death; sin is disconnection. Sin is not our way anymore. Sin's not who we are. Sin doesn't become us. When we remember our baptism, it's a way of remembering who we really are.

And though later in this chapter Paul seems fed up with "the law," he'd agree with all 176 verses of that rhapsody on Torah that the psalmist offers, because it too reminds us of how the family of God looks at its best.

QUESTIONS

How do you "remember who you are" and "who lays claim" to you?

The Baptismal Covenant—in spite of Paul's enthusiasm— assumes that we will "fall into sin" from time to time. How is that a moment of grace for you?

PRAYER

Forgiving God, give me the wisdom to know when I have failed and the grace and courage to turn back to you, through the One who forgave everything and bade us do the same, your son and our brother. Amen.

Day 144

The Rev. Sam Portaro
Author and Retreat Leader
Chicago, Illinois

1 Chronicles 16–18, Psalm 119:33-72, Romans 7

Newly consecrated as king, David establishes the ritual relationship between Israel and God in worship (1 Chronicles 16), appointing (i.e., ordaining) the Levites to priestly service. David's practice of ritual sacrifice, blessing the people, and distributing bread to "every person" foreshadows eucharist and the two-fold dimension of thanksgiving to God in worship of God and generosity to God's people in tangible service rendered equitably (1 Chronicles 17). David's comparison of his own material blessings (a house of cedar) with God's "homelessness" reveals a depth of conscience and relationship; God's generous blessing of David inspires the king to offer more than ritual gratitude in the vision of a temple. But through Nathan, David learns that his priorities are misplaced (1 Chronicles 18). David's role is to build God a different kind of residence, in the strength of God's people. Victory after victory increases Israel's material wealth and welfare, blessings David attributes to God's loving care.

In today's psalm we have a heartfelt prayer, one that may well have been prayed by—and certainly reflects the devotion of—David, whose actions attest that he has indeed learned the ways of God's statutes.

Chapter 7 of Paul's letter to the community in Rome is complex, in part because it struggles to express the dilemma of human motive. Just as David's desire to build a house (temple) for God seems a generous act, it's a misplaced gesture, at least in part because it springs from David's personal appreciation for his own material well-being. David is dissuaded by Nathan and redirects his gratitude to God in a pledge to pursue God's will instead of his own.

The essential point of Paul's tumbling, stumbling message is that through his own experience he has discerned that human will is incapable of self-direction, much less self-correction. A faithful life begins in acknowledging that simply assenting to God's will is inadequate; human motives are often mixed and never pure. This is not a condemnation of humanity but a useful warning against reliance upon one's own convictions.

QUESTION

Recall an instance from your own experience of mixed motives and misplaced priorities. Who was your Nathan, who dared to bring you clarity of purpose?

PRAYER

God of pure wisdom, grant me humility to question even my deepest and most sincere convictions, and grace to submit my own judgment to your scrutiny and the risks of greater clarity in your guidance. Amen.

The Rev. Sam Portaro
Author and Retreat Leader
Chicago, Illinois

Day 145

1 Chronicles 19–21, Psalm 119:73-112, Romans 8

In today's 1 Chronicles reading, Nahash, king of the Ammonites, with whom David has maintained a respectful relationship, has died. David's condolences are met with suspicion by the successor's advisors, who foment a humiliation of David's emissaries. War ensues, escalates, and expands, as do Israel's conquests and riches. As his realm grows, so does David's daring; emboldened by victory, he orders a census—an accounting of his earthly, human capital. His rationale may have been purely practical—to establish a tax system to sustain a growing empire and/or to assess his military capabilities by counting potential warriors. This act is nonetheless an expression of faithlessness, an insult to the God who has promised to provide.

The verses from Psalm 119 express the somewhat ambivalent stress played out in the narrative of 1 Chronicles, where David and his nation are by turns gracious, humiliated, set upon, and challenged, not only by war but by victory as well. Alternating between lament and praise, this portion of the psalm reflects the inner dialogue of any faithful person struggling to balance personal setbacks in the context of God's assurances.

The eighth chapter of Paul's letter to Rome continues his struggle to unravel the perplexities of human will and activity, but it commences with a reassuring assertion that no matter the confusion, God does not condemn humanity for this failing. If it be a shortcoming, it is part and parcel of what it means to be human, to be made distinctly other than God. As poet Alexander Pope succinctly put it, "to err is human." In that confidence, we are encouraged to persevere, as did David, whose own fidelity to God embroiled him in deadly warfare.

For Paul, the central summation of Christ's gospel is the concluding paragraph of chapter 8. No matter the path our lives take, regardless of our missteps, we are not condemned. In the ambiguity of David's experience, in the ambivalence of the psalmist's prayer, in the confusion of Paul's perplexities, there remains the clarity of God's unequivocal promise: God never forsakes us.

QUESTIONS

Have you ever felt caught in a web of complications resulting from your own good intentions? Can you empathize with Paul's torturous struggle to articulate the frustration of such entanglement?

PRAYER

God of truth, help me to unravel the fabric of my own desires that I may see each thread for what it truly is. Then weave my threads into a design of your own delight. Amen.

Day 146

The Rev. Sam Portaro
Author and Retreat Leader
Chicago, Illinois

1 Chronicles 22–24, Psalm 119:113-144, Romans 9

David's reign is nearing its end. He returns to his earlier dream of a house for God and orders that the foundation be laid for the temple. While such an act may seem the obstinate egotism of a man who refuses to surrender a desire deferred by Nathan's prophetic intervention, is it not possible that David undertook this measure in order that all might understand that his conquests and all their benefits are forever to be seen as belonging to God? Thus, as his reign winds down, we find David back where his reign began: attending to the rightful worship of God, provisioning the nation with a temple and the temple with a priesthood now grown to reflect the fullness of Israel's new reality.

Today's portion of Psalm 119 could rest upon David's tongue, commencing with the bold statement, "I hate the double-minded, but I love your law," (v. 113) an assertion lived out in the monarch who is determined to ensure that everything gained in his rule be consistent with his singular devotion to God.

When reading chapter 9 of Paul's letter to Rome, it is helpful to remember that Christianity is bound in profound relationship to Judaism. Like any member of a family struggling to find and establish his or her own identity, the early Christian community, itself a sect of Judaism, is in crisis. Remember, too, that a crisis in one member affects the family as well; the family is also struggling to establish its identity and distinction.

The assertion of chapter 8 that nothing shall ever separate us from the love of God manifest in Christ Jesus moves in chapter 9 to an anticipation of all who might challenge that assertion with logical arguments, many drawn from Scripture. Paul's conclusion, like David's, remains consistent: it is beyond our human capacity to fathom the measure or the mechanics of God's promise of fidelity to humankind. God's promise, like Godself, is what it is. Paul ends with the image of Christ—the incarnation of the promise—as a stone laid in Zion, a stumbling block but also the foundation of a new temple made not of stone but of human hearts filled and aligned with the love of God.

QUESTION

David goes to considerable lengths to ensure his legacy. What is the one principle you wish to leave behind at your death?

PRAYER

In me, on me, you build your temple, God. Make my heart your home and come, dwell therein. Amen.

Day 147: Enjoy hearing the Scriptures read aloud in church.

The Rt. Rev. Catherine M. Waynick
Bishop of Indianapolis
Indianapolis, Indiana

Day 148

1 Chronicles 25–27, Psalm 199:145–176, Romans 10

In the reading from 1 Chronicles, King David continues to make arrangements for the personnel needed to staff and guard the temple and its treasures. Included are detailed lists that can seem mind-numbing to those not included in them! But such lists ground the account in a specific time and place and provide for accountability in carrying out the work. The passage is poignant; David knows he will not build the temple, but seems determined to put his own mark on the project even as he relinquishes it to others.

The psalmist continues to assert his love of Torah and his wholehearted search for wisdom. Those who do not seek wisdom despise and mistreat him. As the psalm nears its conclusion, we encounter discouragement; the situation seems to be getting worse, but the psalmist will remain faithful and hopeful. At the end we find the psalmist's first explicit confession of failure—he has gone astray like a sheep who is lost. Perhaps he is now coming closer to the wisdom he desires.

Our passage from Romans has Paul lamenting that many Jews still seek righteousness through obedience to the law. But the law was given only to the Jews, while God has made it clear that "others" will also be given righteousness. The Jews have not considered that could happen outside the law, so Paul's vocation is to proclaim that salvation through faith in Christ Jesus is for all people. Now both Jews and Gentiles may believe and "call upon the name of the Lord" (v. 13).

QUESTIONS

From your reading of the Bible, how would you say that God responds to those who are proud of themselves? To those who become humble?

PRAYER

Most gracious God, you offer to all people your wisdom and righteousness. Keep me from judgment of others, and give me the courage to be both humble and bold in sharing the Good News of Jesus our Lord. Amen.

Day 149

The Rt. Rev. Catherine M. Waynick
Bishop of Indianapolis
Indianapolis, Indiana

1 Chronicles 28–29, Psalm 120, Romans 11

When David has assembled the leaders and presented the plans for the temple to Solomon, he reminds those present that the young and inexperienced ruler will need their help to complete this holy project. David now tells of his personal donation and invites the leaders to contribute as well. They rejoice at the great size of the offering, and David reminds them of the source of all blessings in words that have become familiar to us (1 Chronicles 29:11-12, 14). Then David prays for Solomon, and the assembly anoints him again (!) to be their king. David's reign as a warrior king comes to a suprisingly peaceful end.

Psalm 120 begins a series known as the "Songs of Ascents," perhaps composed for use on pilgrimage (up) to Jerusalem. The psalmist is remembering a time when his prayers were answered and seeks that consolation once more. He lives, at least figuratively, among barbarous and alien peoples. The journey toward the city of peace is an act that gives him hope.

In the reading from Romans, we are reminded that God's plan is to save all people, not to condemn the Jews. As Gentiles gain righteousness through faith, the Jews will become "jealous" and willing to believe in Christ rather than law. The metaphor of the olive tree provides an image of removing and grafting branches that works both ways: branches once grafted onto the tree can be removed, and branches once removed can be regrafted. No branch need be lost forever, and since all are nourished by the same roots, none has cause to gloat. It is a mystery, this work of God, but Paul is convinced that God can turn the frailty of one to the good of the other, in a dance that makes it possible for all to come to faith.

QUESTIONS

Do you recall a time when you were certain God answered your prayer?

Stewardship is often thought of as giving over to God some of what is ours. All that we have—time, skills, money, relationships, the Good News—are gifts. How can we steward them in ways that would bring us to great rejoicing?

PRAYER

Most gracious God, in your generosity you desire to graft all to Christ, the tree of life. Give us that same generous spirit, and teach us to be faithful stewards of all your gifts. Amen.

The Rt. Rev. Catherine M. Waynick
Bishop of Indianapolis
Indianapolis, Indiana
Day 150

2 Chronicles 1–3, Psalm 121, Romans 12

As Solomon's reign begins in 2 Chronicles, he is invited by God to ask for something. He requests wisdom, so God also promises him "riches, possessions, and honor" beyond compare. Settling in Jerusalem, Solomon negotiates brokerage agreements for trade with other kings, making profitable use of Israel's geographic location.

After four years, he decides to build a temple on the site designated by his father, David. Supplies are purchased from the same kings who provided the materials for David's palace. We see Solomon's wisdom in asking for artisans and craftsmen to come from other countries and enlisting workers from among the resident aliens in Israel—even making some of them overseers. In these ways he gives even foreigners a "stake" in the temple.

Psalm 121 is a song of utter confidence in God, a recital of God's vigilance and loving care. It echoes the request of Solomon for "wisdom and knowledge to go out and come in before this people" (2 Chronicles 1:10). Jerusalem is a high place dedicated unambiguously (at least for a time) to the God of the Jews.

In Romans 12, Paul urges his readers to think of their very lives as offerings—living sacrifices—made to God. What is "slain" in such sacrifice is conformity to the values and behaviors of the world, while a new understanding of what is acceptable to God is gained. There is no room for self-aggrandizement; in Christ we belong to each other and must be mutually supportive in the use of the gifts given to each. There are echoes of Jesus' Sermon on the Mount as Paul exhorts nonviolence and love in response to mistreatment. Enemies are to be won over by treating them with mercy and bringing them to holy shame.

QUESTIONS

Do you find coherence in the practical wisdom and political savvy of Solomon and in Paul's teachings on faithful response to enemies? How do they seem alike to you? Different?

Have you ever been brought up short by someone else's kindness or wisdom? What effect did it have on you?

PRAYER

Most gracious God, help us, like Solomon, to seek your wisdom and, like Paul, to seek new life in Christ. We ask it for the sake of your love. Amen.

Day 151

The Rev. Richard A. Lord
Rector
Church of the Holy Comforter
Vienna, Virginia

2 Chronicles 4–6, Psalm 122, Romans 13

The readings today speak of the power of sacred space to awaken our awareness of God.

The opening chapters of 2 Chronicles describe Solomon's ambitious building program and the central achievement of fulfilling the dream of his ancestor David with the building the Jerusalem temple. Today we read details of the temple's construction and its extraordinary splendor. When the building is completed, the leaders of Israel gather to offer sacrifice and worship. The priests bring the Ark into the Most Holy Place and find that they cannot adequately fulfill their liturgical roles because a billowing cloud—the numinous presence of God—fills the temple. Solomon's prayer of dedication reveals his astonishment that the God of all creation would dwell in a space built by human hands. Solomon prays that the temple will now become a place of divine encounter, a place of prayer, forgiveness, formation, and renewal.

The psalmist expresses gladness at the prospect of going to "the house of the Lord" (Psalm 122:1), where he will give thanks for the sheer goodness of being alive in God's world and pray for peace. In the passage from Romans, Paul exhorts his readers to be up and awake to what God is doing, to wear the clothing of Christ, and to embrace the work of love in the here and now.

Woven through these readings are images of beauty, holiness, and engaging worship. Whether in the context of a sacred space that is magnificent with artistic resources or a space that is simple and austere, we are led to a more conscious relationship with God in those moments and places when the transcendent is truly encountered.

QUESTION

When have you experienced worship that had the quality of God's presence "filling the temple"—the temple of your own mind and heart?

PRAYER

Gracious God, thank you for the gift and beauty of the sacred spaces I have seen and known in my journey of faith. You are worthy of thanksgiving and praise at all times and in all places, Creator of heaven and earth. Amen.

The Rev. Richard A. Lord
Rector
Church of the Holy Comforter
Vienna, Virginia

Day 152

2 Chronicles 7–9, Psalm 123, Romans 14

As he describes the completion of the temple and closes the story of Solomon's building campaign, the Chronicler offers a central theological conviction about standing in covenant relationship with the God of Israel. God will forgive and restore those under judgment when they *humble* themselves, *pray, seek* God's face, and *turn* from their wicked ways (2 Chronicles 7:14). These four verbs will figure prominently in the Chronicler's evaluations of the kings of Judah as further chapters unfold.

The psalmist directs his attentive gaze upward to the God whose "property is always to have mercy" (*The Book of Common Prayer*, p. 337). He reflects the spirit of the Chronicler's four verbs, humbly waiting and watching for mercy in the face of the scorn and contempt of the arrogant and proud.

In Romans 14, Paul urges his readers to unconditionally welcome all in the Christian community and to avoid judging those who observe their faith in ways that seem scrupulous in light of the grace revealed in the life and teaching of Christ. Instead of analyzing the validity of someone else's spiritual practice, we would do better to serve them so that they don't stumble according to what their conscience allows. God's loving reign is not about the food we eat or don't eat, the words we say or don't say, but about a distinctive way of being human—a way of deep goodness, deep trust, and deep joy nourished by the Spirit at work within us.

QUESTION

Prayerfully reread 2 Chronicles 7:13-14. Think of a group of people whose relationship with God needs restoring (e.g., your family, your faith community, your coworkers). How could you, as a part of these communities, begin to contribute to a restored relationship with God?

PRAYER

O God, I lift my eyes and my heart to you, asking that you would bestow mercy on those with whom I live and work today. Help me to humbly accept those with whom I differ and to do all I can to foster relationships of mutual respect and good will. Amen.

Day 153

The Rev. Richard A. Lord
Rector
Church of the Holy Comforter
Vienna, Virginia

2 Chronicles 10–12, Psalm 124, Romans 15

In today's reading from 2 Chronicles, the ideal of a united Israel ruled by a Davidic king and worshiping in the Jerusalem temple ends after Solomon's death, when the nation splits into two kingdoms: Judah in the south, comprised of the tribes which had remained loyal to David's house; and Israel, the ten northern tribes that broke away.

The Chronicler emphasizes that the destiny of the divided kingdom depends to a great extent on the genuine character of its leaders. Faithfulness and repentance yield forgiveness and restoration; complacency and arrogance yield judgment and captivity. What was true in the days of the divided kingdom is no less true for our nation and our world today. How critical it is that we choose wise and tested leaders whose moral character is observable in their respect for and treatment of others, especially those less fortunate than themselves.

The psalmist acknowledges that God's loyal love is the reason that of Israel survives the threats and attacks of her enemies. In God's strong name and by her own faithfulness, Israel will find a lasting help.

In the passage from Romans, Paul offers a unique insight about the essential purpose of Scripture. Paul doesn't write that Scripture provides us with a certain moral code or a theological approach to human life from which there is no deviation. Rather, Paul writes that the primary goal of reading Scripture is to foster encouragement and create hope in us (Romans 15:4-6). Paul prays "the God of hope will fill us with all joy and peace in believing through the Holy Spirit" (v. 13). Perhaps that should be our prayer whenever we approach Scripture and seek to hear the word that God is speaking into the fabric of our daily lives.

QUESTIONS

What personal qualities of character do you most admire in those called to lead the communities to which you belong?

Do you agree with Paul that the primary goal of reading Scripture is to create hope?

PRAYER

Most gracious God, may I find encouragement and hope as I continue to dwell in the transforming narratives of sacred Scripture. Help me to work its wise directives into the way I live, in my words, my judgments, and my actions, that I may be a blessing to others, for your glory and for the sake of the world. Amen.

Day 154: Enjoy hearing the Scriptures read aloud in church.

The Rt. Rev. Greg Rickel
Bishop of Olympia
Seattle, Washington

Day 155

2 Chronicles 13-16, Psalm 125, Romans 16

"But I want you to be wise in what is good and innocent in what is evil." (Romans 16:19)

Ah, if only it were so easy! I think most people do want "to be wise in what is good and innocent in what is evil." On this day, these two compartmentalized realities come to the forefront in every reading assigned. They are prevalent here because they are so prevalent in life. We cannot escape the conflict between these realities, as much as we try and as much as we pray that we be allowed to experience the good instead of the evil.

I may get in trouble here, but I would say both good and evil reside in all of us. The struggle we witness and hear of in Scripture today is just as real for each one of us as it was in the life of a biblical people striving to know God and to loyally follow God. We all know that struggle, which is why these narratives are so real and why they sometimes even seem repugnant to us. We don't want to believe people could be like that, and we surely don't want to believe we could be like that. But, of course, if you are reading this, you know it all too well, both in the context of community and within yourself. If you don't, then this narrative will mean little; but it does call us to look deeply at our role in the struggle of good versus evil, not ignoring the realities, but instead, along with our ancient ancestors, struggling, learning, and growing.

QUESTIONS

What does it mean to be "wise in what is good and innocent in what is evil"?

What story in contemporary life is 2 Chronicles similar to? What could we apply from the ancient story to the contemporary one?

PRAYER

God, help me to be wise in what is good and innocent in what is evil, this day and always. Amen.

Day 156

The Rt. Rev. Greg Rickel
Bishop of Olympia
Seattle, Washington

2 Chronicles 17–19, Psalm 126, 1 Corinthians 1

To be "like those who dream" (Psalm 126:1). Psalm 126 is one of the most beloved psalms. Like all of them, it is a melody. It is about journey, where one moves from carrying the seed to reaping the harvest, experiencing all the joy and struggle that comes with that process. Unlike much of the psalter, this psalm is of a happy time of hope and promise. It is a song of growth and strength.

One thing I love about this psalm is its connection with all we would finally know in Jesus. It seems to speak of the very kingdom he would come to tell us of and that we now strive for.

QUESTIONS

What does it mean to be "like those who dream?"

What can you identify with that begins as a seed and leads to harvest?

PRAYER

God, the lover of souls, help us to dream and to find the happiness that comes from knowing you and trusting you; and may our faith grow just as a seed becomes a mighty oak. Amen.

The Rt. Rev. Greg Rickel
Bishop of Olympia
Seattle, Washington

Day 157

2 Chronicles 20-22, Psalm 127, 1 Corinthians 2

In today's reading from his first letter to the Corinthians, Paul contrasts human wisdom with the true wisdom of God. Recently a friend showed me a photo of his four-year-old grandson, marching proudly in front of a procession at the end of the service one Sunday. He told me something like that happens on most Sundays, and how much he was learning from watching his grandson honor the worship going on around him, being in awe of it. My friend marveled at how his grandson would stop his restless playing with other things when the recessional began. Even at the age of four, he knew something important was going to happen, and he did not want to miss it.

I have experienced the same awe when I take an infant on a blessing tour around the church after a baptism. Many mothers and fathers are a bit nervous about that, mostly because they wonder if the child will behave, but I have never had a problem. Most of the children are spellbound by it all.

We can learn something from this. Children are not yet bound or burdened with human wisdom. Their cues come from the Spirit, and they follow them dutifully. They are miraculous teachers, leading the procession. We would be wise to follow.

QUESTIONS

What is the faith you remember having at the age of four? Or at your earliest memory?

What, through these readings, has been revealed to you by the Spirit?

PRAYER

Holy One, may we rely less on the wisdom we think we have, or that we think we must attain, and instead rejoice in the gift of the Spirit that leads us. Amen.

Day 158

The Rt. Rev. Paul Butler
Bishop of Southwell and Nottingham
Nottinghamshire, England

2 Chronicles 23–25, Psalm 128, 1 Corinthians 3

Children are generally hidden away in history—they are not seen as important. Yet, in today's Old Testament reading, Joash becomes king as a seven-year-old, and as a young person he leads a radical reformation and renewal amongst God's people. Amaziah treats the children rightly in his own day, whilst he is the young king. It is in later life that both kings lose their way and cease listening to the wise counsel of others and the word of the Lord.

The psalmist reminds us that children are a gift from God; they are a blessing, even if at times they are hard work.

We must honour the spiritual lives of children and encourage them to serve the Lord, recognizing that there will be times when they will lead us as well. For wise leadership is needed at all times. Paul understood this, and he saw it personified in his fellow worker Apollos. Unfortunately, the Corinthian Christians decided to set up these two men, along with Peter, as rival leaders. Paul knew that the gifts and talents of each leader were needed to enable the whole people of God to grow and mature.

We still are guilty of putting leaders onto pedestals and creating rival factions within the church. Yet in every church, and across our churches, we need the mutuality of gifts that come with different leaders. No one can do it all. Dividing on the basis of personalities or styles will never produce healthy churches.

QUESTIONS

How much do we recognise the gifts and value of children in our church and community?

What dangers of division on the basis of personality or talent exist where you are?

PRAYER

Lord, thank you for the blessing of children. Teach us to work together across all ages, that our lives may offer you the worship that you deserve. Amen.

The Rt. Rev. Paul Butler
Bishop of Southwell and Nottingham
Nottinghamshire, England

Day 159

2 Chronicles 26–28, Psalm 129, 1 Corinthians 4

Displaying humility before the Lord who made us and calls us into his service can lead to remarkable exploits, growth, and success, as the early years of Uzziah's reign (recounted in today's 2 Chronicles reading) reveal. Arrogance, however, leads people, notably leaders, into some very dangerous places. Uzziah's undoing is his pride; so, too, with Ahaz. We can try and mess with God, his holiness, and the glory of his name, and though in his patience he offers us opportunities to turn around and change, in the end we cannot play games with him. Those who dishonour God will find him cutting their cords.

Paul had been warned from the outset by the Lord that he would suffer much in his service as an apostle. Whether he had anticipated quite so much anguish coming from within the church is not clear. But he certainly discovered that apostolic leadership was not always appreciated or welcomed. The Corinthians had come to faith through his preaching, yet they turned toward others rather than Paul's leadership. In today's reading from 1 Corinthians, Paul sternly warns them, not about turning against him, but about turning away from the truth of the gospel of grace. Paul always saw his own position from a place of humility: he was only an apostle, through the grace of God.

Leadership has responsibilities; it is costly. Most of us are not rulers of nations or apostolic leaders, yet we all have God-given responsibilities. The question is whether or not we are being faithful to our own calling.

QUESTIONS

What responsibility has God given me? Am I being faithful to it?

Who is your "father in Christ"? Take time to thank God for her or him.

PRAYER

Lord, help me to live humbly in the light of the day when all will be revealed by you. Help me to be a faithful steward of all that you have given me. Amen.

Day 160

The Rt. Rev. Paul Butler
Bishop of Southwell and Nottingham
Nottinghamshire, England

2 Chronicles 29–31, Psalm 130, 1 Corinthians 5

The Chronicler's concern for the temple and the worshiping life of God's people shines through very clearly in these three chapters. Hezekiah is applauded for all that he does in reinstating the temple and ensuring that the worshipping life of God's people is once again brought back into line with the law.

As the people of the "new temple" (Jesus himself), the commitment to worship is central to our common life, and the concern that it be truly celebratory and worthy of the God who is loving and gracious to us is a clear challenge from this part of Israel's history. The people of Hezekiah's time recognised that generosity in giving was a central aspect of how they worshiped; indeed, so much was given that they had to create new storage space—how many church treasurers would love to have a similar problem today! Thus the people of God were experiencing the plentiful redemption and forgiveness that the Lord offers us all.

But such redemption and freedom from our iniquity has to lead to holy worship and holy living. In today's New Testament reading, we learn that the Corinthians have fallen prey to the twisted thinking that the liberty Christ brings allows libertarianism in lifestyle—specifically, an incestuous relationship, which Paul notes even unbelievers see as immoral. Paul is stern in his rebuke. He is clear that the lifestyle of Christ's people is to be holy and distinctive—not the holiness that cuts us off from the world, but the holiness that marks us as different. Indeed, Paul encourages the Corinthians to be engaged with all kinds of people so that Christ's redeeming love might be widely known.

QUESTIONS

How generous is our giving as part of our worship?

How might church discipline be exercised wisely today?

PRAYER

Good Lord, pardon all who set their hearts to seek you. We praise you, because with you there is forgiveness and plentiful redemption through Christ our Passover Lamb, sacrificed for us. Amen.

Day 161: Enjoy hearing the Scriptures read aloud in church.

The Rev. Canon Habacuc Ramos-Huerta
Secretary General of the
Iglesia Anglicana de Mexico
Mexico City, Mexico

Day 162

2 Chronicles 32–34, Psalm 131, 1 Corinthians 6

Those who are just will inherit the kingdom of God. And what about those who are not? In today's reading from 1 Corinthians, Paul says that "wrongdoers will not inherit the kingdom" (1 Corinthians 6:9).

In every generation we are called to find the kingdom of God: some generations get closer to it and others go far from it. It would be too risky for this humble servant of God to try to determine what level of justice we are experiencing in different regions of the world today. Some would say that justice cannot be perfect, and, of course, if we go arguing every nuance, then we tend to make all things imperfect instead of looking at the better side of the matter.

Today and always, someone who is just is always searching for justice; but does justice mean to be impartial or to give each person what he or she deserves? Justice is blind, it is said. I am not sure of that. When we close our eyes and pretend not to see what is going on in the local community or the world, we send a clear message that we don't care. My hope is that we don't forget that we as Christians are called to make a difference, to build up the kingdom of God here and now on earth.

Justice is right there in front of us: this is not something subjective. The level of consciousness, the striving to meet goals, the way we do things is so relevant. We are not only in a world with nice concepts or ideas; we are in a world where we have, at a personal level, a very important role. Justice for all is not a slogan; it is something we should always pursue. Justice for those who look for a better life, trespassing across borders in the search for a well-paid job; justice for those who work hard every day in order to get what they need or to send their daughters and sons to university; justice for those who are unheard when they cry out for a change in politics to reverse climate and environmental problems; and justice for those seeking peace.

QUESTIONS

Have you been involved in a peace march or other activity to promote justice?

What do you do to promote justice at home within your family?

PRAYER

Gracious Father, we are your creatures, but we have built up walls and barriers in our lives that have made us walk in different paths. Help us to find ways to encounter our sisters and brothers in need, and give us the willingness to act with justice all the days of our lives. Amen.

Day 163

The Rev. Canon Habacuc Ramos-Huerta
Secretary General of the
Iglesia Anglicana de Mexico
Mexico City, Mexico

2 Chronicles 35–36, Psalm 132, 1 Corinthians 7

You may have heard about the Millennium Development Goals. There are eight, and the first on the list is "End Poverty and Hunger." The Anglican Church in Mexico is contributing to that goal. A wonderful project run by St. Paul's Anglican Church in San Miguel de Allende, Guanajuato, serves breakfast from Monday to Friday to about three thousand kids at several kindergartens and elementary schools in the surrounding area. What began as a social ministry on the streets about thirty years ago is now a great example of what can be done in partnership with local organizations. The challenge is everywhere we look, and we are called to take action now.

Psalm 132 says, "The Lord has chosen Zion; he has desired it for his habitation" (v. 13). Zion is in many ways the people of God in every generation. We are Zion, and we have been chosen by God; we are his place to dwell, and he will give us plenty of bread and feed our souls and bodies; and he will dress us with salvation.

I remember my childhood. Dad and Mom used to go to work meetings every month a little far from home. My mother would get up early to cook food for the three of us so that we could have our meal before they returned. We shared her food with our friends, and Mom used to get pretty upset when she saw that there was no food left.

Years later I laugh about our early experiences—I wish people would act like little kids, sharing what they have, but I see people not willing to share. I see also in our current world that we are being measured as if we were all made of the same character, but no, we are different, every one of us is unique, and we all are loved by God no matter what!

QUESTIONS

Do you participate in any kind of project to help the hungry?

Do you act like a child sometimes, at least for fun?

PRAYER

Most merciful God, don't pay attention to our failures. Give us courage to share your infinite love with our neighbors close to home and far beyond. Amen.

The Rev. Canon Habacuc Ramos-Huerta
Secretary General of the
Iglesia Anglicana de Mexico
Mexico City, Mexico

Day 164

Ezra 1–3, Psalm 133, 1 Corinthians 8

The psalm for today has been a favorite of mine for many years. I can say it by memory, like the canticles for Morning Prayer or Vespers that become so familiar during the days of seminary that you end up saying or singing them while driving or writing or walking. "Oh, how good and pleasant it is, when brethren live together in unity" (Psalm 133:1).

Unity? What is that all about? The love of God has to have an effect in our lives and, of course, in the life of the church. But then we find that we all are human, and we make mistakes, and do what we don't want to do, and say what we don't want to say, and act the way we don't want to act, and finally we find ourselves struggling, fighting, and probably thinking, "I will go away—I don't want to have anything to do with my brother or sister in Christ."

But wait! It is important to sit, to be quiet, to reflect. I suggest reading Psalm 133 and accepting the invitation to receive the fine oil on our head, like the dew of Hermon, and to refresh our existence.

In 1 Corinthians 8, Paul writes, "Now about food sacrificed to idols: we know that 'we all possess knowledge.' But knowledge puffs up while love builds up. Those who think they know something do not yet know as they ought to know. But whoever loves God is known by God."

So, if we love God we are known by him, and this love should direct us straight to the question: what is love for, if we are not willing to live with our neighbor who thinks radically differently? If we believe in God, we have the greatest challenge, and this is to love unconditionally. Unity is love, and love is unity.

QUESTIONS

Have you been tested in hard situations when you must make a decision and there are few options?

How do you act when something controversial or difficult is being discussed: argue, fight, or just leave?

PRAYER

Dear God, give us love and knowledge, and help us to use them to make a better world. Amen.

Day 165

The Most Rev. Dr. Thabo Makgoba
Archbishop of Cape Town
Cape Town, South Africa

Ezra 4–6, Psalm 134, 1 Corinthians 9

Freedom and liberty are hallmarks of the gospel of Jesus Christ, as Paul stresses to those to whom he writes in today's 1 Corinthians reading: freedom from having life ordered by rules and regulations that we are incapable of keeping, and freedom from the consequences of such failures and from the wider power and consequences of sin and death.

But today Paul also reminds us that liberty does not mean license to behave in whatever ways we wish. In yesterday's chapter, Paul promised to give up meat, to avoid upsetting people by eating what was sacrificed to idols. Now he reminds the Corinthians how he also supported himself while he was with them, giving up any expectation that they should support him and Barnabas. Yet he expresses frustration that by curtailing his freedom, his rights, they have devalued him and his teaching and taken it all for granted.

But nonetheless, he will keep on doing all this to preach the gospel, which he feels impelled by God to do. He is prepared to be "all things to all people" (1 Corinthians 9:22) so that his hearers may more readily grasp the good news of Jesus Christ. And, like a runner in a race, he will not give up doing the right thing—nor, he says, should we. All of us should have such dedication.

Our Old Testament chapters recount similar dedication to doing the right thing among the exiles returning to Jerusalem to restore life and worship there, first during the reigns of Persian emperors Cyrus and Darius and later under Artaxerxes. They do not resort to the bullying and bribery exercised by those opposed to their efforts to rebuild the temple, but trust in the Persian authorities to see that justice is done.

And once again they were able to worship in the temple, conscious of being in the presence of the Lord, "lifting up their hands in the sanctuary" (Psalm 134:2), as today's psalm says.

QUESTIONS

Are there areas in your life where you might choose not to exercise your freedom as a Christian, so as to help others find and grow in the faith? And, in contrast, are there areas where you take for granted or exploit such commitment in others?

PRAYER

Lord Jesus, you gave up the glories of heaven to save us. Help me to not "demand my rights" but to strive for the prize that comes through sharing your good news. Amen.

The Most Rev. Dr. Thabo Makgoba
Archbishop of Cape Town
Cape Town, South Africa

Day 166

Ezra 7–9, Psalm 135, 1 Corinthians 10

In today's reading from 1 Corinthians, Paul has more to say about not confusing liberty with license. Saying that "'everything is permissible" is very different from saying that "everything is helpful." When facing choices, we need to give far more weight to asking, "What helps others?" We are not independent individuals with no responsibilities beyond ourselves and our own desires. As Christians, we are reminded of this whenever we share the Lord's Supper and hear Paul's words again: "We who are many are one body, for we all partake of the one bread" (1 Corinthians 10:17). In Christ, our lives are intimately connected with those of other Christians, and our choices must reflect this.

We must also be aware of how our words and actions affect those outside the church and avoid "causing them to stumble" (1 Corinthians 10:32). This does not mean that others exercise a veto over our lives, but it does call us to live with sensitivity. When wondering what others will make of us, we need to ask whether what we do and say will be understood as "all for the glory of God" (1 Corinthians 10:31).

In our Old Testament chapters, we read how Ezra came to Jerusalem, several decades after the first wave of returning exiles. His priority is to restore faithful worship, mirrored in faithful lives. He is appalled by the unfaithfulness he finds, which he sees reflected in the many marriages to neighboring women of other religions. He demands these men separate from their wives (who, according to Persian practices, would have retained custody of the children). To us, this seems very harsh—and indeed, Paul tells Christians to stay with unbelieving spouses who do not oppose our faith (1 Corinthians 7:14-15). But the underlying principle remains to challenge us: is there coherence in our faith—does it reflect Jesus and glorify God and give praise to him (as in our psalm) for all to see, across the whole of our lives?

QUESTIONS

What sort of "giving up" or "putting aside" by your Christian community might help communicate the good news of Jesus Christ more effectively to the society around you?

What church practices are not seen by outsiders as being "for the glory of God"?

PRAYER

Dear Lord, help me to be someone who doesn't just talk the talk, but walks the walk, following you both within the church and for the whole world to see. Amen.

Day 167

The Most Rev. Dr. Thabo Makgoba
Archbishop of Cape Town
Cape Town, South Africa

Ezra 10, Psalm 136, 1 Corinthians 11

The gospel of Jesus Christ comes to all cultures with a message of both judgment and hope, and the difficult question is discerning which applies where.

For most of us today, it goes without saying that God can and does use women in Christian leadership alongside men, gifting individuals by the Spirit for particular tasks that do not reflect one gender or another. Given that in Scripture, the position accorded women is often one of far more equality and justice than in contemporary society (for example, from Deborah in Judges 4 to the gospels), it would be surprising if the church were to lag two millennia behind secular practice.

But the key objective for Paul in this chapter from 1 Corinthians is to ensure holy, reverent worship, especially when Christians gather to celebrate the Lord's Supper (which here may have been combined with a "bring-and-share" meal). Therefore, self-promotion by any cliques, showing off wealth, hierarchies that belittle the poorer and less influential, or anything else that undercuts the message of Jesus' self-giving sacrifice for all is a disgrace. Such behavior has no place within Christian living. In a world that elevates to celebrity status the rich and powerful, this is very countercultural. But the key, says Paul, is for us to emulate him and the best of Christian leaders and their teachings, just as they follow the example of Jesus Christ.

And so, when I read with sadness the final chapter of the Book of Ezra, I wonder how many of the unrecorded wives and children went away knowing that the refrain of Psalm 136, "God's love endures forever," held true for them personally. I recall how another foreign wife, Ruth, was the grandmother of King David, recorded in the genealogy of Jesus (Matthew 1:5). And I also recall Paul's words from another letter, "There is no longer Jew or Greek, there is no longer slave or free, there is no longer male and female; for all of you are one in Christ Jesus" (Galatians 3:28).

QUESTIONS

Where do you find the greatest challenges to living counterculturally?

In what ways does receiving the Lord's Supper help you to reflect the example of Jesus?

PRAYER

Lord, open my eyes so I may see where the norms of life that I take for granted run counter to your gospel, and help me to live by your standards, not those of my culture. Amen.

Day 168: Enjoy hearing the Scriptures read aloud in church.

The Rt. Rev. Michael Perham
Bishop of Gloucester
Gloucester, England

Day 169

Nehemiah 1–3, Psalm 137, 1 Corinthians 12

Today Paul is leaving behind his teaching about *eating* the bread that is Christ's body to think instead about *being* the body of Christ. "Discerning the body," which is what he wrote about in 1 Corinthians 11:29, now becomes a matter of understanding oneself to be a limb or organ of the body, crucial to its well-being, but only in relation to others and always in relation to the head, Christ himself.

Paul wants us to explore the body's diversity. Not everyone has the same gift. The Spirit is at work differently in the variety of people who make up the body. But Paul's principal point is to remind us that, whatever the diversity might be, there is only one body, and by our baptism we were called into that one body. Having a sense of belonging to the body is crucial. The truth is, of course, that the body of Christ, the church, is broken, injured, and wounded by misunderstanding and strife. Rebuilding is needed. Much of 1 Corinthians is about that rebuilding.

Nehemiah is dealing with a similar problem. It's the fifth century before Christ, and Jerusalem has been destroyed. Rebuilding the city will also rebuild the self-respect and the sense of identity of the nation, and Nehemiah sets about the task. Just like the limbs and organs of the body, the priests and Levites bring their differing skills to the task. They work almost as one body as they rebuild.

QUESTIONS

What are the areas of life where God is asking you to do some rebuilding?

The variety of the Spirit's gifts sometimes seems to cause disunity in the church. How can you ensure that your gifts deepen the unity of the Body of Christ?

PRAYER

Holy Spirit, come, renew your gifts within me and make them instruments of unity in the building up of the body of Christ our Lord. Amen.

Day 170

The Rt. Rev. Michael Perham
Bishop of Gloucester
Gloucester, England

Nehemiah 4–6, Psalm 138, 1 Corinthians 13

In today's Old Testament reading, Nehemiah is continuing to rebuild the city walls. The task is daunting, the opposition determined, the need to guard against attack real, and even the support of the Jewish community cannot be taken for granted. That Nehemiah succeeds and the wall is completed says a lot for his energy, generosity, and determination.

Nehemiah is clearly a man of faith and of hope. Those virtues sustain him through all the undermining and opposition. What you don't see in him is much love. You certainly don't see it in his opponents, some of whom even want to kill him—and all of whom resent this wall building and hurl insults at the workers. Nehemiah wants the plotters given over as plunder; he doesn't want their sins blotted out.

This is where the New Covenant and the teaching of Paul are so very different. Paul values faith and hope—they will, he says, last forever—but he adds love, and because he is a follower of Jesus, he means love for God but also for neighbour and even for enemy. Love, he says, is the greatest of the three. At the end of chapter 12 of Corinthians, Paul said that he would show us a still more excellent way, and this is that excellent way: love. It's almost as if all who have gone before, even the activist Nehemiah, have understood God's purposes only as "in a mirror, dimly," but now in Jesus, face to face, we can see that the purpose of God ultimately is love.

QUESTIONS

Loving an enemy is a tall order. Can you identify someone who is akin to an enemy—someone who opposes you—and think through prayerfully how you might love them?

Can you add to Paul's long catalogue of characteristics of love? How would you finish the phrase "Love is…"?

PRAYER

Holy God, in you I put my faith, in you I place my hope, in your overflowing love I receive the grace to love. Help make that love strong in me. Let your love flow through me. Amen.

The Rt. Rev. Michael Perham
Bishop of Gloucester
Gloucester, England

Day 171

Nehemiah 7–9, Psalm 139, 1 Corinthians 14

In today's readings, both Nehemiah and Paul turn to worship. Nehemiah does so with a holy day, a week of festival, a solemn reading of the law to the assembly, and a long prayer of national penitence. For Paul it is more a matter of trying to ensure that all the elements that make up worship—speaking in tongues, interpreting, prophesying, hymns, readings, revelations—come together to create something worthy of God and edifying for the worshipers. The overall aim is that "all things should be done decently and in order" (1 Corinthians 14:40).

You might at first think that both writers are concerned only with ensuring that every-thing goes smoothly, that worship is beautifully performed. But it isn't so. Nehemiah wants the people to listen so intently to the reading of the law that their hearts are touched. Indeed, this happens. They are moved emotionally to grief and weeping by what they hear. Paul wants the worshipers to be able to say "God is really among us" (1 Corinthians 14:25). The outward form is there in order to shape the spirituality of the people, so that they may be genuinely in touch with God and receptive to him. They need to bring to worship the deep feelings of the heart expressed in today's psalm:

"O Lord, you have searched me and known me. You know when I sit down and rise up; you discern my thoughts from far away. You search out my path and my lying down, and are acquainted with all my ways" (Psalm 139:1-3).

QUESTIONS

How do you bring the deep longings of your heart into the church's worship—an undercurrent of spirituality that ensures the service is not just about the words and rituals on the surface?

The reading of the law in a solemn assembly in the public square moved the people of Nehemiah's day. How can the Christian Scriptures be effectively proclaimed outside the church today?

PRAYER

Holy Beloved God, open my heart and make our worship Spirit-filled, transforming of our lives, and beautiful for you. Amen.

Day 172

The Rev. Canon Joseph Galgalo
Vice Chancellor, St. Paul's University
Limuru, Kenya

Nehemiah 10–12, Psalm 140, 1 Corinthians 15

The opening chapter of Nehemiah painted a grim picture. A situation of despair, loss, and ruin was depicted. Nehemiah received the depressing news that "the survivors are in great trouble and disgrace." Taking it hard, he wept and mourned, but through fasting and prayer he kept hope alive.

In today's reading (chapters 10–12), a story of amazing recovery, celebration, and hope begins to unfold. Nehemiah, through faith and godly devotion, exemplary leadership, courage, and hard work, and with God's help, turns the situation around. We see how unwavering faith in God inspires hope and draws out achievements beyond imagination. When we look at life from the vantage point of faith, hope is stirred, and it is possible to see infinite possibilities in God's world and thereby bring light and life into situations that often spell death and gloom.

1 Corinthians 15 presents the hope of resurrection, without which our faith is in vain. Human existence is inauthentic, a story of despair, loss, and ruin if death has the final say. The biblical doctrine of the resurrection of the dead is of utmost importance, yet it is seen by many as incredible. As Paul here says, without the hope of resurrection, our faith is futile: "if only for this life we have hope in Christ, we are to be pitied more than all" (v.19). If we believe in the power of God, it is not difficult to see that resurrection is not only possible but also plausible. The promise of resurrection gives us hope, the courage to face each new day, and the boldness to believe in possibilities beyond imagination.

QUESTIONS

Is the biblical doctrine of resurrection reasonable?

Would the Christian faith be any different had Christ not been resurrected from the dead? How?

PRAYER

Gracious God, thank you for hope and courage in the face of all adversity, and for the blessed assurance of eternal life, through Jesus Christ, the resurrection and the life. Amen.

The Rev. Canon Joseph Galgalo
Vice Chancellor, St. Paul's University
Limuru, Kenya

Day 173

Nehemiah 13, Psalm 141, 1 Corinthians 16

Today's reading from Nehemiah is about commitment. It reminds me of the familiar fable of the chicken and the pig. Motivated by the desire to please their master, and at the chicken's behest, the pig *offers* bacon and ham while the chicken only *contributes* eggs to their master's breakfast table. The difference between the pig and the chicken is that while the pig is totally *committed,* the chicken is only *involved*. The point of the story is that real commitment calls for sacrifice.

It may sound odd to us that Nehemiah condemned mixed marriages. A close examination of this text, however, shows that the situation called for total commitment. Entrusting the reforms to a mixed group raised the real danger of religious apostasy and could have compromised the desired outcome. Tobiah's eviction (v. 8) can be seen in the same light. Faced with the task of rebuilding not only the physical infrastructure but also the people's faith and a covenant community, Nehemiah needed to raise the standard, and this required not just a token contribution but a real sacrificial offering.

Our New Testament reading, addressing an ethnic mix of believers, shows how unity across context and cultural or racial divides can be achieved through common faith in Christ. The closing chapter of 1 Corinthians begins with a plea for contributions to a gift basket for needy Christians in Jerusalem. Toward the close of the chapter, just before sending his final greetings, Paul shifts emphasis from involvement to commitment: "Be on your guard, stand firm in the faith" (v. 13). Pursuance of a genuine life of faith calls for a sacrifice beyond simple involvement. Faith is itself a gift from God, and the appropriation of that gift demands nothing less than total commitment to God. We may choose to determine the level of our involvement in or contribution to the church, but, in the words of the hymn, "Love so amazing, so divine, demands my soul, my life, my all."

QUESTIONS

Do you think Nehemiah was justified in forbidding mixed marriages under the circumstances? Did this injunction have any relevance for the intended reforms?

PRAYER

Merciful God, graciously grant us the will and the strength to give of ourselves and to live only for you as we should, through Christ, the merciful high priest. Amen.

Day 174

The Rev. Canon Joseph Galgalo
Vice Chancellor, St. Paul's University
Limuru, Kenya

Esther 1–3, Psalm 142, 2 Corinthians 1

The opening chapter of 2 Corinthians reads like the memoir of a troubled soul: "the hardship we suffered"; "we were under great pressure"; "beyond our ability to endure"; "we despaired even of life"; "we felt the sentence of death." One could ask, "How bad could it get?" By the same token, the Book of Esther begins with a story I am tempted to entitle "Trouble in Paradise." Death and danger lurk amidst the royal festivity and merrymaking. Queen Vashti is banished, a plot to assassinate King Xerxes is hatched, and a plan to exterminate the entire Jewish community is devised.

These accounts provide powerful testimonies of hope in the face of adversity and despair. They are stories of great deliverance. These testimonies are particularly inspirational in showing how God is often at work against forces of evil. The troubles of life are a sure reminder of our limitations and the fact of our dependency and finitude. Great challenges often humble us to acknowledge God's help, which lifts us to levels we would otherwise not reach. This is Paul's testimony: "But this happened that we might not rely on ourselves but God, who raises the dead. God has delivered us from such a deadly peril, and he will deliver us" (vv. 9b, 10).

We may never fully understand why the world is full of painful experiences and why life is often such a depressing affair. It is possible, however, to grasp by faith the glorious truth that God is able to turn desperate situations into ones of hope and triumph. The possession of this truth, or lack of it, can make all the difference in how we approach life's challenges.

QUESTIONS

Do you see power and greed at play in the story of Esther? How is it possible to see this as a story of hope?

What encouragement or inspiration can we take from Paul's testimony?

PRAYER

Thank you, God, for your constant help in all our troubles, and for your mercies that are new every morning, through Christ our Good Shepherd. Amen.

Day 175: Enjoy hearing the Scriptures read aloud in church.

The Rev. Dr. Cynthia Kittredge
Professor of New Testament and Academic Dean
Seminary of the Southwest
Austin, Texas

Day 176

Esther 4–6, Psalm 143, 2 Corinthians 2

"For if you keep silence at such a time as this, relief and deliverance will rise for the Jews from another quarter, but you and your father's family will perish. Who knows? Perhaps you have come to royal dignity for just such a time as this" (Esther 4:14).

This marks the dramatic moment when Esther, favored member of the harem of King Ahasuerus, shifts from being a person who is acted upon to one who acts decisively and effectively. Mordecai's provocative exclamation about Esther coming to royal dignity expresses the sense of divine destiny.

Yes, this is indeed the critical time for Esther. This colorful biblical book shows how she rises to the occasion and becomes an unexpected hero. Unable to use direct means to gain her objective, even though she has been made queen, Esther, as a female member of a subordinate group (who is keeping her Jewish heritage secret), must use care and subterfuge to prevail in risk and danger. Knowing the king's character, she appeals to his emotions. She proclaims a fast and prepares to confront the king. Attired in her queenly robes, she gains Ahasuerus's favor and develops her strategy to defeat Haman and save her people.

Reading this Jewish novella, we root for the underdog, Esther, and take delight in her eventual triumph against all odds. The plot twists and turns, and whatever spiritual lessons are to be learned come through melodrama, entertainment, and humor. Sometimes human ingenuity and creativity are required to realize God's purposes.

QUESTIONS

What unexpected heroes have you known in your own life?

Times of crisis call forth extraordinary courage. Has your own character or that of another been transformed by severe challenge?

PRAYER

Holy One, grant us in extreme times perceptive wisdom and strenuous courage; in Jesus' name. Amen.

Day 177

The Rev. Dr. Cynthia Kittredge
Professor of New Testament and Academic Dean
Seminary of the Southwest
Austin, Texas

Esther 7–8, Psalm 144, 2 Corinthians 3

"Then Queen Esther answered, 'If I have won your favor, O king, and if it pleases the king, let my life be given me—that is my petition—and the lives of my people—that is my request'" (Esther 7:3).

As elsewhere in the Hebrew Bible, a woman is at the center of this story of deliverance. Through courage and trickery, Shiprah and Puah saved the Hebrew babies from being destroyed at birth. Miriam saved Moses from death as a child and celebrated Israel's salvation in the exodus. Rahab, the Canaanite heroine, saved the Jewish spies and came to represent both works (James 2:25) and faith (Hebrews 11:31). Often, women played the role of trickster figures who use cunning to prevail in the patriarchal society depicted in the biblical world.

Esther, a Jewish woman who advanced in the court of a foreign king, served as an example for Jews in the Persian diaspora, who had to maintain their identity and survive under the domination of foreign rulers. Just as a woman must resort to unorthodox strategies to thrive in a male-dominated society, so must Jews possess extraordinary skill and virtue to make it as members of a minority group in a Gentile world.

Reflecting on the long history of the Jewish people under foreign rule is an inspiring and useful exercise for Christians who have for a long time enjoyed majority status in Western society. When we Christians can no longer take our role as the dominant culture for granted, we may be asked to take risks and to work within hostile power structures, as Esther did to save her people.

QUESTIONS

Do you identify with the female hero of this tale of faith and action? If so, how?

If you do not identify with Esther, what do you learn from her story?

PRAYER

Holy and Loving God, you have saved your people throughout history, and you continue to work for our healing and salvation. Look with your blessing and power upon all those who are oppressed. Help us to work with you for freedom. Amen.

The Rev. Dr. Cynthia Kittredge
Professor of New Testament and Academic Dean
Seminary of the Southwest
Austin, Texas

Day 178

Esther 9–10, Psalm 145, 2 Corinthians 4

Paul writes of himself and his coworkers in ministry: "We are afflicted in every way, but not crushed; perplexed, but not driven to despair; persecuted, but not forsaken; struck down, but not destroyed; always carrying in the body the death of Jesus, so that the life of Jesus may also be made visible in our bodies" (2 Corinthians 4:8–10).

These words have comforted people of faith of every age. They continue to offer sustenance to communities that are persecuted and afflicted.

Although rejection, disappointment, failure, and danger threaten to make sufferers lose heart, Paul is honest about the strength of the opposition and utterly secure in God. Paul grounds his confidence in God's mercy, the integrity of the ministry he shares with his partners, and the knowledge that Jesus is Lord. He uses the vivid image of treasure in "clay jars" or "earthen vessels" (as the King James Bible says) to assert the strength of God and the fragility of humanity. Paul's words express simultaneous confidence and humility as he claims the power of the gospel.

Even though it is sometimes hidden, in every adversity God's power is working, just as the light of creation shines in the darkness. Paul finds in the pattern of Jesus' death and resurrection the pattern of his own life. Life issues out of death: the life of Jesus, visible in the bodies of believers (2 Corinthians 4:10), in mortal flesh (v. 11); "so death is at work in us, but life in you" (v. 12).

Scripture records these words as those of Paul. But they have become words with liturgical and spiritual significance apart from this singular person. When you come, in Paul's letters, to exclamations, laments, or praise that particularly strike you, read them aloud, and then repeat the reading as many times as seems right to you. Imagine them in the mouths of those for whom you care. Let them become your words; let them speak for you.

QUESTIONS

How are clay jars a good metaphor for human beings?

How does the pattern of Jesus' life and death express itself in the pattern of your life?

PRAYER

God of power and might, thank you for the witness of faith of Paul and his coworkers. Thank you for the words of Scripture. May they become our words, our faith, our joy. Amen.

Day 179

The Rt. Rev. Mark MacDonald
National Indigenous Bishop
Anglican Church of Canada
Toronto, Ontario

Job 1–3, Psalm 146, 2 Corinthians 5

Initially, modern readers will find it difficult to enter the world described in the Book of Job. Though the circumstances are exotic, Job's careful attempts to avoid spiritual risk and danger have strong counterparts in the modern obsession to avoid physical, financial, and spiritual distress. Job is best understood by the modern person whose way of life, structured to avoid risk, collapses in an illness, the death of a loved one, or the failure of a business.

Job's response of faith is stunning, a window to the character of a great person. A statement of faith and praise in the face of tragedy, it appears to be a sincere acknowledgment of the gifts of life and the God who gives them. At this point, Job humbly restrains himself from making a human judgment on the ways of God in the world.

Faith in God's ways in the world is a theme of our other passages: the difficulty of being faithful in the midst of an often tragic and corrupt world and, at the very same moment, the affirmation of God's help to us in the midst of that difficulty.

Contrasting the ways of God to the deceptive appearance of human power, Psalm 146 praises God, whose faithful trajectory of justice and mercy to the oppressed is the great and final story of Creation and history. Second Corinthians 5 identifies this trajectory with the life, death, and resurrection of Jesus, whose identification with us has given us a new identity and reveals our destiny in God. Yes, we still groan under the weight of a deceptive and dying counter-reality. But God has not only demonstrated the power of the world to come in the history of Jesus; we also have, through the Spirit, a foretaste of the life to come—a foretaste that empowers us to share its reconciling goodness with the world.

QUESTIONS

Where do you see the ways of God in the world?

Where do you see the ways of God in your own heart and history?

PRAYER

O God of unchangeable power and eternal light: Look favorably on your whole church, that wonderful and sacred mystery; by the effectual working of your providence, carry out in tranquility the plan of salvation; let the whole world see and know that all things are being brought to their perfection by him through whom all things were made, your Son Jesus Christ our Lord. Amen.

The Rt. Rev. Mark MacDonald
National Indigenous Bishop
Anglican Church of Canada
Toronto, Ontario
Day 180

Job 4–6, Psalm 147, 2 Corinthians 6

Like many of the stories that illuminate the life of indigenous peoples, the story of Job functions at quite a few levels of meaning and complexity. Modern Western readers, used to considering things at only one level, may misunderstand a passage like yesterday's second chapter of Job, assuming it is a description of the world view of some ancient primitive mind. On the contrary, the book of Job is a thick description of a complicated topic: humanity's tense and precarious relationship with God in the midst of a world of good and evil, tragedy and blessing.

Chapters 4–6 introduce another element into this profound and intricate mix: the family and friends who are so much a part of the blessings of life can complicate, even hinder, our healing. Their love and loyalty, so cherished in the good times, will often mean that they cannot face the pain of beholding such suffering. In those moments when human affection and community are bent out of shape by suffering, what has been dear can become a threat.

The praise of Psalm 147 shows its author to be acutely aware of the saving and blessing presence of God. Paul, in 2 Corinthians 6, is also aware, but as with our passage in Job, here we are forced to face a challenging paradox: we are saved by a vividly perceptible intervention of God, all too often experienced in the midst of suffering and pain. The saving and satisfying presence of God thrusts us into a pattern of responsibility and, dare we say it, a pattern of suffering that is a recreation and representation of the life of our Saviour. Ultimately, the meaning of suffering is found in the one who suffered with us and for us. Not that this answers all questions neatly or directly, but it is an answer, as we shall see in the rest of Job, that comes through living, praying, and even questioning.

QUESTIONS

How have you interpreted suffering in your own life?

In what ways have friends been a help or a hindrance in your suffering? In your Christian faith?

What is your relationship to the suffering of Jesus?

PRAYER

Heavenly King, the Comforter, the Spirit of Truth, present everywhere and filling all things, treasury of blessing and giver of life, come and dwell in us. Cleanse us of every impurity and save our souls, you who are good. Amen.

—A TRADITIONAL PRAYER
OF THE ORTHODOX CHURCH

Day 181

The Rt. Rev. Mark MacDonald,
National Indigenous Bishop
Anglican Church of Canada
Toronto, Ontario

Job 7–9, Psalm 148, 2 Corinthians 7

The lament of Job is one of the great expositions of human suffering. It is a poem of pain so intense, so vivid, and so personal that his friends cannot bear to listen to it, as we will learn in the next chapters. The lament is still painful to read, but, in our case, that is most likely due to our personal recognition of the sentiment. Anyone who has suffered intensely will identify with the feelings of Job. It is the cry of every person, at some point in their life. It is the cry of Jesus upon the cross.

Psalm 148 is welcome after Job's cry of pain. It is also a reminder of the real dimensions of our relationship to Creation through the goodness of God. Even Job will eventually return to this at the end.

Also a welcome reminder, after reading Job, is the confidence that Paul expresses in 2 Corinthians 7, even in the midst of pain and conflict. In his own suffering and even in the suffering he may have caused others, Paul clings to the promises that God has given him. We should understand that these promises embody much more than a feeling that everything will eventually be all right. The promises are our destiny, demonstrated in the death and resurrection of Jesus, which is not only proclaimed by his followers, but is also vividly experienced in the sacramental life of Christian faith. The promises of God in Jesus call us to courage and hope in the face of difficulties. They also pledge us to a life of compassion, a life we share with all those who live in the promises of God in Christ.

QUESTIONS

Can you remember times when you have felt like Job? How did you overcome those times?

In what ways is Jesus' cry on the cross similar to the lament of Job? What does this mean?

PRAYER

May the power of your love, O Lord, fiery and sweet as honey, wean my heart from all that is under heaven, so that I may die for love of your love, you who were so good to die for love of my love. Amen.

—Francis of Assisi

Day 182: Enjoy hearing the Scriptures read aloud in church.

The Rt. Rev. Stephen Andrews
Bishop of Algoma
Sault Ste. Marie, Ontario

Day 183

Job 10–12, Psalm 149, 2 Corinthians 8

"'I am sickened of life," laments Job in today's Old Testament reading (Job 10:1). It is not just the calamities he has suffered that have brought him to this point. It is the senselessness of it all. The prophets marvel that God has fashioned us as a potter would purposefully mould his clay. But Job can't understand why the divine purpose for his life would seem to be destruction. So, bitterly, he pours out his complaint.

Then a new figure emerges among Job's so-called friends. Zophar the Naamathite remonstrates with Job. He chides him for his insolence, saying that God in his mystery is inscrutable: "Can you fathom the perfection of the Almighty?" (Job 11:7). Zophar has a point. Indeed, it is a point that God himself will make to Job at the end of the story.

But Zophar speaks of God as a smug seminarian might, rigidly applying his propositional truth. He should have stopped with his affirmation of God's enigmatic ways before concluding that Job was being recompensed for some iniquity. Job understands this reasoning all too well, and yet the reality is that "those who provoke God live safe and sound."

By contrast, Paul in 2 Corinthians 8 urges his readers to be generous in providing relief for the poor in Jerusalem. There is no meditation here on what the Jerusalem Christians might have done to deserve their poverty and no profound existential questions are asked. The emphasis is simply on imitating Christ's generosity. He who was "rich for our sake became poor, so that through his poverty we might become rich." The proper Christian response to the suffering of others is not to rationalise it but to enter into it. When we listen with empathy, devote ourselves to heartfelt prayer, and look for ways to alleviate need, even to the point of personal sacrifice, we become God's agents in bringing light into a dark world.

QUESTIONS

In periods of personal trial and suffering, what responses from others have helped you the most?

How does our generosity toward others bring benefit to ourselves?

PRAYER

Be pleased, O Lord, to use me in comforting and relieving those who suffer, that in my care they may come to know your healing love. Amen.

Day 184

The Rt. Rev. Stephen Andrews
Bishop of Algoma
Sault Ste. Marie, Ontario

Job 13–15, Psalm 150, 2 Corinthians 9

"We must be well pleased with God as a friend even when he seems to come forth against us as an enemy," Biblical scholar Matthew Henry wrote about today's reading from Job. While this is a wise word for the faithful who suffer, it is not really Job's meaning. Job is not affirming his trust in God so much as he is steadfastly declaring the injustice of his affliction. And he will not be bullied into a false admission of guilt by Eliphaz—or by God.

While he acknowledges that he is not perfect, it is deeply troubling to Job that his adversity is out of all proportion to his offenses. Indeed, he hints at a kind of perversity in a God who would leave him in his misery without offering him hope.

It is not difficult to understand Job or even to admire him. While our sense of what is just is often skewed, particularly as it affects ourselves, it is nevertheless deeply seated in our consciousness. "That's not fair!" my kids used to complain. And, of course, I would respond, "Life's not fair!" But the complaint is legitimate, and Job's honesty before God is an example for all who suffer.

At some point Job will come to understand that in God's economy, justice is ruled by grace. This is the economy that lies at the base of Saint Paul's understanding of generosity in today's reading from 2 Corinthians. Those who give without compulsion will find God multiplying their gifts, "swelling the harvest of their benevolence" (2 Corinthians 9:11) and spilling over into thanksgiving.

QUESTIONS

Is it better to accept or remonstrate against life's unfairness?

Is your generosity rooted in an economy of justice or an economy of grace?

PRAYER

In hardship or in happiness, in poverty or in plenty, teach me to praise thy name, O Lord. Amen.

The Rt. Rev. Stephen Andrews
Bishop of Algoma
Sault Ste. Marie, Ontario

Day 185

Job 16–18, Psalm 1, 2 Corinthians 10

Today's reading from Job keeps the theme of justice before us. Job still presses for justice, only this time he does not look to his wearisome consolers or even to God directly but to some sort of heavenly witness who can arbitrate on his behalf. He does not realise that there is in fact a courtroom drama underway, with an adversary prosecuting him before the divine throne. As far as he can tell, his protestations of innocence are not being heard on high, and it is certain that he can find no one on earth who will champion his cause before God.

Bildad's callous response, "It is the wicked whose light is extinguished," is a truth that resonates with the last part of today's psalm: "The way of the wicked is doomed." Job himself can affirm this, but it only amplifies our despair. For if God heeds not the innocent, what hope have the sinful?

Thankfully, we have the "comfortable words" of Saint John: "If any one sin, we have an advocate with the Father, Jesus Christ the righteous" (1 John 2:1). There is One who has a personal acquaintance with our moral dilemma and now represents us within the eternal Godhead (Hebrews 4:14-16). He whose loving sacrifice secured our redemption now pleads for us before the seat of a merciful and gracious God. What is more, Christ's work is supplemented by the Holy Spirit, whom Jesus called *"another* Paraclete" (John 14:16), who also intercedes for us.

Paul, in 2 Corinthians 10, is not unaware of this cosmic dimension. He acknowledges that the conflict in Corinth that preoccupies him is, ultimately, not of this world. He teaches us that in meeting evil, error, and the power of darkness, the Christian requires spiritual weapons. Chief among these is the truth of the gospel, which destroys human pride, confounds deception, and brings every thought captive to Christ.

QUESTIONS

How confident are you in your prayers? What is the basis of your confidence?

Does the knowledge that Christ and the Holy Spirit are our advocates change anything for you?

PRAYER

Father, in your mercy look on us in our weakness; and for the glory of your name turn from us all evils. Grant that in all our troubles our whole trust and confidence may be in you; and that we may always seek to serve you in holiness and purity of life to your honour and glory. Amen.

Day 186

The Rt. Rev. Duncan Gray III
Bishop of Mississippi
Jackson, Mississippi

Job 19–21, Psalm 2, 2 Corinthians 11

In today's reading, Job continues to shake his fist at the heavens and demand a just accounting of his life. As far as he can tell, the wicked prosper while the righteous, himself included, suffer unspeakable injustice. His so-called friends are, as has been noted earlier, no help whatsoever, even as they utter traditional pieties about getting what you deserve in life. Job will have none of the clichés that pass for the wisdom of his tradition. "There is nothing left of your answers but falsehood," he shouts at Zophar the Naamathite (Job 21:34).

And yet, in the midst of his agony, convinced that the universe has conspired to destroy him without cause, Job finds the courage to turn his face toward God. The extraordinary gift of Job is his understanding that even if God is, indeed, the source of what has befallen him, God is also his ultimate hope.

Thus, we have in the midst of Job's seemingly unheard cry for justice those great words that create the chorus of hope that begins the Episcopal liturgy for the Burial of the Dead: "I know that my Redeemer lives and at the last he will stand upon the earth…I myself shall see, and my eyes behold him who is my friend and not a stranger" (Job 19:25-27).

Saint Paul is also angry, not so much at God but at the people of Corinth for the ways in which he sees them perverting the gospel he has preached and lived among them. Like Job, Paul is quite capable of sarcasm, and it is evident throughout 2 Corinthians. This is not the way things should have worked out, he seems to be saying—a lament rather similar to Job's.

Life does appear so very unfair at times. In our world, the evil prosper too often to suggest that justice always triumphs. And who has not seen the fruit of his or her labors corrupted by those who do not understand or do not care?

QUESTION

Paul uses anger, sarcasm, and his own keen wit to respond to a church in Corinth that had drifted far from his earlier teaching. How do you respond to dramatic and potentially destructive changes in matters in which you have invested much of your life?

PRAYER

Gracious Lord, make us deeply aware of the frailty of all things. Give us eyes to see you in the midst of all sorrow and courage to ever hold to you as our hope and redemption. Amen.

The Rt. Rev. Duncan Gray III
Bishop of Mississippi
Jackson, Mississippi

Day 187

Job 22–24, Psalm 3, 2 Corinthians 12

After an admonition from Eliphaz the Temonite that he admit his guilt and submit to divine punishment, Job cries out to the emptiness of a universe where God cannot be found (Job 23:3, 8-9). This deep desire to defend himself against his accusers is all the more tragic because the source of his hope has vanished.

Here is both the agony of an inaccessible God and the fear of divine encounter (23:16-17). In the beginning of chapter 24, Job's lament expands beyond himself as he sees what he imagines as God's sovereign indifference toward so much more than his own life.

Psalm 3 begins with a lament not unlike that of Job's, but, unlike Job, the psalmist is assured of God's vindication.

Paul wrestles with the questions of gifts given for ministry and how they should be used. While he is aware that his own training, his post-conversion life experiences of suffering witness, and a powerful mystical moment of revelation (2 Corinthians 12:1-6) give him authority to preach and teach, he is also aware that it is out of his own weakness that God might be more fully known (12:7-10).

I suppose that sense of being ultimately alone is common to many. It is the source of the deepest human despair. Samuel Beckett's *Waiting for Godot* wrestles with that same existential reality as the two main characters wait in vain for the arrival of Godot. And if God is present, God sure seems asleep at the switch.

My state and diocese have known failure and brokenness (poverty, bigotry, natural disasters) far more often than we have known success and power. Yet it is from this tragic history that extraordinary literature, music, and religious faith have come. We know something about God's grace being made perfect in our weakness.

QUESTIONS

When have you felt most alone? Where was God known within that loneliness?

What were those moments in your life when your gifts and strength failed you and it was through your weakness and vulnerability that Christ entered?

PRAYER

Precious Savior, may the loneliness and failures of our lives be an acceptable sacrifice offered to you, and may your power be made perfect in our weakness. Amen.

Day 188

The Rt. Rev. Duncan Gray III
Bishop of Mississippi
Jackson, Mississippi

Job 25–27, Psalm 4, 2 Corinthians 13

Scholars have noted many problems with the order of the text in Job 25–27. Some of the words ascribed to Job seem more consistent with those of his friends, and the reverse may also be true. Nonetheless, Job continues his basic argument that he has lived with integrity, his accusers are wrong, and he will profess his righteousness always (Job 27:1-6).

Psalm 4 is a prayer for the deliverance from enemies and may have been a part of a liturgical rite that included sleeping in the temple (v. 8). Its appropriateness for the evening is evidenced by its use in the service of Compline in *The Book of Common Prayer*.

In the final chapter of 2 Corinthians, we find Paul being clear about his return to visit the community of Corinth. Presumably, a previously canceled visit had resulted in the deterioration of his relationship with the community, a breach that is at the heart of much of this epistle. Paul worries about what he may find upon his return—"quarreling, jealousy, anger, selfishness, slander, gossip, conceit, and disorder" (2 Corinthians 12:20).

He also recognizes that there may be a need for discipline for those who "fail to meet the test" (2 Corinthians 13:5). As Paul deals with the very concrete demands of leadership, we can see a dynamic tension between his deep tenderness toward Corinth (13:9) and his willingness to be quite severe in his discipline (13:10).

This boundary setting is something that every parent must learn to do. Setting limits for the sake of love is never easy but is absolutely essential for the healthy development of the child. So, too, in our relationship with God, these limits, though often abused even by the well-intentioned, are an essential building block for spiritual maturity.

QUESTIONS

What is required for you to "lie down and sleep in peace"?

Where have you discovered the boundaries imposed by God's love?

PRAYER

Deliver me, O Lord, from the pursuit of my own needs that blinds me to your love. May I find you ever near that I may rest eternally in your peace. Amen.

Day 189: Enjoy hearing the Scriptures read aloud in church.

The Rev. Randolph Marshall Hollerith **Day 190**
Rector
St. James's Church
Richmond, Virginia

Job 28–30, Psalm 5, Galatians 1

Today's reading from Job begins with a poem about the mysterious nature of wisdom. Many have suggested that these verses contain some of the most beautiful poetry in all of Hebrew Scripture. Here the poet ponders the origin of wisdom. If everything has a source, where does wisdom come from? It can't be purchased or forged from the earth. Human beings often lack it. Only God knows wisdom's source, and therefore only God is really wise. Job suffers for reasons he cannot understand. The wisdom of suffering eludes him. It is beyond his comprehension.

Like Job, the author of Psalm 5 cries out to God to hear him and protect him from his enemies. The psalmist may be surrounded by evil, but he knows that God is just, and in the end evil will not be allowed to stand. Therefore, both Job and the psalmist trust God, praise God, and live in fear and awe of God, seeking always to do God's will. Only then can they live wisely.

The Christian community in Galatia had heard about Paul's former life as a Pharisee. Paul was infamous as a man who had reached the pinnacle of Jewish society, both in education and position, and then left all that behind to spend his life proclaiming the good news of Jesus Christ. For many of Paul's contemporaries this must have seemed like a foolish, crazy decision. But Paul knew that God's wisdom is different from the world's wisdom. It wasn't crazy to give up everything to follow Christ; for Paul it was the only wise thing he could do once he had been called by God and set apart. Like Job and the psalmist, Paul knew that only by remaining true to God's will for his life could he find any wisdom, any peace, any purpose.

QUESTIONS

In your own life, have you been able to find peace during those times when life does not make sense? Can you see how God's grace was present to you even when life was most confusing?

Can you think of other figures in the Bible who did things deemed foolish by the world's standards and yet who were wise in the ways of God?

PRAYER

God of all wisdom, grant me the faith to cling to you most tightly when my life makes least sense. Help me to see your grace in all things, that trusting in your wisdom I might dare to be a fool for Christ. In the name of the Father, and of the Son, and of the Holy Spirit. Amen.

Day 191

The Rev. Randolph Marshall Hollerith
Rector
St. James's Church
Richmond, Virginia

Job 31–33, Psalm 6, Galatians 2

At the beginning of chapter 31, Job mounts a defense of his own blameless life. He defends himself against a litany of possible transgressions, including adultery, lying, greed, injustice, lack of compassion, idolatry, violence, and wickedness. He proclaims that he is innocent of all offense and would certainly defend himself if only God would bring an indictment against him.

In Job's mind, if he had sinned, if he had broken God's law, he would deserve punishment. But since he is blameless, obedient of God's law, he deserves blessing and vindication. Job wants simple cause and effect, but he learns that God's ways are rarely simple. Like the author of Psalm 6, all Job can do is look to God to heal him and redeem his life. Only God can save him, and Job wonders how long he will have to suffer for reasons beyond his understanding.

In the second chapter of Galatians, Paul proclaims to his readers that it is not our obedience to God's law that makes us righteous because as sinful human beings our obedience is impossible. No matter how hard we try to be righteous, the fact is we all sin; we all fall short of the glory of God. Therefore, the law cannot redeem us because we cannot keep it. The law only serves to reveal our sinful natures. For Paul our justification (being made right with God) is a gift of grace given through our faith in Jesus Christ. Job may have been a righteous person, but we are not. We are dependent on the grace of God as revealed in the death and resurrection of Jesus.

QUESTIONS

When things go wrong in your life for no apparent reason, when something bad happens that you did not cause and do not deserve, where is God in all of that for you?

Paul says that he has been crucified with Christ. What does he mean? What part of Paul has died?

PRAYER

Loving God, there is so much in this life we do not understand. Our vision is limited, and we see life through a mirror dimly. Grant us your peace, that we might rest in your grace and trust in the reconciling work of our Lord Jesus Christ. Amen.

The Rev. Randolph Marshall Hollerith
Rector
St. James's Church
Richmond, Virginia

Day 192

Job 34–36, Psalm 7, Galatians 3

The author of Psalm 7 proclaims, "The Lord judges the people" (v. 8) and "God is a righteous judge" (v. 11). In Job, Elihu argues that "God will not do wickedly, and the Almighty will not pervert justice" (Job 34:12). Both the psalmist and Elihu believe that God is just and will judge people fairly. God will judge what is evil and will establish what is righteous. We may not understand why suffering happens, but we can trust that God will not let evil stand; justice will prevail.

In the third chapter of Galatians, Paul continues to make his case that if God were to judge us fairly, based solely on our behavior, then God's justice would condemn us all. But the wonderful truth Paul has come to understand is that the grace of God found in Jesus Christ frees us from condemnation. When we are baptized we literally put on Christ: we are clothed with Christ and all else falls away. In the waters of baptism we die to one way of life and rise to a new life. We die to a life of sin, and we rise to a life of grace. It is not that we are able to live sin-free after baptism, but sin no longer defines our lives. We are no longer a prisoner of our sins. Now we are one in Christ.

The great joy of our faith is that because of Jesus we have been made into the children of God. We are not condemned; we are loved. We are not judged for our sins but given new lives and invited to be imitators of Christ. Christ offers himself for the life of the world, and in that sacrifice we discover not condemnation and judgment but forgiveness, love, and grace.

QUESTIONS

Have you known the joy of being loved fully and deeply in spite of your shortcomings? Who in your life has been the bearer of that kind of love for you? Are you the bearer of Christ's love for others?

Read Genesis chapter 15 again. What did Abraham do that was "reckoned to him as righteousness"? Did he simply believe in God? What role does trust play in Abraham's righteousness?

PRAYER

Lord Jesus, help me to trust not in my own righteousness but in your gracious love. Give me the joy of knowing that in you there is always life and hope and peace. Daily draw me closer to you that I might learn to walk in your ways. Thank you for the gift of this day. May I use it wisely and always to your glory. In Christ's name I pray. Amen.

Day 193

The Rev. Richard Kew
Author and Development Director
Ridley Hall
Cambridge, England

Job 37–39, Psalm 8, Galatians 4

I have vivid memories of a clear, dark Tennessee night when a small group of us lay on a grassy hillside watching a meteor shower. The starry heavens were breathtakingly beautiful, and if Psalm 8 did not come to mind at that time, it ought to have done! Each year new discoveries show how vast and complex the universe actually is, far larger than the author of Psalm 8 ever imagined—but despite this, then and now we cannot help but wonder at the majesty and magnificence of it all. Just trying to grasp its magnitude demonstrates what it means for God to be "Almighty."

Yet the psalm is not so much about the heavens but about those of us made in God's image who people the earth. The psalmist is showing us in this prayer to the Creator and Sustainer of all things that we are precious and that we matter, not just "in bulk" but as individuals. We may seem to be a tiny part of God's vast creation, but we are fearfully and wonderfully made. We are, as Paul describes it, heirs with a special place in the divine heart, created a little lower than angels but redeemed through the death and resurrection of the Son and equipped by the Spirit to be servants and stewards.

Therefore, I matter to God enormously, and so do you. This means it is important how I live my life today, whether I am suffering like Job, vacuuming the floor, peeling potatoes, managing a major project, or changing a baby's diapers. Within this context the Lord God hears our prayers, listens, and responds—because we matter. Indeed, "God's name is majestic in all the earth!" (Psalm 8:9).

QUESTIONS

How will my actions and thoughts today demonstrate that I matter enormously to God?

How do the cross of Christ and the fact that I matter so much to God fit together?

PRAYER

Lord God, in all that I do and all that I am, may I show forth the refrain of the psalmist that God's name is majestic in all the earth. Amen.

The Rev. Richard Kew
Author and Development Director
Ridley Hall
Cambridge, England

Day 194

Job 40–42, Psalm 9, Galatians 5

Some people are not really sure they like the idea that when God justified Job at the end of all his struggles, he restored all that Job had lost, and then some. Furthermore, Job lived into a deep and satisfying old age. I do not find this at all embarrassing, especially when read beside Psalm 9. Perhaps the preeminent divine characteristic in the tale of Job is the Lord's faithfulness to this faithful man, who certainly experienced a whole range of agonies and emotions when incomprehensibly tested to the uttermost.

In light of his experience, I doubt Job would have been troubled by the psalmist's words. When our backs are up against a wall, when troubles seem to have the upper hand, when we think that we are drowning and going down for the third time, then the Lord is our refuge in time of trouble (Psalm 9:9). Over and over again, the message of the psalm is that the Lord can always be relied upon, even if our full awareness of his protection is only there when we look back at the darkness from a safe distance.

While Paul in Galatians 5 talks eloquently about living a life empowered by the Spirit and bringing glory to God, the psalmist is telling us God is behind the security that enables us to walk in the way of the disciple. This makes the words of verse 10 resonate: "Those who know your Name will put their trust in you, for you never forsake those who seek you, O Lord."

In a world where relationships are often very fragile, this is not only comforting and gratifying but explains why the psalmist launches into his prayer with wholehearted thanksgiving.

QUESTIONS

How do you react when you are passing through a rough patch in life and everything seems to be against you?

What does Psalm 9:10 mean for the way you live your life?

PRAYER

Lord, you are my refuge in time of trouble. Let me never forget to hide in you. Amen.

Day 195

The Rev. Richard Kew
Author and Development Director
Ridley Hall
Cambridge, England

Proverbs 1–3, Psalm 10, Galatians 6

Deficits are something we have been learning a lot about in recent years, and the lessons have not been easy. We have discovered that financial deficits have profound consequences. Yet the Book of Proverbs focuses our attention on the fact that there is a huge and growing surplus of knowledge in our information-driven world, while at the same time there is a growing deficit of wisdom.

In the opening chapters of Proverbs, and in several different ways, the point is made that wisdom originates with God Almighty, and that we are only likely to find it if we take seriously what it means to be in fellowship with God. The contrast is not only drawn between the wise and the foolish, but the point is incisively driven home: "Trust the Lord with all your heart…be not wise in your own eyes…honor the Lord with your wealth… do not despise the Lord's discipline" (Proverbs 3:5-11), and so forth.

There is an echo of these words in Galatians 6, where Paul, drawing upon his own wisdom from above, challenges us to consider our lives to be fields where seed is sown: is it seed whose crop is corruption, or is it seed fertilized by the wisdom of the Spirit, enabling us to reap crops that are from God and bear fruit from time into eternity? Are our lives sowing the wind or the whirlwind?

Having asked us to think in these terms Paul then leads us to the cross in the last paragraph of his letter to the Galatians. The fear of the Lord might be the beginning of wisdom, but we meet wisdom incarnate and personified in Jesus, at the foot of his cross and where the stone is rolled away from the empty tomb.

QUESTIONS

If the source of wisdom is the triune God, then why are Christians so often unwise, even stupid, and sometimes worse?

Which of the images or sayings about wisdom make the most sense to you from Proverbs 1–3?

PRAYER

Lord God, give me the wisdom that comes from walking faithfully in the footsteps of Jesus Christ. Amen.

Day 196: Enjoy hearing the Scriptures read aloud in church.

The Rt. Rev. Gregory Cameron
Bishop of St. Asaph
St. Asaph, Wales

Day 197

Proverbs 4–6, Psalm 11, Ephesians 1

I was paid a compliment once: "You're so wise." Not true, but a big compliment! In the Book of Proverbs, to be wise is to understand how life works, how to be fulfilled; and wisdom comes from studying God's ways and learning to walk in them. These chapters (a father's advice to his son) cover the same ground all parents worry over: the speaker is blunt about sex, debt, laziness, and the company that young men keep. But there's a deeper message as well: being faithful to the handmaid of God's wisdom will bring greater blessing than any superficial pleasures. These words speak to us today, asking if we really do allow our lives to be guided by God's wisdom.

Psalm 11 follows a similar theme: God is the most powerful source of security in life.

The Letter to the Ephesians could be called "The Charter of the Church." It sets out the sweep of God's plans from creation to the place of Jesus as Messiah and the life of God's people. When people talk about the church, they often use words from Ephesians. This language is so developed, and so unlike Paul's words elsewhere, that many scholars agree that the letter was more probably written by his followers, despite the opening verse.

God acts to bring blessing to his people, and Ephesians 1 sets out the promises contained in his plans. It reveals a God lavishing spiritual blessings on his people. We have been chosen, forgiven, gifted, and given a hope and a destiny. The writer prays for God's good gifts to be experienced by God's people. It's an invitation for you and me. But note this too: God's plan was revealed in and through Jesus. It is "in him" that these plans have been established. It is in knowing Jesus and following him that we get woven into God's plans and destiny.

QUESTIONS

What are the real values on which we base our lives?

What do the promises and plans set out in Ephesians 1 mean to you? How might they encourage you in your own journey of discipleship?

PRAYER

Lord God, you are an eternal refuge, and in Jesus, you plan the very best for your people. Help me to live into your promises and walk in your ways. Amen.

Day 198

The Rt. Rev. Gregory Cameron
Bishop of St. Asaph
St. Asaph, Wales

Proverbs 7–9, Psalm 12, Ephesians 2

Sex is still at the forefront of the thoughts of the writer of chapter 7 of Proverbs, which presents a colourful picture of the perils of adultery, expanding on yesterday's theme but hinting at the contrast between wise and foolish ways to live. It's not surprising, then, that in chapters 8 and 9 we find one of the greatest pictures of wisdom in Scripture. Here God's wisdom is personified as a feminine virtue standing alongside God, calling people to maturity and understanding. It's no wonder that the greatest church in the Christian Byzantine Empire, Hagia Sophia, was dedicated to "Holy Wisdom." Many people see a hint of Jesus in this passage, or the Holy Spirit, but the key verse is surely chapter 9, verse 10: this is the road to a full life.

Many of the psalms focus on the enemies that threaten us, and if we live in a country where Christians are persecuted, these passages will come alive for us. Some of the early Christian writers thought that the enemies described here weren't real people but rather the sins that complicate our lives and bring us down. Whichever way you understand the enemies in Psalm 12, the promise is clear: in the teaching of God's words, there is advice that will give us confidence to face life.

In Ephesians 2, the apostle makes a contrast between the way things were before Jesus and the way things are because of God's actions in Christ. He speaks to new Christians who used to be outside of God's promises to his people, without a sense of God's blessing. Through the actions of God in Jesus, however, when Jesus takes up all the brokenness of the world in the sacrifice of the crucifixion, God's mercy is poured out. In accepting that gift, sin is put to death, and we are raised with Jesus to new life.

QUESTIONS

Try and sum up the greatest lessons for living that you've gained over the years—are they a reflection of Holy Wisdom?

What difference does being a Christian make to your life? How do the riches of God's grace show themselves to you?

PRAYER

Show me, Lord, the wisdom on which I can base my life. Help me to abandon things that are destructive to my well-being and in your words and grace to find nourishment for the future. Amen.

The Rt. Rev. Gregory Cameron
Bishop of St. Asaph
St. Asaph, Wales

Day 199

Proverbs 10–12, Psalm 13, Ephesians 3

In the biblical tradition, Solomon is the quintessence of human wisdom, received as a gift from God. These chapters in Proverbs purport to offer a collection of his key sayings as they were handed down and remembered, and each verse stands in its own right. Aphorisms range across many subjects, from advice about honest conversation to suggestions for honest trading. There's a common thread—the way in which we relate to other people is important, and a high standard of personal behaviour reaps its rewards. Integrity is a key element in faithful living.

The psalms speak to the full range of human experience, and today's psalm is for those times when everything seems to be going against us. When times are at their toughest, we need to be on our knees, seeking God's help, and asking for a calm and trusting spirit.

The heart of Paul's ministry is revealed in Ephesians 3 (either his own recollection or another's testimony to its profound effect). Paul was called to proclaim how God's mercy had been made universal, for all people, in the action of Jesus. For the writer of Ephesians, God had always planned to bring reconciliation into the world: the plan was suddenly unveiled in Jesus' sacrificial death, and Paul was called by God to proclaim that truth and that invitation as far and wide as he could. However, there's both a summons and a promise for us as we read this chapter: will we put down deep roots in God's love by spending time in prayer, reflection, and study? In Christ, God offers us the power to win the promise of holiness in our lives.

QUESTIONS

Which of the proverbs of Solomon says the truest thing about your own experience of life?

What are the practical ways in which you pause in life to put down roots in God's love?

PRAYERS

Help me, Lord, to steer a right path through life. Make me honest in my actions and my dealings with other people. Keep me in touch with you and conscious of your blessings. Amen.

Day 200

The Rev. Chip Edens
Rector
Christ Church
Charlotte, North Carolina

Proverbs 13–15, Psalm 14, Ephesians 4

Our Scriptures today invite us to consider what it means to grow in our relationship with God. It's tempting to think that being a Christian is simply a matter of believing or not believing. The fundamental question, though, is not merely, "What do I believe?" The real question is, "How do I live now that I believe?"

I remember when I was new to the faith, and I felt a subtle form of performance anxiety about being a Christian. I thought that by being a Christian, I must do "all the right things." As a result, there were seasons in my life when I felt guilty and unworthy. One of the great gifts the Book of Proverbs offers is the reminder that we are human—that it is even a gift to be human. Trying to be anything else is self-defeating. "The wisdom of the sensible is to understand his way" (Proverbs 14:8).

"But the Lord is our refuge" writes the psalmist (Psalm 14:6). As our refuge, God pulls us back from the temptation to think we must be perfect. Instead, God's desire is to use us, our brokenness as well as our gifts, to teach us how to love. God's desire is not that we live a flawless life but a life of compassion, generosity, and obedience. One translation of the word "obedience" actually means to live "from the heart." I love the image of a person mindful of his or her humanity, living a generous, wholehearted life.

The reading from Ephesians invites us to consider the call to "no longer be children" but to "grow up in all aspects into him who is the head, even Christ" (Ephesians 4:14-15). As you consider this awesome call, remember that the real test is not whether or not you become perfect. The real test is whether or not you are willing to let God work within and through your humanity to share the light of his love with this world.

QUESTIONS

What does it mean to live your life as a Christian?

Do you see your past as an obstacle to being a vessel of God's grace?

Have you ever considered your brokenness to be the gift through which God can work to allow you to understand and embrace others?

PRAYER

God, you have created us in your image. Help us to see our humanity as a gift. In our humility, help us to share with others the good news of your grace, forgiveness, and love. Amen.

The Rev. Chip Edens
Rector
Christ Church
Charlotte, North Carolina

Day 201

Proverbs 16–19, Psalm 15, Ephesians 5

Our lessons today invite us to consider what it means to do the will of God.

Years ago I heard something that caused me to think deeply about my prayer life. A friend and I were talking about how we prayed. He said, "Most of my prayers seem to center around asking things of God. I guess I need to begin to pray more about what God is asking of me." It stopped me in my tracks. Like him, I realized most of my prayers were about asking God for what I wanted. He then said something I will never forget: "We need to make sure we never turn God into a vending machine."

We also need to be careful that we do not go to the opposite extreme: never praying for what we need. Jesus asks us to pray for what we need. But equally important is the need to listen.

One of my favorite stories is about Saint Francis. A man who was captivated by the saint's holiness decided to follow him around to see what made him so special. Late one afternoon he followed Francis to his cell in the monastery where he lived. The man was fascinated by what he witnessed. Francis fell to his knees and prayed simply, "Not my will but thy will." He apparently said that prayer for hours.

"Many plans are in a man's heart, but the counsel of the Lord will stand," says Proverbs 19:21. The invitation of God is to, yes, pray for what we need. We might also work to create the space we need to seek God's will and listen for God's guidance and direction. It is by listening that we discover God's voice and learn how to walk in the light and become "imitators of God" and followers of Jesus.

QUESTIONS

How often do you pray? How many of your prayers are about what you want? How often you do you pray to do God's will?

Have you created a place in your daily routine to listen for God's voice?

PRAYER

Lord, our lives are filled with needs and busyness. Help us to pray that your will be done in our lives, and give us the courage to follow where you lead us. Amen.

Day 202

The Rev. Chip Edens
Rector
Christ Church
Charlotte, North Carolina

Proverbs 20–22, Psalm 16, Ephesians 6

Today's passages invite us to think about where we find strength for the journey we must take in life.

Conventional wisdom says that if you are going to find the strength to face the challenges in life, you must first find it within yourself. Be strong! Don't give up! Work harder! You can do it! We have heard these words many times.

Yet the wisdom of Solomon and the psalms challenges these hollow words. "The glory of young men is their strength, and the honor of old men is their gray hair" (Proverbs 20:29). Indeed, while we may have felt invincible in our younger days, we learn as we grow older that we are quite mortal. While initially this insight may bring concern—when we realize through sickness and hardship just how mortal we are—the insight is actually a gift because we become aware that God can and must be our source of strength in this life.

"Because he is at my right hand, I will not be shaken. Therefore my heart is glad and my glory rejoices" (Psalm 16:8). What joy we feel when we discover that God can be our source of strength in times of trouble! When we are weak, God is strong.

There are times that we will doubt this truth. Therefore, it is essential, as the writer of Ephesians suggests, that we be fervent in prayer, opening ourselves to the love of God, who has the capacity to breathe life into us through the Holy Spirit. As we open ourselves, we will discover a strength that comes not from us but from God, whose greatest desire is to strengthen us with the armor of love.

QUESTIONS

Have you ever thought it was up to you alone to get through life?

What are your greatest assets that you can call upon in times of need? How might God become your strength?

What would it mean for you to trust and rely on God's power in your life?

PRAYER

God, you are God and we are not. Help us to see the limits of our power and the limitless power of your love. Amen.

Day 203: Enjoy hearing the Scriptures read aloud in church.

The Rev. Canon Jan Naylor Cope
Vicar of the Washington National Cathedral
Washington, D.C.

Day 204

Proverbs 23–25, Psalm 17, Philippians 1

In Acts 16:6-10, Paul receives what is known as the Macedonian call. He has a vision of a Macedonian man pleading with him to "come over to Macedonia to help us." Paul immediately sets sail from Troas and makes his way to Philippi. On the sabbath, he encounters Lydia, a purveyor of purple cloth, and she receives and accepts the Good News from him. Lydia and her household are baptized, making them the first European converts.

Since Philippi was his first church in Europe, it is not surprising that the tone of Paul's letter to the Philippians is marked by joy and tenderness for a community that is clearly dear to him. Paul is writing from prison, and he uses the letter to both reassure the faithful that his imprisonment is not impeding the spread of the gospel and to embolden them to continue to "live your life in a manner worthy of the gospel of Christ" (Philippians 1:27) and to "in no way [be] intimidated by your opponents" (1:28).

Some nineteen hundred years later, the Rev. Dr. Martin Luther King Jr. used his own imprisonment to reassure the faithful and to embolden his followers to stand fast in the face of persecution and struggle. In his 1963 "Letter from a Birmingham Jail," Dr. King referenced Paul's Macedonian call and said he was compelled to carry the gospel of freedom beyond his own hometown. "Injustice anywhere is a threat to justice everywhere....But the judgment of God is upon the Church as never before. If today's Church does not recapture the sacrificial spirit of the early Church, it will lose its authenticity, forfeit the loyalty of millions, and be dismissed as an irrelevant social club with no meaning for the twentieth century."

What do the courage and example of Paul and Martin Luther King Jr. have to say to the church today?

QUESTIONS

When has the boldness and courage of another's witness strengthened your faith? How have you responded?

PRAYER

Gracious God, help us to be inspired by the examples of the saints before us in order to be emboldened in our own lives and witness as disciples of Christ. Amen.

Day 205

The Rev. Canon Jan Naylor Cope
Vicar of the Washington National Cathedral
Washington, D.C.

Proverbs 26–28, Psalm 18:1-20, Philippians 2

In today's reading from Philippians, we see Paul shift his focus from his own imprisonment to exhorting the congregation to be in unity and purpose as a church: "be of the same mind, having the same love, being in full accord and of one mind" (Philippians 2:2). Paul begins to marry the theological identity of the community with the ethical demands that emanate from those relationships. "Do nothing from selfish ambition or conceit, but in humility regard others as better than yourselves. Let each of you look not to your own interests, but to the interests of others. Let the same mind be in you that was in Christ Jesus" (2:3-5). The poetry and pairing of the undesirable and desirable attributes is beautiful, but how does one put those ethical demands into practice?

Paul points to the example of Christ, who "emptied himself" (v. 2:7) to take on human form and who humbled himself to the point of death on the cross for our salvation. This theological notion of *kenosis* or "emptying" was posited in the eighteenth century as an explanation for how the Incarnation could be possible; it said in essence that Jesus "made space" in the midst of his divine attributes for his humanness to coexist. Paul exhorts the community to follow Christ's example, and he reminds them that "it is God who is at work in you, enabling you both to will and to work for his good pleasure" (v. 2:13).

Matthias Grünewald's Isenheim Altarpiece depicts a heartwrenching crucifixion. Jesus is hanging on the cross, and John the Baptist is pointing to Christ saying, *Illum oportet crescere, me autem minui*—"He must increase but I must decrease" (John 3:30). As was true for John and the Philippians, it seems that part of our answer lies in being ready to empty ourselves, enabling the very spirit of God to work in and through us.

QUESTIONS

What are the things that fill us, preoccupying and preventing us from emptying space for God to work in and through us?

From what things do you specifically need to fast in order to make space and time available for conversation and communion with Christ?

PRAYER

Holy and loving God, help us to see the things in our lives that need to be relinquished, and give us the courage and strength to do the internal "housekeeping" that will best equip us to serve you. Amen.

The Rev. Canon Jan Naylor Cope
Vicar of the Washington National Cathedral
Washington, D.C.

Day 206

Proverbs 29–31, Psalm 18:21-50, Philippians 3

In today's reading from Philippians, Paul takes on a markedly different tone, warning of the dangerous influence of others and presenting his own life and example as the better path. In an allusion to Greek foot races, Paul writes, "I press on toward the goal for the prize of the heavenly call of God in Christ Jesus. Let those of us then who are mature be of the same mind; and if you think differently about anything, this too God will reveal to you. Only let us hold fast to what we have attained" (Philippians 3:14-16).

This particular passage calls to mind the 1981 film *Chariots of Fire*, which was based on a true story of two athletes in the 1924 Olympics. One of the athletes, Eric Liddell, was born in China of Scottish missionary parents, and his devout sister disapproved of his plans to pursue competitive running. Liddell, however, saw running as a way of glorifying God. As he explained, "I believe that God made me for a purpose. But he also made me fast, and when I run, I feel his pleasure."

On his way to the Olympics, Liddell learned that his race was scheduled for a Sunday, and he refused to compete, despite enormous pressure, because his Christian convictions prevented him from running on the sabbath. One of his teammates, however, yielded his place in a race scheduled for the following Thursday. On the Sunday he was supposed to race, Liddell preached a sermon on Isaiah 40:31: "But those who wait for the Lord shall renew their strength, they shall mount up with wings like eagles, they shall run, and not be weary, they shall walk, and not faint." Liddell went on to win a gold medal, but his convictions remind us that we are to hold fast to what we have attained in Christ, keeping the first things first.

QUESTIONS

When have you been pressured to do something that was in conflict with your Christian convictions?

How did you respond? If you resisted, what enabled you to "hold fast"?

PRAYER

Gracious God, thank you for the gifts you have given us for the upbuilding of your kingdom. Help us always to use them in accordance with your will and for your purpose and to hold fast to that which we have attained in Christ Jesus, our Lord. Amen.

Day 207

The Rt. Rev. Nick Baines
Bishop of Bradford
Bradford, England

Ecclesiastes 1–3, Psalm 19, Philippians 4

Everyone who has ever lived knows well the experience of waking up one day and wondering what life is all about. However full and demanding our lives may be, sometimes we just ask ourselves, "What's it all for?" And sometimes it all seems a bit pointless.

This is where the writer of Ecclesiastes begins. What's the point of it all? We eat and sleep and work; we live and love and weep and breed. Life just goes round in circles and doesn't always seem to get anywhere. So how are we to respond? How are we to think about our lives and what they mean?

Ecclesiastes confronts us with our common starting point as human beings, whoever and wherever we are: our mortality. We are mortal beings in a contingent world. So get used to it, and don't run away from the questions of meaning.

The psalmist, as we know, has asked the same questions. However, he looks up at the stars and sets his own personal experience in the context of the enormity of the universe. He is able to see the bigness of God's creative love, holding together the cosmos and an individual who could otherwise feel as insignificant as a grain of sand. And this perspective—seeing through God's eyes—evokes a response of wonder, praise, and gratitude.

Funnily enough, this is the vision of God (the world and us) that so gripped Paul. In his letters to struggling Christian churches, he repeatedly tried to lift their eyes, so that they could see themselves, their lives and predicaments, through God's eyes and in the context of eternity. So he seems to say to the Philippians, "Sort out your relationships. What do your arguments and power games look like when seen in the light of the cosmic God who loves you?"

QUESTION

Do you look at yourself and wonder why you matter—or look at God and know you matter?

PRAYER

Lord God, Creator of all that is, lift the light of your face upon me, that I might see the world as you see it and love it as you do, in Christ. Amen.

The Rt. Rev. Nick Baines
Bishop of Bradford
Bradford, England

Day 208

Ecclesiastes 4–6, Psalm 20, Colossians 1

Christian faith is invested in a person—God—and not a system or the fulfillment of a particular formula. This is why we Christians should be able to take whatever life throws at us, knowing that God has been among us and knows what it is like, and God will not desert us regardless of what happens. Why this attitude? Simply because our trust is in the God who raised Christ from the dead and sees the "now" in the light of eternity.

The "Teacher" of Ecclesiastes understands this. He knows the human condition—that we are never satisfied, that "people cannot live by bread alone" (Mark 4:4), that our petty competition for stuff and status is a waste of time and of life itself. He wants us to recover a sense of time and see that what looks important now might look silly to the next generation. So we must set our course with humility.

This theme is picked up by the psalmist who recognises that human pride is often misplaced. Do we trust in strength and power? If so, no wonder we find a crucified God a bit embarrassing. Our pride should be placed in the person of the God who sticks by us as time goes by and generation succeeds generation. I was once vicar of a church with Saxon foundations, a Norman font, and an Elizabethan chalice. For over a thousand years, people have prayed in that place…and they are still there. That is the perspective of time that keeps us humble.

And this is Paul's starting point in his letter to the church at Colossae. The gospel "has come to you" (Colossians 1:6)—you did not go and get it. In glorious language, Paul gets the focus right: we inherit the gospel, we don't invent it.

QUESTION

Is your faith in God—or in things working out in a particular way in your life?

PRAYER

Lord God, seen in Jesus Christ, open our eyes to see with humility and confidence our place in the great sweep of your history. Set us free to worry less about now and to put our trust in the eternal you. Amen.

Day 209

The Rt. Rev. Nick Baines
Bishop of Bradford
Bradford, England

Ecclesiastes 7–9, Psalm 21, Colossians 2

Are we getting the message yet? The "Teacher" of Ecclesiastes keeps driving home the point: that wisdom is rooted in a right perspective on God, the world, time, and our priorities. Why are we so shortsighted? Why do we measure our value(s) in terms of the "now" and not as seen through the eyes of the eternal God? Wisdom, we read, is knowing how to enjoy life but not expecting life to be always enjoyable.

Life is often rough, so we shouldn't simply look for God to resolve our problems; God is the God of the whole of life. The world is full of injustice, but God still opted right into it in the person of Jesus. Paul calls this perspective "the knowledge of God's mystery, that is, Christ himself." If Christ went to a cross, why should you be spared? We Christians are plunged into the contradictory realities of life and all that the world can throw at us; this is part of what it means to "be in Christ." Yet, our root conviction is the knowledge that God raised Christ from death, so life's sufferings (which Paul endured in spades) are not the final word.

An English bishop once summarised his creed as follows: "'God is. God is as he is in Jesus. So, there is hope." That's not a bad summary. It reflects the psalmist's recognition of "the steadfast love of God," despite his very human rage against those who perpetrate injustice. God is—and that's enough.

QUESTION

Does Jesus' Resurrection set you free to trust in the God who has been here and has the final word in this world?

PRAYER

Lord God, grant us the wisdom to see ourselves through your eyes, to live our lives wisely, and to put our trust in you at all times. Amen.

Day 210: Enjoy hearing the Scriptures read aloud in church.

The Rt. Rev. Robert Fitzpatrick
Bishop of Hawai'i and the
Episcopal Church in Micronesia
Honolulu, Hawai'i

Day 211

Ecclesiastes 10–12, Psalm 22, Colossians 3

How do I live a life right with God, with my fellow human beings, and within myself? That is the heart of the question for both the "Teacher" of Ecclesiastes and for Paul in the Letter to the Colossians in today's readings.

The Teacher urges his student to put aside "vanity" and to control the tongue. He calls the student to seek "wisdom" and to live life in moderation and with prudence. The Teacher speaks as an elder to a youth: "The end of the matter; all has been heard. Fear God and keep his commandments; for that is the whole duty of everyone (Ecclesiastes 12:13).

Paul likewise offers an ethical view of life grounded in God. Here, however, it is not the commandments—the Law—that ground our life but our baptism in Christ. Paul reminds us that we "have been raised with Christ." He then lists things that we ought not to do, and he describes how our very being is to be shaped in Christ.

For many, the words of the Teacher seem oddly stoic and somehow limiting. Paul's call for living in Christ's inclusiveness—"no longer Greek and Jew" (Galatians 3:28)—and with compassion and kindness seems all well and good, but then he goes and spoils it with wives being "subject to husbands" (Colossians 3:18) and the injunction, "Slaves, obey your masters" (Colossians 3:22).

For both the Teacher and Paul, the core is the call to live in right relationship. I must overcome my own greed, my own desire to control and to manipulate (other people and God), and my own captivity to fear and anxiety about tomorrow. While we might not frame Paul's household rules in the same way, he does get to the core of how we treat those most closely connected to our lives—spouses, children, coworkers, supervisors. It is in the ordinary and the everyday that we live. It is in the here and now that we live for God.

QUESTIONS

How can we extrapolate Paul's rules for his own time to our time (3:18-25)?

The Teacher insists that "all is vanity." How do these words speak to our age? What are examples of the false hopes of our society brought to light in the past few years?

PRAYER

Grant me your grace, Lord Jesus, to live as one of your chosen ones, so that whatever I do, in word or deed, it might be done in your Name, giving thanks to God the Father. Amen.

Day 212

The Rt. Rev. Robert Fitzpatrick
Bishop of Hawai'i and the
Episcopal Church in Micronesia
Honolulu, Hawai'i

Song of Songs 1–3, Psalm 23, Colossians 4

The evocative and even erotic Song of Songs (or Song of Solomon) was likely originally written as a love song celebrating the romance of nobles. It was appropriated by the rabbinic traditions of Judaism to celebrate the relationship of Israel to God and by early Christians to describe the relationship of Christ to the Church.

The words are intimate. The writer exclaims, "Arise my love, my fair one, and come away" (Song of Solomon 2:13) and "My beloved is mine and I am his" (2:16). The images are physical and earthy, with descriptions of love and passion drawn from nature.

Though the familiar language of the divine shepherd in Psalm 23 is not romantic, it, too, is earthy and personal. God is intimate with us, giving food and drink, comfort and protection. The image of God is immediate and practical.

A portion of the second chapter of the Song of Songs is often read at weddings, and Psalm 23 is often read at funerals. Thus our most personal times (celebrations of relationships and the end of life) are marked with scriptural images that are real and physical. The Song of Songs, which offers insights into mutual and sexual love between two persons, also hints at the depth of our human longing for the holy and for genuine connection with God. We seek God to be as close as a lover and a friend. The picture of the shepherd in Psalm 23 provides comfort in the midst of our limited and anxious human condition. We are fed when hungry, we are protected when in danger, and we are comforted when stressed.

These biblical lessons ensure that we encounter God in human life. Here the Holy One is known through images of sexual and romantic love, in the pastures of a shepherd, and in the anxiety of ordinary cares.

QUESTIONS

Consider the divine/human relationship in the very human, romantic/sexual poetry of the Song of Songs. How does such imagery impact your understanding of God?

Reread Psalm 23. What does it mean to have "mercy and goodness" follow you all the days of your life?

PRAYER

Gracious and loving God, grant that I might experience you this day as close as a lover and as near as a friend in the time of trouble. Amen.

The Rt. Rev. Robert Fitzpatrick
Bishop of Hawai'i and the
Episcopal Church in Micronesia
Honolulu, Hawai'i

Day 213

Song of Songs 4–6, Psalm 24, 1 Thessalonians 1

Paul writes to the church in Thessalonica with great love. These are his people and he cares for them. In the opening of Paul's First Letter to the Thessalonians, he celebrates a community close to his heart. He sees God in them through "works of faith and labor of love" (1 Thessalonians 1:3). These are a persecuted people who as the "imitators of the Lord" (v. 6) are an example to others. They serve the "living and true God" (v. 19).

Paul planted the church in Thessalonica, but now God's people in that place show him what faith means. This is the pastoral experience of many who have served congregations as priests and pastors. The people of God help the priest/pastor to see faith lived out in the world and thus have their own faith strengthened. Faith in Jesus Christ is experienced and witnessed in the everyday lives of God's people. It is an understanding of faith planted in the local gathered community.

On the other hand, in today's lesson from Psalm 24, God is encountered as Lord of the entire world. God is ensconced on the holy hill. Only those with "clean hands and pure hearts" (v. 4) can trek up the hill to the temple to join the "King of Glory" (vv.8-10) as the holy one passes through the gates. This is a mighty God. This is the King of Glory entering the beauty of holiness.

God is known through the people, and God is worshiped in splendor. Both encounters with the holy are found in the biblical witness. Like Paul, we often meet God in the touch, loving care, and witness to service of a local community of faith. We also encounter God at worship in "his holy place."

QUESTIONS

Where do you most readily encounter God? Is it in a community amidst a people who serve the living and true God or in the wonder of worship in his holy place?

Have you known a community like the one described by Paul that witnesses to a vibrant faith in Jesus Christ?

PRAYER

Grant, Lord Christ, that I might encounter you this day whether it be in your people gathered in faith, in the wonder of the worship of God, in a holy place, or in the silence of my prayer. Come, Lord Jesus, come. Amen.

Day 214

The Very Rev. Jonathan Lean
Dean of St. David's Cathedral
Pembrokeshire, Wales

Song of Songs 7–8, Psalm 25, 1 Thessalonians 2

The Song of Songs (or Song of Solomon) is a collection of poems. It is good to take them at their face value and to see them as pieces of beautiful writing that set the seal of divine approval on human love and affection.

Psalm 25 is a prayer for help, guidance, and forgiveness. The psalmist reflects on God's mercy, goodness, and tolerance and asks for God to "relieve the troubles of my heart" (Psalm 25:17). It is a prayerful psalm that enables us to draw closer to God and to value his redeeming love.

In the reading from his First Letter to the Thessalonians, Paul encourages the church to proclaim faithfully the message that it has received, in accordance with the will of God. It is a straight-talking and confrontational epistle that reminds its readers of the responsibility of "'living a life worthy of God" (1 Thessalonians 2:12).

QUESTIONS

Do you find consolation and help with personal difficulties when reading the Scriptures?

In the Song of Songs, are you able to see beyond the beauty of the prose to the relevance of God in our lives and in society today?

Are you, like the early church members at Thessalonica, able to face the challenges that sometimes make being a Christian difficult without compromising the gospel and its relevance to today?

PRAYER

Holy and glorious God, in your Son Jesus Christ you have redeemed humankind. You have brought us out of our doubt and fears and enabled us to grow in faith and love. Help us in all things to be your image in the world and reflect your glory to all humanity, through Jesus Christ, our Lord. Amen.

The Very Rev. Jonathan Lean
Dean of St. David's Cathedral
Pembrokeshire, Wales

Day 215

Isaiah 1–3, Psalm 26, 1 Thessalonians 3

In the second half of the eighth century B.C.E., at the beginning of his prophetic ministry, the prophet Isaiah reflects upon the situation of the city of Jerusalem and of God's pronouncement of judgment on the arrogant. Today's Old Testament reading is a hard-hitting prophecy, one that cannot easily be read without seeing parallels with our modern world.

Psalm 26 is attributed to King David. As you read it, reflect upon the life of David as he strives to vindicate himself before God. This psalm is an offering to God of a life dependent upon God.

In today's reading from Paul's epistles, he is frustrated that he is unable to be with the church in Thessalonica. Paul knows that the fruits of his ministry are beginning to ripen there, and he rejoices in the witness of the church. Unable to be with the Thessalonians as they face persecution and difficulties, he appeals to them to be strong despite his absence and to rely upon God and God's providence.

QUESTIONS

In the light of these readings, how do you see the world?

Do you consider that our society makes it difficult to be a Christian? Do you derive strength from the foundations set by the early Christians (reflecting upon what they went through and the hardships that they endured in the face of persecution)?

Is our "labour in vain," or are we encouraging the world as did the church in Thessalonica with our witness and uncompromising stand regarding the truth of the gospel?

PRAYER

Heavenly Father, give us strength in this troubled world to be strong for your sake, to live according to your word, and to proclaim your gospel faithfully, in the name of Jesus and in the power of the Holy Spirit. Amen.

Day 216

*The Very Rev. Jonathan Lean
Dean of St. David's Cathedral
Pembrokeshire, Wales*

Isaiah 4–6, Psalm 27, 1 Thessalonians 4

From chapter 4 of the prophecy of Isaiah, we see a reflection of the glory intended for the faithful. Chapter 5 seems to suggest that a spirit of goodwill toward God can be distorted by the world and its intent. If we can see beyond these negativities, there is a chance God can use us, as he did the prophet, for a higher purpose in proclaiming his word.

Psalm 27 is a prayer for help that falls neatly into three distinct sections. It is a reflection upon the journey of life and the psalmist's dependence upon God, who will lead him out of a forsaken way into the life God intends for him.

In 1 Thessalonians, chapter 4, a common theme of sanctity is endorsed by Saint Paul; he calls upon Christians to be pure and holy. This can be achieved by faithfulness to God in everyday things, so that at the end, all things that belong to God will return to God.

QUESTIONS

How do you feel about your own calling to be a Christian in the light of these readings? Are you prepared to respond by saying, "Here am I; send me!"?

Are you prepared to respond to God by seeing "the resurrection promise" not as something that is to come but as something that is relevant to your situation today?

Is it possible to trace a thread of negativity in these readings that can be applied to your own life? By recognising these threads, do you realise your dependence upon Jesus? Despite the recognition of your failures, do you trust in God to fulfill his will in you and the world today?

PRAYER

Heavenly Father, may we grow in faith and love, trusting in your will and purpose. Give us strength and guide us in all things so that in all things we may glorify your holy name, through Jesus Christ our living Lord. Amen.

Day 217: Enjoy hearing the Scriptures read aloud in church.

Dr. Judy Fentress-Williams
Associate Professor of Old Testament
Virginia Theological Seminary
Alexandria, Virginia

Day 218

Isaiah 7–9, Psalm 28, 1 Thessalonians 5

The oracles in Isaiah 7–9 are delivered against a background of political and social turmoil. Judah faces a very real threat in the impending attack of Aram and Israel. The prophet Isaiah delivers a strange message to the king of Judah: "Take heed, be quiet, do not fear" (Isaiah 7:4). The prophet's instructions are based on his understanding of God's role in world affairs. His words reflect the larger themes of Isaiah, that God's holiness, power, and might are greater than any earthly threat. Moreover, this mighty God is "with us." The prophecy that God is with us, "Immanuel" (Isaiah 7:14), is a promise and a reminder that reorients us by replacing the realities of our world with an ultimate reality.

The psalmist understands this when he says, "My heart trusts in him" (Psalm 28:7). No matter what the circumstances, the response of the psalmist is consistent. We can avail ourselves of the goodness of God.

Centuries later, in our New Testament reading, the members of a small church in Thessalonica are struggling with their identity as followers of Christ in a tumultuous world. Paul reminds them to live in light of the hope that Jesus will return soon and that "the one who calls you is faithful."

The circumstances of our life do not define us. Rather, it is God's presence with us that informs our reality.

QUESTION

How do the words of Scripture "reorient" us so that we can be encouraged in difficult circumstances?

PRAYER

Gracious God, help me to remember that regardless of my circumstances, you are with me and that you are faithful. Amen.

Day 219

Dr. Judy Fentress-Williams
Associate Professor of Old Testament
Virginia Theological Seminary
Alexandria, Virginia

Isaiah 10–12, Psalm 29, 2 Thessalonians 1

Judah is a small nation that lives in the shadow of the powerful Assyria. Her fate is tied to the whims of this mighty nation. In response to this reality, in today's Old Testament reading Isaiah offers prophetic words that may have been received as mixed messages. On the one hand, he prophesies utter destruction for Judah. On the other hand, he offers hope when he declares that the destruction will not be complete. There will be a "remnant," and the line of David will be continued. With his words the prophet creates a picture of a peaceable kingdom where the lion will lay down with the lamb. This God wields power and establishes peace.

Psalm 29 describes a God who is God over all of creation. The potential chaos of the creation is subject to the God of creation. Even as the church anticipates the end of the world, as described in today's chapter from 2 Thessalonians, we are reminded that the God who brought the world into being with his power and might will see us through to the end.

QUESTIONS

Are you uncomfortable with the idea of God wielding power in the world? Why?

To what extent do you, like Judah, assume that forces other than God have primary power over your life?

PRAYER

God, who formed order out of chaos, speak peace to the chaos of our lives. Remind us that you are the Creator and Sustainer of all that is and bless us with your peace. Amen.

Dr. Judy Fentress-Williams
*Associate Professor of Old Testament
Virginia Theological Seminary
Alexandria, Virginia*

Day 220

Isaiah 13–15, Psalm 30, 2 Thessalonians 2

When we are under duress, our sense of community is often lost. In today's Old Testament reading, the prophet Isaiah delivers oracles of judgment against Babylon, Moab, and Philistia—and in the midst of this judgment, there is a word of promise for the small nation of Judah. Isaiah's prophecies reflect a world view of winners and losers, victors and victims. The inhabitants of Judah were often in the role of potential victims and were most likely encouraged to hear that their powerful enemies would be taken down. Within the larger context of Isaiah, however, the message broadens somewhat. It is not only Judah's enemies that will fall, but Judah herself. God plans to take Judah down as a precursor to rebuilding the nation. One wonders, then, if God has similar plans for Judah's enemies.

As long as we view the world from the perspective of our own location and our own concerns, we will forever be cut off from the larger perspective of the God of creation. If Judah's story doesn't end with punishment, perhaps it is not the end for others, even when they are our enemies. Psalm 30 asserts that God's anger "is but for a moment; his favor is for a lifetime" (Psalm 30:5). Might that promise extend to others?

QUESTIONS

To what extent is your understanding of God's saving work in the world limited to your own communities and experiences?

How does your understanding of God's saving work change when you consider that you are simply one part of a larger story?

PRAYER

We are grateful, Lord, that you desire to be in relationship with us. Thank you that your love extends not only beyond our shortcomings but beyond our world views, so that your plan of salvation might be achieved. Amen.

Day 221

Dr. Stephen Cook
Professor of Old Testament
Virginia Theological Seminary
Alexandria, Virginia

Isaiah 16–18, Psalm 31, 2 Thessalonians 3

Listen! Nations are massing together, roaring! You can hear it in the thunder of the people in Isaiah 17:12–14. This is a deafening Niagara roar, a tsunami rush!

Jerusalem's enemies roar in our ears, a tumult of watery chaos (cf. Psalms 18:16; 29:3; 32:6; 46:2–3; 93:3–4). We hear the din of army ranks swelling: perhaps the joining of Syria and the Northern Kingdom in enemy alliance (735 B.C.E.); perhaps the muster of the forces of Assyria (701 B.C.E.). From its inscriptions, we know that Assyria portrayed its armies this way, as raging waters, as a primeval chaos-flood. The "gait" of its emperor, Assyria boasted, was nothing other than *"the* Flood" itself.

Without spiritual imagination, we tremble before such boasts. We melt in fear before the enemy tumult. Assyria's king is bursting all bounds, pouring into Judah, sweeping away everything; water is up to our necks. But with blinders removed, we see all this rumbling and hubbub as hot air. The threat of Assyria is empty; nothing can come of it. It is but smoke and mirrors up against God's heavyweight substance.

In Isaiah 17:13-14, God silences all the roaring with a word, making the enemy run. God unveils the threat as mere "chaff," light and easily blown away. The foe is mere tumbleweed before God's divine gale. Assyria's downfall comes quickly, with the morning's dawn—the dawn of salvation (cf. Psalms 30:5; 46:5).

Isaiah lived to see the sunrise of God's heavyweight salvation unveiled for all to see. In 701 B.C.E. the forces of the Assyrian King Sennacherib abandoned their siege of Jerusalem. God's reality proved to be what's really real, what's really substantial.

QUESTIONS

C. S. Lewis once described heaven as a place where humans at first feel very insubstantial, transparent as ghosts. He imagines that in God's reality, our feet cannot even bend God's grass beneath them. How would entering this ultra-solid world of God make you feel? Disturbed? Indignant? Challenged to grow more substantial, more solid?

PRAYER

God Almighty, we say your reign is real to us. But the truth is, world news and world politics feel most really real. Free us from fascination with this present world so that we may see the world around us through your eyes—as something flimsy and transient, which shall be fully transformed, at the coming of your rock-solid reign. Amen.

Dr. Stephen Cook
Professor of Old Testament
Virginia Theological Seminary
Alexandria, Virginia

Day 222

Isaiah 19–21, Psalm 32, 1 Timothy 1

Isaiah 19:18-25 sits amid gloomy judgments as a shining vision of God's *universal* reign (cf. Isaiah 2:2-4, 11:10, 49:6). In God's time, God will step out so that earth's superpowers can get to know God. Then earth's nations will worship God seriously. Some cities will abandon their native tongue and learn the language of faith.

Isaiah 19:23 speaks of a wondrous superhighway stretching from Egypt to Assyria, connecting the endpoints of Isaiah's historical purview. With this highway built, the people of Earth unite as a worship community—a congregation that includes Egypt and Assyria, the worst of enemies. As elsewhere in Isaiah (vv. 11:16; 35:8; 40:3; 49:11; 62:10), the "highway" is a bridge to God's values, to God's world of reconciliation.

Verses 20-21 describe God delivering the foreigners of Egypt. Then they make sacrifices and vows to the Lord. The message is clear: God's worship is for the whole world, not for just one people.

But this message is not all sweetness. God first wounds Egypt—hits first and then heals (v. 22). It's not enough to "live and let live" in God's storm-tossed world. We've got to reconcile with each other and unite amid life's gales and tempests.

Isaiah 19 may make Israel feel less special. Verse 19 allows an altar to God in Egypt. Verse 25 puts Egypt, Assyria, and Israel on the same footing. God has *de-centered* the covenant people! And yet, like Jonah, has not Israel become God's intermediary, through which reconciliation comes to the world? Has not Israel, the land bridge between Assyria and Egypt, now become God's highway of blessing in Earth's midst?

QUESTIONS

In the Bible, God and God's world are stormy, not benign. Have we lost the skill to see God in life's storms today?

In Isaiah 19:25 God claims to be the grower and tender of the Assyrians, archenemies of Israel. Do we, God's elect, feel betrayed at having to share God's attention? Can we broaden our horizons to imagine sharing "our" God?

PRAYER

Loyal God, we are far too comfortable in our personalized, parochial relationships with you. Push our egos off center stage, so that we find a truer center in your mysterious, broad loyalty to all Earth's far-flung strangers and enemies. Amen.

Day 223

Dr. Stephen Cook
Professor of Old Testament
Virginia Theological Seminary
Alexandria, Virginia

Isaiah 22–24, Psalm 33, 1 Timothy 2

In traditional Africa, burial on ancestral land is a *big* deal. One must be buried with one's family. No one wants to be cut off from the bonds that connect the generations.

Paralleling African belief, the biblical texts attest that a traditional Israelite longed to be "gathered" to his or her people upon death. Since cold, dank Sheol's menace is isolation, its antidote is the warmth of community found in the company of one's ancestors, to whom one hopes to be "gathered" when one's time comes (e.g., Genesis 25:8).

As Israel's society grew as a monarchy, older ways got pushed aside. New practices contradicted and threatened the beliefs and norms of traditional biblical faith, which stressed family loyalty as the means to counter the threats of Sheol. Some of Judah's new elite built personalized tombs located far from kith and kin. Isaiah 22:15–25 blasts the royal steward Shebna for doing just that.

Shebna and other owners of the new royal-style tombs at Silwan had no interest in being gathered with their ancestors. These new tombs no longer had benches so family members could lie together in death. They no longer had repositories for the gathering of bones of multiple generations.

Individualized to fit particular bodies, designed with lids to seal off each corpse, and decorated with personal inscriptions, the new tombs of Silwan had nothing to do with old Israel's family ties, its bonds of kinship. The owners of these new tombs had death as their shepherd, not their kinfolk (cf. Psalm 49:14; Isaiah 28:15; 18; 57:9)!

QUESTIONS

In the biblical world, people enacted faith in the first person *plural*. How can *we* today find power by building "family ties" of faith—tight-knit circles of nurture, formation, and economic commitment?

The spiritual bonds that nourished our forebears embraced generations long passed. How might we again find power in a vision of the communion of saints?

PRAYER

Rabbi Abraham Heschel wrote, "Israel is the tree, we are the leaves." Lord, remind me that I am a leaf. Make me cling to the stem that I might be kept alive. Amen.

Day 224: Enjoy hearing the Scriptures read aloud in church.

The Rev. Richard Corney
Professor Emeritus of Old Testament
The General Theological Seminary
New York, New York

Day 225

Isaiah 25–27, Psalm 34, 1 Timothy 3

Today's reading from the Old Testament concludes that section of the Book of Isaiah known as the "Isaiah Apocalypse." These chapters look forward to that final day when God will punish the oppressors of the poor and needy—not just their human oppressors, but the ultimate oppressor of the human race, death itself. At that time the righteous, those who have remained steadfast in their adherence to the one true God, will participate in a glorious future. Among the images used to portray this future is that of a great feast, an image that to Christian readers brings to mind that messianic banquet of which every eucharist is a foretaste.

Psalm 34 offers thanksgiving for deliverance from trouble. The psalmist uses his own deliverance from affliction as a means of instructing others in the right way to live. Like the author of today's reading from Isaiah, the psalmist displays trust in the ultimate triumph of God over oppression and evil.

The first part of today's chapter from 1 Timothy sets forth the qualifications for and behavior expected of two classes of officials in the church: bishops and deacons. It does this not only in relation to their duties within the church, but also, like the psalmist who used his own experience as an object lesson, in relation to how they are perceived by those outside the Christian community. The chapter concludes with a statement of the purpose of this letter, together with a brief summary of the Christian faith.

QUESTIONS

How does God's concern for the down-trodden suggest we should act in our world today?

Do you understand your everyday behavior as a form of bearing witness to God?

PRAYER

Lord, help me so to live that my words and actions may bear witness to your saving love, that love which triumphs over every evil. Amen.

Day 226

The Rev. Richard Corney
Professor Emeritus of Old Testament
The General Theological Seminary
New York, New York

Isaiah 28–30, Psalm 35, 1 Timothy 4

The chapters that constitute our Old Testament reading for today are focused on Jerusalem and the Assyrian invasion of 701 B.C.E. The fundamental indictment of the inhabitants of Jerusalem is their failure to trust in God, which manifests itself in various ways. It is seen in the failure of priest and prophet to listen to the divine word, thereby neglecting their duty to communicate God's will to the people of God. It is seen also in the nation's reliance for protection on an alliance with Egypt. The result of such lack of trust, says Isaiah, will be the destruction of Jerusalem by an alien people. Interspersed with these prophetic oracles of doom are other texts of a more hopeful character. Two agricultural parables make the point that destruction is creative, and these chapters of the Book of Isaiah close with a prophecy of post-destruction hope.

The author of today's psalm is a victim of malicious attacks by others, in spite of, rather than because of, the way he has acted toward those who are now his tormenters. The psalmist pleads with God to take action against those persecutors.

The fourth chapter of 1 Timothy opens with an attack on the teaching of certain ascetical practices. These practices, in the view of our epistle's writer, are wrong because they deny the goodness of God's creation. The rest of the chapter contains instructions for teaching the leader of the church, who, like an athlete, is to train rigorously. The leader's teaching is to be accomplished both by example and by word.

QUESTIONS

Thinking about your spiritual life, can you come up with an example of destruction that is at the same time creative?

How does the time you spend in physical training compare with the time you spend in spiritual training?

PRAYER

Lord, give us the ears to hear and the grace to heed your word, that we may function as your witnesses in the world. Amen.

The Rev. Richard Corney
Professor Emeritus of Old Testament
The General Theological Seminary
New York, New York

Day 227

Isaiah 31–33, Psalm 36, 1 Timothy 5

Our Old Testament reading today alternates between oracles of disaster related to the Assyrian invasion and oracles of hope that look beyond the coming destruction to a post-destruction restoration. These chapters open with another attack on Jerusalem's forming an alliance with Egypt instead of relying on God. Egypt is characterized as "flesh," signifying that which is transitory, in contrast to "spirit," which is eternal. It is only with God that Jerusalem's protection is to be found, and when the people return to God, the power of the oppressor Assyria will be destroyed. Then the nation will enjoy a properly ordered society under a king who will rule with justice and in righteousness.

Next the text warns the complacent women of Jerusalem of the coming destruction of their city, a destruction that, in God's time, will be followed by security and peace, for the destroyer will be destroyed. Then a prayer for divine assistance is followed by a description of present disastrous conditions. Our reading concludes with another promise of the destruction of the destroyer, followed by another description of a bright future.

Psalm 36 contrasts the behavior of the wicked who ignore God with the protection that God is able to provide; it concludes with a prayer that God provide such protection from the wicked for those devoted to God.

Today's chapter from 1 Timothy is primarily concerned with proper behavior within the Christian community—how the young should act toward the elderly, how widows should behave and how they should be supported, the treatment of the clergy, and the way to deal with sinners.

QUESTIONS

In different ways, the readings from Isaiah and 1 Timothy provide pictures of relationships within a properly functioning society. What do you think should constitute relationships within a properly functioning society in our time? What modifications in behavior would have to be made for such a society to function?

PRAYER

Lord, in time of distress give us hope; when all is well, keep us from complacency. Amen.

Day 228

The Most Rev. Bolly Lapok
Archbishop of South East Asia
Kuching, Malaysia

Isaiah 34–36, Psalm 37:1-18, 1 Timothy 6

These are three very contrasting chapters from Isaiah. Chapter 34 is a stern prophecy of God's judgment on the nations, a "year of recompense for the cause of Zion" (v. 8b). There will be total devastation, and nature will claim back its heritage. Chapter 36 is a repeat of material in 2 Kings: the Assyrian king attacks Jerusalem, which is ruled by Hezekiah, one of the few kings praised for following King David and "doing right in the eyes of the Lord" (2 Chronicles 29:2). The attack is portrayed as a battle between the Lord and the pagan gods of Assyria. Hezekiah instructs his envoys to keep silent in the face of the seductive words of their enemies.

The re-use of this material may have served to encourage trust in the Lord as the nation faced the judgment portrayed in chapter 34, and it gives a heightened value to chapter 35. God, who has acted in the past, can be trusted to act, again, in the future! So the prophet looks forward to a beautiful and fertile world, where all those who are hindered and who stagger through life will sing and leap for joy. God's plan is for renewal and for "'sorrow and sighing to flee away" (Isaiah 35:10).

Psalm 37 echoes Hezekiah's trust in the Lord and the prophet's confidence in God's redemptive action. "Be still before the Lord," (v. 7) he says, and "commit your way to the Lord, trust in him" (v. 5). In 1 Timothy 6, Paul continues this theme of trust in God, challenging his readers to live by love and encouraging Timothy to "fight the good fight of faith" (v. 12), so that God's work of renewal may be furthered.

QUESTIONS

What helps you to trust in God when life is difficult?

Where do you see Isaiah's vision of heaven becoming a reality in the world today?

PRAYER

Lord, help us always to trust in you and hold on to the vision of your renewal of the world, so that we may be good servants in the work of the kingdom, after the example of Jesus Christ our Lord. Amen.

The Most Rev. Bolly Lapok
Archbishop of South East Asia
Kuching, Malaysia

Day 229

Isaiah 37–39, Psalm 37:19-42, 2 Timothy 1

In today's reading from Isaiah, the excerpt from 2 Kings continues; under attack, King Hezekiah leads the people in penitence and seeks the prayers of the prophet Isaiah. The prophet assures him that all will be well. God is in control and "will put his hook in Sennacherib's nose!" (Isaiah 37:29). The king is to get on with life and be confident that "the remnant of Judah will take root downward and bear fruit upward" (Isaiah 37:31). The reader may understand that God still needs his servant people. In spite of this assurance, Hezekiah finds trust in God difficult; when he falls sick, he immediately sends for Isaiah, who treats him and promises recovery.

The text of chapter 38:9-20, surely a later interpolation, exemplifies the place of prayer in healing and finds an echo in the words of the psalmist, who appears naïve about the fate of the wicked but challenges the disciple to depart from evil and do good, whilst waiting patiently for the Lord. This is all good advice, but King Hezekiah reveals where he really stands in chapter 39, when he expresses himself glad about his own recovery and the promise of fifteen further years of life (Isaiah 38:5) but is indifferent to the fate of his children (v. 39:7-8). Although the writer probably needs to make this point, it also serves to remind us that God's work is bigger than the part we play in it.

The need for tenacity of trust and faith in the face of adversity can also be seen in the opening passage from 2 Timothy. Paul encourages Timothy to "testify to the Lord" (2 Timothy 2:8) and take on his share of the suffering that this brings. He is to keep the faith and guard the truth.

QUESTIONS

Do you spend enough time building your trust in God through prayer?

How easy is it to "keep the faith and guard the truth" in the face of those around you?

PRAYER

Heavenly Father, as you strengthened Jesus in Gethsemane and Paul on his demanding mission, so give us the strength to witness to your truth and the power of faith in a sceptical world. Help us to see where we have an opportunity to speak out in love and in the name of Jesus, our Lord. Amen.

Day 230

The Most Rev. Bolly Lapok
Archbishop of South East Asia
Kuching, Malaysia

Isaiah 40–42, Psalm 38, 2 Timothy 2

The message of Isaiah changes dramatically, and chapters 40–55 are surely the work of a later prophet, when the people of God are suffering in exile. The people may even have used Psalm 38, lamenting their sad plight and pleading for God to save them. Now this longed-for time of God's action is at hand. So "prepare the way of the Lord" (Isaiah 40:1), the way for the "Creator God" (37:37) scorned by Sennacherib, who does not "faint nor grow weary" (40:31) but will father his flock like a shepherd (40:11) and renew all those who wait for him (40:31). His progress is unstoppable. He will strengthen his servant people (41:9-10), quenching their thirst as he did in the wilderness and showing the nations' idols to be worthless.

This message of hope is addressed to God's people, but it is not simply about their restoration: the opening verses of chapter 42 (often referred to as a "servant song'") call on the servant to bring justice and new life to the nations; to be a "light to the nations" (42:6). The restored people have a task to perform! Inevitably, this servant image has also been applied to Christ, but the two ideas are not mutually exclusive. Indeed, if Christ is the true Israelite, the true servant of God, then those who are called, now, to be "in Christ" also have a task to perform. No wonder Paul challenges Timothy in today's epistle to follow his example and "endure everything for the sake of the elect." He and his people are not to be distracted from their task, in which all can play a part.

QUESTIONS

Should we be looking for, and pleading for, God's renewal in our lives today?

Do you think that churches today are distracted from their main task?

PRAYER

Lord, forgive what we have been, help us to amend what we are, and direct what we shall be, so that we may focus on your call to walk the way of Christ, the way of love, without distraction, through the same Jesus Christ our Lord. Amen.

Day 231: Enjoy hearing the Scriptures read aloud in church.

The Rev. Canon Harold T. Lewis   **Day 232**
Rector
Calvary Episcopal Church
Pittsburgh, Pennsylvania

Isaiah 43–45, Psalm 39, 2 Timothy 3

All of today's lessons make clear the basic difference between God and humankind. The words of Isaiah 45:9—"Does the clay say to the one who fashions it, 'What are you making?'"—foreshadow the image of God in Isaiah 64:8, "I am the potter, you are the clay." We are, in a very real sense, in God's hands. God reminds us of the great works he has wrought on our behalf and describes what he has done as "a new thing" (43:19).

Psalm 39 might well have been the inspiration for the prayer in the Burial Office in *The Book of Common Prayer* that contains the words, "O God, make us, we beseech thee, deeply sensible of the shortness and uncertainty of life." It reminds us of our human frailty and at the same time of our necessity to put our trust in the changelessness of God. David's words, "I am your passing guest," are as poignant as they are poetic and serve to remind us "rugged individualist" types that we are ultimately not in charge of our fate.

Having learned this lesson, our role is to live lives worthy of our calling. The end of the third chapter of 2 Timothy is familiar to most of us; it is one of the places in the Bible where Holy Scripture commends itself. Paul tells us that all Scripture is inspired by God and is useful, indeed indispensable, in our spiritual formation. But by reading the verses that precede chapter 3:16-17, we understand why. The perilous times and the enemies of the gospel, of which Paul warned Timothy and that in the words of a Lenten collect, "assault and hurt the soul," are still present among those of us who seek to work out our salvation in the twenty-first century.

QUESTIONS

What do today's lessons teach us about humility?

What are some ways in which you, as clay, have asked the Potter what he is making?

How successful have you been, in today's perilous times, in avoiding the unsavory influences which Paul describes in 2 Timothy 3:2-5?

In what ways have you been guilty of "holding to the outward form of godliness but denying its power?"

PRAYER

O Lord, our Potter, remind us that we are but clay. Mold us, bend us, and shape us to do your will and not ours, through Christ our Lord. Amen.

Day 233

The Rev. Canon Harold T. Lewis
Rector
Calvary Episcopal Church
Pittsburgh, Pennsylvania

Isaiah 46–48, Psalm 40, 2 Timothy 4

The temptation of the twenty-first century Christian is probably to dismiss any biblical discussion of idols, believing them to be creatures of ancient times. So we move on to the next verse when confronted, for instance, by Bel and Nebo in the prophecy of Isaiah. The words of a great hymn, "O for a Closer Walk with God," remind us, however, that idols can be part of our contemporary spiritual landscape: "The dearest idol I have known, whate'er that idol be, help me to tear it from thy throne, and worship only thee" (*The Hymnal 1982*, #684).

An idol can be a false god, something (or someone) adored, often blindly or excessively, or something visible and without substance. An idol is anything that gets in the way of our goal to worship God alone.

The word "pit" appears more than a hundred times in the Bible. It always represents a place (physical or psychological) of despair. Sometimes, because we have worshiped idols of one kind or another, we find ourselves in pits of depression, degradation, isolation, alienation. Today's psalm paints a picture of deliverance from a pit that is not only deep but miry, making escape virtually impossible. But the Lord inclines his ear to the psalmist, and that sets his feet firmly upon a rock. Then the psalmist sings the Lord's praises and tells the glad news of his deliverance. Do we not see here a paradigm for the life of faith? Our journey is not just from perdition to salvation, but to a salvation that inspires rejoicing and proclamation—sharing the Good News.

Paul, who progressed from being a persecutor of the Christian faith to its greatest apologist, can identify with that story. As he lays dying in 2 Timothy 4, he offers this stirring valedictory to his protégé and son in the ministry. He exhorts Timothy to be unswerving in his ministry, to avoid being unduly influenced by those who will fashion the gospel to their own ends. He admonishes Timothy to preach the gospel with conviction, "in season and out of season" (v. 2), or as my favorite translation reads, "when it is convenient, and when it is inconvenient." Paul's words should serve as a warning to preachers who water down the gospel and who live in dread of offending their listeners or rocking the boat.

Day 233, continued

QUESTIONS

What are the idols that you must "tear from God's throne"?

What pits have you experienced? Did you fall into them or dig them yourself?

Have you preached the gospel when it is both convenient and inconvenient to do so?

PRAYER

O Lord our Deliverer, help us to climb out of those pits into which we have fallen and those pits of our own making, that we may sing your praises and proclaim your message of salvation, through Christ our Lord. Amen.

Day 234

The Rev. Canon Harold T. Lewis
Rector
Calvary Episcopal Church
Pittsburgh, Pennsylvania

Isaiah 49–51, Psalm 41, Titus 1

In today's Old Testament reading, Isaiah emphasizes the importance of ministry to others, especially for the purpose of kingdom building. The prophet was called from his mother's womb for this very purpose (Isaiah 49:5); he has been given the gift of utterance in order that he might teach others and bring them back to the Lord (50:4); he will bring justice and deliverance to his people (51:4-5) and cause the oppressed to be released (51:14).

According to Psalm 41, the person of faith must "consider the poor" (v. 1), that is, take them into account and minister to them. But compassion for the poor consists of far more than providing their physical necessities. The poor are protected from their enemies, sustained in their suffering, and healed of their infirmities.

Complementing the theme of service, the Epistle to Titus continues to address matters raised in Paul's letters to Timothy. This is especially true as regards the ministry. The qualifications for the office of bishop, as outlined in this chapter, are as meaningful today as they were when Paul first wrote them. They address such categories as reputation (blamelessness); holiness (setting an example for spouse and children); temperament (even-temperedness); personality (prudence, uprightness); and theology. In this final category, Paul reminds bishops that it is not enough to be a teacher of sound doctrine; the preacher must also be able to refute those who preach false doctrine—in other words, be a defender of the faith. There is also a not-too-veiled warning about the evils of hypocrisy, exhibited by professing to know God but denying him through one's actions.

QUESTIONS

To what extent do we hold up the psalmist's standards in our ministry to the poor and oppressed?

To what biblical standards do we hold our ordained leaders, especially our bishops?

PRAYER

Lord, you have entrusted us with the ministry of service and reconciliation. Give us the grace, patience, and fortitude to carry out this work of him who came not to be ministered unto but to minister, even Jesus Christ our Lord. Amen.

The Rev. Dr. Ephraim Radner
Professor of Historical Theology
Wycliffe College
Toronto, Ontario
Day 235

Isaiah 52–54, Psalm 42, Titus 2

The author of today's psalm, beset by sorrows, here searches for hope. Where does he find it? It seems to emerge from deep waters like a rock pushing out of a raging stream, a witness to the mystery of God's coming, of God's upholding goodness. This hope stands before all things, even our sorrows and troubles, and it discloses itself anew out of the midst of these very sorrows.

In the Old Testament reading, Isaiah speaks to this in terms of God's "free" grace. Israel's fate was one of destruction and very real exile, all due to her forgetfulness of God and disobedience. Israel, as it were, "disappeared" from the international scene, swallowed up by the forces of rapacious empire around her. Worthless in the world's eyes, she vanished without notice. But God announces the way that Israel will now emerge from her time of disappearance just as mysteriously, just as astoundingly, as she had first succumbed. Why? Because God acts in a way that is utterly "free"; more than that, this freedom is the freedom of the One who is ultimately good. Hence, God is "gracious" and acts as grace itself.

In chapter 53, Isaiah points to the broken servant, buried in a criminal's grave, who nonetheless is revealed to the world as someone restored and fruitful, to the amazement of many. This image became the prophetic lens through which God's victorious love in Christ Jesus could be apprehended, and it was early seen as pointing to Jesus. To the faithful child of God who waits in hope for deliverance from sorrow, Israel and then Jesus himself seem to carry all burdens for the sake of finding within them God's very grace for renewal at work. So Paul, in Titus 2, proclaims Jesus as our "hope," "redeemer," and "savior."

QUESTIONS

Where does hope come from?

Is hope something we can manufacture ourselves?

What does hope point us to?

PRAYER

Dear God, as I am overcome by the waters of sorrow, let your grace be my rock, and let me be borne on the back of your Son Jesus as he rises up from the currents of trouble to new life. Amen.

Day 236

The Rev. Dr. Ephraim Radner
Professor of Historical Theology
Wycliffe College
Toronto, Ontario

Isaiah 55–57, Psalm 43, Titus 3

Life with God is not given in a single moment, for all time. It is lived out over weeks, months, and years. And during this drawn-out life, God works with us. This is important to grasp; otherwise we can easily be overcome by events where it seems as if our previous relationship with God was for naught. "Why are you cast down, O my soul?" the author of today's psalm asks (Psalm 43:5).

It is true that God's mercy is decisive for us. In today's New Testament passage, Paul gives Titus one of the clearest expressions of how God "saves" us purely out of God's own love, not in response to some good deed we may have done to "earn" God's favor. This decisive act of love, enacted by God's own self-giving in Christ Jesus, is not negotiable. "The saying is true," Paul says (Titus 3:8). It forms the foundation of everything else about our life with God.

But it *is* still a life lived over time. Today's reading from Isaiah describes how Israel can still turn from God, still reject God's love, still act in ways that deny God's righteousness. So there is a struggle at work, even in the face of grace. Yet God promises to "heal," a promise already made good from the start, ever ready to be proven true. So Paul can call Christians to a life of purity, goodness, and righteousness, not so that they can "win" God back, but because they are already assured of God's love and are freed to return and give thanks ever again.

QUESTIONS

Do you think God ever ceases to be forgiving? What does God's promise of forgiveness "depend on"?

What is the fuel or motivator for your life of faithfulness with God?

PRAYER

Loving Father, you have drawn me to you in Jesus as your child; help me to remember this embrace at all times, and help me ever to be ready to turn back to you in faith. Amen.

The Rev. Dr. Ephraim Radner
Professor of Historical Theology
Wycliffe College
Toronto, Ontario

Day 237

Isaiah 58–60, Psalm 44, Philemon

Paul's letter to Philemon is perhaps the shortest work with the most social punch ever written. In it, Paul asks his friend Philemon to take back a runaway slave, Onesimus, who became a Christian after his escape. Take him back, Paul urges, "no longer as a slave, but as a beloved brother" (Philemon 16). This is what being joined to Christ has done: turned Paul, Philemon, and Onesimus into blood relatives, members of one another's "very heart."

In today's Old Testament chapters, Isaiah goes into detail about Israel's failures to treat her members fairly and justly. (Israel might well have remembered what it is like to be mistreated, as is described in today's psalm!) Reading God's complaint, one has to think of our own society and, of course, our own personal disdain and mistreatment of others. But in the Letter to Titus that we read on days 234-236, Paul tells us that this is about much more than following laws and rules regarding what is "right," tallying up good deeds and injustices, and then issuing a score card. God has joined our own flesh in Christ, and we are joined to his. And in this new "oneness," we not only discover the source of love for one another, but we are impelled to and empowered in it through the very presence of God in our common life. We come face to face with real love, because God is "one of us" now. When that happens, we not only know what we *should* do toward one another, we embrace it with joy.

QUESTIONS

Why should we treat one another fairly? How does God enter into this?

What is the difference between treating someone justly and "loving" them?

PRAYER

Lord Jesus Christ, you are the God who has become one with us, and you have done this out of love for us. Lead me into that love for all those you have joined, and who are now my sisters and my brothers in you. Amen.

Day 238: Enjoy hearing the Scriptures read aloud in church.

Day 239

Dr. Harold Attridge
Professor of New Testament and
Dean of Yale Divinity School
New Haven, Connecticut

Isaiah 61–63, Psalm 45, Hebrews 1

Today's marvelous poetic text from Isaiah celebrates the return of the people of Israel from their Babylonian exile. Yet deliverance is coupled with a sense of calling. The opening verses of chapter 61 will later be found on the lips of Jesus (Luke 4:18-19) as a description of his mission. That mission, as Isaiah depicts it, is to work for justice, which the Lord loves (Isaiah 61:8). To embrace that calling is not simply to do what is right. It is to enter into an intimate relationship with God, likened to the relationship of bride and groom (61:10-11). Dedication to the cause of justice is a mission that produces joyous restoration of what has fallen, elaborately detailed in chapter 62. It can also have a hard edge of judgment, as suggested in chapter 63.

Psalm 45 also proclaims a message about the justice that the Lord desires, although this time the focus is not on the mission of a prophet but that of a king. Addressed to a Davidic monarch, the psalm celebrates him as a god to his people precisely because he is bound up with equity and righteousness (vv. 6-7).

The Christian homilist who wrote Hebrews used Psalm 45 as a part of his depiction of Christ, exalted by God to a position of glory at his right hand (Hebrews 1:8-9). This epistle will go on to call all Christians to follow in the footsteps of Christ, faithful to the mission that he had from God, which will be described in terms of priesthood, a notion shared with Isaiah 61:6.

These passages together remind us that we, too, are called to the same mission, whether as priests, prophets, or the modern equivalent of kings—a mission that aims to bring true justice to humankind.

QUESTIONS

In what ways do you work for justice in your own life?

Is human justice the same as God's justice?

PRAYER

O Lord, give us the insight to understand the justice that you desire and the courage to work for it. Amen.

Dr. Harold Attridge
Professor of New Testament and
Dean of Yale Divinity School
New Haven, Connecticut

Day 240

Isaiah 64–66, Psalm 46, Hebrews 2

The final chapters of Isaiah sound two themes: first, repentance for not living up to the ideals of God's call, admitting that "we sinned" (Isaiah 64:5). The prophet understands that sin primarily as idolatry, worshiping as God what is not God (65:2-7), and suggests that God will continue to punish this (65:11-15). Yet the God of Israel is not simply a God of wrath and judgment. God is also the merciful one who will not destroy the vineyard in which there remains something blessed (65:8), the gracious one who will provide pasture for his flock (65:10).

The second theme, an image of God's creative compassion framed in extravagant language, then overwhelms the theme of wrathful judgment. God is setting out to create a new heaven and a new earth (65:12), a reign of peace and justice in which all will flourish, when wolves and lambs, lions and oxen, will live together on God's holy mountain (65:25); this evokes imagery used in earlier chapters (6 and 7) of Isaiah. The concluding chapter paints another hopeful vision in which a purified and restored Jerusalem (66:10-13) will welcome survivors from all nations (66:18-21).

The images of a new creation and restored Jerusalem appear also in Psalm 46, which expresses awe in the presence of God, who calls on all to "be still and know that I am God" (v. 10).

Hebrews continues its homily with a message that, like Isaiah's offering of words of admonition (Hebrews 2:1-4) and hope, now focuses on the story of Christ, who has become human (2:5-8a) so that his "brothers and sisters" might share his "heavenly glory" (2:8b-18).

QUESTIONS

Do you see evidence of God's judgment at work in today's world?

How do you reconcile the pain and sadness of life with the hope given to us in Christ?

PRAYER

O Lord, help us to find the stillness that will enable us to hear your challenge to abandon the idolatries that tempt us and to live in the hope for the realm of peace that you have promised. Amen.

Day 241

Dr. Harold Attridge
Professor of New Testament and
Dean of Yale Divinity School
New Haven, Connecticut

Jeremiah 1–3, Psalm 47, Hebrews 3

Jeremiah, writing (as he tells us in Jeremiah 1:1-3) in the tumultuous days at the end of the Kingdom of Judah in the early sixth century B.C.E., offers a challenging message to the people of Israel. The disaster (1:14) that has overtaken them is, he argues, a result of their own behavior, their infidelity to their God, graphically compared to the actions of an unfaithful wife (3:1-5), a harlot who has committed her acts of unfaithfulness "on every high hill and under every green tree" (2:20; cf. 3:13). Jeremiah's call to repentance from idolatry sounds as plaintive as the weeping that it describes (3:21-22). Yet in the middle of this forceful message of judgment and condemnation, there are moments of hope, as there will be throughout the book. God promises not to be "angry forever" (3:12) and holds out the hope of a return to Zion, under new shepherds blessed with "knowledge and understanding" (3:15).

Today's psalm offers a striking contrast in tone, with its celebration of God enthroned over all the earth and its call to sing God's praise. Hebrews 3, an admonition based on Psalm 95, sounds rather like Jeremiah, warning its Christian hearers against the kind of faithlessness that characterized the Israelites in the desert on their way to the Promised Land. Yet the warning is prefaced with a hopeful reminder that Christians are "partners in a heavenly calling" to which they should, like Christ, be faithful.

QUESTIONS

How can we offer hymns of praise in a time of desolation?

Can you remember unhappy times in your own life when you experienced the presence of God?

PRAYER

O Lord, in the midst of the dark moments of my life, grant me the grace to face my faults, but also to draw strength from your call, knowing that you are merciful and faithful. Amen.

The Rev. Christopher Webber
Author and Episcopal Priest
Sharon, Connecticut

Day 242

Jeremiah 4–6, Psalm 48, Hebrews 4

Jeremiah has been called "the prophet of my people" because of the way he identifies himself with those whose disaster he foresees. He is no outsider condemning others, but a part of the society whose sins he sees so clearly. Some might look at a society heading for disaster and say, "You have failed. You have sinned. God will destroy you and you deserve it; you had it coming," but Jeremiah looks at the impending disaster and says, "I am in anguish when I see what is coming on *my* people." In the Book of Lamentations Jeremiah spells this out even more clearly and with deeper anguish, but in today's reading he is searching for any evidence of repentance among poor or rich and, finding none, can only weep for the coming destruction he sees so clearly.

Psalm 48 comes from another time and portrays the Jerusalem that Jeremiah sought in vain, a strong and peaceful city relying on God as its defender.

The Epistle to the Hebrews is well matched with Jeremiah and this psalm. These readings, like the whole of the Old Testament, portray good times and bad in the relationship between God and God's people, but the epistle lays out what God has done, and which we could never do, to reconcile and unite humanity with God. Chapter 4, verses 13–15, may be the best summary in the Bible of the meaning of Christian faith. Often, when we need assistance we have friends unable to help and no access to the one who *could* help us. But these verses tell us that because Jesus is one with us and one with God, we can "come boldly" to him and there "receive mercy and find grace to help in time of need." Isn't that the gospel in a nutshell?

QUESTIONS

Would Jeremiah have more or less to lament about in today's world? Do we also weep for a society we feel deeply a part of? Is it "my people" for whom we weep—or those others we can easily condemn?

Does the fact that God in Christ identifies himself with us encourage you to come to him freely and openly in your prayers? Do you feel a distance still from God? If so, who creates that distance?

PRAYER

Thank you, Lord Jesus, for coming into my life; draw me always closer to you so that I can find the forgiveness and strength I need to serve you. Amen.

Day 243

The Rev. Christopher Webber
Author and Episcopal Priest
Sharon, Connecticut

Jeremiah 7–9, Psalm 49, Hebrews 5

I had a friend once who named his cat Jeremiah because, he said, the creature was "full of lamentations." Jeremiah is not cheerful reading. How can he be cheerful when he knows that God asks us only to "obey my voice," but he sees his friends and neighbors thinking that traditional sacrifices and "business as usual" will save them. Would Jeremiah have anything more cheerful to say about our world? Why is it that we trust in military power and economic policy and traditional patterns of worship—business as usual—to save us? Israel tried all that long ago and was destroyed. How can we not weep with Jeremiah when we also know what God asks, yet we seem unable and unwilling to respond?

The psalmist, by contrast, lays out calmly and rationally the human predicament: life ends in death; it would be foolish to trust in human accomplishment, wealth, or wisdom, but we remain foolish just the same.

The author of Hebrews spells out Jesus' role as "high priest" by talking about the role of the priests in Jewish history and in the Jerusalem temple of Jesus' time. He wants us to see how Jesus is both the same and different. The human priest is weak and understands human weakness; Jesus, for our sake, experienced human weakness and suffering. Likewise, no human being claims the priesthood by right nor did Jesus glorify himself. Hebrews stresses again and again that Jesus is one with us here and yet eternally available for us there, at God's right hand. The author never pretends that what he says is easy to understand, but he chides his congregation for being satisfied with baby food when stronger nourishment is available—and needed if we are to serve God as we are called to do.

QUESTIONS

How might you in your Christian life be settling for baby food when there is stronger nourishment available?

How might you seek and obtain this stronger nourishment?

PRAYER

Lord Jesus, let me never assume that "business as usual" is good enough. Help me to see the world with new eyes, with your eyes, and to respond as you would respond. Amen.

The Rev. Christopher Webber
Author and Episcopal Priest
Sharon, Connecticut

Day 244

Jeremiah 10–12, Psalm 50, Hebrews 6

In today's Old Testament reading, Jeremiah, like Isaiah, mocks the pagans who make gods of wood and stone and bow down to what they have created. Perhaps they would also mock us for centering our lives on the bits of plastic and silicone that we mold into computers and cell phones. Again and again, Jeremiah tells us that God asks one thing: "obey my voice." We are useless to God when we ignore God's plain directions for living lives connected to the source of life. Yet Jeremiah reminds us that God has compassion for us; there is always hope if only we respond.

The psalm puts any pattern of worship over against the glory of God the Creator and asks, in effect, what does such a God need? The obvious answer is not simply rituals of sacrifice but "the sacrifice of thanksgiving" (Psalm 50:14)—in other words, thankful hearts and transformed lives. Don't take God's patience for granted, the psalmist says; walk in the right way and God will walk with you.

The author of the Letter to the Hebrews preaches obedience as Jeremiah does and, like the psalmist, has much to say about the sacrifice of thankful lives as the proper response to Jesus' sacrifice. In chapter 6, however, he is simply encouraging his readers to set a higher standard for themselves. We ought not to be satisfied with the lessons we learned in Sunday school when there is so much more we need to know in order to serve God in the midst of so many distractions and temptations. Don't be satisfied with the basics; don't, in effect, crucify Christ again by ignoring what he has done; grow up and move along. God can always be trusted completely, and Jesus is there with God for us.

QUESTIONS

With the aid of cellphones and computers, we can be in touch with each other. Are we in touch with God as freely and fully as with our family and business contacts? If not, what could we change?

When did you last read a serious book about the Christian faith, one that was intellectually challenging, not merely emotionally satisfying?

PRAYER

Help me, Lord Jesus, to continue to grow in faith and to rely on you ever more completely. You have given your life for me; help me to give my life ever more fully to you. Amen.

Day 245: Enjoy hearing the Scriptures read aloud in church.

Day 246

The Rev. Marek P. Zabriskie
Founder of the Center for Biblical Studies
Rector of St. Thomas Church, Whitemarsh
Fort Washington, Pennsylvania

Jeremiah 13–15, Psalm 51, Hebrews 7

Hebrew prophets often acted prophetically: their actions sometimes spoke louder than words. In chapter 13 of the Book of Jeremiah, the Lord instructs him to buy a linen belt used by priests and hide it in the crevice of a rock. Many days later, God instructs him to dig up the belt, which is now ruined. The Lord tells Jeremiah, "In the same way, I will ruin the pride of Judah…These wicked people, who refuse to listen to my words." God is angry that the Israelites have worshiped false gods. "Your adulteries and lustful neighings, your shameless prostitution…How long will you be unclean?" asks the Lord.

This leads perfectly into Psalm 51—the greatest of the penitential psalms, ascribed to King David, who wrote it after being confronted by the prophet Nathan for committing adultery with Bathsheba (see 2 Samuel 12:1-14) and breaking the fifth, sixth, seventh, eighth, ninth, and tenth commandments. David's humble prayer for forgiveness represents the only fitting response to God when we commit significant sins.

Just as Jeremiah's belt was ruined, David's sin has stained his character and ruined relationships. "Wash away all my iniquity and cleanse me from my sin," pleads David (v. 2). "Against you, you only, have I sinned and done what is evil in your sight….Do not cast me from your presence or take your Holy Spirit from me."

The reading from Hebrews reintroduces the historical figure of Melchizedek, the King of Salem and priest of the God Most High, whose name means "king of righteousness." He is a precursor of another king of righteousness, king of peace, and priest of the Most High God—Jesus. Hebrews notes that Jesus did not become a priest through ancestry but through the "power of an indestructible life" (v. 16). Unlike other priests whose sacrifices must be performed constantly, Jesus "sacrificed for their sins once for all when he offered himself" (Hebrews 7:27). We come full circle with sin, cleansing, and forgiveness.

QUESTIONS

Why does David say to God, "Against you, you only, have I sinned and done what is evil in your sight"?

When we sin, do we not hurt God, hurt others, and ourselves simultaneously?

PRAYER

Almighty God, you alone have the power to forgive us and wash away our sins. Cleanse us from the wrongs we have done that have stained our integrity and marred your image within us. Create in us a pure heart that will allow us to will one thing—to love you with all our heart, mind, and soul. Amen.

The Rev. Marek P. Zabriskie
Founder of the Center for Biblical Studies
Rector of St. Thomas Church, Whitemarsh
Fort Washington, Pennsylvania

Day 247

Jeremiah 16–18, Psalm 52, Hebrews 8

In today's Old Testament reading, Jeremiah chastises Israel for fabricating false gods and being unfaithful. He praises those who trust God in an ode reminiscent of Psalm 1, saying, "But blessed is the man who trusts in the Lord, whose confidence is in him. He will be like a tree planted by the water that sends out its roots by the stream" (Jeremiah 17:7-8).

A key to flourishing like this is, as Jeremiah notes, to "keep the sabbath day holy, as I commanded your forefathers" (17:22). He then offers one of the great images of God found in the Bible, comparing God to a potter shaping Israel like a piece of clay.

After watching a potter at work, Jeremiah says, "The clay was marred in his hands; so the potter formed it into another pot, shaping it as seemed best to him" (Jeremiah 18:4). The Hebrew word for "marred" is the same word that is translated as "ruined" in Jeremiah 13:7, referring to the priest's linen belt that had rotted. God clearly can only do so much with clay that is marred or a priest's ruined belt. God's imperfect followers must allow God to form them into righteousness.

The psalmist builds on this image of a thriving plant, describing the righteous man as being like "an olive tree flourishing in the house of the Lord" (Psalm 52:8). An olive tree can survive for several thousand years. These sturdy trees are reminders that those who root themselves in God's teaching build upon a sure foundation.

The author of Hebrews quotes Jeremiah 31:31-34, saying, "The time is coming, declares the Lord, when I will make a new covenant with the house of Israel and with the house of Judah" (Hebrews 8:8). God's laws will serve as inner principles to guide God's followers and enable them to delight in following God's will. Their sins will be forgiven forever. "I will put my laws in their minds and write them on their hearts," says Jeremiah (31:33).

QUESTIONS

How good are you at keeping the sabbath?

Do you worship every Sunday, and do you allow the sabbath to be a time where God can recreate you and restore your soul?

PRAYER

Most Merciful God, we have been like hard clay that resists being shaped in your loving hands. Help us to maintain the sabbath and to root our lives in worship so that we might be like trees planted by streams of living water and have leaves that do not whither and bear fruit in all seasons. Amen.

Day 248

The Rev. Marek P. Zabriskie
Founder of the Center for Biblical Studies
Rector of St. Thomas Church, Whitemarsh
Fort Washington, Pennsylvania

Jeremiah 19–21, Psalm 53, Hebrews 9

In today's Old Testament reading, Jeremiah continues his prophetic work. He buys a clay jar and invites some elders to join him at the entrance to the Potsherd Gate, overlooking Jerusalem's dump for broken pottery. After chastising the Israelites for worshiping pagan gods, he smashes the jar and says, "This is what the Lord Almighty says: I will smash this nation and this city just as this potter's jar is smashed and cannot be repaired" (19:11).

Jeremiah predicts that God will punish Israel by allowing the Babylonians to destroy Jerusalem and take its citizens captive. Unable to endure this prophecy, the priest Pashhur orders Jeremiah to be beaten and imprisoned. This is the first of many acts of violence against Jeremiah. Speaking prophetically can be costly, but Jeremiah must prophesy. He notes, God's "word is in my heart like fire, a fire shut up in my bones" (20:9).

As Nebuchadnezzar, King of Babylon, and his army attack, King Zedekiah sends Pashhur to see if Jeremiah can mediate and convince God to spare Israel. Instead, Jeremiah predicts that Zedekiah and his officials will be handed over to their enemies. Jeremiah offers advice similar to Deuteronomy 30:15-20, saying, "See, I am setting before you the way of life and the way of death. Whoever stays in this city will die by the sword, famine, or plague. But whoever goes out and surrenders to the Babylonians who are besieging you will live; he will escape with his life" (21:9).

The psalmist offers a similar lament, saying, "Everyone has turned away, they have together become corrupt; there is no one who does good, not even one" (Psalm 53:1). The reading from Hebrews compares Moses' manmade tabernacle with Jesus, whose tabernacle is with God. Just as the priest approached the tabernacle on the Day of Atonement, Christ passed through the tabernacle of death to obtain our eternal redemption. His unblemished blood purchases our forgiveness and frees us from our sins.

QUESTIONS

What aspects of your life does God lament and shed tears over? How are you being called to account by God?

In what ways are you called to be prophetic in your present circumstances?

PRAYER

Gracious God, help us to accept your acceptance of us and to put our trust in Jesus, who is the mediator of the new covenant that you have established with us. May we trust that you have forgiven our sins and live gratefully knowing that we are to serve you and others in a sacrificial life of service. Amen.

The Rt. Rev. Jeffery Rowthorn
Retired Bishop of the Convocation
of Episcopal Churches in Europe

Day 249

Jeremiah 22–24, Psalm 54, Hebrews 10

Many people in the United States these days assume that religion and politics should have nothing to do with each other. They cannot conceive of God being directly involved in human affairs. Today's chapters from Jeremiah confront us with witness to the contrary: "Why has the Lord dealt in this way with that great city? Because they abandoned the covenant of the Lord their God, and worshiped other gods and served them" (22:9).

Jeremiah leaves us in no doubt about what God expects of us, not just as individual believers but as members of our society. Greed, self-interest, cheating others of their due, indifference to the poor and needy, violence and oppression—all these are specifically cited and condemned by the prophet. Speaking in the Lord's name, he calls instead for social justice and civic righteousness. Only then will the king and the people be blessed.

Jeremiah believes that the future well-being of the nation is at stake, and that accounts for his fierce condemnation of those who keep saying, "It shall be well with you....No calamity shall come upon you" (23:17). Because of these false prophets, "ungodliness has spread throughout the land" (23:15).

Undergirding all that Jeremiah says and does is the powerful realization that God is the Sovereign Lord who, for the achievement of his good purposes, intervenes in national and international affairs. That is why, in the face of many social ills, the prophet can still foresee the coming of a just and righteous ruler, raised up by God to enable the land to live in safety. For Jeremiah, to worship and serve this God faithfully is the only guarantee of national security.

QUESTIONS

On the fourth Sunday after the Epiphany, we pray, "Almighty and everlasting God, you govern all things both in heaven and on earth." What light do today's readings from Jeremiah shed on this affirmation that God governs all things?

Does God still speak to our society and our world through prophets like Jeremiah? If so, call to mind some of those faithful prophetic voices.

PRAYER

Almighty and everlasting God, open my eyes to see your judging and healing love at work in our nation's affairs, and help me to live believing that in Jesus Christ our Lord you have the whole world in your hands. Amen.

Day 250

The Rt. Rev. Jeffery Rowthorn
Retired Bishop of the Convocation
of Episcopal Churches in Europe

Jeremiah 25–27, Psalm 55, Hebrews 11

Our reading today from the Letter to the Hebrews begins with one of those Bible verses that once read is not quickly forgotten: "Now faith is the assurance of things hoped for, the conviction of things not seen" (11:1). Again and again the Bible introduces us to people whose faith is so strong that they move mountains and overcome what may seem to us insuperable odds as they do what God is asking of them.

Chapter 11 of Hebrews is like a great canvas depicting the heroic figures of the Old Testament who defied those odds: "Gideon, Barak, Samson, Jephthah, David and Samuel and the prophets" (v. 32). And, equally important, countless men and women, now nameless, who faithfully endured suffering and privation because, more than anything else, they desired "a homeland…a better country…a city prepared for them by God" (vv. 13-15).

The book that bears his name witnesses to the hostility that Jeremiah faced time and again from his fellow citizens. He dared to challenge his people to turn from their evil ways and live instead by God's laws—and he did this in the house of the Lord at the heart of his nation's capital, Jerusalem. It was only because some recognized the authentic voice of God in what the prophet said that Jeremiah escaped being put to death. Even that threat could not silence him, and he continued to prophesy.

In our day, Jeremiah's experience has been the experience of Martin Luther King Jr., Oscar Romero, Dietrich Bonhoeffer, and so many others, mostly unknown to us, who have paid what Bonhoeffer called "the cost of discipleship." They have done so with faith and conviction and, above all, with trust in the Lord who "will never let the righteous stumble" (Psalm 55:22).

QUESTIONS

Has daily reading of the Bible strengthened your faith and given you a deeper conviction of things hoped for but not yet seen? In what ways?

Imagine that you are painting a canvas depicting people who have witnessed boldly to the Christian faith over the past hundred years. You can only depict eight men and women. Whom will you choose?

PRAYER

O God, the protector of all who put their trust in you, help me to do what you ask of me, counting not on my strength alone but on your power, which can do infinitely more than we can ask or imagine. This I pray in the name of Jesus Christ our Lord. Amen.

The Rt. Rev. Jeffery Rowthorn
*Retired Bishop of the Convocation
of Episcopal Churches in Europe*

Day 251

Jeremiah 28–30, Psalm 56, Hebrews 12

Back in the days when East Germany was a communist state, Christians in that country turned to the Bible for solace and direction. In those radically changed circumstances, how they could stay faithful to the Lord who had called them? Many found the answer in the letter Jeremiah sent to the exiles whom King Nebuchadnezzar had carried off to Babylon.

What did Jeremiah tell the people of Israel in the name of the God who had sent them into exile? "Build houses, plant gardens, get married, and give your children in marriage" (29:5-6). And then the prophet said something extremely hard for the exiles in his day, or the East German Christians, to hear: "Seek the welfare of the city where I have sent you into exile, and pray to the Lord on its behalf, for in its welfare you will find your welfare" (v. 7).

In other words, do not listen to the false prophets who say that this "exile" is only temporary. Instead, live faithfully where you are, caring for those around you, however different and foreign they may be. And realize that this time of painful separation from "the good old days" is part of God's design: "For surely I know the plans I have for you, says the Lord, plans for your welfare and not for harm, to give you a future with hope" (29:11).

Much is changing in our church, our country, and our world, so much so that at times we may feel as Christians that we are living in exile in a secular wilderness. Alien as it seems, this "brave new world" is part of God's design—for God intends not a return to "the good old days" but rather a future with hope, a future that as yet is hidden from us. In the meantime, we can take heart from "the great cloud of witnesses" surrounding us on every side and look, as they did, to Jesus, "the pioneer and perfector of our faith" (Hebrews 12:1-2).

QUESTIONS

If a modern prophet sent you a letter similar to Jeremiah's letter to the exiles, what sense would you make of it?

Who among "the great cloud of witnesses" encourages you most by their examples of faithfulness?

PRAYER

God of each time and place, thank you for the saints who surround us on every side; help me, like them, to look to Jesus and to run with perseverance the race you have set before me. Amen.

Day 252: Enjoy hearing the Scriptures read aloud in church.

Day 253

The Rt. Rev. Dr. Stephen Pickard
Assisting Bishop of Canberra and Goulburn
Canberra, Australia

Jeremiah 31–33, Psalm 57, Hebrews 13

Today's reading from Jeremiah belongs to the collection of writings that scholars have referred to as the Book of Consolations. In chapter 31 we hear the voice of Rachel in Ramah who is "weeping for her children" and "refuses to be comforted." In response, the voice of God says, "Keep your voice from weeping and your eyes from tears; for there is a reward for your work" (31:16). This chapter reads like a conversation between human suffering and God. What may Ramah hope for? What might the nation hope for, given the people's disobedience? Are they cut off from God forever?

Similarly, in Psalm 57 David pleads, "Oh God, be merciful to me…in the shadow of your wings I will take refuge, until the destroying storms pass by" (v. 1). In both of these readings, the suffering depicted reflects a foreboding of annihilation, both from without and within, to which there does not seem to be any antidote.

As human beings we are all vulnerable to the forces of destruction that affect our personal lives and the nations. It is hard to know what to hold on to in such times, and it is natural to ask, "Where is God in this, and is there any hope for us?" Often all we can do is learn to wait faithfully.

In Jeremiah, God responds to human suffering (whether self-inflicted or at the hands of others) with the promise that "I will put my law within them, and I shall write it on their hearts…for they shall all know me" (31:33). In Hebrews 13, the author implies that to know God in the midst of our suffering means not turning away from pain but rather allowing it to stretch and open our hearts to one another.

Discovering hope in our afflictions comes from deeper knowledge of God as our refuge and involvement in the sufferings of others. This is to walk the way of the Lord.

QUESTIONS

What does the consolation of God mean for you?

How has your knowing of God been connected to caring for others?

PRAYER

God of infinite consolation, come to us in our failures and unfaithfulness, and sow a seed of hope that we might truly serve you in the world. Amen.

The Rt. Rev. Dr. Stephen Pickard
Assisting Bishop of Canberra and Goulburn
Canberra, Australia

Day 254

Jeremiah 34–35, Psalm 58, James 1

Today our reflections begin with the Epistle to James. Chapter 1 goes directly to the trials and temptations that beset human life. The apostle exhorts the reader to stand firm under temptation and reminds us that God tempts no one. There is a warning about how desire lures and entices us into sin and deception. The dynamics are complex; one result is that we become absorbed with ourselves and care little for the practice of real religion, "to care for orphans and widows in their distress" (v. 27) and purity of life. The apostle offers sound practical advice for living well with others under God. But his words have a social, economic, and political edge.

This wider dimension comes to the fore in the Jeremiah reading. Here the prophet delivers unwelcome messages to kings Zedekiah and Jehoiakim of Judah. The temptation of the national leaders is to play the political game and thus sacrifice faithfulness to God. Jeremiah is unrelenting in his announcement of God's word to the leaders who are lured and enticed away from the way of the Lord. He introduces the "house of the Rechabites" (35:2), a people who remain faithful to their vows and live a life of purity, neither drinking wine nor buying property or vineyards. They stand as a witness against the kings of Judah who do not keep faith, do not resist temptation, and fall prey to the violence of other nations, in this case the Babylonians. God's constant faithfulness to Israel will be traced through the descendants of the Rechabites, for they exemplify true religion.

Keeping faith in adversity is a significant challenge in human life. Oftentimes we are tested very hard, and oppressors can be fierce. This is echoed in Psalm 58, where the author appeals to God's gracious favour and protection in the face of trials. And the psalmist feels justified in making this claim upon God because as he says in Psalm 56:8, "you have kept count of my tossings; put my tears in your bottle."

QUESTION

Who have been examples for you of faithfulness under temptation?

PRAYER

Dear Lord, come to our aid when we are tempted to give in to those voices that would lead us away from your love and freedom. Amen.

Day 255

The Rt. Rev. Dr. Stephen Pickard
Assisting Bishop of Canberra and Goulburn
Canberra, Australia

Jeremiah 36–38, Psalm 59, James 2

In today's readings we meet people who do not know how to listen and seem to be closed to hearing the subtle word of God.

In Psalm 59, David complains about the people, who are "bellowing with their mouths, with sharp words on their lips" (v. 7). Similarly the Epistle of James chastises the people: "Have you not made distinctions among yourselves and become judges with evil thoughts?" (James 2:4). And Jeremiah, who has heard the word of God, is not received well: the people asked him to "'sit down and read it to us" (Jeremiah 36:15), but they "would not listen to him and arrested him" (37:14).

After being asked to speak, thrown in prison, dragged before the king, arrested, and tortured, Jeremiah becomes shrewd about expressing his message: "'If I tell you, you will put me to death, will you not? And if I give you advice, you will not listen to me" (38:15). All the while, Jeremiah does not lose his integrity; he does not change his words to suit the mood around him, even though his constancy has caused him much suffering at the hands of those who do not listen.

These passages hint at what it means to hear the word of God and offer advice on how to act once we have heard such a message of truth. The psalmist says, 'I will sing aloud of your steadfast love" (Psalm 59:16). But what if we speak a truth that may not be welcomed by those who need to hear it? Jeremiah and James both ask boldly for their audiences to listen to them anyway. But this requires courage to speak truthfully and with integrity in the face of opposition. At the same time, we need not necessarily sing loudly to those who do not listen. Rather, we should be shrewd and wait for the right moment to speak our piece without compromising the integrity of what we have to say. And in the distress this may cause us, God provides a fortress of strength.

QUESTION

What has been your experience of trying to speak the truth in difficult situations?

PRAYER

Loving God, give us the ears to hear your voice, courage to speak it, and wisdom to know when to say it. Amen.

The Rev. Canon Petero Sabune
Africa Partnership Officer for
The Episcopal Church
New York , New York

Day 256

Jeremiah 39–41, Psalm 60, James 3

In today's reading from Jeremiah, we are faced with the fall of Jerusalem, the city of God, the *shalom* city. In chapter 39:15-18, "the Word of the Lord came to Jeremiah." The oracle is an assurance of safety and security, in spite of the evidence. Chapter 40 shows Jeremiah choosing exile, for unknown reasons. Why would he do that? Why not stay in Judah? Chapters 39 and 41 give us the chronology of exile of the people of God. Murder, assassinations, and exile are themes of Jeremiah's time—and ours.

The author of Psalm 60 cries out to God to deliver loved ones. When God speaks through us, we need to be still and hear so that we can heed his call and warn the people.

Today's reading from James is a radical reminder of true wisdom. Preachers and teachers need to be reminded that true wisdom comes from God. Concerning the evils of the tongue, James warns us to be mindful of our words. They could cause conflicts and harm to the body of Christ. His practical suggestions are still applicable to our time.

The recent death of Pope Shenouda III, who led the Coptic Orthodox Church in Egypt for four decades, was a reminder that we may not be as far from Jeremiah's era as we think. In 1981 Pope Shenouda was forced into exile by President Anwar Sadat. Like Jeremiah and James, he would not keep his mouth shut when he saw the people of God being persecuted. After four years, he was allowed to return, but the discrimination against Christians continued. For the ten million Christians in exile in their own land, he was the voice of reason, calling for tolerance and interfaith dialogue. What words can we say to our brothers and sisters in Egypt who are being persecuted for their faith?

QUESTIONS

Who are the people in exile in your country today?

What can you do to support the struggle of those being denied their rights?

PRAYER

God became human that we might be made divine. God endured humiliation at men's hands that we might inherit incorruption. God endured these things for the sake of suffering men, and through his own impassibility he preserved and saved us. Amen.

—SAINT ATHANSIUS

Day 257

The Rev. Canon Petero Sabune
Africa Partnership Officer for
The Episcopal Church
New York, New York

Jeremiah 42–43, Psalm 61, James 4

On this 257th day of our journey though the Bible in one year, we encounter Jeremiah being consulted by fugitives as to whether they should go to Egypt or remain in Judah. They reject his answer and are taken to Egypt against their will.

The author of Psalm 61 calls on God for protection. Whether we are in exile or out of exile, rich or poor, in Egypt or at home, God is always ready to hear us when we cry out. When we go into exile, voluntarily or against our will, God never ceases to listen to our prayers. The presence of the divine crosses ocean floors and snow-capped mountains and passes through prison walls. God will oppose the arrogant and give grace to the humble, in exile or at home.

In chapter 4 of the Epistle of James, we are again warned to draw near to God. If we repent, God will grant us forgiveness. James warns those who are wealthy to avoid greed and indifference to social justice. As James reminds us, there is only one lawgiver and judge, the One who is able to save life and destroy it.

The attacks on people of faith have continued in West Africa, the Middle East, South Asia and Oceania. On Christmas Day 2011, a church in Nigeria was bombed, and three people were killed and thirty-eight wounded. At another church, thirty-two were killed on the day we celebrate the birth of the Prince of Peace. We need to hear the words of the prophet calling on rulers to heed the Word of God, the word of *shalom, salaam,* peace.

QUESTIONS

Do you regularly pray for those who are persecuted for their faith?

Do you remember to pray for those in authority?

PRAYER

The source of being is above, which gives life to all people; for people are satisfied and do not die, for the Lord gives them life. Amen.

—ZULU PRAYER

The Rev. Canon Petero Sabune
Africa Partnership Officer for
The Episcopal Church
New York, New York

Day 258

Jeremiah 44–45, Psalm 62, James 5

In today's readings, Jeremiah forecasts Nebuchadnezzar's invasion of Egypt. The time is around the fall of Jerusalem in 587 B.C.E. or possibly the earlier deportation in 597 B.C.E. In Jeremiah 44:26-27, it is interesting to compare the doom of those in Egypt with the hope extended to the exiles in Babylon. Jeremiah proposes a sign that when the Pharaoh is taken by his enemies, God's punishment of his people will be imminent. This prediction concludes the story of God's people in Egypt and the biography of Jeremiah.

Psalm 62 proclaims confidence in God's protection: "He alone is my rock and my salvation" (v. 2). When we hear those words, we are assured of God's protection, unconditionally. No matter what happens, God will never abandon us, whether we are at home or in prison.

The Letter of James concludes with a discussion of healing: "Are any among you suffering? They should pray....Are any among you sick? They should call for the elders of the church and have them pray over them, anointing them with oil in the name of the Lord" (James 5:13-14). The prayer offered in faith will save a sick man.

From the call of the psalmist to the words of the prophet and the apostle, we are reminded of our need to call on the name of the Lord. Our sin-sick society needs prayer. I am writing these meditations on Passion Saturday in 2012, the day before Passion week, in the aftermath of the shooting to death in Florida of a young boy named Trayvon Martin by George Zimmerman. I tremble to contemplate what both families are going through right now. Like Jeremiah and James, we do not choose the age into which we are born, but we do chose how to respond to "thus says the Lord."

Is there a balm in Gilead? Is there healing for the people of Florida and Egypt? James and Jeremiah responded to their time; may we respond to our time with calls to justice and *shalom*. Amen.

QUESTIONS

Are there immigrants living in exile in the community where you live? What are their lives like?

Have you ever visited a prison or a detention center?

PRAYER

*There is a balm in Gilead
to make the wounded whole.
There is a balm in Gilead
to heal the sin-sick soul. Amen.*

Day 259: Enjoy hearing the Scriptures read aloud in church.

Day 260

The Rt. Rev. Humphrey Sarfaraz Peters
Bishop of Peshawar
Peshawar, Pakistan

Jeremiah 46–47, Psalm 63, 1 Peter 1

In today's Old Testament reading, Jeremiah, prophet to the nations, predicts defeat for Egypt, whose army arrogantly marches out as if it will bring back laurels. But the Egyptians' pride and arrogance simply ruins their glory. Their intention to expand becomes a humiliation for them because God is not on their side (chapter 46). Egypt's defeat on the Euphrates is not an end to its humiliation: there is also an attack by the Babylonians directly on Egyptian territory. Jeremiah 46:14-26 tells of the vulnerability of a great nation that always attacked and conquered others but is helpless now, like a dove before a cat. Arrogance, false hope, and pride have invited judgment upon Egypt.

Jeremiah's prophecies for Egypt foretell the vengeance of God. Yet God's mercy transforms the entire scene, as the fragrance of fresh flowers drives away a bad odour. God our Father promises restoration after judgment. The key is to listen to his voice.

Philistia, a mighty power, was badly defeated by the Egyptians. The wickedness of the Philistines led to their punishment. For when the Lord intends to destroy the wicked, even their friends leave them.

Jeremiah 46-47 remind us that if God grants gifts of strength, power, skill, or wealth, we had better desire God's satisfaction, assurance, and safety. In Psalm 63, David reminds us of the same. He was hiding from Absalom in the wasteland of Judah and said, "O God, my flesh is dry and burning like a land where there is no water" (v. 1). We need to seek protection from pride, arrogance, and false hope; this will be given if we try not to live in ignorance but become holy in all we do (1 Peter 1:14-15).

QUESTIONS

Can you count the blessings you enjoy every day, even the smallest ones, and find God's satisfaction, assurance, and safety in all of them?

If you feel that God is not listening to your prayers, do you review your countenance and conduct?

PRAYER

Most gracious Heavenly Father, you have given me many blessings for which I greatly rejoice. Grant me serenity to enjoy your blessings and strength to realize and overcome my many weaknesses, in the name of Jesus. Amen.

The Rt. Rev. Humphrey Sarfaraz Peters
Bishop of Peshawar
Peshawar, Pakistan

Day 261

Jeremiah 48–49, Psalm 64, 1 Peter 2

Even today, the prophecies of Jeremiah are a signal for us to overcome our weaknesses. The prophecy to Moab in Jeremiah 48 reveals that the Moabites enjoyed a comfortable lifestyle. Their leisure not only made them self-righteous—they often made fun of others. Their overweening pride, conceit, arrogance, haughtiness, insolence, and boasting became a snare for their destruction. Yet God in his mercy promised the restoration of Moab for the sake of the righteous Lot, as the Moabites were his descendants.

In Jeremiah 49, which concerns the people of Ammon, their boastful attitude about their treasures and their enmity and forceful possession of the Israelites' land was a sin in the sight of God. Edom's hostility against Israel, assistance to Babylon against Judah, and boasting about wisdom and knowledge was not pleasing to God. Damascus was involved in the punitive raid on Judah in 601/600 B.C.E. That people's enmity and hostility against God's chosen ones was an offense. Kedar and Hazor, Arab nomadic tribes, were involved in the raids against Israel. Elam had some excellent archers—there is a reference to four winds, which indicates God's might—but the best archers with their cloud of arrows were no match for God's power. Later, there is a promise that Elam will be restored.

Chapters 48 and 49 tell about different enemies against God's chosen people—enemies who were self-righteous, arrogant, cunning, crafty, and cruel. But God is a shield for his chosen ones. In Psalm 64, we find anxiety and complaint, yet the poet is confident that God's righteousness will inevitably punish the evil. 1 Peter 2 prepares us to become God's chosen ones, with advice to put off our sinful ways and attitudes: malice, craftiness, envy, insincerity, and slander.

Almighty God in his mercy has always favoured his chosen people, provided they are also faithful to him.

QUESTIONS

How do you overcome malice, craftiness, envy, insincerity, and slander?

How do you share the concept of God's chosen ones with others?

PRAYER

Almighty and most gracious Heavenly Father, through the grace of our Lord Jesus Christ enable us to become your chosen ones. Amen.

Day 262

The Rt. Rev. Humphrey Sarfaraz Peters
Bishop of Peshawar
Peshawar, Pakistan

Jeremiah 50–51, Psalm 65, 1 Peter 3

Chapters 50 and 51 of Jeremiah tell of the destruction of Babylon and the restoration of Judah and Israel. Although God had used Babylon as his instrument for the judgment of other nations, yet the time came for Babylon's own judgment. God's designs are beyond human conception. Babylon's judgment became inevitable because the Babylonian people were faithless. They worshiped idols and mocked God. God grieved about the judgments, while Babylon rejoiced at the plunder. All these facts warn us that wickedness and oppression ruin individuals and nations.

These chapters tell us that the real power behind the affairs of nations is the Lord. Israel, once conquered, was vindicated, while Babylon, once the conqueror, was not. Israel had hope while Babylon did not. Babylon was punished while Israel was restored. The penitent nations of Israel and Judah were brought back to their land to be united in an everlasting covenant by God. They were judged because they disclaimed guilt and turned away from God, but the Lord in his mercy became their Redeemer.

In Psalm 65, God is praised for his control over the creation and history. He is praised for the forgiveness of our sins and the privilege of worshiping him as his people. He is the hope for all those who have confidence in him.

We see obedience, respect, hope, and reverence for God in 1 Peter 3. When individuals and nations overlook these essentials, God leaves them to their foolishness. To attain God's blessings, we had better try to overcome our harshness, anger, and arrogance, letting in gentleness as part of our personality.

QUESTIONS

Can you see in your life those weaknesses that grieve the Holy Spirit?

How can you give full reverence to God in order to attain his favour?

PRAYER

Our Heavenly Father, let hope in the Holy Spirit become my strength, so that I may enjoy and share your many blessings. In the name of Jesus I ask. Amen.

The Very Rev. Walter B. A. Brownridge
Dean of St. Andrew's Cathedral
Honolulu, Hawai'i

Day 263

Jeremiah 52, Psalm 66, 1 Peter 4

The Book of Jeremiah is a prelude, a warning of the disaster that is to befall God's people who have chosen to walk away from their covenant with the Lord. The text describes a prophecy, a vision of pending doom. The Babylonian Empire is on the march. It will lay siege, capture, and destroy Jerusalem, the capital of Judah. In addition, a great number of Jews will be sent into exile. The government in Jerusalem will be destroyed. When the Book of Jeremiah was written, all the warnings had come to fruition.

However, God's vision to Jeremiah is given several years in advance and predicts defeat for the vicious Babylonian empire. Jeremiah's prophecy then describes the vengeance that God will exact on Babylon. "May the violence done to our flesh be upon Babylon" (Jeremiah 51:35), say the inhabitants of Zion. The Lord will avenge the violence enacted against his people, according to his plans.

It is difficult to grasp—but why do we need to look at the image of a vengeful God returning the suffering the Jews endured by inflicting it on Babylon? For Christians who claim to follow the Lord of Peace, we are naturally and rightfully uncomfortable with this violence.

Yet, as human beings, we are not immune to sin, including acts of violence. So we need to respect our shadow side. Trying to repress or submerge violent desires can result in our darker angels coming out in spiritually deadly ways. We need to acknowledge that we are violent creatures, but God calls us to be transformed by the renewing of our minds (Romans 12:2). We must rest in the hope that God and our faith communities will form us so that we turn from our atavistic impulses and seek to pursue peace.

QUESTION

What would be a spiritually healthy way of dealing with our darker forces and the desire for vengeance against our enemies?

PRAYER

O God, the Father of all, whose Son commanded us to love our enemies: Lead them and us from prejudice to truth: deliver them and us from hatred, cruelty, and revenge; and in your good time enable us all to stand reconciled before you, through Jesus Christ our Lord. Amen.

Day 264

The Very Rev. Walter B. A. Brownridge
Dean of St. Andrew's Cathedral
Honolulu, Hawai'i

Lamentations 1–2, Psalm 67, 1 Peter 5

The Book of Lamentations consists of five mournful poems. Together they constitute a powerful expression of grief over the destruction of Jerusalem and exile of its people by King Nebuchadnezzar and the Babylonians in 586 B.C.E. If the Book of Jeremiah was a narrative account of the danger that was to befall Judah and Israel because of their unfaithfulness, then Lamentations is the poetic lament of an author (either Jeremiah or an anonymous poet or poets) writing during the exile.

This poetry is an eloquent expression of the anguish, bewilderment, and loss felt by many of the people. The words of chapter 1 evoke the mood from the start: "How lonely sits the city that once was full of people! How like a widow she has become, she that was great among the nations! She that was a princess among the provinces has become a vassal" (v. 1).

The images of a distraught widow, a mother torn from her children, or a homeless old woman dressed in rags give us an insight into the horror that the people must have endured. The sting of loss is all the more painful because we are repeatedly told that "there is no one to comfort her" (Lamentations 1:2, 17).

Chapter 2 confirms that the author agrees with the pre-exile prophets (Isaiah, Amos, Hosea, Micah and Jeremiah) that the destruction of the holy city was the just judgment of God for Israel's and Judah's sins. People in ancient times understood the cosmos as functioning this way, and that type of thinking still permeates some forms of Christianity and other religions.

This again poses the problem of theodicy: how do we reconcile the reality of evil and suffering with an understanding of God as all-powerful, all-knowing, and especially all-loving? We'll explore this more tomorrow.

QUESTIONS

Have you ever written down or recorded your feelings when you are going through difficult times?

Might you consider doing so in the future?

PRAYER

O merciful God, you have taught us in your holy word that you do not willingly afflict or grieve your children: Look with pity upon the sorrows of your servants. Remember us, O Lord in mercy, nourish our souls with patience, lift up your countenance upon us and give us peace. Amen.

The Very Rev. Walter B. A. Brownridge
Dean of St. Andrew's Cathedral
Honolulu, Hawai'i

Day 265

Lamentations 3–4, Psalm 68, 2 Peter 1

One of the themes in the Book of Lamentations poses the problem of theodicy: How do we reconcile the reality of evil and suffering with an understanding of God as all-powerful, all-knowing, and especially all-loving? All religions, if they are serious, must wrestle with this issue.

Theologians far greater than I have attempted to address this, in far more detail than this meditation will allow. The concise answer is that evil and suffering are part of the human condition. Human beings have free will, coupled with the fact that humanity lacks control over the forces of nature, so we have no reprieve from ills unlimited.

Despairing news? Perhaps, but even in Lamentations there is a ray of hope. Chapter 3 says that the Lord will not reject Israel and Judah forever: "The steadfast love of the Lord never ceases, his mercies never come to an end; they are new every morning; great is your faithfulness. 'The Lord is my portion,' says my soul, 'therefore I will hope in him'" (v. 3:22–24); "I called on your name, O Lord, from the depths of the pit; you heard my plea, 'Do not close your ear to my cry for help, but give me relief!' You came near when I called on you; you said, 'Do not fear!'" (v. 3:55-57).

I think the American music idiom known as the blues can help us here. The best of the blues acknowledges that pain is the result of human folly and irresponsibility. The blues singer expresses poetry in music and lyrics that allow him or her to process suffering without blaming God. It has been said that in African American history, especially during the dark days of Jim Crow segregation and deep poverty, the community used the blues on Saturday night and the church on Sunday morning to maintain spiritual health.

QUESTIONS

Have you found solace in the blues? If so, how?

If not, could you consider trying it? The expression "laugh instead of cry" is the operating principle.

PRAYER

Loving God, inspire by your Holy Spirit all those who are afraid of losing hope. Give them a fresh vision of your love, that they may find again what they fear they have lost. Grant them your powerful deliverance through the One who makes all things new. Amen.

Day 266: Enjoy hearing the Scriptures read aloud in church.

Day 267

The Rev. Dr. Lloyd Lewis
Professor of New Testament
Virginia Theological Seminary
Alexandria, Virginia

Lamentations 5, Psalm 69, 2 Peter 2

Does anyone really believe that life is easy? One thinks of Job the righteous and the series of messengers who washed over him with such a plethora of bad news that his reaction was to turn swiftly to sackcloth and ashes. Today's psalm catches the drift of that moment with the image of one facing opposition from both the mighty and the lowly, gasping for air to breathe while the waters rise up neck high.

The early Christian church was no stranger to the uneasy life, lashing out against those it perceived to be false teachers. The language was strong, but given the danger that false teaching posed to the faithful and the tentative, one is hardly surprised that the reaction was as sharp as it was. So the author of 2 Peter cried out for deliverance from the way things had become. As one author has said, "When we hurt physically, we cry out in pain; when we hurt religiously, we lament!"

One need only think of the ongoing recovery efforts in Haiti, or closer to home in New Orleans, to be cognizant of why sometimes the only thing we can do is to cry out. I remember a conversation I had with a restaurant owner whose deluged business had been on the edge of the French Quarter. What had been established by his grandparents and passed down to him, and from him to his sons, had been all but swept away. Only extraordinary faith had anchored him and his family and made it possible for them to rebuild.

"Restore us to yourself, O Lord, that we may be restored; renew our days as of old" (Lamentations 5:21). The cry of lament finds its answer in the light of the providence of the living God, who through flood and wandering and the cross has never abandoned his own.

QUESTIONS

Where do you look for confidence when the waters rise up in your life?

When it comes to matters of faith, is there a difference in your mind between lament and nostalgia?

PRAYER

When we face what we do in life, God of the people restored, we are awed by the certain knowledge that you are a steadfast companion to us on our way. Amen.

The Rev. Dr. Lloyd Lewis
Professor of New Testament
Virginia Theological Seminary
Alexandria, Virginia

Day 268

Ezekiel 1–2, Psalm 70, 2 Peter 3

We like to live in the "hurry-up" world, do we not? We would just as soon forego watching paint dry or the grass growing. So we microwave the food, we "speed interview" for the job, and "speed date" to find a life partner.

As one who teaches ancient languages to adults, I have always been amazed by the courage that some exhibit when taking on Greek or Hebrew. But I have been equally amazed at the impatience with which other adults approach language learning, seeing it as something that should be instant and forgetting that the long trial-and-error refining process that accompanied their transition from baby talk to speaking in sentences is happening again.

In today's reading, Ezekiel's vision of the glory of God stands in tension with the "hurry-up" world. In almost excruciating detail, the heavenly vision unfolds like a flower: wheels and wheels within wheels. Likewise the prophet's own call to his task seems strangely postponed by a series of symbolic actions. A scroll is provided for him, not to be read but to be consumed. Then a valley appears, filled with the nation's skeletal remains, bones expectant of the breath that will bring them to life. Then the revived temple appears, but first it must be described before the waters can flow from beneath its altar to revive the land. Are these descriptions belabored? Do we chafe to "get on with it"? Do we echo the psalmist's cry, "O Lord, make haste!"?

I wonder if part of what God has graciously done has been to free us from refashioning his activity to meet our "hurry-up" expectations. The reading from 2 Peter tells us that when it comes to the end of time and even the fervent desire for the *maranatha* prayer to be answered immediately, God's intentional stretching out of things is an act of patient love for those of us who are coming along more slowly, but who are coming along nonetheless.

QUESTIONS

What is truly worth waiting for when it comes to what God has planned for us?

What does it mean when Saint Paul says in Galatians 4:4 that in "the fullness of time" God sent his son?

PRAYER

Help us, Lord, to wait on the working out of your will, as we consider the pressing needs of this world and of our own lives. Amen.

Day 269

The Rev. Dr. Lloyd Lewis
Professor of New Testament
Virginia Theological Seminary
Alexandria, Virginia

Ezekiel 3–4, Psalm 71, 1 John 1

The toughest audience is the one closest to you. I still remember a sermon about the problem encountered by the two children of the prophet Hosea's wife: they had to preach to their own mother, knowing well that without their mother and her troubled history they would not have existed. We can think of what Jesus experienced when he went home to the synagogue at Nazareth: he first met acceptance, but later encountered hostility when the welcoming message he preached, based on God's graciousness to Naaman the Syrian general, the leper, and the widow of Zarephath, ran headlong into the face of those who recognized that the one they knew as Joseph's son was challenging them. We can think of what happens whenever we speak the words of the gospel to those who know us very, very well.

In today's Old Testament reading, when Ezekiel gets the word from God that he has to read, mark, learn, and literally digest, he is sent to proclaim it to his own people, not to a people of obscure speech or difficult language. This is done with God's conviction that the prophetic word would not go down lightly. Such a mission required as hardheaded an attitude from the prophet as what the prophet would inevitably encounter from his audience. All of this requires extraordinary confidence in the God who is with the one speaking his word: a God who was present in the psalmist's youth and remains even as age and the gray hairs increase.

Crucial to all of this is the message that is meant to be proclaimed. In the first chapter of 1 John, this message is foundational to both belief and action. God is light: darkness is not found in him. And you can see that light whenever you see Jesus, in the fact of his Incarnation and his Resurrection, but also in every moment of his life and ministry. What else does the tough audience really need to hear?

QUESTIONS

To whom are we called to preach the Good News?

Read God's words to Ezekiel again. Where else in Holy Scripture do you hear the words given to Ezekiel, "Do not fear"?

PRAYER

We hear your challenge to stand as boldly as those who are sent to keep watch by you, God, and we are helped in our fear and uncertainty when faced with that task by your abiding and strengthening presence. Amen.

The Rt. Rev. Barry Beisner
Bishop of Northern California
Sacramento, California
                                                                                Day 270

Ezekiel 5–6, Psalm 72, 1 John 2

In the sacrament of baptism, we renounce "the spiritual forces of wickedness that rebel against God," "the evil powers of this world which corrupt and destroy the creatures of God," and "all sinful desires that draw you from the love of God" (*The Book of Common Prayer*, p. 302). Moving from the cosmic to the personal, we are then asked to commit ourselves to Jesus Christ as our Savior and Lord.

The horrors that the prophet Ezekiel describes in today's Old Testament reading are a picture of those rebellious spiritual forces at work at a moment in history, when some who were called to be God's servants in this world chose instead to join in rebellion against God. They may not have thought of it that way, but by putting things and persons in a place in their lives that properly belonged to God—idolatry—and by making their society a place of injustice, oppression, and violence, they brought a terrible turn of events upon themselves. The prophet seeks to find meaning in those events. He sees a nation strategically placed by God in order to be a light to all nations, a model of God's agenda of justice and peace, and he sees that that nation has failed and is reaping the results of its failure. Nevertheless, God is still at work and still seeks to be known.

In the epistle reading for today, John also has a sense of God at work in the world and of human history moving in a trajectory according to God's ultimate purpose. The nature of that purpose is revealed to us in Jesus Christ. The way to live according to that purpose is to live in the way that he taught and showed us—to love others as he loves us. That is the basis for our life and work and relationships in this world, as God works with us to create a new world.

QUESTIONS

Where do you see God at work in the events of our time?

Where is the issue of idolatry most real for you?

PRAYER

Gracious God, help me to see you at work around me today, and help me to join you in your work. In Jesus' name. Amen.

Day 271

The Rt. Rev. Barry Beisner
Bishop of Northern California
Sacramento, California

Ezekiel 7–8, Psalm 73, 1 John 3

In today's reading from Ezekiel, the disaster continues to unfold, and there is no escape for the failed nation from the inevitable results of corrupt leadership, bad foreign policy, inauthentic religion, gross inequality, chronic violence and injustice, and cynical disregard for the common good. At the heart of all this is idolatry—letting things and persons take the place of God in our lives, letting other agendas come before God's agenda. For the prophet, all this is summed up in the word "abomination." Nothing could be more distant from what God has in mind for his beautiful creation.

If the prophet calls upon us to witness what the world looks like when it turns its back on its Creator, the writer of 1 John points to just the opposite: "See what love…." (v. 1:1). Jesus has overcome the evil that is at work in the world. His love for us is the most real and important thing about us; his love reaches through us to others, to build a new human community, a new society, a world in which everyone is understood to be a child of God.

The church is meant to be the model of that society and God's instrument in creating that new world. The church is where, as for the psalmist, perspective shifts, and it is clear that nothing is more important than God. There is still a struggle with the forces that rebel against God, a struggle that goes on in us and in the world around us. But God is with us in that struggle. We are partners with God in God's work, including the work of repenting and returning to God whenever we ourselves fall away.

QUESTIONS

Where do you most experience God's love for you?

When in your experience has the church been most effective in demonstrating God's love?

PRAYER

Lord, help me to put your agenda before my own and to be a faithful partner with you in your work. In Jesus' name. Amen.

The Rt. Rev. Barry Beisner
Bishop of Northern California
Sacramento, California

Day 272

Ezekiel 9–10, Psalm 74, 1 John 4

In today's reading from Ezekiel, the prophet sees the glory of God depart from the temple, a visible demonstration that the desolation of that terrible time in the life of the nation is total—and yet, even at such a moment, there is God's assurance that a remnant of the people will be spared. The psalmist writes from a vantage similar to that of the prophet (that is, after the actual destruction of the temple by enemy forces); he remembers God's saving actions in the lives of his people in times past, and prays not to be forgotten by God in a very difficult present time.

The work of God continues even amidst such great disaster, and the prophet is assured that those who do not condone the abominations of idolatry, who have not lost their moral compass, or their sense of call to serve God and accomplish his agenda, will be invited to be God's partners in that continuing work.

That same invitation is extended to us. It is an invitation to love the world as God loves it, and it is possible for us to do that because God himself loves us and loves through us. The source of life and love and all that is good and true and beautiful is at work in us and through us. Nowhere is that source better known to us than in Jesus Christ. And so we are given the criteria by which to assess our agendas, the commitments we make, and the work we do, and to determine how they measure up to what God has in mind for us.

In Jesus Christ, we are given a surprising ability to live without fear in our own difficult times, knowing that he has overcome the forces that are at work in this world to corrupt and destroy the creatures of God, and confident that, in his love for us, he will never abandon us.

QUESTIONS

Where is God's help most needed in this world today?

What part is God asking you to play in that work?

PRAYER

God of love, help me to be aware of your love for me today, and help me to show that love to someone else whom Jesus loves. In his name. Amen.

Day 273: Enjoy hearing the Scriptures read aloud in church.

Day 274

The Rev. Canon Louis C. Schueddig
Executive Director of the
Alliance for Christian Media
Atlanta, Georgia

Ezekiel 11–12, Psalm 75, 1 John 5

In today's reading from Ezekiel, the Israelites are uprooted and feeling cranky. Caught in a regional power shuffle, they find themselves forced out of their homeland by Nebuchadnezzar's army and living in captivity along a water canal in Babylon. They are not happy campers and need to understand why this calamity had befallen them. Their God is a God of the nation; without a country, God is absent and they are devastated.

Ezekiel, from a high priestly family, is called to prophesy to Israel. He begins with a vision journey back to Jerusalem to judge those who had remained and to tell them to shape up and take some responsibility for what has happened. His language is vivid and dramatic, but by the end of the vision, he realizes that the true Israel lies with those who live beside the river in exile, and he returns to prophesy to them with a message of hope.

Ezekiel needs his people to see the truth and to admit their loss and know for themselves what they have become. In Psalm 75, we hear that "at the set time that I appoint I will judge with equity" (v. 2). God's judgment is not cruel despite the prophet's harsh tone. It is set out before us as equitable truth-telling, so we can start anew with the facts as they are in our lives. Our human condition is what God comes to treat, in good times and in bad. We must diagnose the disease to receive the cure.

We read at the end of the last chapter in the First Letter of John: "We know that the Son of God has come and has given us understanding so that we may know him who is true, and we are in him who is true, in his Son Jesus Christ" (1 John 5:20).

QUESTIONS

What hard truth about yourself do you need to acknowledge today?

Will you present this part of your life honestly to God, to be loved into wholeness in God's name?

PRAYER

God, grant us the strength and wisdom to see ourselves truly as we are and to humbly ask for your forgiveness. Come, Holy Spirit, and enter in. Be with me this day to heal all my sins that I may serve God fully in heart, mind, and body. Amen.

The Rev. Canon Louis C. Schueddig
Executive Director of the
Alliance for Christian Media
Atlanta, Georgia

Day 275

Ezekiel 13–14, Psalm 76, 2 John

"Don't worry about it. Everything will be just fine." When the news is not good, some people will always avoid reality by looking unrealistically on the bright side. Sometimes things are just what they are, and it might mean we are looking into one of life's black holes.

There were those who thought the Israelites' captivity in Babylon would be short-lived: soon they would be back home worshiping in the temple in Jerusalem, reunited with family and friends. Nothing was further from the truth.

In today's reading, Ezekiel judges harshly those "false prophets" who are feeding the captives unwarranted good news. As it turned out, he was right. It would be a long time until they returned, and when that day came, they found that the temple and most of Jerusalem had been destroyed.

As we learn more about God's ways and the message of the prophets, we learn that to judge is not to condemn but, as a seminary professor of mine once said, "God's judgment is turning the light on and seeing things in plain view." In Psalm 76 we hear that God's judgment comes "to save all the oppressed of the earth" (v. 9).

In the Second Letter of John we read in the fourth verse: "I was overjoyed to find some of your children walking in the truth, just as we have been commanded by the Father." Let us all search for the truth and find it in the embrace of the everlasting grace of Jesus Christ.

QUESTIONS

Are judgments you hear people making about you saying something you may need to hear, or are they just displaying anger?

How can you better understand the judgment of God as a positive aspect of your spiritual life?

PRAYER

Dear Lord, give me grace to humbly know myself and the truth about me. Help me to be liberated by it to better serve those who are in need; through Jesus Christ our Lord. Amen.

Day 276

The Rev. Canon Louis C. Schueddig
Executive Director of the
Alliance for Christian Media
Atlanta, Georgia

Ezekiel 15–16, Psalm 77, 3 John

Today's chapters from the Book of Ezekiel contain some of the most violent language in the Bible. In fact, biblical scholars have suggested that they are unsuitable for public reading in church! Most of the images, however, are rooted in other passages, stories, and prophecies in Scripture. At first blush, we must assume Ezekiel is out of his mind and speaking in a fit of rage against his own people. The author of Psalm 77 asks, "Has God forgotten to be gracious?" (v. 9).

Again and again, however, God has worked through the prophets to call God's people back into a covenant relationship, assuring them of God's abiding love. As harsh as his language gets, even Ezekiel ends up offering a message of hope, envisioning the restoration of Israel and the spread of God's love not only to Israel but also even to Sodom and Samaria.

As shameful as Ezekiel's words might make us feel, the good news is that we can leave our shame at the foot of the cross and know that Jesus has indeed restored the covenant to all creation without limitation. This is why the Old Testament must always be read in light of the saving life, death, and resurrection of Jesus Christ.

We all know people whose feelings of shame drive them to sickness and broken relationships. In response to this shame, Jesus offers us freedom and security in his eternal love, the restored covenant that Israel longed for throughout its history. We are called, therefore, by John in his Third Letter, verse 4, to walk in that truth: "I have no greater joy than this, to hear that my children are walking in the truth." The ultimate truth is not in shame but in glory. Praise be to God!

QUESTIONS

Are you conscious of any feelings of shame inside yourself today? Are you willing to let go of this shame and leave it at the foot of the cross?

PRAYER

God, by your mercy, grant me the grace and strength to see beyond my shame and embrace the sacrifice you have made for me. Let it mean for me freedom and joy to always to love and serve you; through Jesus Christ our Lord. Amen.

Alice Shirengo
Professor of the Bible
St. Paul's University
Limuru, Kenya

Day 277

Ezekiel 17–18, Psalm 78:1-39, Jude

In chapter 17 of Ezekiel, we learn that the captives do not understand that it was because of their sins that they were taken into captivity. Ezekiel embarks on teaching them about the cause of their suffering. He does this through a parable, using the zoomorphic image of two eagles. The political alliances made by Israel's leaders were in themselves big mistakes. But since Zedekiah had made an oath in the name of the God of Israel, it was political suicide and an irreligious act for him to rebel against the Babylonian king. Moral decline leads to national disaster, and judgment is passed on the wicked.

Although judgment is passed on the wicked, the prophet is careful to state in chapter 18 that the father will not die for the sins of the son and vice versa, setting out clearly the notion of individual responsibility. Only the soul of the one who sins shall die.

The prophet Ezekiel wonders at the moral decay and the hypocrisy of Israel's religious acts. The Letter of Jude picks up on this theme of moral decay and judgment, reminding readers of Sodom and Gomorrah. Being saved by grace through Jesus Christ does not give us license to sin without judgment or consequences.

QUESTIONS

As you read through these passages, what comes to your mind about universal sin and punishment?

PRAYER

God, our heavenly father and father of our Lord Jesus Christ, open our minds so we are able to worship you in truth and spirit; in Jesus' name we pray. Amen.

Day 278

Alice Shirengo
Professor of the Bible
St. Paul's University
Limuru, Kenya

Ezekiel 19–20, Psalm 78:40-72, Revelation 1

In today's Old Testament reading, Ezekiel continues to use zoomorphic imagery. This time it is a lioness that cares for her cubs. The theme of Israel's rebelliousness runs throughout these chapters. God recounts how Israel sinned against him by refusing to follow his statutes, even though he had brought them out of Egypt and cared for them in the wilderness. Their history is retold as if to justify the punishment rendered on Israel when she rebelled against God.

The elders go to the prophet to make inquiries. It is not clear what they want to ask, but the context suggests that they might have wanted to know the length of their exile or to ask the prophet to pray to God on their behalf for forgiveness. But it appears that the Lord will not listen to these elders of the exiles. God has already passed judgment; in other words, it appears already to be too late. (Ezekiel 20:1-32). But in verse 33, the Lord God begins to speak of a future kingdom and the restoration of Israel. God has not given up on them.

We see a vision of this future kingdom in the book of Revelation which we begin reading today. Revelation 1 introduces Jesus as the coming Son of Man who will judge the living and the dead. He holds the keys of hell and heaven (v. 18).

QUESTIONS

Consider these readings in reference to your own country. How is the political situation there? Are the leaders religious in any way? How do they influence the ordinary people to follow God?

PRAYER

O God Almighty, do not count on our rebelliousness but forgive us our trespasses. Help us to imitate godly men and women among our leaders and to resist the wicked ones, through Jesus our Lord and Savior. Amen.

Alice Shirengo
Professor of the Bible
St. Paul's University
Limuru, Kenya

Day 279

Ezekiel 21–22, Psalm 79, Revelation 2

In today's reading, Ezekiel uses imagery of swords to describe the defeat of Israel and God's punishment of the exiles. God points out that the punishment they are undergoing is one that they have brought upon themselves; hence his call to them in the previous chapters to repent and turn away from their sins.

The prophet is especially concerned that it is the leaders—the princes, priests, officials and prophets—who have led God's people into committing political as well as spiritual adultery. He enumerates the sins that were committed by the leaders (Ezekiel 22:25-28).

In Revelation 2, letters are written to the leaders of the seven churches outlining their sins and weaknesses. The chapter ends with the promise of a reward to those who respond obediently and hold fast to the faith.

QUESTIONS

Are the sins enumerated by Ezekiel (22:25-26) still seen in some church leaders today?

How do you feel when you hear about religious leaders who have misused their power by abusing others? Do you wonder why God does not rain fire on them?

PRAYER

God who judges all, reveal to us when you see the Church going astray. Give us the courage like Ezekiel to point out these sins in our leaders and ourselves. Help us to be instruments of change in your church. Amen.

Day 280: Enjoy hearing the Scriptures read aloud in church.

Day 281

The Rev. Paul Thaxter
Director of Transcultural Ministries
Church Mission Society
Oxford, England

Ezekiel 23–24, Psalm 80, Revelation 3

Whose warnings do you take seriously? Irresponsible parents admonish their children but do not follow through appropriately. Children develop ways of coping with such parental "threats." In the same way, those living in Judah had heard it all before, but Jerusalem always escaped destruction.

In today's Old Testament reading, Ezekiel continues to present extreme parables to the people, such as the story of two sisters, Oholah and Oholibah, who are flagrantly prostituting themselves. The people have paid little attention to prophetic warnings. The prophet indicates that these two communities—Samaria and Jerusalem—are out of control. Samaria has already been judged by God and destroyed by the Assyrian Emperor; Jerusalem, the more wanton sister, is now to be judged by the Babylonians. God's warnings always have an ultimate delivery deadline—"this very day."

God will radically cleanse his holy city Jerusalem. Ezekiel himself will experience a divine burden of pain as his wife, "the delight of [his] eyes" (Ezekiel 24:16), will die on the same day as Jerusalem's judgment. The people need to understand the prophet's life and pronouncements. As Ezekiel signals by his own life, they, too, will become numb and dumb as the awful realities of judgment begin to sink in and even their children left in Jerusalem will die.

In Babylon, the people make painful silent sighs, not traditional ritual wails. Then Ezekiel will find his voice again, a voice that will be heard by the Babylonian exiles so "they shall know that I am the Lord."

In Revelation 3, Christians are exhorted to have ears to hear what the Spirit is saying to the churches as the "hour of trial that is going to come upon the world" approaches (v. 10.) These early Christians have to be attentive to the Spirit and to what is going on in the church and in the world.

QUESTIONS

Do you think calamity will never happen to you?

Which signs should you pay attention to?

What does it mean for you to "watch and pray"?

PRAYER

O God Almighty, help us to hear you when you warn us. Give us ears to hear and hearts to obey. And Lord, for those who fail to hear you and come under your judgment, may you at the right time restore them, O Lord God Almighty. Amen.

The Rev. Paul Thaxter **Day 282**
Director of Transcultural Ministries
Church Mission Society
Oxford, England

Ezekiel 25–26, Psalm 81, Revelation 4

In today's reading from Ezekiel, judgment may begin with God's people, but it does not end there; it is also for Judah's historic enemies who proved to be unreliable political allies at a time of crisis—Ammon, Moab, Edom, and Philistia. Loyalties can be lost when the benefits cease, and expedient alliances gave way to deeper enmity between Judah and its historic neighbours. The surrounding nations would not escape God's justice.

It is the same in our personal lives: tough times reveal true friendship. Superficial friendships may lead to the use and even abuse of people. Deeper friendships are shaped in the hard times. Judah, though, could not count on its neighbours; they even exploited Judah's demise. The city of Tyre is highlighted as a centre of commercial exploitation, a place of business with few ethics. Judah's "divine disaster" was yet another profit opportunity for Tyre's merchants. Powerful Tyre became the proverbial example of luxurious greed that we see amplified in the larger imperial cities of Babylon and Rome. The prophet reveals that God will judge all.

There is a sense of satisfaction when people get their just deserts. Such a prevailing sentiment may be encapsulated in the phrases, "serves them right," "I have no sympathy for them!" But Jesus was concerned not only about how we treat our friends, but also our enemies. In Revelation, the Lion of the tribe of Judah is named as the one who has conquered, but it is the slain Lamb whom the four living creatures and the twenty-four elders declare is "worthy to take the scroll and to open its seals, for you were slaughtered and by your blood you ransomed for God saints from every tribe and language and people and nation" (Ezekiel 5:9).

QUESTIONS

How do you deal with the judgment of others?

Who are your real friends and why? Is God calling you to love your enemies as a brave lamb?

PRAYER

O Lord, help us to remember to love our friends who are in tough times now. Give us the courage of your Son to love our enemies as brave lambs amongst wolves. Amen.

Day 283

The Rev. Paul Thaxter
Director of Transcultural Ministries
Church Mission Society
Oxford, England

Ezekiel 27–28, Psalm 82, Revelation 5

Ezekiel 28 can be very difficult to interpret—it has some phrases or words that appear rarely elsewhere in the Bible. Ezekiel's funeral lament over Tyre displays a comprehensive knowledge of the role the Phoenicians played in world trade (compare it with Revelation 18). Tyre, likened to an abundant cargo ship, will be sunk into "the heart of the seas" by the east wind of Babylonia.

The prophet is particularly scathing about the king of Tyre, whose arrogance and pride in his wealth and abilities will lead to his downfall. Ezekiel's funeral lament for the king of Tyre is devastating. Some see this passage as saying that the king of Tyre is a form of Satan or spiritual adversary (Ezekiel 28:13a), presented first in Eden. Others note that ancient temples had gardens like Eden, and the king of Tyre reigned in his own kingdom like a god. Clearly, the king is an embodiment of supreme pride that has usurped the place of God, and so he will be brought low.

In our world today, global strategies, plans for commercial expansion, status, brands, and profit lines are not sufficient or even always desirable in God's economy. Losing sight of the purpose of Eden (Genesis 1:26-31) and excessively "commodifying" creation and making God redundant will lead to judgment.

In Revelation 5, heavenly authorities know their status and roles and ascribe greatness and holiness only to God. Global exploitation is replaced by sacrificial service to the world. The vanguard of a new world order is led by the Lamb, who trains his diverse people to reign on earth by serving.

QUESTIONS

Do you have excessive confidence in your own wealth or status? Are you proud about the right things?

In what ways can you reign through service?

PRAYER

O Lord, Judge of all gods and nations, establish the rights of the lonely, the weak, and the orphan in our global commerce. May we remember that the manager and worker all share the same mortality. Help us to share our time, talent, and treasure with all in need. Amen.

The Rev. Riaz Mubarak
Vicar
St. Luke's Church
Abbottabad, Pakistan

Day 284

Ezekiel 29–30, Psalm 83, Revelation 6

Throughout the book of Ezekiel, the prophet asserts that God spoke to him. Almost every chapter in this section of the book begins with "the word of the Lord came to me." As we put the scenes together, we see that there was no way that Ezekiel could know those things were going on unless it was God speaking to him.

We can't get away from it: the Bible over and over affirms that "this is what God has said." And, in today's reading, God pronounces judgment.

The judgments of God which we hear in Ezekiel are meant to make people realize that they have been sinning against themselves and against God. The fact is that God is the God of love, peace, and mercy. God speaks to those whom he loves and guides, the ones whom he has chosen—through Scripture, the Word of God.

Scripture may seem old-fashioned to us, with its harsh or rude or even boring language. Yet, we see life lessons in the texts; for example, to obey, to receive peace, and to love and trust in God. The spirit of such passages may apply to our lives as we learn to trust God in our distrust and thus to see hope in our hopelessness. We so easily see the harsh words and ignore the essence. Thus we are unfaithful to him who trusts us to live so that we will see the world in its beauty, in its wrongs, in its good, and in its reality. God is always faithful in his promises and, like the father in the parable of the prodigal son, will receive us as his loving children and embrace us (Luke 15:20).

QUESTIONS

Can I be sensitive to the voice of God?

Can I trust myself to be obedient to God?

PRAYER

Lord, grant me the spirit of trust in the midst of so much distrust, so that I may embrace all that you have said in your Word and live today in the your light. Help me to believe that what you do for me is sufficient for my life. Amen.

Day 285

The Rev. Riaz Mubarak
Vicar
St. Luke's Church
Abbottabad, Pakistan

Ezekiel 31–32, Psalm 84, Revelation 7

Ezekiel chapters 31 and 32 contain the final three of the seven prophetic oracles. The birds nesting in the branches of the great "tree" and the beasts living beneath them illustrate all of the nations that were under the power and control of the great empire of Assyria. It was foolish for Egypt to think she was greater than Assyria, because Egypt had been successfully invaded by Assyria, who destroyed Egypt's major city of Thebes in 633 B.C.E. Then Assyria was conquered by the Babylonians. Now Egypt has had a skirmish with Babylon and has been defeated.

Nebuchadnezzar has not yet invaded the land of Egypt, which he later conquered. So God is saying, "What shall we liken Egypt to?" (Ezekiel 31:2). He likens it to Assyria. It was Assyria that conquered the Northern Kingdom of Israel. Had it not been for God's intervention and the destruction of the Assyrian army when it sought to take Judah and Jerusalem, Assyria would probably have remained one of the major world powers.

However, God destroyed the power of the Assyrians when they came against Jerusalem. Thus, Assyria was defeated by Babylon, as Babylon began to emerge as a world power. The sin of the empire of Assyria was pride in its greatness, and the Lord was using Assyria and its fall as a lesson for the other nations.

Sometimes we go through low or hard experiences in life. God never leaves us in the depths but always brings us out. The end of the story is always one of restored glory, of restored blessings. God is always multiplying the grace and love and mercy he shows to human beings.

QUESTIONS

Do you perceive how God intervenes in your life?

Can you sense God's presence in the failures or successes of your life?

PRAYER

Dear God, we thank you for the hope that you give us in Christ Jesus. Help us to overcome the pride that may take us away from your love and grace. Restore us and fill us with your Holy Spirit, so that we may be humble channels of your grace to others. We ask in the name of Christ Jesus, who is the hope of all humanity. Amen.

The Rev. Riaz Mubarak
Vicar
St. Luke's Church
Abbottabad, Pakistan

Day 286

Ezekiel 33–34, Psalm 85, Revelation 8

In chapter 33 of Ezekiel, God likens the prophet's role to a watchman. Historically, when a land is at war, watchmen have given advance warning of attacks. If a watchman does his duty and gives a warning, it is not his responsibility if the people do not heed it. The person responsible is the one who does not heed the warning. His death is his own fault. If a watchman doesn't give warning, then people will still die, but the responsibility then moves from the people to the one who doesn't warn them (Ezekiel 33:1-6). As watchman, Ezekiel's task was to warn the Israelites of the consequences of their sin. But the Israelites objected that their sins were too great to do anything about! It is common among the wicked to hope to remain in sin and go unpunished, yet simultaneously to despair of escaping punishment because God will never forgive their sins.

However, God isn't looking to destroy the wicked: his priority is offering them repentance so that they may live. Each person is judged by his or her own actions. We can't save up righteousness to balance future sins, nor do we have to pay back for all our past sins when we repent, because God is going to forgive them all (2 Chronicles 7:14).

Ezekiel 34:1-6 is the prophecy directed to the shepherds of Israel—the kings—who had a responsibility to care for others under their authority. They had placed their own wants over the needs of those under their care. Those under them starved, while the kings had more than they needed (Isaiah 56:11). They made no attempt to heal their wounds (Zechariah 11:15-17). They ruled by force, something specifically forbidden (Leviticus 25:43). The result was that the people scattered as if they had no shepherds.

We have no excuse for our inequities, for not leading a life of commitment, because we are personally accountable to God. Even being in a good environment with righteous friends will not shelter us from unfortunate personal choices.

QUESTIONS

Do you sometimes blame your church, its organizations, or your friends for your faults or sins or your failure to be obedient?

If you are a leader in the community, is your role that of a shepherd or just a paid worker? (See John 10:11-13).

PRAYER

Dear Lord, grant me your grace so that I may serve you with all my heart, soul, mind, and strength, becoming a true and humble servant. Amen.

Day 287: Enjoy hearing the Scriptures read aloud in church.

Day 288

The Rev. Dr. John Lewis
Assisting Priest, St. Mark's Church
Co-director, The WorkShop
San Antonio, Texas

Ezekiel 35–36, Psalm 86, Revelation 9

Sometimes we find ourselves in the midst of chaos and destruction brought about by our own sinful ways. It seems the whole world is set against us, and God has abandoned us. This is the plight of the Israelites in today's reading from Ezekiel. Their beloved temple is destroyed. The elite members of Israelite culture and religion have been exiled to Babylon because the people defiled the Promised Land with their sinful ways and deeds (Ezekiel 36:17).

In despair, Ezekiel could well have prayed Psalm 86: "Incline your ear, O Lord, and answer me, for I am poor and needy. …Give ear, O Lord, to my prayer: listen to my cry of supplication. In the day of my trouble, I call on you, for you will answer me" (vv. 1, 6-7).

The answer lies solely in God's grace. Only the life-giving power of God can move us out of our dangerous place of alienation and restore our relationship with God.

That is Ezekiel's message today for the dispossessed: God will act graciously and generously to preserve God's holy name (36:22). No less than twenty times in the succeeding verses, God says "I" will act: to deliver God's people; to cleanse them from their idols; to implant within them a new heart and a new spirit; to bring forth abundance from the land. Why? So God's people will remember their evil ways, repent, and turn back to the Lord (36:31-32).

This is also the good news we hear in the judgment woes of Revelation's trumpet plagues. God judges our sinful ways, not to punish us but to call forth our repentance and reorientation to God.

QUESTIONS

Where do you see chaos and destruction among God's people in your life, suggesting the need for repentance and reorientation toward God?

Where do you see God already at work in the midst of such chaos and destruction, bringing new life out of death?

How is God calling you to respond?

PRAYER

O God, open our eyes to see your gracious hand at work in the midst of our own sinfulness and despair, and so move us to repent that we may once again faithfully bear witness to your holy name by walking only in your holy ways; through Jesus Christ our Lord. Amen.

The Rev. Dr. John Lewis **Day 289**
Assisting Priest, St. Mark's Church
Co-director, The WorkShop
San Antonio, Texas

Ezekiel 37–38, Psalm 87, Revelation 10

In Revelation 10, we catch our breath in a momentary interlude from the intensity of the earlier judgment scenes. During this interlude, John's prophetic commission is renewed. He must take the angel's scroll and eat it (Revelation 10:9-10), just as Ezekiel was instructed to do in his own day (Ezekiel 2:8–3:3). The prophet is not only to hear and proclaim the Word of God; he is to ingest the prophecy. That means he is to embody it, bearing witness to everyone about how to walk faithfully in the ways of God.

Thus the prophecy will be sweet, because speaking the Word of God brings a pleasing flavor to the prophet's mouth. But it will also be bitter in the stomach, because when the Word is embodied, when God's people walk according to God's ways, they become vulnerable and exposed to opposition.

We see this unfold in Ezekiel 38. Ezekiel prophesies against Gog and the land of Magog, mythical representatives of God's archetypal enemy among the nations. At some future time, says Ezekiel, Israel will be restored and once again live by God's ways in the land: peacefully, quietly, without walls, and having no bars or gates. And, because the people are living vulnerably in these peaceful, unguarded ways of God, invaders will attack them (38:10-16). Ultimately, though, God will save Israel and destroy the aggressors (38:17-23).

This is Ezekiel's word of hope: by living faithfully, yet vulnerably, we bear witness to God's ways. And God will finally deliver us, thereby vindicating God's holy name before all the world.

QUESTIONS

Where are you and your church being called to "eat the scroll," to speak and embody God's Word, that may render you vulnerable to the world around you?

What does it look like in our modern world for God's people to live peacefully, quietly, without walls, and have no bars or gates? Do you sufficiently trust God's word of hope to embody this way of living? Why or why not?

PRAYER

O God of all creation, give us strength and courage to proclaim by word and deed your never-failing love for all people, so that by living vulnerably, peacefully, and openly toward everyone, we might bring your word of new life and hope to people throughout the world. Amen.

Day 290

The Rev. Dr. John Lewis
Assisting Priest, St. Mark's Church
Co-director, The WorkShop
San Antonio, Texas

Ezekiel 39–40, Psalm 88, Revelation 11

The American actor George Clooney was jailed for protesting outside the Sudanese embassy in Washington, D.C. He was arrested while trying to bring attention to a human crisis underway in Sudan. Tens of thousands of people are at risk of dying from starvation, not because of famine, but because of repressive policies and violent persecution by the government of Sudan.

Today's reading from Revelation also reminds us that being God's faithful witnesses comes with a cost. When God's two witnesses finish confronting the nations, calling them to repentance, they are savagely killed and their bodies left in the streets. God's enemies celebrate and gloat over the deaths (Revelation 11:7-10). The witnesses suffer the same fate as their crucified Lord (Revelation 11:8).

Those who witness this slaughter must certainly ask God the question we find in Psalm 88:10 "Do you work wonders for the dead? Will those who have died stand up and give you thanks?"

The resounding answer is yes! God gives the people the divine promise of protection. Even in death, the breath of life from God will enter them, and they will be taken up into heaven in a resurrection from the dead (Revelation 11:11-12; see also Ezekiel 39:25-29). Beginning with the resurrection of our crucified Lord, God's faithful servants are rewarded. God's great power has begun to reign in the world, for which we give God thanks and praise (Revelation 11:17-18).

QUESTIONS

Where are the nations of the world, or the church, in need of repentance?

How might you or your church, "wearing sackcloth" (Revelation 11:3), prophesy to the nations or the church, calling them to repent of the things you have identified?

PRAYER

O God of life-giving power, fill us with the hope of eternal life, that we, despite the dangers and difficulties of opposition we are bound to provoke, might be emboldened to steadfastly bear witness to your holy name throughout the world; this we ask through him who was crucified and raised for us, Jesus our Lord. Amen.

The Very Rev. Jeffrey John
Dean of St. Alban's
Hertfordshire, England

Day 291

Ezekiel 41–42, Psalm 89:1-18, Revelation 12

In today's Old Testament reading, Ezekiel is preaching to the Jewish exiles in Babylon after the temple in Jerusalem has been destroyed. In his thinking, the destruction is God's punishment for unfaithfulness, but his vision looks forward to the temple's rebuilding. The measurements of the temple are minutely relayed. These are not simply building instructions but reflect symbolically the holiness and perfection of God, since the sanctuary of the earthly temple was believed to reflect the sanctuary of God in heaven.

John's vision in Revelation derives from the same belief. At the end of chapter 11, we were told "God's temple in heaven was opened." Now John sees a woman clothed with the sun, the moon at her feet, crowned with twelve stars (Revelation 12:1).

This vision has many layers of meaning. Historically the woman must be Mary, since she gives birth to the Messiah; and the fact that she escapes with her newborn child into the desert reflects Matthew's story of the flight into Egypt. She appears with the Ark of the Covenant, and Luke also identifies Mary and the Ark. When Gabriel tells Mary, "The Holy Spirit will come upon you and the power of the Most High will overshadow you" (Luke 1:35), he uses language that recalls the cloud of God's presence entering the Ark in the desert. Mary is a new Ark, holding in her womb the presence of God on earth.

She also symbolises Israel. Part of her description comes from Joseph's dream in Genesis, where the sun stands for Israel and the twelve stars are the twelve sons, the twelve tribes. She is also the new Israel, the church. It is her offspring against whom the dragon is continuing to wage his war—a reference to the Christians being persecuted when John wrote his vision in exile.

QUESTIONS

Visionary passages like Ezekiel and Revelation are mostly about events in the authors' own time. To interpret them, we need the help of a biblical commentary. Can you think of examples of how these passages can be dangerous if we attach them to events in our own time?

Does it surprise you that in Revelation 12 Mary's story is seen as the fulfillment of many Old Testament themes?

PRAYER

God our Father, help us to trust like Ezekiel and Saint John that all things are in your hand. Give us wisdom to read the signs of the times and to see and serve your will in the events of today. Amen.

Day 292

The Very Rev. Jeffrey John
Dean of St. Alban's
Hertfordshire, England

Ezekiel 43–44, Psalm 89:19-52, Revelation 13

Once the temple has been rebuilt, Ezekiel looks forward to the presence of God returning to it, but he warns that this will be strictly on condition that its ordinances are observed. Only those who are qualified by race, family descent, and the rules of cultic purity may serve there. Foreigners are strictly excluded.

The vision of the beast from the sea and the beast from the earth in Revelation 13 is very close to similar visions in Daniel. John has adapted Daniel's allegory, which referred to the Greek Empire persecuting the Jews, to the Roman Empire persecuting Christians. In both cases, political power is the tool of supernatural power. The dragon (or Satan) gives the beast (the Roman Empire) his own power and authority to rule over all nations and to make war on Christians. The account of one of the beast's heads receiving a mortal wound is almost certainly a reference to Nero, who after his suicide was widely believed to have been resurrected in the form of various impostors. The mysterious number 666 also probably refers to him. (Hebrew letters are also used as numbers, and "'Emperor Nero" written in Hebrew is 666).

It is remarkable how the Roman Empire's work of evil parodies the work of God, with references to the Trinity and the church. The first beast receives the dragon's authority just as Christ receives the Father's, and like the Son of Man in Daniel, "rules over every tribe and tongue and nation" (Revelation 13:7). People cry, "Who is like the beast?" as the psalmist cries, "'Who is like God?" (Psalm 89:6). The second beast resembles a lamb but speaks like a dragon. Nero's supposed resurrection mimics that of Christ. The second beast "breathes life" into the first as a parody of the Spirit and puts a mark on his servants, just as the church marks her own with the seal of the Spirit and the sign of the cross.

QUESTIONS

How does Ezekiel's vision of the new, purified temple compare with your idea of the church, the "spiritual temple built of living stones" that Christ came to build?

John saw the powers of evil working through the Roman Empire in its persecution of Christians. Do you see God and evil at war in the world today?

PRAYER

Grant, O Lord, we beseech thee, that the course of this world may be so peaceably ordered by thy governance that thy church may joyfully serve thee in all godly quietness; through Jesus Christ our Lord. Amen.

The Very Rev. Jeffrey John
Dean of St. Alban's
Hertfordshire, England

Day 293

Ezekiel 45–46, Psalm 90, Revelation 14

In today's reading, Ezekiel continues his list of ordinances for the new temple of his vision. Large tracts of land are apportioned for the upkeep of the prince and of the priests. The prince is enjoined to maintain justice, especially in respect of weights and measures, but the main emphasis remains on cultic purity. The hierarchical boundaries are emphasised: to preserve the temple's holiness, common people must not be allowed to defile the areas and activities restricted to the prince and the priests.

Revelation 14 is a vision of God's judgment and triumph over the forces of oppressive evil. The 144,000 who rejoice in the Lamb represent the first fruits of the saved, those who have stayed faithful to Christ under persecution. The number is symbolic and unlimited: twelve (12 x 12 = 144) recalls the twelve tribes, and 12 x 12 x 100 represents the totality of God's "true Israel," the church. The "chastity" of the saved is not necessarily sexual but more probably refers to spiritual faithfulness—Revelation regularly uses "fornication" to mean apostasy and idolatry.

The angels pronounce God's judgment on "Babylon," John's code word for the Roman Empire. The Son of Man comes on the clouds, recalling Christ's prophecy in Mark 14:62, and judgment is "reaped" by the avenging angel. As when reading Daniel 7 (from which this vision ultimately derives), it is important to remember that "Son of Man" is simply the ordinary Hebrew term for "human being."

The nations have made themselves less than human—they have become "'beasts" by practising idolatry and oppression. As Son of Man, Christ shows us what true humanity is. And this vision, for all its bloodiness, is a promise that in the end humanity will win out against all that can make us beastly and subhuman.

QUESTIONS

What is the difference between holiness as Ezekiel conceives it and your understanding of holiness?

Why do you think Jesus chose the title Son of Man, rather than Son of God or Messiah or Saviour, as the way he normally referred to himself?

PRAYER

Lord God, you have made us human beings in your image. Forgive and heal all that spoils and hides your image in us and makes us less than fully human. Help us grow in the likeness of Christ, so that we may become the people you created us to be. Amen.

Day 294: Enjoy hearing the Scriptures read aloud in church.

Day 295

The Rt. Rev. Henry Scriven
Mission Director for Latin America
Church Mission Society
Oxford, England

Ezekiel 47–48, Psalm 91, Revelation 15

The last two chapters of Ezekiel's prophecy deal with the division of land among the twelve tribes of Israel. The theme is one of order and concern for the detail of human life; the tribes each have their own portion of land. Theology is here expressed through geography; issues of space, access, and position relative to the temple are significant. At the center is the restored temple from which the healing river flows.

God's presence with his people is the source of life for the world. The land has been so defiled, and evil has so affected every part of life, that the promise of restoration is a great comfort for every believer. God's power and authority is absolute and cannot abide the presence of evil, as Revelation 15 shows. Ultimately, it's all about God's sovereignty. In Psalm 91, the same powerful God promises protection for his people, shelter in the midst of the hardest of times.

QUESTIONS

How is theology expressed in geography today?

How do you experience the healing river, and how can you be an agent of that healing for others?

Can you abide in the shelter of the Most High, even when everything seems to be going wrong? Can you lift others into God's refuge?

PRAYER

Great and amazing are your deeds, O Lord God the Almighty. You alone are holy, and you answer me and are with me in trouble. You deliver me from the snare of the fowler and from the deadly pestilence, and under your wings I find refuge. Amen.

The Rt. Rev. Henry Scriven
Mission Director for Latin America
Church Mission Society
Oxford, England

Day 296

Daniel 1–2, Psalm 92, Revelation 16

Daniel is a model for Christians of a disciplined, holy lifestyle. He accepted his new culture to a degree, learning the language and literature of the Babylonians (Daniel 1:4) and accepting his new name (1:7), but he drew the line at accepting the king's diet. This is a great example of cultural discrimination. Every culture is a mixture of good and evil, truth and error, beauty and ugliness. Daniel and his friends resolved to assimilate all that was good in the Chaldean culture, but they were equally determined to reject everything that was incompatible with their revealed faith. God honored their faithfulness (1:15-17) and gave them understanding, and he gave to Daniel the gift of interpreting dreams.

In Revelation 16, the key verse is 17. "It is finished" was the same cry Jesus gave from the cross. No one can successfully fight with God; this scene pictures an end to rebellion against God.

QUESTIONS

What are the good and the evil elements in your culture? Where does God ask you to draw the line?

Can you trust in God's judgments today, even though there is so much that is beyond your understanding?

PRAYER

It is good to give thanks to you, O Lord, to sing praises to your name, O Most High. Give me grace today, Lord, to be faithful to your word and to trust in your sovereignty. Amen.

Day 297

The Rt. Rev. Henry Scriven
Mission Director for Latin America
Church Mission Society
Oxford, England

Daniel 3–4, Psalm 93, Revelation 17

The telegram from the besieged troops in Dunkirk in 1940 had only three words: "But if not." That was enough to spur the nation of Britain to send thousands of small boats to rescue the 350,000 men trapped on the beaches.

Biblical knowledge was greater at that time than it is today, but those three words are still inspirational. The three young men in the Book of Daniel would not be shaken from their faith in their God, come what may. They were far from home and all the odds were against them, but they knew, as Nebuchadnezzar had to learn, that "The Most High has sovereignty over the kingdom of mortals and gives it to whom he will" (Daniel 4:32).

Similarly, Revelation's chapter 17 alludes to the persecutions of the Roman Empire, but the theme of sovereignty is clear there, as it is in Psalm 93.

QUESTIONS

Do these passages help you to pray for those suffering under unjust rulers? Identify two or three situations for your prayers today.

Does the apocalyptic literature help you to trust in God's sovereignty?

PRAYER

Pray Psalm 93 for yourself and for all who suffer today.

The Rev. Canon Mark Oakley
Treasurer
St. Paul's Cathedral
London, England

Day 298

Daniel 5–6, Psalm 94, Revelation 18

It is said that we spin ourselves into a circle of spending money we don't have on things we don't want in order to impress people we don't like. Today's readings suggest this is nothing new.

In both Daniel and Revelation we are introduced to great wealth, power, and puzzlement. King Belshazzar, surrounded by his possessions, "praised the gods of gold and silver" (Daniel 5:4), and John, using all the strength of the old prophetic oracles against Babylon, turned on the Rome of his day. For him the Empire's prosperity rested on a contempt for human lives (Revelation 18:13) and therefore "the fruit for which your soul longed has gone from you" (v. 14).

Set in the midst of all this is the figure of Daniel, who showed his fidelity to God by praying regularly and without apology. Having condemned Belshazzar for acting proudly, he showed in his own actions that a human self is most itself when not being selfish. He bowed down three times a day to praise his God and to place himself in proportion.

Prayer distils us and, like a snowfall in the soul, creates a new landscape from which to explore the spiritual adventure of being alive. The ancient Assyrians had the same word for prayer as the word they used for opening a clenched fist. Prayer does not so much demand as receive—and when your life is centered on it, not even lions can touch you.

QUESTIONS

Do you have the same public and private commitment to God as Daniel? If not, what holds you back?

Your bank statement reveals where you place value: what gods are you praising at the moment?

PRAYER

Loving God, open me, and this day give to me to your eternal freshness. Deepen my relationship with you, my neighbour, and myself, and teach me what to leave behind so I travel with you more lovingly, more closely; through Jesus Christ our Lord. Amen.

Day 299

The Rev. Canon Mark Oakley
Teasurer
St. Paul's Cathedral
London, England

Daniel 7–8, Psalm 95, Revelation 19

The readings today remind us of the importance of poetry to faith. So much of our talk of God has all the depth of a bumper sticker—sound bites that we are meant to honk at if we agree or to drive by if we don't. The seductions of quick clarity and the easy answer lure us into reducing God to another bit of downloadable information. To read the Bible, however, is to realise that we are not here to resolve the mystery of God but to deepen it, and that God remains the question, not the answer.

So, in Daniel we read of dreams, visions, and the patient search for interpretation. The easy answers are not the ones worth pursuing, and Daniel confronts all the ingredients of his soul that come out to play in his dreaming to see what God might be saying.

The author of Psalm 95, a poet of great skill, likewise tells us not to harden our hearts as we fall down before the God of heights and depths. In Revelation, John sees heaven open, and the imagery that ensues is riotous, confusing, and dislocating. What's going on? What am I supposed to make of all this?

In the life of faith, what we long for most eludes us. It could not be otherwise, for it is desire that is the pulse of our relationship with God. Our belief in God nourishes us by the hunger it creates in us, intensifying rather than satisfying our longing for God. God is the depth, not the surface, and is to be found in the later discernment, not the first impression. As Daniel says, "My thoughts greatly terrified me and my face turned pale; but I kept the matter in my mind" (Daniel 7:28).

QUESTIONS

Today's texts invite us to wonder whether God is in the world as poetry is in the poem. If so, how do we read that world?

How we hear a text differs according to how we approach it. We hear something that begins "Here is the news…" differently from something that starts "Once upon a time…" How do you hear the Bible?

PRAYER

God of beauty, ever ancient and ever new, refresh my eyes, relight my heart, warm my affections, so that I might live in and for you, willing to be stretched and moulded into the likeness of your Son, Jesus Christ. Amen.

The Rev. Canon Mark Oakley
Treasurer
St. Paul's Cathedral
London, England
Day 300

Daniel 9–10, Psalm 96, Revelation 20

In his poem "Prayer Before Birth," which voices the call of an unborn child from the womb, the Anglo-Irish poet Louis MacNeice writes: "I am not yet born; O hear me, Let not the man who is beast or who thinks he is God come near me."

Toward the end of the poem the child prays for strength to resist all that will come to drown his or her individuality and self-confidence. Having already identified the "wise lies" that can allure, the poet recognizes that acumen will be needed to keep one's integrity when belittled by officialdom or intimates, isolated by stranger and relation alike. We can be led all too easily by loud or charming types, often with frightening consequences.

In today's Old Testament reading, Daniel begins a thorough self-scrutiny by putting on sackcloth and ashes, reminding himself of what he is truly made and placing himself in the presence of the majesty of God. Such recognition is a means of grace. Hard full stops in life can be transformed into commas as God refreshes by forgiveness and encouragement.

Similarly, in Revelation 20, John tells us of the dragon who has wickedly deceived people and nations, of false prophets and Satan's misleading charm. All of their voices are convincingly loud. Can we refuse to live down to them and instead live up to the voice that comes from the heavenly throne?

Those of us in the church can be caught up in a net of compromises that dilute the gospel we hope to be transformed by. If, as Martin Buber said, nothing can mask the face of God so much as religion, then we need prayers for exposure, for that true gift of prophecy that tells it as it is, such as we find in Daniel and in the raw reality of Revelation. We need the nerve to pray to be judged, for ultimately judgment is liberating when, finally, we are told who we are and see ourselves for whom we have become.

QUESTIONS

What has the world made of me? How can I amend what needs to be changed?

What prayer would I now pray from the womb before birth, knowing what I know today?

PRAYER

Holy God, may the noise of angry voices be submerged and drowned in your love. May I come up from the waters and hear only your heavenly voice telling me I am your child, called to help others hear your transforming word, which we have encountered in Christ Jesus, our Lord. Amen.

Day 301: Enjoy hearing the Scriptures read aloud in church.

Day 302

The Most Rev. Barry Morgan
Archbishop of Wales
Cardiff, Wales

Daniel 11–12, Psalm 97, Revelation 21

The Book of Daniel, like the Revelation of John, is full of profound theological and prophetic insights. Both books are difficult to understand because they belong to a genre of literature called apocalyptic, which literally means "unveiling." Both writers claim that the future has been unveiled to them by God. These books were written at a time of persecution: Daniel in the second century B.C.E., when the Jews were being severely oppressed by the Hellenistic Syrian Seleucids, and Revelation during the first century C.E., when the Christian church was being persecuted by the Roman Empire. They give reassurance that in spite of all appearances to the contrary, the future is in God's hands and he will ultimately be victorious. God's people are challenged not to give in to the forces of darkness but to continue their faithful witness.

Psalm 97 sums up this theme by asserting the supreme Lordship of God over the earth and his faithful watch over his people. The abiding message in today's readings is that whatever difficulties we face, God is greater than them and will ultimately triumph.

But both Daniel and Revelation also look to new life with God beyond this world. The earliest canonical reference of life after death comes in Daniel 12:1-3. Up until then, Old Testament writers believed that those who died went to Sheol, described by one commentator as "a mythical version of the tomb, a place of darkness and silence from which no one returns."

Revelation sees the union of heaven and earth, of God living with his people, and in this new cosmos, the end of suffering, sorrow, and death. It is God's new creation for a redeemed humanity where all nations live in total harmony. In the language of richly poetic imagery, the book speaks of God's future and the gifts he will shower on his people; the writing is full of hope and promise.

We are the object of God's deepest desire; as such, the healing of the nations, the reconciliation of men and women everywhere, is the promise he holds before us, as invitation and gift.

QUESTIONS

Do you sometimes think that tragedies mean that God is absent from his world?

Do you really believe that you are precious to God and totally loved by him?

PRAYER

Lord God, help us to renew our confidence in your love, and strengthen us with the gift of your Spirit, so that we might acknowledge you, our Creator and Redeemer; through Jesus Christ our Lord. Amen.

The Most Rev. Barry Morgan
Archbishop of Wales
Cardiff, Wales

Day 303

Hosea 1–2, Psalm 98, Revelation 22

Hosea prophesied in the eighth century B.C.E., when the Northern Kingdom of Israel was eventually captured by Assyria and some of its people carried off into exile. Hosea saw this as God's response to Israel's unfaithfulness to the covenant. Gomer, Hosea's wife, was either a prostitute or committed adultery during their marriage, and she is compared to Israel, lusting after the gods of Baal. In the end, God, like Hosea, woos back his erring wife because his nature is one of mercy, forgiveness, and love. The nature of that kind of God is echoed in Psalm 98: "who is faithful to the house of Israel" (v. 3). Mercy, not punishment, has the last word.

That mercy and compassion of God is shown in the Book of Revelation as God's new creation where the nations are healed and people respond in love to God's divine love. In such a world, God is encountered face to face—something hitherto regarded as being too terrifying for any human being. Such is the nature of God's new world.

These passages signify that the heart of God's nature is compassion, love, and grace. Like Hosea taking back his erring wife, God forgives Israel again and again. So, too, God through Jesus forgives his disciples in spite of their failure to live up to the challenges of the gospel. This is the good news to which we are asked to respond. As one hymn writer puts it, "He who breathes through all creation, he is love, eternal love" (*The Hymnal 1982*, #379).

Revelation is written in language that ought not to be interpreted literally, but its underlying message is that of God's faithfulness to, and hope for, his people. In the end, it is the promise of God's faithfulness that invites us to participate in his life, no matter who we are, where we have come from, or what we have suffered. All our weaknesses and failures are, ultimately, eclipsed by the strength of God's love for us.

QUESTIONS

How often have we made promises and broken them? Is that why we find it so difficult to accept that God promises us new life? Do we judge God's ability to keep promises by our own standards?

PRAYER

Lord God, creator of all that is seen and unseen, we thank you for your faithfulness to us; as we renew our faith in you, so take what we are and who we are to your generous heart and renew us through your Spirit. We ask this in the name of Jesus Christ, our light and our salvation. Amen.

Day 304

The Most Rev. Barry Morgan
Archbishop of Wales
Cardiff, Wales

Hosea 3–4, Psalm 99, Matthew 1

The woman in this passage from the Book of Hosea is commonly thought to be his wife, who has committed adultery. Her sin is compared to Israel's adultery with other gods. Yet in spite of Israel's apostasy and unfaithfulness, God is merciful; this is dramatically illustrated by Hosea's buying back of his wife after she has left him.

The link with the first chapter of Matthew seems very obscure at first. Matthew traces Jesus' origins back to Abraham, perhaps because some people had leveled accusations of illegitimacy about Jesus. Illegitimate children were not regarded as children of Abraham, and Matthew is therefore anxious to emphasise that Jesus is a true child of Abraham. Matthew's genealogy also includes four women, unusual since they were not the matriarchs of Israel. They all have a whiff of scandal about them: Bathsheba, who committed adultery with David; Tamor who slept with her father-in-law, Judah; Rahab, who was a prostitute; and Ruth who propositioned her kinsman, Boaz.

Matthew links these women to Joseph's shame about Mary's pregnancy until he was told in a dream how Mary had conceived. The link of Hosea's wife to Mary and these four other women then becomes obvious: all of them were involved in unusual relationships and yet were used by God in different ways to save his people. God's providence cannot ultimately be thwarted.

God powerfully uses even our most inglorious moments and what we are sometimes most ashamed of to bring us new life and healing. Wilfred Owen's poem "Spring Offensive" uses a powerful image of the soldiers' boots being "blessed with gold." It was, in fact, an image from the poet's childhood, when buttercups left golden pollen on his shoes when he walked through a meadow. God's very life irradiates us with a blessing that can reflect his glory, even in the most inglorious of situations. It is, after all, what the Incarnation has brought about—the life of heaven and earth, brought together.

QUESTIONS

Do you find it easy to forgive those who have let you down?

Do you believe that God's purpose can work out through the most unpromising of circumstances?

PRAYER

Loving Father, bless with the life-giving dew of your presence our lives, our homes and families, and the places where we work, live, and witness. May we reflect your peace and light in the darkest corners of your world, to bring harmony and justice. We ask this in the name of your risen Son, Jesus Christ our Lord. Amen.

The Rev. Dr. Libby Gibson
Senior Associate Rector
Church of the Holy Comforter
Vienna, Virginia

Day 305

Hosea 5–6, Psalm 100, Matthew 2

Jubilate Deo! This song of praise has been offered in the Judeo-Christian tradition for centuries; it was part of ancient temple liturgies in Jerusalem. As Anglicans, we are familiar with this psalm of thanksgiving and pray it often as part of Morning Prayer. "Make a joyful noise to the Lord, all the earth" (Psalm 100:1). As I write this meditation, the sounds and sights of spring surround me—gorgeous cherry trees, chirping birds, tulips—the Lord is good indeed!

I love the hymn "Earth and All Stars" (*The Hymnal 1982*, #412) for the variety of ways we see all the earth making a joyful noise to God. Loud rushing planets, hail, wind, trumpets, engines, pounding hammers, boiling test tubes, cheering crowds, and loud praying members all sing to the Lord a new song. From the experiences of your life, what might you add?

When I listen to people in prayer groups offer their praise and thanks, I regularly hear gratitude for health, family, friends, shelter, meals, our pets, seasonable weather, and our church families. But as Saint Ignatius reminds us, all the things of this world are gifts of God, created so we can come to love and serve God more completely. This is easy to feel when we see a new baby or hear a glorious piece of music, but what about construction on the highway, bickering children, and sudden illness?

As Archbishop Rowan Williams and Sister Joan Chittister remind us in *Uncommon Gratitude: Alleluia for All That Is*, even in times of uncertainty, suffering, and disappointment, we can offer praise and thanksgiving to God. For God's love is everlasting and enduring, reaching out to us in times of great joy and sorrow and helping us find the "Alleluia"!

QUESTIONS

Is it easier for you to give thanks to God when things are going well in your life? Can you praise God when times are difficult?

How have you experienced life-giving, holy moments in times of darkness and suffering? Can you sing, "Alleluia for all that is"?

PRAYER

We thank you and bless you for all of the gifts of this life, O Lord, and ask for the grace to see your hand in all that is. Amen.

Day 306

The Rev. Dr. Libby Gibson
Senior Associate Rector
Church of the Holy Comforter
Vienna, Virginia

Hosea 7–8, Psalm 101, Matthew 3

Do you ever feel unworthy to do something that is asked of you? When I was in seminary, one of my professors worshiped at my field-education site. At that parish, after the celebration of the Holy Eucharist, we offered healing prayers at the communion rail. As I was moving down the line of people, I looked up and caught sight of my professor. I froze. Instantly I was flooded with self-doubt. She offered healing prayers at the seminary, and I needed prayers from her. What was she doing coming to me?

When John the Baptist sees Jesus approaching him to be baptized and expresses his hesitation, I love Jesus' response, offered here from Eugene Peterson's translation *The Message:* "Do it. God's work, putting things right all these centuries, is coming together right now in this baptism" (Matthew 3:15). John's hesitation and my hesitation are human and understandable. But when we get stuck in our human ways of thinking, we may miss the possibility that God is using us in ways that we cannot understand to "put things right."

The theme of God using unlikely people in unexpected ways can be read throughout the Bible. The Hebrew midwives saved the Hebrew people when they were in Egypt. Rahab the prostitute protected the Hebrew spies when they were in Jericho. As you approach the last part of this Bible Challenge, where do you see this theme in the Bible? Have you ever been used by God in some unexpected way, in a way that you felt unworthy to perform?

I finally collected myself, and offered healing prayers with my professor. My personal insecurities momentarily made me forget that it's not I who heals, but God. It's not I who protects, but God. Our job is to recognize these moments and consent.

QUESTIONS

Why do you think that Jesus asked John to baptize him?

The other gospels don't show John's hesitation. Why do you think that is?

PRAYER

Gracious God, grant us the grace to do what you ask even when we feel unworthy, trusting that all of our good works are for your glory. Amen.

The Rev. Dr. Libby Gibson
Senior Associate Rector
Church of the Holy Comforter
Vienna, Virginia

Day 307

Hosea 9–10, Psalm 102, Matthew 4

As we continue to read Hosea, we feel God's fury with the people of Israel. In the early chapters of this book, their repeated violations of the covenant are represented as adultery, with Ephraim—one of the tribes of Israel—accused of "playing the whore." We hear God's pain and deep sense of betrayal and God's judgment of the people. Intertwined in God's expressions of outrage, we hear Israel's expressions of repentance.

As painful as it is to read about God's judgment and to consider the ways that we betray God, I find it comforting to have this image of God enraged by the chosen people. When the people worshiped other gods, their idolatry was not merely a violation of religious laws (which is bad enough!) but deeply cut into the bonds of the covenant with God. God has a complaint with the people and makes sure they know it by using this language of whoredom and betrayal.

Do you ever feel that you have angered God, that you have violated God's covenant with you? Or do you ever feel as if you have a complaint against God? Do you call God names and demand an accounting when you feel abandoned and betrayed?

Hosea reminds us that when we are in a covenant relationship with someone, including God, each party has a right to complain against the other. God doesn't walk out on the people of Israel no matter how much they stray, and God never walks out on us. Yet, do we walk out on God? When our lives are full of suffering, we may feel our faith falter. In these times, we don't have to be polite! If you have a complaint against God, be of strong courage and speak to God in whatever language will express your pain and outrage. This is what people do when they are in relationships—they communicate with each other and are faithful to each other, no matter how hurt and disappointed they may be.

QUESTIONS

Does it surprise you to hear God speaking to the chosen people in such harsh language? Is this comforting? Upsetting?

Have you ever felt betrayed by God? Were you willing to take your complaint to God, using whatever language best expressed your feelings?

PRAYER

Give us strength, Gracious God, to seek forgiveness when we betray our relationships and to openly express ourselves when we feel hurt and abandoned. Amen.

Day 308: Enjoy hearing the Scriptures read aloud in church.

Day 309

The Rev. Canon Dr. Alyson Barnett-Cowan
Director for Unity, Faith and Order
Anglican Communion Office
London, England

Hosea 11–12, Psalm 103, Matthew 5

Earlier in his prophecy, Hosea used the example of his unfaithful wife to contrast God's steadfast love with Israel's sin. In chapter 11, he uses another family metaphor. Here God is a loving parent whose emotions are in conflict over the behaviour of a wayward child. God remembers the early days of the child's growth and nurture. God is furious that the child has now rebelled, yet cannot forsake one who has been loved so much.

"Ephraim," the nickname for the northern tribes, and "Judah," the south, have both turned to the worship of idols, to greed, dishonesty, and violence, and God is uncertain whether to unleash great anger against them or to restore them. "My heart is changed within me, all my compassion is aroused" (Hosea 11:8), says God, who, unlike humans, will turn from anger.

The same theme runs through Psalm 103, which is a hymn of praise. God is a parent who has compassion for God's children and in spite of anger will forgive and heal.

Matthew 5 begins the Sermon on the Mount. Through the next three chapters, Matthew gathers various sayings of Jesus to provide moral instruction for the gathered community of a primarily Hebrew Christian church. The teaching to the disciples is to form them into a community different from both the synagogue and the nations. The Beatitudes (vv. 3–10) set out the values of those beloved by God; the series of statements beginning "You have heard it said…but I say" (vv. 21–48) exhort Christians to a higher standard even than the Law of Moses: the standard of the love and righteousness of God. It is the God who shows infinite love and mercy to God's people, and who asks them to aspire to that same perfect love.

QUESTIONS

In what human relationships have you most experienced the love and compassion of God?

Which of the Beatitudes do you find most challenging at the moment?

PRAYER

Praise the Lord, O my soul, and all that is within me praise God's holy name! Loving God, thank you for your infinite mercy and love, which has forgiven and healed me whenever I have turned away from you. May I never forget all that you have done, and give me the grace to walk in your ways. Amen.

The Rev. Canon Dr. Alyson Barnett-Cowan
Director for Unity, Faith and Order
Anglican Communion Office
London, England

Day 310

Hosea 13–14, Psalm 104, Matthew 6

In Hosea's prophecy today, God continues to remember all that God has done in bringing the people of Israel through the wilderness. Though they turn from God to worship idols, though they put their trust in earthly rulers instead of in divine guidance, God will still deliver and redeem them. "Return, Israel, to the Lord your God!" is the constant plea of the prophets. Death and destruction follow from the choices of sin; life and flourishing are found with God. We are constantly putting things of our own creating in the place of God, and we find that life is empty as a result. In God alone is our true life to be found.

Psalm 104, another hymn of praise, recounts all the great works of God in creation and in continuing to provide for all that God has made. Everything receives its life and nurture from God. What a contrast to lifeless idols!

In Matthew 6, Jesus continues to lay out a way of life for his disciples. It is a way of quiet and private discipline, not done for show. He urges them to follow the traditional Jewish practices of prayer, fasting, and alms giving and provides a model for prayer that we know as the Lord's Prayer.

In a way of life oriented to God, there is no need for the anxious worry that is so characteristic of our society. Our trust should be in God's grace and providence rather than in getting and spending. As Psalm 104 says, God will provide all that we need.

QUESTIONS

What things are in danger of becoming idols for you?

The Lord's Prayer lays out a way of life. Which line of it is the greatest challenge for you?

PRAYER

Holy God of all creation, you are great and good! Help me to see and treat the world as your gift to all of your creatures, and help me to trust that you provide me with all that I truly need. Amen.

Day 311

The Rev. Canon Dr. Alyson Barnett-Cowan
Director for Unity, Faith and Order
Anglican Communion Office
London, England

Joel 1–2, Psalm 105, Matthew 7

Scholars have had a hard time determining exactly when the prophet Joel lived. It was probably after the time of the Exile, when the temple had become the focal point of Jewish life. It was in a time that followed a devastating invasion of flying locusts that, like an invading army, laid waste to the land. The crops are completely ruined, and there is famine and drought. The destruction caused by the locusts is compared to an even greater, apocalyptic judgment, "the day of the Lord." Joel exhorts the people to repent: everyone is to fast and to gather to implore God to spare the people. And God promises in faithfulness to restore the land to its previous plenty. Finally, there is a promise that Peter will recall on the Day of Pentecost, that the Spirit of God will be poured out on all people to sustain them in the last days.

Psalm 105 is another hymn of praise to the God who led Israel out of Egypt. It recalls the plagues that fell on the Egyptians in the time of Moses and the gift of bread and water in the wilderness as God remembered the covenant with Abraham and blessed the people.

Matthew 7 concludes Jesus' teaching in the Sermon on the Mount with some of the most familiar verses in the Bible, including the Golden Rule that is common to the great religions of the world: "treat others as you would have them treat you" (Matthew 7:12). Jesus contrasts the narrow gate of life with the wide road of destruction, the true with the false prophet, the house built on rock with the one built on sand. Disciples are to be more critical of themselves than of others, to search persistently for the truth, and to act on Jesus' words, for it is by our "fruits" and not our words that we will be measured in God's eyes.

QUESTIONS

While times of devastating destruction can be called "the day of the Lord," the Bible portrays them as times when God's goodness provides people the means to come through them. When have you experienced God's goodness in the midst of what might have seemed a disaster?

To what extent do you live by the Golden Rule?

PRAYER

God, grant me the serenity to accept the things I cannot change, courage to change the things I can, and the wisdom to know the difference. Amen.

The Rev. Dr. Barney Hawkins IV
Vice President and Associate Dean
Virginia Theological Seminary
Alexandria, Virginia

Day 312

Joel 3, Psalm 106, Matthew 8

The Book of Joel is a hymn that is both lament and praise. We first sing a stanza about ruin and devastation, with the people of God like a "virgin dressed in sackcloth." In the last stanza there is no lamenting. Judah and Jerusalem have passed through a "valley of decision" (Joel 3:14), and the mountains are dripping "sweet wine" (v. 3:18). The persecutors (Egypt) are punished and become a "desolate wilderness" (v. 3:19) because of what they did to the people of Judah.

Judah's victory is Jesus' vocation for the whole world. In Matthew's Gospel, the Messiah, Israel's consolation, is the Son of Man, actually the son of David, the son of Abraham. In chapter 8 we discover Jesus living out his vocation. He is healing the inhabitants of the land that Joel wrote about. The leper is cleansed; a paralyzed man is cured; Peter's mother-in-law is made well; and the demon-possessed are set free. Jesus even "heals" nature when he stills the storm after people cry out, "Lord, save us! We are perishing!"

Joel and Matthew wrote to people of "little faith" who were "perishing." Most of us have called out to Jesus, "Lord, save us!" We long for wholeness—in our own lives and in the broken life of the world. But we often search for it in all the wrong places—we look to philosophers and great thinkers for the answers we need. It takes more than a "little faith" to finally say that Jesus is the answer. In Matthew 8:14-17 we read the lovely account of Peter's house being made whole. The people reflected on what Jesus did, and they said, "He took our infirmities and bore our diseases" (Matthew 8:17). The Messiah comes as the Son of Man, and his vocation is to heal our brokenness. Jesus empties himself, and the world God loves is healed.

QUESTIONS

When have you called out to Jesus from your little boat saying, "Lord save me!"?

The leper chose to be made clean. Must we choose to accept the healing touch of Jesus?

PRAYER

Loving God, we draw near to an untenanted cross. Once we said, "Crucify him!" Now we pray for healing. Now we cry out, "Lord save me!" Heal our infirmities and make us whole; and this we ask in the name of Jesus, who is our Lord and Savior. Amen.

Day 313

The Rev. Dr. Barney Hawkins IV
Vice President and Associate Dean
Virginia Theological Seminary
Alexandria, Virginia

Amos 1, Psalm 107, Matthew 9

Most of us would not enjoy having cocktails with one of the Old Testament prophets! They are unpredictable, and they say things that are not polite: they would ruin a civilized evening. And they seem to talk a lot. Amos is no exception. Who of us wants a "plumb line" held over our city or "in our midst"? Amos' parable about "a basket of summer fruit" leaves my stomach a bit queasy. Amos 1 leaves little to write home about. Israel's neighbors do not have a chance—they are all consigned to the outer rungs of Dante's Inferno. Neighboring kings will go into exile. Gaza, Ashdod, Tyre, Edom, the "strongholds of Bozrah" are doomed. The Ammonites will suffer forever because they have "ripped open pregnant women in Gilead in order to enlarge their territory" (Amos 1:13). There is no good news from Amos, who "was among the shepherds of Tekoa."

The Old Testament is full of God's judgment. Is God vengeful? Does God choose one people over another? Clearly, the Lord was and is the God of Abraham, Isaac, and Jacob. God identified with Israel and called that people into covenant.

This is all rather perplexing. Most of us believe in a God who is inclusive, a God who loves the whole world. But in the Old Testament, it is clear: God loves concretely in space and time. Israel's story is grounded in a covenant relationship with not just any God but, rather, the God of Abraham and those who came after him. In Amos, God is angry with Israel's neighbors, but the same God also rains judgment down on Judah because they have "rejected the law of the Lord and have not kept his statutes" (Amos 2:4). Destruction and restoration are chapters in Israel's stormy relationship with God.

So, let us be clear: to be chosen by God does not lead to a peaceable kingdom. No, being called by God, being in a covenant relationship with God, carries life-giving responsibility.

QUESTIONS

Where is God's judgment in the New Testament?

As a Christian, are you in a covenant relationship with God?

PRAYER

Gracious God, hold back your judging hand. Give us time to be found by you. Let your grace and mercy carry us to a place where the grass is green and the water fresh and flowing. We pray in the name of Jesus who cures our souls. Amen.

The Rev. Dr. Barney Hawkins IV
Vice President and Associate Dean
Virginia Theological Seminary
Alexandria, Virginia

Day 314

Amos 2, Psalm 108, Matthew 10

As Israel with its twelve tribes was called by God, so Jesus called his twelve apostles, giving them instructions to travel lightly as they shared God's good news with the "lost sheep of the house of Israel." He told them they would be persecuted in Matthew 10:16: "I am sending you out like sheep into the midst of wolves." He invited them into a servant ministry. Jesus charged the twelve to have no fear. The position description in Matthew 10 concludes with the promise of a reward: "and whoever gives even a cup of cold water to one of these little ones in the name of a disciple—truly I tell you, none of these will lose their reward" (v. 42).

Let us focus on that phrase, "in the name of a disciple." Jesus gave great authority to his apostles. Their names mattered. He entrusted his message, ministry, and mission to them. Jesus gave them his name, but they also kept their own names, their own identities. It seems that Jesus held nothing back. He gave full instructions to the twelve.

We are Jesus' disciples in our time. We should take heart: Jesus does not call the perfect or the trained or the most pious. He calls ordinary people and gives them authority "over unclean spirits, to cast them out, and to cure every disease and every sickness" (Matthew 10:1). The dour Welsh poet R. S. Thomas believes that God calls the "crippled soul" to invite people to the table where the broken body and shed blood are served. Thomas is convinced that it is only the "crippled soul" who knows in the deepest places that if we follow Jesus and are his disciples, then we must limp through life on our prayers. Jesus looks for disciples who discover that we begin and end our serving on our knees.

QUESTIONS

What does servant ministry mean?

How does a "crippled soul" proclaim the wholeness of God?

PRAYER

Loving God, you call us each by name. You give instructions to those who follow you. Make us joyful servants who stay on our knees as we do the work you have given us to do. Heal us and make us whole as we tell others of Jesus Christ in whose holy name we pray. Amen.

Day 315: Enjoy hearing the Scriptures read aloud in church.

Day 316

The Rev. Dr. Tim Perry
Rector
Church of the Epiphany
Sudbury, Ontario

Amos 3, Psalm 109, Matthew 11

God's judgment is often downplayed. We prefer to talk about God's love and patience. The Scripture lessons, however, all speak of judgment, of a God who takes the side of sufferers and opposes those who reject his salvation.

The prophet Amos speaks of judgment coming upon the Israelites precisely because of the grace and favour they have been shown (Amos 3:2). Jesus, in our gospel today, speaks similarly. The cities in which he ministered will suffer more than Tyre, Sidon, and even Sodom because of their lack of repentance in response to his teaching and miracles (Matthew 11:20-24).

How discomfiting! Being called by God in the Exodus, and later being encountered by God Incarnate, was both the grace and mercy of God turning toward God's people and the judgment of God upon their lack of repentance. Gospel and Law, grace and judgment, love and wrath come together. They are not polar opposites set against each other. They are different ways of naming God's jealous love, which enters into history to heal and to restore and set it aright. God promises to annihilate every "no" to his intervention.

Perhaps we are more comfortable praying like today's psalmist, who wishes God to take vengeance on his enemies and show mercy upon him. Grace and mercy are for us; judgment is for others. There are times when those kinds of prayers are inevitable and even appropriate—otherwise, they would not be found in Holy Scripture. They give to the voiceless words with which to call to God for justice. And if God is the God of mercy and judgment, then such prayers do indeed move his heart.

But they are dangerous prayers. Asking God to come in judgment is to place ourselves— not just our enemies—under that judgment. And when we do that, we are invited again to repent and believe, to assent to God's "yes" to us in Christ, and therein to find mercy. It is a "yes" that judges and finally overcomes every "no."

QUESTIONS

How do the Scripture readings for today challenge the idea that "God is for us and against our enemies"?

What does living faithfully under the grace and judgment of Jesus look like for you?

PRAYER

Lord Jesus Christ, in grace you turned toward me and called me to repentance. Give me faith and strength to repent and believe your Holy Gospel. Through your holy name, I pray. Amen.

The Rev. Dr. Tim Perry
Rector
Church of the Epiphany
Sudbury, Ontario

Day 317

Amos 4, Psalm 110, Matthew 12

"Religion is unfaith. It is the one great affair of godless humanity." So wrote the great twentieth-century theologian Karl Barth. He echoes the prophet Amos in our Old Testament lesson today.

Amos continues his message of judgment of the people of Israel. They oppress the poor and the needy, live in prosperity (Amos 4:1), and remain very religiously devout (4:4-5). Religion has become a cover under which evil can hide and thrive. In spite of repeated judgments sent by God (4:6-11), the people will not repent. It seems that they are too religious to recognize that they are doing evil in oppressing the poor or to understand that a repentant response has more to do with pursuing God's justice than being liturgically pristine.

Similarly, in today's gospel Jesus condemns the religious experts of his day for misunderstanding the law, thereby turning it into a burden rather than a joy (Matthew 12:1-14). Their expertise renders them blind to the presence of God in their midst; they attribute the power of Jesus to the devil (12:24) and are stone deaf to God's Spirit (Matthew 12:32). No repentance comes from such willful blindness and deafness, and therefore there can be no forgiveness.

We live in a world where religion, far from fading away as the disciples of Karl Marx once predicted, is thriving. Islam and Christianity are growing exponentially in South Asia and Africa, with violent clashes sometimes the tragic result. In the West, secularism has ceased to be a practical way for differing religious views to live together and has become instead its own increasingly intolerant "Religion of No Religion."

In such a world, the prophet's and Jesus' condemnations of religion are needed! They remind us that religion, as a human invention, is as tainted by human sinfulness as every other human artifact. Religion—even liturgically beautiful religion—can blind us not only to the needs of our fellow human beings, but to the presence of God in our midst.

QUESTIONS

In what ways does religion—even the Christian religion—continue to blind us in the ways that Amos and Jesus describe?

How might Amos and Jesus describe our religious situation today?

PRAYER

O God, instill in us your true religion, which is love for you and for our neighbour. Open our eyes to your presence in our world; open our ears to the truth of your gospel, that we might see and hear and be saved; through Jesus Christ our Lord. Amen.

Day 318

The Rev. Dr. Tim Perry
Rector
Church of the Epiphany
Sudbury, Ontario

Amos 5, Psalm 111, Matthew 13

The gospel for today is a collection of parables through which Jesus describes the kingdom of heaven.

The first two parables draw from farming practices. The kingdom is one in which the good news of the gospel is extravagantly proclaimed to all kinds of people, not all of whom respond and persevere. It is one where "wheat" and "weeds"—again, different kinds of people—must grow together until the end and only then be separated. On the one hand, the call to repent and believe goes forward in the most inefficient and even prodigal way. On the other, not only will not all respond, but it is not easy to discern just who repents and believes and who does not.

The next two parables also take imagery from the everyday. The parable of the mustard seed emphasizes the growth of the kingdom. The seed begins puny but grows to a size one could not have foreseen, given its small start. The parable of the yeast has to do with influence. Just as yeast works its way through a whole lump of dough, so the kingdom has an impact on its location that far exceeds its original size.

The next parable has to with the kingdom's value. It is like a treasure in a field or a beautiful pearl. It is rare, but those who know its value will do anything to obtain it. And the last— the parable of the net—reintroduces the theme found in the story of the wheat and the weeds. All kinds of people will be caught up in the kingdom's scope, but only in the end will the righteous be revealed.

What ties all these parables together? The kingdom of God comes in ways and is found in places that we do not expect. It resists becoming a programme; it sometimes looks insignificant; its influence outpaces its size; and we cannot say who's in and who's short of the end. It is dynamic—always moving, shifting—always present but never obvious.

QUESTIONS

Where will you look for signs of the kingdom of God today?

What are you willing to relinquish to be included in it?

PRAYER

O Lord, you have used the foolish things to confound the wise. Grant us eyes of faith to see your kingdom among us and courage to give up all we have to obtain it. This we ask in Jesus' name. Amen.

The Rt. Rev. Mathayo Kasagara
Bishop of Lake Rukwa
Mpanda, Tanzania

Day 319

Amos 6, Psalm 112, Matthew 14

In Amos 6, the prophet directs his words toward the leaders of Israel. They are engrossed by their luxurious lifestyles, as though the word of the Lord doesn't apply to them. While the ordinary people are suffering, the leaders remain heedless, enjoying their own pleasures and deaf to God's repeated warnings.

This is a common evil, even in the present day. When disaster strikes, it is often the poor who suffer and the rich who profit. Those who are in authority often make more gains during war, famine, and other calamities than during times of peace and prosperity. When the poor are famished, the rich grow fat.

There is a similar situation in our reading in Matthew 14. The Jewish people were suffering under Roman occupation, while King Herod was living a luxurious lifestyle. The prophet John warned him that it was not lawful for him to have Herodias as his wife. But Herod was deaf to John's warnings. Herod even abused his authority by having John put to death.

What a contrast with the rich and powerful described in Psalm 112, who fear the Lord and find great delight in God's commands.

QUESTIONS

Think about the passages we have just read. Do leaders in our communities behave like the leaders of Israel and King Herod?

What effect do leaders who are concerned only about lining their own pockets have on their communities? Or the global community? How can this be changed?

PRAYER

Almighty God, help those who are in authority and in favour at the courts of princes, that they may fear God and do justice to those whom they are leading, through Jesus Christ our Lord. Amen.

Day 320

The Rt. Rev. Mathayo Kasagara
Bishop of Lake Rukwa
Mpanda, Tanzania

Amos 7, Psalm 113, Matthew 15

In Matthew 15 we learn of the compassion of our Lord Jesus. He heals the lame, the blind, the mute, and the deaf and feeds the multitudes. Psalm 113 is a hymn of praise to the same compassionate God. He comforts the poor, helps the needy, and gives children to the barren woman. So it is no surprise that in Amos 7, God listens to Amos' pleas and postpones the punishment that Israel deserves.

Amos records three visions: a plague of locusts, a firestorm, and a plumb line. God responds to Amos and holds back the locusts and fire. Yet God is just, as well as merciful, and sin has to be punished. The plumb line shows clearly that the people of Israel are not upright before God, so God has no option but to tear down the political and religious structures of Israel.

Amaziah, the priest of Bethel, reports what Amos is saying to King Jeroboam. Amaziah mocks Amos and commands that he go back to his home and earn his keep there. Even though Amaziah is a priest, he doesn't understand the crucial importance of the presence of God in Israel. He warns Amos, "Don't prophesy anymore in Bethel because it is the sanctuary of the king as well as God's temple" (Amos 7:13). Amaziah honours the king before God.

Similarly in Matthew 15, Jesus says, "These people honour me with their lips, but their hearts are far from me" (v. 8).

QUESTIONS

As you read these stories, do you see parallels between Amos and Amaziah, then and now? Pray for our spiritual leaders and ask God to change their hearts.

Do you see parallels with yourself? Ask God to forgive you.

A priest is to be the mediator between God and his people. But we don't see that in the priest Amaziah. What can we learn from Amaziah's attitude?

PRAYER

Almighty God, teach us to appreciate your favour and grace in our lives, and help us turn back to you for your forgiveness, through Jesus Christ our Lord. Amen.

The Rt. Rev. Mathayo Kasagara   **Day 321**
Bishop of Lake Rukwa
Mpanda, Tanzania

Amos 8, Psalm 114, Matthew 16

Amos 8 is the final vision: a basket of ripe fruit reveals that Israel is ripe for destruction.

God's judgment falls upon the rich and powerful who oppress the poor and marginalized. The leaders of Israel are so focused on making money that they consider even religious festivals to be a nuisance because they interfere with business. Seeing their greed and dishonesty, God withdraws his presence. That is what he means when he says, "I will send a famine … a famine of hearing the word of the Lord" (Amos 8:11).

The leaders of Israel have rejected God's word and warning. Their punishment is that they will never again hear God's word of comfort. They will stagger to every corner of the land, searching for the word of the Lord, for a word of explanation, of forgiveness, or of hope, but they will never find it.

According to Psalm 114, Israel had once been God's dominion, God's sanctuary, where even the earth trembled at the Lord's presence and his people lived in a close personal relationship with him. But now they can expect only disaster—no smile but a frown, no mercy but justice.

In Matthew 16, Jesus finds a similarly tragic situation. The Jewish leaders were supposed to lead people to God and his Messiah, but when they meet him, they attack him venomously. Proudly they demand a sign to prove that Jesus really is the Messiah, but the sign that is given is one that only the humble will recognise—the cross.

QUESTIONS

Nowadays God's one, universal church is broken up into many denominations. This is particularly so in Africa. Why do you think this is?

In some countries the number of Christians is not growing but diminishing, and even those who do attend services are mostly elderly. Do you have any ideas on how to change this trend?

PRAYER

God, help us to obey your command-ments. May we not reject your word but rejoice in it and understand it more deeply. This we pray through Jesus Christ our Saviour. Amen.

Day 322: Enjoy hearing the Scriptures read aloud in church.

Day 323

The Rev. George Sumner
Principal of Wycliffe College
Toronto, Ontario

Amos 9, Psalm 115, Matthew 17

Chapters 17–19 of Matthew follow the gospel's pivot or hinge passage, the confession by Peter of Jesus as the Christ, the coming Son of Man (Matthew 16:13-20, 24-28). He is the one coming to usher in the kingdom of heaven in place of the kingdom of this world. Jesus' rebuke of Peter reinforces the disturbing manner in which he will bring it; we, too, run the risk of hearing and yet not hearing this news. Today's chapters elucidate the nature of this coming kingdom, even as they maintain the "scandalous" relation between the two kingdoms that we straddle. Chapter 17 insists that we can only think about the two as we fix our gaze on Jesus himself; chapter 18 describes the common life of the present kingdom of heaven; chapter 19 takes up the same question with respect to individual ethics of discipleship.

We are interested in our time in "transformation": we expect it for development, personal growth, spirituality. In church life the watchword is "culture." How can the gospel be "incarnate" in our context? In Richard Niebuhr's famous typology in *Christ and Culture*, Anglicans are flattered to find their hero (F. D. Maurice) illustrating "Christ transforming culture," the most appealing option. It is a short step to imagine the church transforming culture—but Matthew 17 offers us no such thing.

Beginning with verse 24, we hear this very question: should the disciple pay Caesar's tax? Jesus' answer is typically cryptic: you are free of the obligation and yet should meet it. Then he who rules all nature commands a miracle, that they haul a fish from the sea with a shekel in his mouth. Try to draw a theory of Christ and culture from that! His word alone elicits the answer. There is no balancing of kingdoms, no incarnation between them, only the Son of Man, at once God and human. The only transformation chapter 17 offers is the vision of Jesus himself (17:1-8).

QUESTION

How does Matthew 17 challenge our way of thinking about culture?

PRAYER

Father, let your kingdom come in on your son Jesus. Let it break into my life and my world, in its surprise, its power, its strangeness. Show us your glory in the suffering person of Jesus our Lord. Amen.

The Rev. George Sumner
Principal of Wycliffe College
Toronto, Ontario

Day 324

Obadiah, Psalm 116, Matthew 18

Though we live in a time intent on overcoming Cartesian "body-mind" dualism, our lives as Christians tell a different story. What could be further from spirituality than the fractious, unedifying spectacle of church politics and governance? But in Matthew 18, these domains are as one in the life of the kingdom that is more real than what we call the "real world."

When Jesus teaches us how to pray, the Lord's Prayer is in fact a précis of his own life: his relation to his Father is summed up in "Abba"; he himself is the coming of the kingdom; Gethsemane, the surrender of his own will; his passing through suffering, the great tribulation, his death offered for the forgiveness of his tormentors' sins. To live the Lord's Prayer is to live hidden with Christ in God his Father.

In this light, consider Matthew 18. Now the oversight of the church, the kingdom community, indwells in his same prayer. Children and the simple are to be honoured, for they embody the trusting relation to Abba. Nothing is to be put before standing with Christ in the "great tribulation," when solidarity with the truth of the gospel of Jesus Christ is publicly at stake. The spirit of governance and discernment in the community is exercised under the sway of forgiveness, for we who judge are forgiven sinners. Whether on our knees or in church councils, we are to live out the Lord's Prayer, whereby we are conformed to his own life and death in the hope of his resurrection.

QUESTION

How would church life in the spirit of Matthew 18 look different?

PRAYER

Father, infuse the life of our church, especially where we are most fractious, with your spirit. Keep us faithful to our calling, and remind us that we speak on your behalf only as forgiven sinners, in Christ's name. Amen.

Day 325

The Rev. George Sumner
Principal of Wycliffe College
Toronto, Ontario

Jonah 1, Psalm 117, Matthew 19

"Behold the new has come, the old has passed away" (2 Corinthians 5:17). The chapters of Matthew we have just read expand on the nature of the kingdom of heaven, which is nothing other than Christ who has come, and is coming, into our world, the kingdom of the old aeon. But what is the nature of this newness? For this old world of distortion and rebellion is also the created order God has made and loves. Christ's followers are not Gnostics, who thought that the new had erased that created order, nor are we Savanarolas who anticipate the old order's explosion. How then has the new come, and what exactly has passed away? These are the questions chapter 19 addresses.

In a manner most pertinent to our own confounded church, Jesus begins by reconfirming the shape of our social and biological life. Marriage as the union of man and woman, from which the family grows (Genesis 1 and 2), is rooted in the creative purposes of God himself. The "new thing" God is doing builds on the shape and intent of creation; God intends us to be creatures redeemed and restored in the image.

Does this mean that there is no place for the celibate life devoted entirely to the service of God? Not at all, for there is a diversity of callings. Different callings may witness to different aspects of the kingdom, coming and come. When it comes to the relation of wealth to life in the kingdom, no such ready path is offered (Matthew 19:24). The only hope for the rich is the sheer grace of God and costly discipleship in the moment of testing.

Are we left then to choose the option we prefer? Hardly. Christ's real presence—to the Pharisees, the disciples, the children, the young man, the wealthy—is what binds the cases in this chapter of Matthew together, and it is from Christ as king that each question is determined.

QUESTION

What difference does it make to consider ethical questions in light of the real and risen presence of Christ?

PRAYER

Father, teach us how impossible all things are to us alone and how utterly unconstrained you are. Remind us continually who is who, in Christ's name. Amen.

The Rev. Canon Paul Avis
Author and Theological Consultant to the
Anglican Communion Office
Devon, England

Day 326

Jonah 2, Psalm 118, Matthew 20

The story of Jonah shows a person running away from God, closing his ears to God's call, then getting into a life-threatening situation and turning back to God with a cry for help.

This scenario rings true for us. When things are going smoothly and life is good, it's easy to forget God and become cool toward spiritual things. Prayer and Bible reading get squeezed out, and we soon find excuses why we need not go to church so often. But when our circumstances turn around and life starts to fall apart, we soon find new motivation to seek God's face. Out of bitter adversity we cry to God for help. Our prayer doesn't deserve to be heard—but it will be!

Jonah's fate—thrown into the sea, swallowed by a great fish, dragged down to the depths, and then cast up on dry land after three days—prefigures the destiny of Jesus in his death and resurrection (Jonah 1:17; Matthew 20:19).

Today's liturgical and processional psalm follows the same pattern: a cry to God for deliverance, turning into confidence in God's mighty aid and victory over one's foes. Then the psalmist comes to offer sacrifice, in thanksgiving for God's mercy.

The labourers in today's reading from Matthew all receive the same pay, regardless of what work they have put in. When God is good to us, it is not a reward for our merits—we cannot earn God's love and blessing; it is all a gift of grace.

The mother of James and John seeks special privileges for her sons, but Jesus responds that those who are close to him must share his destiny without thought of reward. Two blind men cry to Jesus as Messiah out of their affliction. They have no other claim on him, but, moved with compassion, Jesus heals them. Today we have come full circle.

QUESTION

How hard is it to rid ourselves of the notion that our blessings are rewards and our afflictions are punishments?

PRAYER

God of generosity and compassion, we owe everything to your grace. Help us to serve you out of love and gratitude, without thought of reward; through Jesus Christ our Lord. Amen.

Day 327

The Rev. Canon Paul Avis
Author and Theological Consultant to the
Anglican Communion Office
Devon, England

Jonah 3, Psalm 119:1-32, Matthew 21

In today's readings we place ourselves, with the biblical authors, in the light of God's truth, which judges and reshapes our lives.

Jonah's message of judgment on the wicked city of Nineveh has the opposite effect to what he expects. In the Bible, God's word, spoken by prophets, affects what it foretells. But here the unlooked for effect is profound and sincere repentance, so that God—depicted in very human terms—changes his mind and withdraws the threat of judgment.

In the gospel reading, Jesus enters the temple in Jerusalem as its rightful "owner" and passes judgment on its corrupt practices. He comes as king, yet in humility and peace, on a donkey, not a warhorse. He also passes judgment on a fig tree, a symbol of Israel. These two acts prefigure the destruction of Jerusalem and its temple by the Romans in 70 c.e. The same truth of judgment is contained in the parable of the vineyard, another biblical symbol of Israel.

Between these two sections of the chapter, we have the parable of the two sons, with its judgment on the "official" religious institutions that failed to respond to Jesus' mission, and its punch line that instead, social outcasts are embracing the kingdom of God in the person of Jesus.

This is the first hint that the kingdom will be offered to others—those currently excluded—who will welcome it. The second hint is in verse 43: this is a rare intimation in the gospels that the Gentiles— non-Jews, the rest of the world—will receive the gospel and enter the kingdom.

Psalm 119 is a prolonged meditation on the truth of God and its power to purify and reshape our lives. The psalmist dwells on God's law, that part of the Hebrew Bible (the Christian Old Testament) known as the Torah, the first five books of the Bible. As you reflect on this psalm, make it your prayer for the light and truth of the Scriptures to refresh and renew your life.

QUESTION

Why are we so reluctant to allow God's truth in the Scriptures to shine a searchlight on our lives and to transform us into the people God wants us to be?

PRAYER

Open our eyes, O Lord, that we may behold wondrous things coming out of your word and be changed by them; through Jesus Christ, our Lord. Amen.

The Rev. Canon Paul Avis
Author and Theological Consultant to the
Anglican Communion Office
Devon, England

Day 328

Jonah 4, Psalm 119:33–72, Matthew 22

Today as we conclude the story of Jonah, we learn, as he did, something of the infinite scope of divine compassion. Jonah is sulking because he feels that God has made a fool of him: what he has prophesied has not come to pass. His vocation as a prophet has been undermined; his life is not worth living. But he waits, hoping that, after all, Nineveh will feel God's wrath. Jonah has not yet learned his lesson.

When the plant that is sheltering him from the blazing sun shrivels, Jonah again curses his lot and asks to die. His concern is self-centred and petulant. He is not on God's wavelength. We recall some words from the parable of the vineyard: "Are you envious because I am generous?" (Matthew 20:15).

God's concern is with the vast population of the city, who are not believers, and also (surprisingly, perhaps) with their livestock. God does not want them to perish. God's compassion and care are universal; God's concerns and purposes are broader than ours. No one is outside of God's love and care. "There's a wideness in God's mercy, like the wideness of the sea" (*The Hymnal 1982*, #469).

The gospel reading begins with the parable of the wedding banquet: do we or do we not heed God's call and accept God's invitation in the gospel message? Those initially invited violently abuse the king's hospitality, so he turns to others who did not expect to attend. Are they the socially excluded or the Gentiles, both of whom were mentioned in yesterday's reading?

Matthew 22, from verse 15 to the end, recounts a series of four rabbinic disputations in which Jesus confounds his opponents and teaches an important theological truth. In each case, he speaks with divine authority as an interpreter of the Scriptures.

QUESTION

Can you identify the punch line in the four rabbinic disputations (Matthew 22:15-46)?

PRAYER

Lord, teach us to think in tune with your will and purpose and not in a petty, human way. Be our teacher and renew our minds by your truth; through Jesus Christ, our Lord. Amen.

Day 329: Enjoy hearing the Scriptures read aloud in church.

Day 330

The Rev. Carol Pinkham Oak
Rector
St. John's Church
Ellicott City, Maryland

Micah 1, Psalm 119:73-112, Matthew 23

The pattern of these Scripture passages is disconnect, connect, disconnect. The prophet Micah speaks not only to God's people, but from his world view, to all people. God will continue to be God and bring his power of judgment and restoration to the earth. God will undo all the places that are disconnected from him. God will lament for the people who have disconnected from God's life.

Psalm 119 is a long acrostic that was likely used in public worship and intended as a guide for staying in God's way of life. The source of that way is the connection God created within humankind from the beginning. Our desire to be in God's way is as intimate as our deepest longing, and the separation from God's way is as painful as our deepest grief.

Jesus condemns those who have disconnected themselves from God's source of life. In this reading from Matthew, he points to those who are the most learned of the community but are disconnected from living. The acts of study, prayer, or sacrifice stand alone. These actions are more important than the source from which they come.

QUESTIONS

How often do we turn to others to solve our struggles with living instead of exploring the depths of our relationship with God?

How often do we turn to self-help books when instead we could ask for God's help?

PRAYER

Gracious God, we give you thanks that you are always connected to us, even when we feel disconnected from you. Make us aware of your presence in all we do. Amen.

The Rev. Carol Pinkham Oak
Rector
St. John's Church
Ellicott City, Maryland

Day 331

Micah 2, Psalm 119:113-144, Matthew 24

If one takes a broad and long view, today's Scripture texts look to a future of downfall and destruction. Matthew is particularly familiar as an apocalyptic text, the Advent God reordering creation.

There is another closer and more intimate view of these passages. They entreat us to be sensitive—not sensitive in that we put forth our raw and hurt places and see our life with God through that lens, but rather sensitive to our physical state of being, attuned to the stimuli around us—sensitive beings in a world filled with distractions and with delights. Psalm 119:120, 123: "My flesh trembles for fear of you and I am afraid of your judgment"; "My eyes fail from watching your salvation." Our muscles feel the tension of anticipation. Our eyes strain to look past the smoldering horizon to the yet unseen.

A beloved mentor once said to me, "You are too sensitive. You need to toughen up." He meant that I was overly attuned to the stimuli around me. In Myers-Briggs terms, I was living too fully out of one side of my personality while neglecting the other. I am grateful that I took his advice, for the most part.

However, I realized that I could not toughen up every part of my awareness because doing so would cut me off from a delicate, intricate, and essential sensitivity to God's presence working through my body, in the people around me, and in my physical environment. I have paid a price for this vulnerability. I have also been deeply aware of God's enduring love, no matter how the world around me feels.

QUESTIONS

What are the sensitive places within you that bring you closer to God?

Where are the places that are too raw and sensitive? Where are the places that are too hard and crusty?

PRAYER

God, help me to serve you faithfully, through both sensitivity and strength. Amen.

Day 332

The Rev. Carol Pinkham Oak
Rector
St. John's Church,
Ellicott City, Maryland

Micah 3, Psalm 119:145-176, Matthew 25

"What are the goals, actions, and measurements?" "Does income exceed expenditures?" "Were the objectives met?" These are words about measurement we use every day. And they are appropriate when a group, an institution, or a congregation points its resources in a specific direction.

In the parable of the talents found in chapter 25 of Matthew, the measurement is different. It is assumed by the landowner that the stewards and slaves will care for the resources entrusted to them. The amount the first two stewards make at first appears to be what the landowner values most. They have increased his wealth. But when the third steward returns in full exactly what he was given, we learn that the landowner values taking risks. At the very least, he says, you could have taken one action and invested the money. His praise for the first two stewards is based on the risk they took to use the resources they had.

I wonder what the landowner would have said if the parable included a fourth steward who came and said, "I am returning less than what you have given me. I took a risk on rehabbing an old school building in the city. I am looking for a tenant to pay the rent."

QUESTIONS

How would you end this hypothetical story of a fourth steward?

What risks have you taken with your talents?

PRAYER

God, help us to measure our lives by your standards—not the world's—and make us good stewards of all that you have given us. Amen.

The Rev. Dr. Jane Patterson
Assisting Priest, St. Mark's Church
Co-director, The WorkShop
San Antonio, Texas

Day 333

Micah 4, Psalm 120, Matthew 26

In the turmoil of day-to-day events—both in our personal lives and in global struggles—it can be hard to find the larger purposes of God. Today's readings give us a glimpse of the larger framework of God's purposes, so that we may grasp the challenge of being God's faithful people in our own time and place.

Chapter 4 of Micah begins by repeating an oracle of Isaiah: "They shall beat their swords into plowshares, and their spears into pruning hooks" (v. 3), a vision that seems to echo a response to the wistful ending of Psalm 120, "I am for peace; but when I speak, they are for war" (v. 7). This fourth chapter of Micah is the first of two that express hope in the midst of exile and domination by a foreign power.

Psalm 120 is the first of the Songs of Ascents, perhaps songs that were sung when going on pilgrimage to Jerusalem. Meshech is a place far to the north of Jerusalem, while Kedar is far to the south. Perhaps these two places of exile are speaking of a spiritual exile, far from God's dwelling place. From that distance, God's ways may be hard to discern.

In Matthew 26, we enter into both the tenderness of Jesus' last Passover meal with his disciples and the trauma of his arrest and abuse at the hands of his captors. Remembering the Passover is key to seeing God's hand in these events. In this Passover, it is Jesus' blood that will be spilled, his life poured out in a way that will prove to be the gateway to freedom for his followers. It is Jesus alone who seems to grasp both the pathos of what he must endure and also the power of God that is on the move in these serious events.

Every week, at the celebration of the eucharist, we recall and proclaim the Passover of the Lord. No matter what is going on in the world about us, the eucharist draws us into God's larger vision for all people: the peace that comes from being at last in right relationship with God and our neighbor.

QUESTIONS

What issues in the world are hard for you to bear? How do you think God is calling you in the midst of these events?

What issues in your life seem to be farthest from God's goodness? Is it possible, in light of today's readings, to see a larger framework of God's purposes for you?

PRAYER

God of peace, show me how to find you in the midst of all that troubles me and give me the courage to follow your path into a freedom I can hardly imagine. This I ask for Jesus' sake. Amen

The Rev. Dr. Jane Patterson
Assisting Priest, St. Mark's Church
Co-director, The WorkShop
San Antonio, Texas

Micah 5, Psalm 121, Matthew 27

If we imagine a golden thread running through today's readings, it might be the assurance from Psalm 121, "The Lord is your keeper. ... The Lord will keep you from all evil; he will keep your life" (vv. 5, 7).

The reading from Micah, addressed to the Israelites in exile, calls for their trust in the Lord's keeping. Micah 5:2-5 is a poem that may have been familiar to early Christians, expressed in their proclamation of Jesus as the one who came forth from Bethlehem to rule for God in Israel. No matter who or what appears to have power and authority in our world, for good or for ill, it is truly God who keeps us in life.

Remembering this fact as we read Matthew 27 gives us a window into how some of the characters lose their way. In one of the most poignant scenes in the gospel, Judas repents of betraying Jesus for thirty pieces of silver, but his repentance is too late. What he has done cannot be undone, and he cannot live with his guilt. The chief priests and elders seem to think that if they help to do away with Jesus, then their positions will be secure. They incite the crowd to turn against Jesus, to the point that the people call out, "His blood be on us and on our children!" (Matthew 27:25). In all of these attempts to place their security in money or public position or violence, each of these people illustrates Jesus' earlier teaching: "Those who find their life will lose it, and those who lose their life for my sake will find it" (Matthew 10:39).

Only Jesus holds the golden thread of perfect trust in God as his ultimate keeper. As you read Matthew 27:27-50, pay attention to the ways in which Jesus shows us how to live out each of the Beatitudes (Matthew 5:3-11), even at the extreme edge of human endurance. Throughout his suffering and crucifixion, Jesus courageously retains his poverty of spirit and offers himself in mourning, in gentleness, hungry for righteousness, merciful, pure in heart, a peacemaker, persecuted for righteousness' sake, subject to slander. Matthew invites us to see the crucifixion of the wholly innocent Jesus, not from the point of view of the soldiers or the taunting crowds, but through the eyes of God, who alone sees through to the heart.

Those who have been truly absorbing the teachings of Jesus will be able to see through the cruel posturing of the people around him and have confidence that his faithfulness will result in all the blessings of the Beatitudes: this Jesus who is being treated as a criminal is actually the one who will be filled with righteousness and mercy, who will see God, who will inherit the earth, who will receive the kingdom of

Day 334, continued

God, who will be called Son of God. As you read, receive his final teaching, his example of how to live the Beatitudes with unwavering trust in God as his keeper.

QUESTIONS

Imagine that you are among the women "looking on from a distance," who had come all the long way with Jesus from Galilee. What detail in the story is especially vivid to you today?

Is there something in your life that is stretching your faith that God is truly your keeper?

PRAYER

We lift our eyes to you, O God, our Creator and Helper, our Keeper and Redeemer: teach us through the trials of our lives how to keep our eyes always on you, and where our faith fails, multiply our efforts by your grace, for the love of Christ Jesus our Lord. Amen.

Day 335

The Rev. Dr. Jane Patterson
Assisting Priest, St. Mark's Church
Co-director, The WorkShop
San Antonio, Texas

Micah 6, Psalm 122, Matthew 28

All three readings for today, filled with the emotions and drama of human life, witness to the concrete reality of our relationship with God.

In the reading from Micah, God asks, "O my people, what have I done to you? In what have I wearied you? Answer me!" (Micah 6:3). And the people, for their part, ask, "With what shall I come before the Lord?" (v. 6). What God desires is not an empty gift, but the knowledge that we will do God's own work in our world, the work of mending a broken, but beloved Earth: "to do justice, and to love kindness, and to walk humbly with our God" (v. 8). Psalm 122 is a love song to Jerusalem, the holy city of the Lord's house, the temple. And at the very end of the Gospel of Matthew, the risen Jesus promises that he will be with us always.

But to ask the question raised by Micah, what does the risen Lord require of us? One of the interesting aspects of Matthew 28 is the way in which the women and the other eleven disciples are described as having very mixed reactions to the resurrection of their beloved Christ. The women have a mixture of "fear and great joy" (Matthew 28:8), enough fear that when they meet Jesus on the road, he tells them not to be afraid. The eleven, likewise, recognize and bow down before their risen Lord, while at the same time, some are hesitant. None of these reactions seem to bother Jesus. He commissions all the eleven, no matter their level of faith. Even faith worn thin and ragged by fear or hesitation may, by the grace of God, be a means of God's power.

Jesus commissions the eleven to "disciple the nations" (Matthew 28:19)—in other words, to pass on the teachings of Jesus concerning how to live in right relationship with God and with our neighbor. And they are to baptize people of all nations "in the name of the Father and of the Son and of the Holy Spirit." In doing so, the disciples will help to create a new Israel, not bounded by national borders, but everywhere that people walk in God's paths. The Holy Spirit was God's agent in the conception of Jesus (Matthew 1:18, 20), and is the vehicle of God's empowerment for those who are baptized into Jesus (Matthew 3:11). The Holy Spirit is perhaps the most internal way in which Jesus is with us always, empowering us to be God's hands and feet in the world, even "to the end of the age" (Matthew 28:20).

Day 335, continued

QUESTIONS

Think of the patterns of your life. How might God use you to disciple others, to teach them how God's ways look in an ordinary human life?

How do you treat others? How do you honor God's presence in your life? Who is learning about Jesus from watching you?

PRAYER

Most gracious God: I am humbled that you have commissioned me not only to be a disciple, but to disciple others in your ways. Grant me wisdom, courage, and above all, the gift of your Holy Spirit, that I may carry out your commission to all whom you are drawing to yourself. I pray this in the Name of Jesus, your Son and my Lord. Amen.

Day 336: Enjoy hearing the Scriptures read aloud in church.

Day 337

The Rev. Dr. John Yieh
Professor of New Testament
Virginia Theological Seminary
Alexandria, Virginia

Micah 7, Psalm 123, Mark 1

Micah describes it well. The world is indeed a woeful place. It is difficult to find a faithful or upright person. Self-interest is the ultimate concern in a competitive society. Friends tread on each other to get to the top and lie without shame to make profits. Public officials and judges are supposed to uphold justice for all, but they are the first to be corrupted by bribes. Even loved ones cannot be trusted. Divorce and lawsuits are sadly frequent, and broken relationships have become too common. Unless we close our eyes to what is happening in and around us, we cannot help feeling betrayed, enraged, and cynical. This cannot be the world in which God wants us to live.

In today's reading, the prophet refuses to be discouraged by what he sees in the world. Holding firm to God's mercy, he says, "But as for me, I will look to the Lord. I will wait for the God of my salvation" (Micah 7:7). He also looks inside himself and admits that he is part of the problem. Having been reconciled with God, he looks to God for hope and is reassured of God's compassion and faithfulness.

The psalmist expresses the same hope when he encourages us to worship God and sing together, "so our eyes look to the Lord our God, until he has mercy on us" (Psalm 123:2). When we change our perspective from the earth to the heavens, we are given the courage to confront the evil in us and in the world and granted the joy of knowing the compassionate God is fully in charge.

In fact, God has begun to fix the world. Mark the Evangelist tells us how God sent Jesus Christ to usher in the kingdom of God. By healing the sick and casting out demons, Jesus Christ demonstrated his mercy and power to give us new life. In great confidence, therefore, we can thank God that our lives can be blessed and the world can be renewed. All we need to do is look to Jesus Christ and follow him.

QUESTIONS

What are the conditions of your life, your church, and your society? Are you satisfied with them?

What divine acts of mercy have you experienced? What did you do in response?

PRAYER

Merciful God, the world is cruel and stifling, and we have nowhere to look for help but you. Thank you for sending your Son Jesus Christ to show us your compassion. Guide our eyes to always look to you, and grant us your peace that we may follow Jesus to preach his gospel and bring your hope to those who suffer. Amen.

The Rev. Dr. John Yieh
Professor of New Testament
Virginia Theological Seminary
Alexandria, Virginia

Day 338

Nahum 1, Psalm 124, Mark 2

In today's Old Testament reading, Nahum's oracle is a judgment against Nineveh but a comfort to Israel. The metropolis of Nineveh enjoyed power, prestige, and prosperity, but it was also the center of idolatry, evil, and violence that brutalized God's people trying to live righteously. God will not look away from his suffering people, however, and will relentlessly punish their wicked oppressors. As Nahum says, God's marvelous way can be seen in whirlwind and storm. God rebukes the sea, and it becomes dry. The mountains quake before God, and the hills melt. Before the Creator God, even the mightiest city cannot escape its due punishment. Thus the prophet declares, "A jealous and avenging God is the Lord" (Nahum 1:2) and challenges any opponent of God saying, "Who can stand before his indignation?" (v. 6).

Seeing violence and wars destroying innocent lives, we often feel helpless and hopeless. No one seems able or willing to do anything about it. But Nahum's oracle reassures us of God's justice. Evil will not last forever. God's people can be confident of God's plan to mend the world and vindicate their plight; even though they are not exempt from misfortune, they can always count on God's protection. As the psalmist says, "We have escaped like a bird from the snare of the fowlers" (Psalm 124:7). It is in such salvation moments that we learn to sing in praise even as we face new ordeals: "Our help is in the name of the Lord, who made heaven and earth" (v. 8).

Jesus is also powerful and merciful. He brings justice to his people by casting out demons with a single command and reveals his grace by healing those suffering from all kinds of illness. In Mark 2, he holds the divine authority to forgive sins and is the lord of the sabbath. Why is Jesus Christ so kind to us, the sin-stricken, the weary, and the heavily burdened? Thanks be to God! It is the sheer grace of God.

QUESTION

New wine needs new wineskins. What new frame of mind should you have in order to appreciate God's justice and grace as shown in Jesus Christ?

PRAYER

Gracious Lord, you render justice to the wicked and show mercy to those who take shelter in you. Give us new hearts that we may understand the depth of your grace and follow Jesus Christ to share your goodness with people around us, that they may also love you. Amen.

Day 339

The Rev. Dr. John Yieh
Professor of New Testament
Virginia Theological Seminary
Alexandria, Virginia

Nahum 2, Psalm 125, Mark 3

What a horror! Nineveh's mighty chariots are burned and its swords melted in smoke. The wealthy city is completely destroyed and left in ashes. The ferocious lion's den is raided—its gold and silver looted, and its lionesses and cubs slaughtered. This apocalyptic scene tells a sober story, a divine drama in which God's wrath is finally unleashed to execute justice on earth. Everybody should be afraid, and even the most powerful kingdom of the world should take heed. It does not pay to defy God.

Empires rise and fall, and arrogant leaders often forget they are nothing but fragile creatures before the almighty God. They fool themselves into believing that they are invincible, that their city or nation will stand forever. Leaders of the church, in whom spiritual authority is invested, can easily fall into the same sin of pride. In contrast to the arrogant leaders who bring a terrible fate on their cities or churches, those who trust in the Lord, says the psalm, will stand upright and firm like holy Mount Zion (Psalm 125:1).

In the stories of Mark 3, Jesus continues to heal the sick and free the demon-possessed, even though the Pharisees refuse to recognize Jesus' remarkable acts of mercy that change lives. Determined to thwart Jesus' work of salvation, some Pharisees commit the unforgivable sin of blasphemy against the Holy Spirit by calling it Beelzebub, the leader of demons.

Without the inspiration of the Holy Spirit, no one can repent of their sins or accept Jesus' forgiveness. Anyone who blasphemes against the Holy Spirit, therefore, effectively removes themselves from the first step to reconciliation with God. Between Jesus and the Pharisees, alas, we see the contrast between Mount Zion and Nineveh. In view of the potential consequences, let us follow Jesus closely and do God's will so that we may become members of his family rather than his enemies. Let us also pray often for our political and church leaders.

QUESTIONS

What can we do as Christians to make sure that our city is blessed like Mount Zion rather than doomed like Nineveh?

What is the relationship between Jesus Christ and the Holy Spirit?

How can we become members of Jesus' family?

PRAYER

Holy God, you are slow to anger, but in justice no one can escape your wrath. You are also quick to forgive, calling us ever patiently to return to your blessings. Grant us your Holy Spirit, so that we may see your grace, be healed, and become family members of your Son our Lord. Amen.

The Rt. Rev. Suheil Dawani
Anglican Bishop in Jerusalem
Jerusalem, Israel

Day 340

Nahum 3, Psalm 126, Mark 4

Today's reading transports us to the place where we are able to listen, hear, and understand. Parables and metaphorical language were, and still are, an important method to relay messages, lessons, and words of wisdom. The Bible is full of texts that enable the readers and the hearers to draw nearer to God and God's creation.

The last chapter of the book of Nahum uses very strong metaphorical language and delivers a powerful message of sin and punishment. Exile and captivity were an inevitable consequence to sin; fragility and shame lead to defenselessness. Yet, the psalmist offers a song of joy and restoration for the people of God. God does great things for God's holy people; if they will open their eyes and their ears in order to see the Lord and to hear the voice of God—then they will understand.

According to Mark's Gospel, one of the greatest challenges the disciples of Jesus had was their inability to understand, in particular, Jesus' parables. One expects that those who claim to be insiders will be the first to know and understand. This was not the case with the disciples and other religious leaders of the time. Yet, the most unlikely people, those who were considered to be the outsiders, were able to see and understand.

Jesus was aware of the ability of the people around him to understand his message. Parables were means of communication, a window into the divine realm or the kingdom of God—a place where there is only one circle, one faith, and one Lord of all.

QUESTIONS

What has helped you most in your Christian journey to understand your faith?

How do you see the role of teaching in the process of healing and restoration?

PRAYER

O Lord, I do not understand, but I trust. Amen.

Day 341

The Rt. Rev. Suheil Dawani
Anglican Bishop in Jerusalem
Jerusalem, Israel

Habakkuk 1, Psalm 127, Mark 5

Listening is an important spiritual instrument that helps those who seek the face of the Lord to understand the will of God in their lives, both as individuals and as a community. Especially in the holy season of Advent, we focus on the importance of preparedness, readiness, and watchfulness; all three require some kind of listening.

Whether we are standing on the threshold of the Nativity of our Lord and Savior or are living through other times in the Christian year, we are called to walk in wholeness. Much of the anticipation and watchfulness of our Christian journey depends on our readiness to listen to the Spirit of God that makes us whole. Wholeness does not mean perfection! Rather, it reminds us that our dependence on the Lord is what brings about grace and prosperity. The psalmist was very clear that without the Lord our God, all that we do will be in vain (Psalm 127:1-2).

Today's reading from Mark focuses on two main aspects of Jesus' ministry, teaching and healing. Chapter 5 recounts three healing miracles, all performed around the Sea of Galilee. All three recipients of healing were considered outsiders: a demoniac, a bleeding woman, and a dead girl. Jesus' intention was to bring holistic healing to the person as well as to the community. He empowers the person to be fully restored within the community and enables the community to embrace all people.

As Christians we must listen to the needs of the world around us. Indeed, we look in anticipation and listen in eagerness to the voice of the Lord in a troubled world.

QUESTIONS

How faithful are you toward those in need around you?

To what extent does the church's teaching involve listening?

PRAYER

God of mercy and love, we ask you to open our eyes and ears in order that we may see and hear the cries of your people and be faithful to them. Take our lips and speak through them; take our hands and heal through them. Amen.

The Rt. Rev. Suheil Dawani
Anglican Bishop in Jerusalem
Jerusalem, Israel

Day 342

Habakkuk 2, Psalm 128, Mark 6

It is with anticipation that we await the coming of the kingdom, at the celebration of the Nativity of the Babe of Bethlehem and throughout the year. The coming of God into our midst reminds us of the purpose of our own being and asks to consider how we will respond to the hungry world around us.

The prophet Habakkuk also questions when and how God would answer his prayers and complaints. God's reply was to be found in waiting and anticipating through faith. The will of God for us suggests that if the vision of God "seems to tarry, wait for it… the righteous live by their faith." God's promise is that "the Lord is in his holy temple" (Habakkuk 2:20)—that the Lord is within the church and will nourish and feed God's people.

There are many different stories in Mark 6 that tell of the ministry of Jesus in and around Galilee. Proclaiming the coming of the kingdom of God is one of the main themes in Mark's Gospel, and the feeding of the five thousand is a central event in this chapter. It is about nourishing God's people. We are told that as they reached the shore, the disciples were overwhelmed by a huge crowd. The people were hungry for righteousness and truth, and Jesus was there to satisfy even their physical hunger.

It is important to remember that after Jesus fed the crowd, he took himself off to pray. When we go to a deserted place, we may anticipate feeling hunger, thirst, and eagerness. A retreat, although a time to shut out the busyness around us and be in the presence of the Holy, is also a time when we can hear and see the world around us through the eyes of God, in whose presence we sit. This is our time to be nourished by the Holy.

QUESTIONS

Jesus was born in a manger, a place where animals go for nourishment. How can you share the incarnate Word with the world around you, so that all may learn to "feed on him in faith"?

In a world full of hunger and thirst, how can the church assist in the distribution and sharing of the world's resources?

PRAYER

O Lord, in the stillness of our lives, help us listen to your will, walk in your ways, and offer ourselves in love for you and for those around us. Amen

Day 343: Enjoy hearing the Scriptures read aloud in church.

Day 344

The Rev. Dr. Peter Carrell
Director of Education
Diocese of Christchurch
Christchurch, New Zealand

Habakkuk 3, Psalm 129, Mark 7

Israel lives a precarious existence. That is true today, but it was also true of ancient Israel. Psalm 129 is raw emotion, telling of Israel's affliction and wishing shame and worse on those who hate Israel. Technically, this psalm is difficult to follow (verse eight is ungainly, relative to the first seven verses), but the sense is easy enough to get: those who love God will love and not hate God's people.

The precariousness of Israel is threatened by external enemies and by internal rebellion against God's ways. Habakkuk 3 presents God as a terrifying judge—no more awesome (or awful) vision of the Divine Judge is found in Scripture. Yet, the terror is mitigated. The prophet's prayer asks God to "in wrath remember mercy" (v. 2), and in the last verses of the chapter, 17-19, the prophet sees beyond the terror and resulting devastation of crops and flocks to happy days in God's presence.

We are still with Israel in Mark 7. Jesus judges some of Israel to be clever, conniving hypocrites. He then turns the point he makes into a call to all humanity to understand that evil comes out from a person rather than going into the person. Then a cleverness of a different kind is experienced, as a Gentile woman seeks a way into Jesus' kingdom. Finally, a deaf man (probably also a Gentile) is healed. The notion of "Israel," who belongs to it and what behavior is counted righteous within it, is being turned upside down by Jesus.

QUESTIONS

Do you love God's people?

If your life is devastated and desolate, what prevents you, nevertheless, from acclaiming the joy of the Lord as your strength?

Think about the people of God with whom you identify most closely (perhaps a local congregation). Is it easy for others to join in? Are there barriers to belonging that you think Jesus would toss aside?

PRAYER

God, mighty in judgment, unfathomable in mercy, grant us your joy, especially in the midst of desolation; increase our love for your people everywhere; and challenge us to remove all barriers to people joining your kingdom; through Jesus Christ our Saviour. Amen.

The Rev. Dr. Peter Carrell
Director of Education
Diocese of Christchurch
Christchurch, New Zealand

Day 345

Zephaniah 1, Psalm 130, Mark 8

The day of the Lord is at hand (Zephaniah 1:7). Today's reading continues the theme of divine judgment begun yesterday. Here judgment is against idolatry (vv. 4-6), as well as compromising behavior that crosses the boundaries between Israel and foreign states (v. 8). There is also a strong message for those who "rest complacently" on what could be described as bad theology (v. 12).

In Psalm 130 we breathe a different air than that of Psalm 129. No concerns about Israel's enemies—rather, there is an attentive, patient waiting for God to redeem Israel. Noticeable here is the confidence of the psalmist: the Lord will hear his prayers and forgive his sins. This Lord is marked by "steadfast love" and "great power to redeem" (v. 7). Who would not have confidence in such a wonderful Lord!

The eighth chapter of Mark is a busy one, but a common thread through its many sections is the difficulty people have in grasping just who Jesus is. Even Peter, who gets it precisely right with his confession, doesn't understand the true meaning of that confession. Jesus' rebuke to him confronts us with the question: are our minds on divine things or human things? Then we have one of the most striking sayings of Jesus about the true character of discipleship. Verses 34–38 deserve slow reading and rereading. The heart of being a Christian disciple lies here.

QUESTIONS

Are there idols, compromises, or complacencies in your life that God is asking you to do something about today?

Do you have the confidence of the author of Psalm 130? If not, why not ask the Lord for that confidence?

What does taking up the cross mean for you today?

PRAYER

Lord of all the earth, abounding in steadfast love and powerful to redeem us, may we know your love in every aspect of our lives; drive out of our lives all idols, compromises, and complacencies; and enable us to be true followers, denying self and taking up our cross; all for the sake of the gospel of Jesus Christ our Lord. Amen.

Day 346

The Rev. Dr. Peter Carrell
Director of Education
Diocese of Christchurch
Christchurch, New Zealand

Zephaniah 2, Psalm 131, Mark 9

Perhaps the only common thread throughout the stories in Mark 9 is Jesus himself. Certainly three sections here take Jesus closer to the ultimate "transfiguration," that is, from crucifixion to resurrection (Mark 9:2-8, 9-13, 30-32). These sections are woven into material about the disciples, but Mark's account does them no favours: they cannot cast out an evil spirit; they do not understand what Jesus says about his death and resurrection; they argue over who is greatest; and they mistakenly try to stop an exorcist because "he was not following us" (9:38). In the end, the disciples merit some strong teaching from Jesus and a warning not to lose their saltiness.

Perhaps we find ourselves in the position of the disciples, feeling we do not understand, we have made mistakes, and we have let Jesus down. Worse, our saltiness may feel distinctly lacking in flavor! Is there hope for us? Can we be restored to full spiritual health? Yes, we can!

The psalmist encourages us to be calm and quiet our souls while putting our hope in God. In the Old Testament reading, Zephaniah offers a fierce prophecy against the enemies of Israel at that ancient time, but he tucks into the prophecy a word of encouragement for all times: "the seacoast shall become the possession of the remnant....For the Lord their God will be mindful of them and restore their fortunes" (Zephaniah 2:7).

Through the cross and resurrection of Jesus, that promise of prosperity to ancient Israel becomes God's promise of restoration for God's people in every generation. No matter our mistakes and misunderstandings as disciples of Jesus, God will restore us and make us salty again.

QUESTIONS

In what ways might have you let Jesus down recently?

What is missing from your life and godly service that you long for God to restore and make salty again?

What agitation and anxiety within you needs calming and quieting?

PRAYER

God of restoration, take my life and let it be reconsecrated in your service. Forgive my faults and correct my misunderstandings. Calm my soul and quiet my mind with your peace that passes all understanding. Above all, restore your Spirit within me that I may be your salt on this earth, through Jesus Christ your Son. Amen.

The Rt. Rev. Victoria Matthews
Bishop of Christchurch
Christchurch, New Zealand

Day 347

Zephaniah 3, Psalm 132, Mark 10

Today's readings ask us to consider depths and shades of desire and meaning. God's kingdom is often overlooked and discounted, yet it is our true heart's desire. There are many things that glitter and seem to shine but actually have little true worth.

Zephaniah 3, Psalm 132, and Mark 10 remind us of eternal values that are ours for the asking, yet are easily overlooked. The gift of spiritual sight is granted to those who seek God and are able not to be distracted by the quick pleasures and heady ambitions of this world. The gift of salvation is offered to those who wait upon the Lord.

QUESTIONS

What is the distraction that most easily causes you to stray from seeking God and following Christ?

What allowed blind Bartimaeus to see what Jesus had to offer him while many who could physically see were blind to Jesus' identity and giftedness?

PRAYER

Gracious and holy Lord, by your grace and mercy, grant us the desire to know you, see you, and follow you in the service of your kingdom both now and in eternity. We ask this in the strong name of Jesus the Christ. Amen.

Day 348

The Rt. Rev. Victoria Matthews
Bishop of Christchurch
Christchurch, New Zealand

Haggai 1–2, Psalm 133, Mark 11

There are times in each of our lives when a major transition takes place, and we are faced with choosing priorities for our new situation. It is always tempting to choose the easy way.

Haggai was born in Babylon during the captivity and was part of the remnant that returned to Jerusalem in 539–538 B.C.E. He faced the question of what would govern his new life and what familiar things must be left behind. For many, the old life had become very attractive, and a certain prosperity was hard to abandon. Haggai's prophecy consists of four oracles challenging the status quo.

In the same way, the temple in Jerusalem in Jesus' time had lost its sense of being a house of prayer, above all else. In Mark 11, Jesus calls it "a den of robbers" (v. 17).

QUESTION

The crowds in Jerusalem at the time of the Passover were immense, and there were many exciting distractions. What allowed the crowd that shouted "Hosanna to the Son of David!" to see a king, not a peasant, riding on a donkey?

PRAYER

Gracious God, many who shouted "Hosanna!" later cried "Crucify!" Grant us eyes to see the Christ in every situation and the grace to honour his presence whatever the cost. Amen.

The Rt. Rev. Victoria Matthews
Bishop of Christchurch
Christchurch, New Zealand

Day 349

Zechariah 1–2, Psalm 134, Mark 12

Zechariah, like Haggai, is one of only three prophets who wrote after Israel's return to Jerusalem from Babylonian captivity. Both prophets wrote approximately fifteen years after the captivity ended, and both were very concerned that the temple in Jerusalem be rebuilt. However, the people who returned from exile were not wealthy—they had to work hard even to earn a living. Overall, the situation was bleak. Zechariah, in the power of the Spirit, called first for repentance and then for the temple to be built. But that is not what the people wanted to hear.

In Mark 12, there are also those who questioned who had the authority to make decisions and call the people to account. Jesus told them to give to God what is owed to God. He also clearly said that physical might should not dictate the moral code.

QUESTION

If you give to God the things that are God's, what does that leave for the emperor?

PRAYER

Compassionate and loving God, your people over many centuries have turned away and sought to satisfy their own desires before obeying you. Yet you are always more ready to forgive than we are to repent. Thank you for your loving care and boundless mercy. Guide us to walk in your paths and heed your call. In Christ we pray. Amen.

Day 350: Enjoy hearing the Scriptures read aloud in church.

Day 351

The Rev. Dr. Helen-Ann Hartley
Dean of Tikanga Pakeha
The College of St. John the Evangelist
Auckland, New Zealand

Zechariah 3–4, Psalm 135, Mark 13

These prophetic chapters of Zechariah present us with two powerful images: the trial of the high priest, Joshua, and the vision of the golden lamp and olive-tree people. The landscape is of the temple realm, of the role and function of leaders and those who are "anointed," and the "fitness" of the people to fulfill the role that God has bestowed upon them. Prophetic writings are challenging to understand, so it is important to think carefully about the context that produced them and the context to which they speak. Because these chapters are presented with two other readings, it might be helpful to see what light they shed on our understanding of some of the deeper rhythms of the story.

Psalm 135 has a liturgical role in ascribing praise and glory to God. It consists of two elements: commands to praise and reasons why the Lord should be praised. These reasons may indeed be summed up in the clauses: "for the Lord is good…for he is gracious" (v. 3). The Lord chose Israel as his personal possession, so the relationship of the covenant is key. More than that, the Lord should be praised because, put simply, he is "great"; he is "above all gods" (v. 5). The Lord endures forever and ultimately is in control of all ages, past, present, and future.

Mark 13 presents an apocalyptic vision of the temple and its destruction. Whether or not this gospel was written before or after the tumultuous events of the year 70 c.e. does not take away from the sense of anxiety that must have prevailed when Mark was writing and proclaiming the "good news" (the gospel) of Jesus Christ. Reading these verses, we wonder along with those who heard them first when these events might take place and what it might mean. This is all the more real because so much of Mark is written in the present tense, as if the events were part of our narrative, too—as indeed they are.

QUESTIONS

As you read these passages, where do you see yourself in the story or stories?

What are the signs of God's presence in your world today, in your local community? Where is the "good news"?

PRAYER

God of all ages, be with us as we wrestle with challenging texts, engage us where we are, and help us to seek your presence and proclaim your good news. Amen.

The Rev. Dr. Helen-Ann Hartley
Dean of Tikanga Pakeha
The College of St. John the Evangelist
Auckland, New Zealand

Day 352

Zechariah 5–6, Psalm 136, Mark 14

The visions continue in Zechariah with a flying scroll of huge dimensions, a measuring basket (ephah), and a final vision reminiscent of the first with four chariots coming out from between two bronze mountains. The final vision affirms that God's rule extends over the whole earth and God's empire is beyond anything that imagination can create—or indeed beyond any known power of the day. That, in its context, was a very bold and challenging message to proclaim!

Psalm 136 echoes the sense of God's sovereignty and majesty found in yesterday's psalm, offering a hymn of praise to God as creator and deliverer.

Mark 14 then takes us into the story of Christ's passion. Mark's telling of the final days of Jesus' life is incredibly powerful. Proportionately these chapters far outweigh the previous ones in their focus on just a few days. Mark's narrative has hurtled along at great speed up to this point, and suddenly we are made to slow down and dwell with Jesus' death in a way that again, as with the previous chapter we explored, invites us into the drama of the moment. The plot against Jesus, the anointing, the sinister role of Judas, the Passover meal, the Last Supper, the denial of Peter, the prayer at Gethsemane, the betrayal and arrest, and the trial: all these crucial events are recounted in a way that calls our attention and engagement into being. We cannot ignore this story, nor should we.

The enigma of verses 51-52 is interesting. Archbishop Rowan Williams was once asked, "Who is that young man in the story?" Expecting an in-depth answer, the questioner was perhaps left surprised, yet I hope thoughtful, at the wise words in response: "Maybe we are not meant to know exactly who that young man was." Part of Mark's clever narrative technique is to leave us with a sense of mystery. We are invited to "wonder"—and so we do.

QUESTIONS

What role can the visionary wonderings of Zechariah play in your contemporary attempts to read and understand Scripture?

What part would you have played in Mark 14?

PRAYER

Gracious God, as we begin our journey with Jesus to the cross, teach us patience in recalling how your precious Son gave his life for us so that we might know you better. Amen.

Day 353

The Rev. Dr. Helen-Ann Hartley
Dean of Tikanga Pakeha
The College of St. John the Evangelist
Auckland, New Zealand

Zechariah 7–8, Psalm 137, Mark 15

Words about fasting and a reassurance in the midst of economic turmoil: these characterise chapters 7 and 8 of Zechariah. Again, reading these chapters in their context is crucial to how we engage with them. The closing verses of chapter 8 present a vision of the city as being at the heart of the hopes of all nations. Jerusalem's universal appeal, of course, resonates powerfully and profoundly with that city today as the focus of so much tension, yet still a sign of great hope. Sometimes the prophets can leave us overwhelmed with the impossibility of our role in proclaiming the Scriptures. How can we understand and make sense of where we are? Yet, we are reminded, too, of the importance of attending to glimmers of light and hope where we find them, often in unexpected places.

Psalm 137, well-known to many, is an expression of lament, of the impossibility of keeping faith in the midst of great unrest. How can a people in exile sing praises to God? How to remember not only *who* we are but *whose* we are is crucial. And then of course, verse 9—often this verse is skipped, but how might it be read? How should it be read? When interpreting the psalm, it is important to take into account that the author uses different genres or styles of writing in order to create certain effects. Verse 9 is therefore deeply ironic in its context.

The journey to the cross reaches a climax in Mark 15 where the ultimate irony and tragedy is the shame of the Christ crucified. How can this be? Jesus is buried, but as we know, this is not the end of the story.

QUESTIONS

How do you read Psalm 137?

In Mark 15, where are you in the narrative? Mark's Greek here is again in the present tense. Read the chapter aloud in the present tense. What difference does this make to our understanding?

PRAYER

Loving God, be with us in the words of Scripture that are tough and challenging. Help us to read and interpret with great care. Amen.

The Rev. Canon Andrew McGowan
Warden of Trinity College
University of Melbourne
Melbourne, Australia

Day 354

Zechariah 9, Psalm 138, Mark 16

Zechariah's prophecy addresses Israel's misery after destruction and captivity. The famous call to Jerusalem, "Rejoice greatly, O daughter of Zion" (Zechariah 9:9), is set among predictions of calamity for those who have acted unjustly. The prophet assures the people of God's persistent love and care, manifest in, and despite, historic reversals.

Things will get better. The way to restoration does not sound easy or even pleasant, however. God promises joy, but not at the expense of avoiding truth about how dire our circumstances may be. Reversal implies that we needed it.

The ultimate reversal is the resurrection of Jesus, which overcomes the despair of his friends at the first Easter. As three later "daughters" of God's promise confront their own desolation in Zion at the tomb, God's capacity to overcome our deepest adversities is shown in the transformation of their grief—eventually.

The women are afraid at first, not overjoyed. Mark's version of the story, which ends at 16:8, leaves us with a reminder that transformation is not the same as cockeyed optimism or a "glass half full" mindset. The women left the tomb in fear. We know that their fear was turned to joy, not as a "happy ending" to the gospel but rather as an extraordinary new beginning. This is what God offers for our sorrow, our need, our brokenness, too, and the world's.

QUESTIONS

Is there a difference between optimism and hope?

Where do we need to hear God's promise to bring justice and to overcome oppression?

PRAYER

Risen Christ, you overcame death to set us free; raise us up from despair to hope, and make us signs of your power and love for all. Amen.

Day 355

The Rev. Canon Andrew McGowan
Warden of Trinity College
University of Melbourne
Melbourne, Australia

Zechariah 10, Psalm 139, Luke 1

The stories of Jesus' and the Baptizer John's origins are simultaneously intimate and earth-shattering. History is about to change, but it begins not in palaces, with battles, or in the distance, but in the intimate recesses of minds and bodies.

In the reading from Luke, Mary's encounter with the angel is "perplexing"—well might she wonder what kind of greeting this might be (Luke 1:29). God's intentions seem to concern her very self, and their depth and impact are staggering.

God's intimate engagement with us is also the theme of Psalm 139. God's knowledge of us is extraordinary, but it's not easy to accept. How fully do we really want to be known?

Reading this psalm, we may be (rightly) caught up in the "nice" parts, the sense of transcendence and intimacy with the one who searches us out and knows us. If we realise the full extent of this knowledge, however, it is not just overwhelming but difficult to live with.

Most of us rely on not admitting at least some part of who we are, whether in our buried present or our forgotten past. The psalmist's own unattractive aspects, however, are fully on show in verses 19–22, as the text shifts with disconcerting speed from the heights and depths of the divine encounter to an ironic and unattractive intolerance of God's enemies (whom God presumably knows, too, and can cope with better than we or the psalmist can). Skipping these verses is appealing—feel free to do so if you've never entertained a violent or hateful thought. Otherwise, consider again that God really does know you and loves you anyway. And that, as for Mary, God's willingness to engage with our real and truest selves intimately is what may make us who we are really meant to be.

QUESTIONS

How well do you think you know yourself? Do others know you better?

How do you deal with aspects of Scripture that express difficult or unattractive feelings or ideas? Are those feelings worse than your own?

PRAYER

God, you search me out and you know me. Help me to know myself more and more as you know me, and to become who I truly am for you. Amen.

The Rev. Canon Andrew McGowan
Warden of Trinity College
University of Melbourne
Melbourne, Australia

Day 356

Zechariah 11, Psalm 140, Luke 2

There are plenty of biblical shepherds, and while those in the gospel stories of Jesus' Nativity are acknowledged good guys, they may actually be in the minority.

Often the "shepherds" of Israel are kings and rulers, and, more often than not, when we encounter them in the pages of Scripture, they are failing in their duty or actively abusing their "sheep." Zechariah tells us that, in good prophetic fashion, he acted this out literally: he was called by God to take on a shepherd's job as a sort of lived parable, to show his contemporaries through symbolic action what God had in store for the false shepherds.

Shepherds seem to have provided such obvious imagery because they are so powerful, relative to the sheep, but their role in life depended on the sheep, too. The careless or wicked shepherd is not merely a villain out of central casting but someone who has missed the opportunity to find his or her real calling.

The shepherds at the Nativity bring this image with them to the manger, but they seem themselves to be poor, marginalised people. The true shepherd is the even more powerless one to whom the angels lead them. He has come to be with them, and with us: a true shepherd whose rule and leadership consist of sharing the plight of the sheep.

Our response is likely to have both "shepherd" and "sheep" aspects. We all exercise power of one kind or another, in family, community, workplace, church. We are all accountable for our actions and for the welfare of those whose vulnerability is somehow in our hands. Getting this right entails understanding the other side—our own vulnerability and our own need to understand whom we follow and obey.

QUESTIONS

Where in your own life can or must you exercise power? Where are you the one led or cared for?

Where do you see power misused? What light does the gospel shed on that misuse?

PRAYER

Lord, you are my shepherd; may I lead those entrusted to my care, remembering your own care for them and for me. Amen.

Day 357: Enjoy hearing the Scriptures read aloud in church.

Day 358

The Rev. Emma Percy
Chaplain and Welfare Dean
Trinity College
Oxford, England

Zechariah 12, Psalm 141, Luke 3

"What should we do?" This is what the people ask John the Baptist in response to his preaching. In today's reading from Luke, we are told that crowds were journeying out to the banks of the Jordan to hear this preacher who, like so many of the prophets before him, Zechariah included, was calling people to repent and refocus their lives on living in a way that would please God.

The city of Jerusalem, the countries of Israel and Judah, were part of the Roman Empire—Luke's historic note at the start of the chapter reminds us of this. Jerusalem is not the invincible city of Zechariah's vision; it is occupied by foreign soldiers. It is into this political situation that John preaches repentance and a sense that God's reckoning of his people is imminent. Again, like many prophets before him, John tells the people that it is not enough to make claims to be God's chosen people, the children of Abraham, if they do not behave like God's children.

John uses the imagery of bearing good fruit, what he calls the fruit of repentance. In response to the questioning crowd, he gives practical specific examples of such fruit: if you have two tunics give one to the man who has none; share your food with the needy; do not misuse positions of power to cheat or bully people. The fruits of repentance can thus be seen in lives that look outward, that show compassion to others. Turning to God involves turning to one's neighbours.

John prepares the way for Jesus, who comes to him to be baptised. And Jesus will reinforce this message in action and story. To live right with God, to be righteous, involves us in learning to live right with our neighbours. It sounds so simple, and yet we find it so hard—which is why we constantly need to repent and pray for forgiveness and grace.

QUESTIONS

What should the fruits of repentance look like in my life?

What simple things could I change to make me more outward-looking, more concerned for the well-being of others?

In the Bible, repentance is not just personal but political. How can I play my part in campaigning for a more compassionate world?

PRAYER

Gracious and generous God, forgive me for the self-centeredness that limits my vision. Grant me your grace to see where I can make changes in my life and in my world, so that I may bear good fruits; for the sake of your son, Jesus Christ our Lord. Amen.

The Rev. Emma Percy
Chaplain and Welfare Dean
Trinity College
Oxford, England

Day 359

Zechariah 13, Psalm 142, Luke 4

We live in a world where quick fixes and instant results are prized by many. Advertisements continually tell us that with this cream, this food, this lifestyle, we can look younger and be healthier and more fulfilled. And it is all because we are worth it! Some of these things may well be true, but it is rarely as simple as the advertisers would wish us to believe; often, they give us false hope and a false picture of what we should be valuing.

In today's reading, Zechariah's harsh words are directed at the false prophets of his day—those who have told lies to the people, promising false hope and a false sense of security. And Luke's Gospel recounts the meeting in the wilderness between Jesus and the Prince of Lies. The temptations present Jesus with the opportunity to show that he is worth it, to use his powers to instantly satisfy his hunger and increase his prestige. He counters each temptation by pointing away from himself to his Father in heaven.

Jesus then begins his public ministry, first by teaching with authority in the synagogue and then by casting out demons and healing the sick. The power and authority that he was not tempted to acquire for his own sake now become apparent in his compassionate ministry for others. The demons declare him to be the Son of God, and the people come flocking because he can give them the healing they long for.

The one who refused to make the stones bread to feed himself becomes the bread of the world, feeding people with the truths of God's love. The one who refused to accept the power promised by the devil has the power to drive out demons and illness in the name of God. And we know that his ministry will lead not to a miraculous avoidance of death but to a dying that in the end triumphs over death, giving real hope to all who put their trust in him.

QUESTIONS

In what ways am I tempted to trust in false hope? How can I learn to discern the true prophets from the false?

What need do you long for Jesus to meet?

PRAYER

Lord Jesus, you were tempted as we are but were without sin; grant us the wisdom to discern your truths, that we may resist false hopes and trust in your compassionate goodness. May we worship the Lord our God and serve only him in all that we do and say. Amen.

Day 360

The Rev. Emma Percy
Chaplain and Welfare Dean
Trinity College
Oxford, England

Zechariah 14, Psalm 143, Luke 5

In today's reading, Zechariah draws his prophecy to its end with a vision of salvation and the true kingship of God. Living waters will flow out of Jerusalem, and the Lord will become king over all the earth. It is a vision of kingship brought about by the smiting of enemies, with dire warnings for those nations who do not come up to Jerusalem to worship the Lord God.

Yesterday's chapter in Luke's Gospel ended with Jesus' words that he was to preach the good news of the kingdom of God. Today, chapter 5 outlines this work. We find that the kingdom of God is not brought about by smiting of enemies and dire warnings but by the invitation to follow, the healing of the sick, and the forgiving of sins.

The fisherman Simon and his colleagues James and John are amazed by the vast catch of fish after their night of catching nothing. Yet they are even more amazed by Jesus. They leave their boats and follow him. A leper is healed, and a paralysed man not only has his sins forgiven but is commanded to get up from his bed and walk. Levi the tax collector finds himself hosting a meal in which those who were outsiders are welcomed by Jesus, and he, too, leaves everything to follow Jesus. "And amazement seized them all" (Luke 5:26).

Yet these events are unsettling to those who feel they know the law and know how a good religious man should behave. The Pharisees and teachers of the law are disturbed by the words of forgiveness, perplexed by the healings, and outraged by the company Jesus keeps. This does not look like the holiness they understand—this does not look like the kingdom of God. This is new wine that demands new ways of understanding God's kingdom and the people who are welcome in it.

QUESTIONS

What is your vision of the kingdom of God?

Are you sometimes like the Pharisees, holding on to your understanding and judging those who unsettle you?

If Jesus called you, could you leave everything behind and follow him? And what would that mean?

PRAYER

Lord Jesus, you taught us to pray, your kingdom come, on earth as it is in heaven. Help us to share your vision of that kingdom and through our discipleship play a small part in making it a reality in our world. Amen.

The Rev. Canon Rosalind Brown
Canon Librarian at Durham Cathedral
and Columnist for Church Times
Durham, England

Day 361

Malachi 1, Psalm 144, Luke 6

Malachi lived in the post-exilic period when the people were rebuilding their temple and their national life. God declared his love for them, but their harsh question, "How have you loved us?" (Malachi 1:2), reflects discouragement with the severity of post-exilic life. Their perspective was blinkered because things had not gone as easily as they had hoped, and they faced ongoing hardship.

In return, God challenged the people about their less than wholehearted worship. They expected God to turn a blind eye to the poor quality of their sacrificial offerings, but God criticised their narrow vision, which meant they were in danger of being bypassed. In the great post-exilic vision of universal blessing outlined at the end of Isaiah, God's name is great and will be revered among all the nations, way beyond their borders.

Just as God accused the returned exiles of breaking the commandments about worship, so the religious leaders accused Jesus of doing so. He had dared to bring God's blessing on the sabbath day! Again, God's purposes are bigger than the leaders' religious boundaries would allow.

Among the disciples called by Jesus was one who would betray him and others who would, at times, let him down. Like the returned exiles, the disciples were not perfect. It was up to them what they would make of their discipleship. Jesus set out topsy-turvy blessings and woes and described how they should live with generosity and love for all, not just calling him Lord but doing what he commanded. Faith must lead to action, shown in love for God and for neighbour.

If the religious leaders and the disciples were not perfect, neither are we. Yet God calls us to a faith that dares to live in a radically bounteous way because God's vision for the world is so good.

QUESTIONS

As you look back on a year of reading the Bible, what stands out to you about God's way with the world?

Whom can you love more generously or bless more radically this week?

PRAYER

Gracious God, help us to live more graciously and in a more Christlike way. Amen.

Day 362

The Rev. Canon Rosalind Brown
Canon Librarian at Durham Cathedral
and Columnist for Church Times,
Durham, England

Malachi 2, Psalms 145–146, Luke 7

Today's psalms are extolling God's goodness, singing how the Lord sets prisoners free and lifts up those who are bowed down. In the reading from Luke we find Jesus doing just that. He healed the Roman centurion's servant because he was asked to do it and then raised the dead man without being asked, probably out of compassion for a widow in the devastating situation of having no one to support her (the reason the Bible keeps reiterating God's concern for orphans and widows).

In contrast to Jesus' life-giving actions, Malachi had to censure the priests of his day who perverted justice and religious tradition, calling evil good and complaining when God did not respond as they wanted. God condemned the priests for causing people to stumble because of their teaching. Jesus, too, was exercised by people who were never satisfied with what God was doing but always found something to complain about. Things had slipped badly from the delight of the psalmist in God's goodness!

Then there was John the Baptist, in prison. Jesus didn't set that captive free despite John's unwavering fidelity in preparing the way for Jesus. If anyone could expect God's blessing of release, surely it was John? Instead, Jesus told John's disciples to report all the good things that were happening and to challenge John not to take offence that they weren't happening to him.

Sometimes that same challenge comes to us. We have to learn to trust God's life-giving goodness that we see elsewhere in the world, even when we do not experience it ourselves. We can complain and blame God or, like John, we can trust that we will find blessing in not taking offence at God.

QUESTIONS

What do you think causes God offence in the world today? What can you do about it?

Look back on your life: have you experienced the gratuitous goodness of God at any time? How do these experiences help you to remain faithful to God in times when God's blessing seems to be withheld?

PRAYER

Lord Jesus Christ, please help me to follow your example and bring light and life in the world, trusting you to care for me and my needs as I serve others. Amen.

The Rev. Canon Rosalind Brown
Canon Librarian at Durham Cathedral
and Columnist for Church Times
Durham, England
Day 363

Malachi 3, Psalms 147–148, Luke 8

Things come to a head in today's reading from Malachi: God stirs into action and sends the messenger the people are expecting to prepare the long-awaited day of God's coming. But the shock is that this will mean refining and judgment before there can be blessing. God's righteousness has not changed, and neither has the people's waywardness. The whole biblical story has been building to this climax: time and again in the Old Testament, there have been warnings of the consequences of unfaithful action alongside the promise of blessings for fidelity.

A last plea is made: bring the full tithe into the warehouse so that there is food in God's house. This food could feed the hungry of the land, just as the women who accompanied Jesus offered their resources to provide for Jesus and his companions (Luke 8:3). In response, God would rebuke the locusts that destroyed their harvests, a promise of restoration previously given through the prophet Joel (Joel 2:18–27).

At the end of the Old Testament, things come full circle from Genesis where God gave humans everything that was good for food (Genesis 1:29; 2:9). God's provision has never been in doubt because God does not change. Indeed, the psalmist sings that God gives the animals and birds their food (Psalm 147:9); it is only the people's defiance that has brought them to disaster time and again.

It is timely that we read the parable of the sower in Luke as well as this challenge from God in Malachi. When the sower sows in good soil there is an abundant harvest; when he sows in poor soil there is failure. God has been pleading with the people throughout the biblical story to be that good soil in which righteousness can take root and grow. That promise still holds true centuries later.

QUESTIONS

What connections can you make between your duty to God and God's blessing of the world? How would you strengthen those connections?

As you near the end of your journey through the Bible, what themes have you noticed throughout it? How have they been developed as the story unfolds?

PRAYER

Holy God, guide us to sow in good soil and to produce harvests in our lives. Accept the offerings that we bring today, and use them to bring blessing in your world. Amen.

Day 364: Enjoy hearing the Scriptures read aloud in church.

Day 365

The Rev. Marek P. Zabriskie
Founder of the Center for Biblical Studies
Rector of St. Thomas Church, Whitemarsh
Fort Washington, Pennsylvania

Malachi 4, Psalms 149–150, Luke 9

We started our journey in Genesis as God's Spirit moved over the waters, and we close with fire and brimstone. Malachi warns, "Surely the day is coming; it will burn like a furnace" (Malachi 4:1). We hear echoes of Isaiah, "The mighty man will become tinder and his work a spark; both will burn together with no one to quench the fire" (Isaiah 1:31).

There is hope, if we abide by God's teaching. Malachi exhorts, "Remember the law of my servant Moses" (v. 4). Elijah will return on the day of the Lord to turn "the hearts of the fathers to their children, and the hearts of the children to their fathers" (v. 6). Five hundred years later, an angel tells Zechariah that his son, John the Baptist, will turn "the hearts of the fathers to their children" (Luke 1:17). Could John the Baptist be Elijah, preparing the way for Jesus?

The final two psalms remind us that the Psalter was Israel's prayer book, full of prayers of praise. Psalm 150 strikes a fitting finale of Hallelujah praise, with an orchestra to glorify God.

Today's reading from Luke reminds us that God always calls his disciples to mission and to confess that Jesus is the Messiah, the Christ, and the keystone of our lives. This confession of faith does not protect us from all evil, for just as Jesus suffered, so will his followers. We must therefore pick up our cross daily and follow him.

Yet, we can expect rare moments of spiritual transcendence—like the disciples witnessing the Transfiguration—reminding us that we follow not a man but the Son of Man. Luke knows that prayer is vital. It guides us to the transfigured Christ. Jesus prays before multiplying the fish and loaves, before questioning his disciples, and before being transfigured.

QUESTIONS

How does prayer and reading the Bible prayerfully transfigure you and allow you to see the glory of God in Jesus, in others, and in yourself?

Are God's praises frequently on your lips, and is your life a song of praise to God?

PRAYER

Almighty God, as you allowed the disciples to witness the transfigured glory of Jesus on the Mount of Transfiguration, be now the God who transfigures us, so that our lives may reveal your glory as we journey among your people and carry your Word deep within our hearts. Amen.

Afterword

Congratulations!

You have finished and have done something truly memorable and spiritually rewarding. I hope that this has transformed your life in a special way. God will surely honor the significant effort that you have made.

Rather than rest upon your laurels, I strongly encourage you to begin reading the Bible again, this time moving more slowly and deliberately, but ensuring that each day you read a portion of the Scriptures. You may wish to read a different translation this time so that you read passages, which are now more familiar to you, and see slight differences that will reveal deeper meanings and more truths to you. As always, I encourage you to put yourself in the presence of God before you read any portion of the Bible.

If you chose to re-read the Bible and let daily Bible reading become a lifelong spiritual practice for you, I recommend that you read the article on "Lectio Divina" on the Center for Biblical Studies website to help you discover a slow, meditative way of reading the Scriptures that can be life-transforming.

If this spiritual experience has touched your heart and nourished your soul, I invite you to contribute to the Center for Biblical Studies to help us promote *The Bible Challenge* globally so that others may benefit from the daily reading of God's Word and participate in *The Bible Challenge*. Your gift can be made out to "St. Thomas Episcopal Church" with a memo for "The CBS" and sent to St. Thomas Episcopal Church, P.O. Box 247, Fort Washington, Pennsylvania, 19034.

Once again, congratulations on achieving a major spiritual goal in your life. You can build greatly on the important spiritual work that you have done.

With gratitude for your achievement and prayers for your continued daily reading of God's Word,

—The Rev. Marek P. Zabriskie

Founder of *The Bible Challenge* and
the Center for Biblical Studies

Rector of St. Thomas' Church, Whitemarsh
Fort Washington, Pennsylvania

Daily Readings

You can start The Bible Challenge *on January 1 or any day of the year of your choice. The schedule of this book works best if you begin "Day 1" on a Monday. We encourage readers to read portions of the Bible Monday through Saturday, and assume that on Sunday they will be in church hearing the Scriptures read aloud.*

Day 1 –   Genesis 1-3, Psalm 1, Matthew 1

Day 2 –   Genesis 4-6, Psalm 2, Matthew 2

Day 3 –   Genesis 7-9, Psalm 3, Matthew 3

Day 4 –   Genesis 10-12, Psalm 4, Matthew 4

Day 5 –   Genesis 13-15, Psalm 5, Matthew 5

Day 6 –   Genesis 16-18, Psalm 6, Matthew 6

Day 7 –   Enjoy hearing the Scriptures read aloud in church

Day 8 –   Genesis 19-21, Psalm 7, Matthew 7

Day 9 –   Genesis 22-24, Psalm 8, Matthew 8

Day 10 –   Genesis 25-27, Psalm 9, Matthew 9

Day 11 –   Genesis 28-30, Psalm 10, Matthew 10

Day 12 –   Genesis 31-33, Psalm 11, Matthew 11

Day 13 –   Genesis 34-36, Psalm 12, Matthew 12

Day 14 –   Enjoy hearing the Scriptures read aloud in church

Day 15 –   Genesis 37-39, Psalm 13, Matthew 13

Day 16 –   Genesis 40-42, Psalm 14, Matthew 14

Day 17 –   Genesis 43-45, Psalm 15, Matthew 15

Day 18 –   Genesis 46-48, Psalm 16, Matthew 16

Day 19 –   Genesis 49-50, Psalm 17, Matthew 17

Day 20 –   Exodus 1-3, Psalm 18:1-20, Matthew 18

Day 21 –   Enjoy hearing the Scriptures read aloud in church

Day 22 –   Exodus 4-6, Psalm 18:21-50, Matthew 19

Day 23 –   Exodus 7-9, Psalm 19, Matthew 20

Day 24 –   Exodus 10-12, Psalm 20, Matthew 21

Day 25 –   Exodus 13-15, Psalm 21, Matthew 22

Day 26 –   Exodus 16-18, Psalm 22, Matthew 23

Day 27 –   Exodus 19-21, Psalm 23, Matthew 24

Day 28 –   Enjoy hearing the Scriptures read aloud in church

Day 29 –   Exodus 22-24, Psalm 24, Matthew 25

Day 30 –   Exodus 25-27, Psalm 25, Matthew 26

Day 31 –   Exodus 28-30, Psalm 26, Matthew 27

Day 32 –   Exodus 31-33, Psalm 27, Matthew 28

Day 33 –   Exodus 34-36, Psalm 28, Mark 1

Day 34 –   Exodus 37-39, Psalm 29, Mark 2

Day 35 –   Enjoy hearing the Scriptures read aloud in church

Day 36 –   Exodus 40, Psalm 30, Mark 3

Day 37 –   Leviticus 1-3, Psalm 31, Mark 4

Day 38 –   Leviticus 4-6, Psalm 32, Mark 5

Day 39 –   Leviticus 7-9, Psalm 33, Mark 6

Day 40 – Leviticus 10-12, Psalm 34, Mark 7

Day 41 – Leviticus 13-15, Psalm 35, Mark 8

Day 42 – Enjoy hearing the Scriptures read aloud in church

Day 43 – Leviticus 16-18, Psalm 36, Mark 9

Day 44 – Leviticus 19-21, Psalm 37:1-18, Mark 10

Day 45 – Leviticus 22-24, Psalm 37:19-42, Mark 11

Day 46 – Leviticus 25-27, Psalm 38, Mark 12

Day 47 – Psalm 39, Mark 13

Day 48 – Numbers 1-3, Psalm 40, Mark 14

Day 49 – Enjoy hearing the Scriptures read aloud in church

Day 50 – Numbers 4-5, Psalm 41, Mark 15

Day 51 – Numbers 6-8, Psalm 42, Mark 16

Day 52 – Numbers 9-11, Psalm 43, Luke 1

Day 53 – Numbers 12-14, Psalm 44, Luke 2

Day 54 – Numbers 15-17, Psalm 45, Luke 3

Day 55 – Numbers 18-20, Psalm 46, Luke 4

Day 56 – Enjoy hearing the Scriptures read aloud in church

Day 57 – Numbers 21-23, Psalm 47, Luke 5

Day 58 – Numbers 24-26, Psalm 48, Luke 6

Day 59 – Numbers 27-29, Psalm 49, Luke 7

Day 60 – Numbers 30-32, Psalm 50, Luke 8

Day 61 – Numbers 33-35, Psalm 51, Luke 9

Day 62 – Numbers 36, Psalm 52, Luke 10

Day 63 – Enjoy hearing the Scriptures read aloud in church

Day 64 – Deuteronomy 1-3, Psalm 53, Luke 11

Day 65 – Deuteronomy 4-6, Psalm 54, Luke 12

Day 66 – Deuteronomy 7-9, Psalm 55, Luke 13

Day 67 – Deuteronomy 10-12, Psalm 56, Luke 14

Day 68 – Deuteronomy 13-15, Psalm 57, Luke 15

Day 69 – Deuteronomy 16-18, Psalm 58, Luke 16

Day 70 – Enjoy hearing the Scriptures read aloud in church

Day 71 – Deuteronomy 19-21, Psalm 59, Luke 17

Day 72 – Deuteronomy 22-24, Psalm 60, Luke 18

Day 73 – Deuteronomy 25-27, Psalm 61, Luke 19

Day 74 – Deuteronomy 28-30, Psalm 62, Luke 20

Day 75 – Deuteronomy 31-33, Psalm 63, Luke 21

Day 76 – Deuteronomy 34, Psalm 64, Luke 22

Day 77 – Enjoy hearing the Scriptures read aloud in church

Day 78 – Joshua 1-3, Psalm 65, Luke 23

Day 79 – Joshua 4-6, Psalm 66, Luke 24

Day 80 – Joshua 7-9, Psalm 67, John 1

Day 81 – Joshua 10-12, Psalm 68, John 2

Day 82 – Joshua 13-15, Psalm 69, John 3

Day 83 – Joshua 16-18, Psalm 70, John 4

Day 84 – Enjoy hearing the Scriptures read aloud in church

Day 85 – Joshua 19-21, Psalm 71, John 5

Day 86 –	Joshua 22-24, Psalm 72, John 6
Day 87 –	Judges 1-3, Psalm 73, John 7
Day 88 –	Judges 4-6, Psalm 74, John 8
Day 89 –	Judges 7-9, Psalm 75, John 9
Day 90 –	Judges 10-12, Psalm 76, John 10
Day 91 –	Enjoy hearing the Scriptures read aloud in church
Day 92 –	Judges 13-15, Psalm 77, John 11
Day 93 –	Judges 16-18, Psalm 78:1-39, John 12
Day 94 –	Judges 19-21, Psalm 78:40-72, John 13
Day 95 –	Ruth 1-4, Psalm 79, John 14
Day 96 –	1 Samuel 1-3, Psalm 80, John 15
Day 97 –	1 Samuel 4-6, Psalm 81, John 16
Day 98 –	Enjoy hearing the Scriptures read aloud in church
Day 99 –	1 Samuel 7-9, Psalm 82, John 17
Day 100 –	1 Samuel 10-12, Psalm 83, John 18
Day 101 –	1 Samuel 13-15, Psalm 84, John 19
Day 102 –	1 Samuel 16-18, Psalm 85, John 20
Day 103 –	1 Samuel 19-21, Psalm 86, John 21
Day 104 –	1 Samuel 22-24, Psalm 87, Acts 1
Day 105 –	Enjoy hearing the Scriptures read aloud in church
Day 106 –	1 Samuel 25-27, Psalm 88, Acts 2
Day 107 –	1 Samuel 28-30, Psalm 89:1-18, Acts 3
Day 108 –	1 Samuel 31, Psalm 89:19-52, Acts 4
Day 109 –	2 Samuel 1-3, Psalm 90, Acts 5
Day 110 –	2 Samuel 4-6, Psalm 91, Acts 6
Day 111 –	2 Samuel 7-9, Psalm 92, Acts 7
Day 112 –	Enjoy hearing the Scriptures read aloud in church
Day 113 –	2 Samuel 10-12, Psalm 93, Acts 8
Day 114 –	2 Samuel 13-15, Psalm 94, Acts 9
Day 115 –	2 Samuel 16-18, Psalm 95, Acts 10
Day 116 –	2 Samuel 19-21, Psalm 96, Acts 11
Day 117 –	2 Samuel 22-24, Psalm 97, Acts 12
Day 118 –	1 Kings 1-3, Psalm 98, Acts 13
Day 119 –	Enjoy hearing the Scriptures read aloud in church
Day 120 –	1 Kings 4-6, Psalm 99, Acts 14
Day 121 –	1 Kings 7-9, Psalm 100, Acts 15
Day 122 –	1 Kings 10-12, Psalm 101, Acts 16
Day 123 –	1 Kings 13-15, Psalm 102, Acts 17
Day 124 –	1 Kings 16-18, Psalm 103, Acts 18
Day 125 –	1 Kings 19-21, Psalm 104, Acts 19
Day 126 –	Enjoy hearing the Scriptures read aloud in church
Day 127 –	1 Kings 22, Psalm 105, Acts 20
Day 128 –	2 Kings 1-3, Psalm 106, Acts 21
Day 129 –	2 Kings 4-6, Psalm 107, Acts 22
Day 130 –	2 Kings 7-9, Psalm 108, Acts 23
Day 131 –	2 Kings 10-12, Psalm 109, Acts 24
Day 132 –	2 Kings 13-15, Psalm 110, Acts 25

Day 133 – Enjoy hearing the Scriptures read aloud in church

Day 134 – 2 Kings 16-18, Psalm 111, Acts 26

Day 135 – 2 Kings 19-21, Psalm 112, Acts 27

Day 136 – 2 Kings 22-24, Psalm 113, Acts 28

Day 137 – 2 Kings 25, Psalm 114, Romans 1

Day 138 – 1 Chronicles 1-3, Psalm 115, Romans 2

Day 139 – 1 Chronicles 4-6, Psalm 116, Romans 3

Day 140 – Enjoy hearing the Scriptures read aloud in church

Day 141 – 1 Chronicles 7-9, Psalm 117, Romans 4

Day 142 – 1 Chronicles 10-12, Psalm 118, Romans 5

Day 143 – 1 Chronicles 13-15, Psalm 119:1-32, Romans 6

Day 144 – 1 Chronicles 16-18, Psalm 119:33-72, Romans 7

Day 145 – 1 Chronicles 19-21, Psalm 119:73-112, Romans 8

Day 146 – 1 Chronicles 22-24, Psalm 119:113-144, Romans 9

Day 147 – Enjoy hearing the Scriptures read aloud in church

Day 148 – 1 Chronicles 25-27, Psalm 119:145-176, Romans 10

Day 149 – 1 Chronicles 28-29, Psalm 120, Romans 11

Day 150 – 2 Chronicles 1-3, Psalm 121, Romans 12

Day 151 – 2 Chronicles 4-6, Psalm 122, Romans 13

Day 152 – 2 Chronicles 7-9, Psalm 123, Romans 14

Day 153 – 2 Chronicles 10-12, Psalm 124, Romans 15

Day 154 – Enjoy hearing the Scriptures read aloud in church

Day 155 – 2 Chronicles 13-16, Psalm 125, Romans 16

Day 156 – 2 Chronicles 17-19, Psalm 126, 1 Corinthians 1

Day 157 – 2 Chronicles 20-22, Psalm 127, 1 Corinthians 2

Day 158 – 2 Chronicles 23-25, Psalm 128, 1 Corinthians 3

Day 159 – 2 Chronicles 26-28, Psalm 129, 1 Corinthians 4

Day 160 – 2 Chronicles 29-31, Psalm 130, 1 Corinthians 5

Day 161 – Enjoy hearing the Scriptures read aloud in church

Day 162 – 2 Chronicles 32-34, Psalm 131, 1 Corinthians 6

Day 163 – 2 Chronicles 35-36, Psalm 132, 1 Corinthians 7

Day 164 – Ezra 1-3, Psalm 133, 1 Corinthians 8

Day 165 – Ezra 4-6, Psalm 134, 1 Corinthians 9

Day 166 – Ezra 7-9, Psalm 135, 1 Corinthians 10

Day 167 – Ezra 10, Psalm 136, 1 Corinthians 11

Day 168 – Enjoy hearing the Scriptures read aloud in church

Day 169 – Nehemiah 1-3, Psalm 137, 1 Corinthians 12

Day 170 – Nehemiah 4-6, Psalm 138, 1 Corinthians 13

Day 171 – Nehemiah 7-9, Psalm 139, 1 Corinthians 14

Day 172 – Nehemiah 10-12, Psalm 140, 1 Corinthians 15

Day 173 – Nehemiah 13, Psalm 141,
1 Corinthians 16

Day 174 – Esther 1-3, Psalm 142,
2 Corinthians 1

Day 175 – Enjoy hearing the Scriptures
read aloud in church

Day 176 – Esther 4-6, Psalm 143,
2 Corinthians 2

Day 177 – Esther 7-8, Psalm 144,
2 Corinthians 3

Day 178 – Esther 9-10, Psalm 145,
2 Corinthians 4

Day 179 – Job 1-3, Psalm 146,
2 Corinthians 5

Day 180 – Job 4-6, Psalm 147,
2 Corinthians 6

Day 181 – Job 7-9, Psalm 148,
2 Corinthians 7

Day 182 – Enjoy hearing the Scriptures
read aloud in church

Day 183 – Job 10-12, Psalm 149,
2 Corinthians 8

Day 184 – Job 13-15, Psalm 150,
2 Corinthians 9

Day 185 – Job 16-18, Psalm 1,
2 Corinthians 10

Day 186 – Job 19-21, Psalm 2,
2 Corinthians 11

Day 187 – Job 22-24, Psalm 3,
2 Corinthians 12

Day 188 – Job 25-27, Psalm 4,
2 Corinthians 13

Day 189 – Enjoy hearing the Scriptures
read aloud in church

Day 190 – Job 28-30, Psalm 5, Galatians 1

Day 191 – Job 31-33, Psalm 6, Galatians 2

Day 192 – Job 34-36, Psalm 7, Galatians 3

Day 193 – Job 37-39, Psalm 8, Galatians 4

Day 194 – Job 40-42, Psalm 9, Galatians 5

Day 195 – Proverbs 1-3, Psalm 10,
Galatians 6

Day 196 – Enjoy hearing the Scriptures
read aloud in church

Day 197 – Proverbs 4-6, Psalm 11,
Ephesians 1

Day 198 – Proverbs 7-9, Psalm 12,
Ephesians 2

Day 199 – Proverbs 10-12, Psalm 13,
Ephesians 3

Day 200 – Proverbs 13-15, Psalm 14,
Ephesians 4

Day 201 – Proverbs 16-19, Psalm 15,
Ephesians 5

Day 202 – Proverbs 20-22, Psalm 16,
Ephesians 6

Day 203 – Enjoy hearing the Scriptures
read aloud in church

Day 204 – Proverbs 23-25, Psalm 17,
Philippians 1

Day 205 – Proverbs 26-28, Psalm 18:1-20,
Philippians 2

Day 206 – Proverbs 29-31, Psalm 18:21-50,
Philippians 3

Day 207 – Ecclesiastes 1-3, Psalm 19,
Philippians 4

Day 208 – Ecclesiastes 4-6, Psalm 20,
Colossians 1

Day 209 – Ecclesiastes 7-9, Psalm 21,
Colossians 2

Day 210 – Enjoy hearing the Scriptures
read aloud in church

Day 211 – Ecclesiastes 10-12, Psalm 22,
Colossians 3

Day 212 – Song of Songs 1-3, Psalm 23,
Colossians 4

Day 213 – Song of Songs 4-6, Psalm 24,
1 Thessalonians 1

Day 214 – Song of Songs 7-8, Psalm 25,
1 Thessalonians 2

Day 215 – Isaiah 1-3, Psalm 26, 1 Thessalonians 3

Day 216 – Isaiah 4-6, Psalm 27, 1 Thessalonians 4

Day 217 – Enjoy hearing the Scriptures read aloud in church

Day 218 – Isaiah 7-9, Psalm 28, 1 Thessalonians 5

Day 219 – Isaiah 10-12, Psalm 29, 2 Thessalonians 1

Day 220 – Isaiah 13-15, Psalm 30, 2 Thessalonians 2

Day 221 – Isaiah 16-18, Psalm 31, 2 Thessalonians 3

Day 222 – Isaiah 19-21, Psalm 32, 1 Timothy 1

Day 223 – Isaiah 22-24, Psalm 33, 1 Timothy 2

Day 224 – Enjoy hearing the Scriptures read aloud in church

Day 225 – Isaiah 25-27, Psalm 34, 1 Timothy 3

Day 226 – Isaiah 28-30, Psalm 35, 1 Timothy 4

Day 227 – Isaiah 31-33, Psalm 36, 1 Timothy 5

Day 228 – Isaiah 34-36, Psalm 37:1-18, 1 Timothy 6

Day 229 – Isaiah 37-39, Psalm 37:19-42, 2 Timothy 1

Day 230 – Isaiah 40-42, Psalm 38, 2 Timothy 2

Day 231 – Enjoy hearing the Scriptures read aloud in church

Day 232 – Isaiah 43-45, Psalm 39, 2 Timothy 3

Day 233 – Isaiah 46-48, Psalm 40, 2 Timothy 4

Day 234 – Isaiah 49-51, Psalm 41, Titus 1

Day 235 – Isaiah 52-54, Psalm 42, Titus 2

Day 236 – Isaiah 55-57, Psalm 43, Titus 3

Day 237 – Isaiah 58-60, Psalm 44, Philemon

Day 238 – Enjoy hearing the Scriptures read aloud in church

Day 239 – Isaiah 61-63, Psalm 45, Hebrews 1

Day 240 – Isaiah 64-66, Psalm 46, Hebrews 2

Day 241 – Jeremiah 1-3, Psalm 47, Hebrews 3

Day 242 – Jeremiah 4-6, Psalm 48, Hebrews 4

Day 243 – Jeremiah 7-9, Psalm 49, Hebrews 5

Day 244 – Jeremiah 10-12, Psalm 50, Hebrews 6

Day 245– Enjoy hearing the Scriptures read aloud in church

Day 246 – Jeremiah 13-15, Psalm 51, Hebrews 7

Day 247 – Jeremiah 16-18, Psalm 52, Hebrews 8

Day 248 – Jeremiah 19-21, Psalm 53, Hebrews 9

Day 249 – Jeremiah 22-24, Psalm 54, Hebrews 10

Day 250 – Jeremiah 25-27, Psalm 55, Hebrews 11

Day 251 – Jeremiah 28-30, Psalm 56, Hebrews 12

Day 252 – Enjoy hearing the Scriptures read aloud in church

Day 253 – Jeremiah 31-33, Psalm 57, Hebrews 13

Day 254 – Jeremiah 34-35, Psalm 58, James 1

Day 255 – Jeremiah 36-38, Psalm 59, James 2

Day 256 – Jeremiah 39-41, Psalm 60, James 3

Day 257 – Jeremiah 42-43, Psalm 61, James 4

Day 258 – Jeremiah 44-45, Psalm 62, James 5

Day 259 – Enjoy hearing the Scriptures read aloud in church

Day 260 – Jeremiah 46-47, Psalm 63, 1 Peter 1

Day 261 – Jeremiah 48-49, Psalm 64, 1 Peter 2

Day 262 – Jeremiah 50-51, Psalm 65, 1 Peter 3

Day 263 – Jeremiah 52, Psalm 66, 1 Peter 4

Day 264 – Lamentations 1-2, Psalm 67, 1 Peter 5

Day 265 – Lamentations 3-4, Psalm 68, 2 Peter 1

Day 266 – Enjoy hearing the Scriptures read aloud in church

Day 267 – Lamentations 5, Psalm 69, 2 Peter 2

Day 268 – Ezekiel 1-2, Psalm 70, 2 Peter 3

Day 269 – Ezekiel 3-4, Psalm 71, 1 John 1

Day 270 – Ezekiel 5-6, Psalm 72, 1 John 2

Day 271 – Ezekiel 7-8, Psalm 73, 1 John 3

Day 272 – Ezekiel 9-10, Psalm 74, 1 John 4

Day 273 – Enjoy hearing the Scriptures read aloud in church

Day 274 – Ezekiel 11-12, Psalm 75, 1 John 5

Day 275 – Ezekiel 13-14, Psalm 76, 2 John

Day 276 – Ezekiel 15-16, Psalm 77, 3 John

Day 277 – Ezekiel 17-18, Psalm 78:1-39, Jude

Day 278 – Ezekiel 19-20, Psalm 78:40-72, Revelation 1

Day 279 – Ezekiel 21-22, Psalm 79, Revelation 2

Day 280 – Enjoy hearing the Scriptures read aloud in church

Day 281 – Ezekiel 23-24, Psalm 80, Revelation 3

Day 282 – Ezekiel 25-26, Psalm 81, Revelation 4

Day 283 – Ezekiel 27-28, Psalm 82, Revelation 5

Day 284 – Ezekiel 29-30, Psalm 83, Revelation 6

Day 285 – Ezekiel 31-32, Psalm 84, Revelation 7

Day 286 – Ezekiel 33-34, Psalm 85, Revelation 8

Day 287 – Enjoy hearing the Scriptures read aloud in church

Day 288 – Ezekiel 35-36, Psalm 86, Revelation 9

Day 289 – Ezekiel 37-38, Psalm 87, Revelation 10

Day 290 – Ezekiel 39-40, Psalm 88, Revelation 11

Day 291 – Ezekiel 41-42, Psalm 89:1-18, Revelation 12

Day 292 – Ezekiel 43-44, Psalm 89:19-52, Revelation 13

Day 293 – Ezekiel 45-46, Psalm 90, Revelation 14

Day 294 – Enjoy hearing the Scriptures read aloud in church

Day 295 – Ezekiel 47-48, Psalm 91, Revelation 15

Day 296 – Daniel 1-2, Psalm 92, Revelation 16

Day 297 – Daniel 3-4, Psalm 93, Revelation 17

Day 298 – Daniel 5-6, Psalm 94, Revelation 18

Day 299 – Daniel 7-8, Psalm 95, Revelation 19

Day 300 – Daniel 9-10, Psalm 96, Revelation 20

Day 301 – Enjoy hearing the Scriptures read aloud in church

Day 302 – Daniel 11-12, Psalm 97, Revelation 21

Day 303 – Hosea 1-2, Psalm 98, Revelation 22

Day 304 – Hosea 3-4, Psalm 99, Matthew 1

Day 305 – Hosea 5-6, Psalm 100, Matthew 2

Day 306 – Hosea 7-8, Psalm 101, Matthew 3

Day 307 – Hosea 9-10, Psalm 102, Matthew 4

Day 308 – Enjoy hearing the Scriptures read aloud in church

Day 309 – Hosea 11-12, Psalm 103, Matthew 5

Day 310 – Hosea 13-14, Psalm 104, Matthew 6

Day 311 – Joel 1-2, Psalm 105, Matthew 7

Day 312 – Joel 3, Psalm 106, Matthew 8

Day 313 – Amos 1, Psalm 107, Matthew 9

Day 314 – Amos 2, Psalm 108, Matthew 10

Day 315 – Enjoy hearing the Scriptures read aloud in church

Day 316 – Amos 3, Psalm 109, Matthew 11

Day 317 – Amos 4, Psalm 110, Matthew 12

Day 318 – Amos 5, Psalm 111, Matthew 13

Day 319 – Amos 6, Psalm 112, Matthew 14

Day 320 – Amos 7, Psalm 113, Matthew 15

Day 321 – Amos 8, Psalm 114, Matthew 16

Day 322 – Enjoy hearing the Scriptures read aloud in church

Day 323 – Amos 9, Psalm 115, Matthew 17

Day 324 – Obadiah, Psalm 116, Matthew 18

Day 325 – Jonah 1, Psalm 117, Matthew 19

Day 326 – Jonah 2, Psalm 118, Matthew 20

Day 327 – Jonah 3, Psalm 119:1-32, Matthew 21

Day 328 – Jonah 4, Psalm 119:33-72, Matthew 22

Day 329 – Enjoy hearing the Scriptures read aloud in church

Day 330 – Micah 1, Psalm 119:73-112, Matthew 23

Day 331 – Micah 2, Psalm 119:113-144, Matthew 24

Day 332 – Micah 3, Psalm 119:145-176, Matthew 25

Day 333 – Micah 4, Psalm 120, Matthew 26

Day 334 – Micah 5, Psalm 121, Matthew 27

Day 335 – Micah 6, Psalm 122, Matthew 28

Day 336 – Enjoy hearing the Scriptures read aloud in church

Day 337 – Micah 7, Psalm 123, Mark 1

Day 338 – Nahum 1, Psalm 124, Mark 2

Day 339 – Nahum 2, Psalm 125, Mark 3

Day 340 – Nahum 3, Psalm 126, Mark 4

Day 341 – Habakkuk 1, Psalm 127, Mark 5

Day 342 – Habakkuk 2, Psalm 128, Mark 6

Day 343 – Enjoy hearing the Scriptures read aloud in church

Day 344 – Habakkuk 3, Psalm 129, Mark 7

Day 345 – Zephaniah 1, Psalm 130, Mark 8

Day 346 – Zephaniah 2, Psalm 131, Mark 9

Day 347 – Zephaniah 3, Psalm 132, Mark 10

Day 348 – Haggai 1-2, Psalm 133, Mark 11

Day 349 – Zechariah 1-2, Psalm 134, Mark 12

Day 350 – Enjoy hearing the Scriptures read aloud in church

Day 351 – Zechariah 3-4, Psalm 135, Mark 13

Day 352 – Zechariah 5-6, Psalm 136, Mark 14

Day 353 – Zechariah 7-8, Psalm 137, Mark 15

Day 354 – Zechariah 9, Psalm 138, Mark 16

Day 355 – Zechariah 10, Psalm 139, Luke 1

Day 356 – Zechariah 11, Psalm 140, Luke 2

Day 357 – Enjoy hearing the Scriptures read aloud in church

Day 358 – Zechariah 12, Psalm 141, Luke 3

Day 359 – Zechariah 13, Psalm 142, Luke 4

Day 360 – Zechariah 14, Psalm 143, Luke 5

Day 361 – Malachi 1, Psalm 144, Luke 6

Day 362 – Malachi 2, Psalm 145-146, Luke 7

Day 363 – Malachi 3, Psalm 147-148, Luke 8

Day 364 – Enjoy hearing the Scriptures read aloud in church

Day 365 – Malachi 4, Psalm 149-150, Luke 9

Author Index